Southern Legal Studies

SERIES EDITORS

Paul Finkelman, *Gustavus Adolphus College*
Timothy S. Huebner, *Rhodes College*
Charles Zelden, *Nova Southeastern University*

ADVISORY BOARD

Alfred L. Brophy, *University of North Carolina School of Law*
Lonnie T. Brown Jr., *University of Georgia School of Law*
Laura F. Edwards, *Duke University*
James W. Ely Jr., *Vanderbilt University Law School*
Sally E. Hadden, *Western Michigan University*
Charles F. Hobson, *College of William & Mary*
Steven F. Lawson, *Rutgers, The State University of New Jersey*
Sanford V. Levinson, *University of Texas at Austin School of Law*
Peter Wallenstein, *Virginia Polytechnic Institute and State University*

Constitutional History of Virginia

Constitutional History of Virginia

Brent Tarter

The University of Georgia Press
ATHENS

Published with support from the 1971 Virginia Constitution Commemoration Steering Committee through the Library of Virginia Foundation

Paperback edition, 2025
© 2023 by the University of Georgia Press
Athens, Georgia 30602
www.ugapress.org
All rights reserved
Designed by
Set in 10.25/13.5 Minion Pro by Copperline Book Services

Most University of Georgia Press titles are available from popular e-book vendors.

Printed digitally

Library of Congress Cataloging-in-Publication Data
Names: Tarter, Brent, 1948– author.
Title: Constitutional history of Virginia / Brent Tarter.
Other titles: Southern legal studies.
Description: Athens : The University of Georgia Press, 2023. | Series: Southern legal studies | Includes bibliographical references and index.
Identifiers: LCCN 2022042545 | ISBN 9780820363356 (hardback) | ISBN 9780820363349 (epub) | ISBN 9780820363363 (pdf)
Subjects: LCSH: Constitutional history—Virginia.
Classification: LCC KFV2801.5.T37 2023 | DDC 342.75502/9—dc23/eng/20221101
LC record available at https://lccn.loc.gov/2022042545

Paperback ISBN 978-0-8203-6988-4

CONTENTS

Acknowledgments   ix
Introduction   1

CHAPTER 1 The Constitution of the Colony   5
CHAPTER 2 The Constitution of 1776   40
CHAPTER 3 The Constitution of 1830   78
CHAPTER 4 The Constitution of 1851   106
CHAPTER 5 The Constitution of 1864   132
CHAPTER 6 The Constitution of 1869   157
CHAPTER 7 The Constitution of 1902   195
CHAPTER 8 The Constitutional Revision of 1928   246
CHAPTER 9 The Constitution of 1971   272
CHAPTER 10 The Age of Constitutional Amendments   312

Notes   315
Select Bibliographies   367
Index   377

ACKNOWLEDGMENTS

For advice, research assistance, critical commentary, and other valuable help and encouragement, I gladly thank the archivists and librarians at the Library of Virginia, especially David Grabarek and his colleagues in interlibrary loan; John E. Stealey III, professor emeritus of history at Shepard College; Frances Pollard, retired librarian of the Virginia Historical Society; John Ruston Pagan, University Professor and Professor of Law emeritus, T. C. Williams School of Law, University of Richmond; John O. Peters, of Richmond, retired lawyer and historian; John K. Nelson, professor of history emeritus at the University of North Carolina at Chapel Hill; Jon Kukla, former director of publications at the Library of Virginia and retired executive director of Red Hill; A. E. Dick Howard, professor of law at the University of Virginia School of Law; Trenton E. Hizer, private papers archivist at the Library of Virginia; Kevin Hardwick, professor of history at James Madison University; Mark Greenough, of the Virginia state Capitol; Greg Crawford, senior local records archivist at the Library of Virginia; Trevor S. Cox, of Richmond, attorney and former acting solicitor general of Virginia; Preston L. Bryant, of Richmond, Senior Vice President of McGuire Woods Consulting; Warren M. Billings, distinguished professor emeritus of history at the University of New Orleans; and Barbara C. Batson, exhibitions coordinator at the Library of Virginia. I also thank clerk of the House of Delegates and enrolling clerk for the General Assembly, G. Paul Nardo, and his successor, Suzette Denslow, for supplying electronic texts of enrolled constitutional amendments that were then in their offices before depositing them in the legislative archive in the Library of Virginia. And a special word of thanks to Patrick Gallagher who volunteered to participate in the oral proofreading of the texts of all the Virginia constitutions and their amendments.

INTRODUCTION

When members of the Revolutionary generation began to write the first constitutions for the new American states in 1776, George Washington sent advice on that subject to his brother, who was a member of the convention that wrote the first constitution for the independent state of Virginia. "To form a new Government, requires infinite care, & unbounded attention," the general explained to the convention delegate, "for if the foundation is badly laid the superstructure must be bad"; therefore, "every Man should consider, that he is lending his aid to frame a Constitution which is to render Million's happy, or Miserable, and that a matter of such moment cannot be the Work of a day."[1]

Written constitutions of government were one of the most important innovations that Americans made as part of their gaining independence from Great Britain. Unfortunately, Americans have often taken that revolutionary part of their national founding for granted. State constitutions are one of the most essential parts of the social contract in a democratic republic. They embody fundamentally important ideas about the relationships between people and their governments.

To a larger extent than most people ordinarily perceive, each state's constitution and laws influence how people live and how they live differently than people in other states. The operations of a state's constitution and the workings of its legal and political systems are confined within clear, though often artificial, political boundaries. Each state's constitution has evolved in its own way so that no two are entirely alike. Within Virginia, and under its constitution and laws, some people live in very different legal and political environments than their near neighbors who live on the other side of a state border. At the same time, residents of Virginia who live very far from one another live within the same legal and political systems however much the natural, manmade, cultural, and economic environments where they live may differ.

The legal and political systems of Virginia, which its constitutions both create and reflect, have influenced people's lives in many ways: offering economic opportunity to some people and condemning others to lifelong slavery; determining what kind of public education their children can receive, if any; and at the most basic level of participation in self-government decreeing who may vote and who may not. That is what makes the constitution and the legal and political culture of Virginia—and of every other state—of primary importance to the people who live within its political boundaries.

Each of the fifty state constitutions is embodied in one specific document but, as with the Constitution of the United States, each constitution is also much more than the single document. The meanings and modes of operation of all American constitutions are understood, animated, and amplified in judicial decisions, legislative acts and processes, executive actions, and political institutions and practices. The many glosses on state constitutions and the numerous changes that people have made to them demonstrate the extent to which those texts have been living documents that are in all respects different from the Constitution of the United States. Unlike the nation, which has had only one constitution since 1789, most states have had at least two constitutions and several have had more. The Commonwealth of Virginia has had seven constitutions—eight if the numerous changes ratified together in 1928 be counted as a new constitution that replaced that of 1902 rather than as a revision. The past of even the most recent of the Virginia constitutions stretches all the way back to or beyond the founding of the colony.

When contemplated in the long history of Virginia, which now extends for more than four centuries, the most salient features of each of the constitutions provide milestones for identifying and assessing historical changes and continuities. The continuities illustrate how resistant to change the political leadership of Virginia has sometimes been, and some of the changes show that events outside Virginia and outside Virginians' control forced some important changes in the relationships between the people and the government.

Legal scholars and political scientists have created a large and important body of scholarship on state constitutions beginning in 1868 with Thomas M. Cooley's *Treatise on the Constitutional Limitations Which Rest Upon the Legislative Power of the States of the American Union* and inspired in the final decades of the twentieth century by Justice William J. Brennan's 1977 article "State Constitutions and the Protection of Individual Rights" in the *Harvard Law Review*.[2] They have assessed the role and significance of state constitutions in the overall American constitutional system; similarities and differences between the United States Constitution and state constitutions generally; similarities and differences among state constitutions; evolving trends in state constitutional development; methods, frequency, and topics of constitutional amendments; and whether, if state and federal constitutions contain the same language, state judges should interpret state constitutional provisions in the same manner that federal judges interpret the federal constitution.

State constitutional history is not so well developed a field of scholarship as state constitutional law. The majority of the scholarship on state constitutions focuses on constitutional conventions rather than on constitutions and for the most part highlights regional variations, particularly in the age of slavery and after its abolition. Few historians or political scientists have traced the constitutional histories of any of the states. We have no thorough and comprehensive constitutional history of Virginia that takes the long view of the whole four centuries or permits a comparison of the state's constitutional history with national or regional trends.[3] We have two studies that treat the constitutional history of the state between the American Revolution and the American Civil War,[4] and we have three very brief and superficial summaries compiled at the turn of the twentieth century and one short reference guide published in 1967.[5]

None of the existing scholarship exhibits a full recognition of how much the constitution of colonial Virginia provided institutions, precedents, practices, and principles that merged into the first constitution of the state at the moment of independence. The constitutional history of Virginia did not begin in June 1776 with the first constitution of the state but in April 1606 when King James I issued the first charter for the Virginia Company. Without understanding the colonial constitution, it is easy to misinterpret the state's first constitution. Through the Constitution of 1776 and its successors, the laws and legal practices of the state evolved and operated in ways that preserved, sometimes in disguised or hidden form, some of those first colonial constitutional institutions and practices.

This book begins with a chapter on the constitution of the colony and includes chapters on each of the constitutions that Virginians wrote in 1776, 1829–30, 1850–51, 1864, 1867–68, 1901–2, and 1969–70 and the revised constitution that the governor and General Assembly proposed and voters ratified in 1928. Each chapter is self-contained and can be read apart from the others. Each chapter after the first therefore necessarily includes references back to provisions of earlier constitutions. That unavoidably requires some repetition for the benefit of readers who seek information on a particular constitution rather than on the state's whole, long constitutional history.

Chapter 1 on the constitution of the colony and chapter 2 on the Constitution of 1776 can (and should) form a unit and be read together the better to understand how the constitution of the colony shaped the first constitution of the state, which changed some provisions of the colonial constitution and preserved others, in some instances more or less silently. Chapters 4 through 6 can also be read together as another unit because during the two decades of 1850–70, which they encompass, Virginians wrote five constitutions and went through the most dramatic and fundamentally important constitutional transformation in the state's history. And chapters 7 and 8 can form a third unit that traces the long history of, and many changes made to, the Constitution of 1902 before, in, and after 1928. Read together and consecutively, these chapters form a long narrative arc of change and continuity across more than four hundred years of Virginia's English-language history.

Dates between 1 January and 24 March and references to events that happened during that interval for years before the British calendar reform of 1752 appear in a style common at the beginning of the eighteenth century (as 14 February 1698/9) that indicates that by the old Julian Calendar, which began the new year on 25 March, it was 1698 and that by the new Gregorian Calendar, which began the new year on 1 January, it was 1699. All quotations preserve the original spelling, capitalization, and punctuation. I have verified the texts of the constitutions, schedules, and amendments for quotation here from the most authoritative sources that are available, in most instances the authenticated enrolled texts in the state archives in the Library of Virginia. Full, verified texts of all of Virginia's state constitutions with schedules and amendments are available on the Library of Virginia's website.

CHAPTER 1

The Constitution of the Colony

"It is in vain to search into the civil Constitution of *England*," Virginian Richard Bland wrote in his influential 1766 treatise, *Inquiry into the Rights of the British Colonies*, "for Directions in fixing the proper Connexion between the Colonies and the Mother Kingdom; I mean what their reciprocal Duties to each other are, and what Obedience is due from the Children to the Parent."[1] It is also in vain to search in any one place for the "civil Constitution" of what official documents sometimes described as the English king's most ancient colony and dominion of Virginia. The constitution of the colony was not, as twenty-first-century Americans think of constitutions, a formal structural outline, a superior body of law that specified grants of and limitations on governmental authority, or a legal document that embodied the governmental elements of the social contract. Instead, the constitution of colonial Virginia very closely resembled the constitution of England. Both constitutions were the sum of all the documents, practices, and precedents that people obeyed and understood as good fundamental law. In the tradition of the common law, the elements of the constitutions had become good law through "immemorial" or "customary" usage because they had remained settled, acknowledged, and in force for so long that "the memory of man runneth not to the contrary."[2]

Government under the Virginia Company

The first English-speaking residents of Virginia lived under rules and regulations that the Virginia Company of London made. The company, in turn, operated under a series of three royal charters that King James I issued. The charters resembled those of the older trading companies, the predecessors of modern limited liability companies, that operated with permission of the king to conduct their business in different regions of the world.[3] James I issued the first charter to the Virginia Company of London on 10 April 1606. The charter authorized the investors to occupy and to exploit the natural resources of a designated portion of the Atlantic coast of North America. The charter declared that the company's officers and employees who resided in North America "shall have and enjoy all liberties, franchises and immunities within anie of our other dominions to all intents and purposes as if they had been abiding and borne within this our realme of Englande or anie other of our saide dominions." As subjects of the king, the residents of its settlement also expected to enjoy the protection of the king's army and navy. The company's charter did not dictate how the company was to manage its settlers in Virginia or specify an institutional structure or mode of governance.[4] The institutions and practices that the company created for or permitted to arise in the little settlement led directly to the formation of the first quasi-governmental institutions, which during the ensuing years developed into the government of the colony and eventually gained constitutional legitimacy.

The charter of 1606 gave the Virginia Company royal permission, and therefore authority under English law, to use and control an area fifty miles north, south, and inland from the point of settlement. A council of the company's principal shareholders met from time to time in London and made all decisions concerning the company. When the company sent out the first three shiploads of settlers late in 1606, the council created a second, subordinate seven-member council of officers to command the Englishmen on the ground in Virginia.[5] It soon became obvious (as is well-known to every student of Virginia's early history) that the council quickly became hopelessly dysfunctional. Its members quarreled among themselves, deposed their presidents, and died or returned to England. By the autumn of 1608, of the original members only the council's fourth president, Captain John Smith, remained. He alone among the council's members seemed able to take charge and make things happen; but he too returned to England after being wounded in an explosion of gunpowder in 1609.[6]

The king issued the second charter to the Virginia Company on 23 May 1609. He then granted to the company all of North America west and northwest of the Atlantic coast for two hundred miles south and two hundred miles north of the latitude of Point Comfort.[7] That charter fixed the boundaries of Virginia according to English law and, within international legal conventions, established England's right to own and settle the area without the acquiescence or even knowledge of any of the native peoples whose ancestors had lived there for centuries.

The company then overhauled its administration of the settlement and sent out military governors to supplant the council. In 1610, the first two military governors, Sir Thomas Gates and Thomas West, baron De La Warr, issued the first of the so-called Lawes Divine, Morall, and Martiall, the earliest recorded laws for Virginia. The first of the 1610 laws "divine and moral" were merely orders and regulations that the company's officers promulgated and enforced, not laws in the then- or now-accepted sense in which acts of Parliament were laws because the entire political nation in the form of the House of Commons, the House of Lords, and the Crown jointly enacted them and relied on an established set of royal courts and officials to enforce them. The law "martial" that Sir Thomas Dale imposed in 1611 probably applied primarily to the military force he commanded rather than to the whole population, although he enforced it however and against whomever he pleased.[8] For a brief time, the military regime worked brutally and effectively and it put the settlement in order, but the company still did not earn any profits for the investors.

The king issued a third charter for the Virginia Company on 12 March 1611/2,[9] which created the civil office of governor to replace the military regime. Instructions that the company sent to Virginia in November 1618, also known as the Great Charter,[10] authorized the governor and his advisory Council of State to summon a new body to be known as the General Assembly consisting of the governor, members of the council, other company officers such as the secretary, and two representatives from each of the principal settlements. The assembly's records identified the two men elected from each of the eleven settlements as burgesses, a term which in England signified responsible men entitled to take part in municipal affairs.[11] The first General Assembly of Virginia met in unicameral session in the church in Jamestown from 30 July to 4 August 1619. The laws and orders that the first assembly adopted and issued were in several respects laws in the accepted modern sense, and in adopting them the members generally followed then current parliamentary procedures.[12]

As the name indicates, the General Assembly was a general assembling of men from throughout Virginia, though not a full assembling of everybody, of the whole polis as in an ancient Greek democracy. The word *assembly* did not then ordinarily even imply a legislative body.[13] In 1619, the governor issued a summons for the assembly and stipulated that the burgesses be "Chosen by the inhabitants."[14] The January 1623/4 summons directed that "all freemen" in each settlement select their burgesses "by pluralitie of voices."[15] That was probably the case in 1619 too. It is highly unlikely that any but respectable free adult men—no indentured servants, no hired laborers, no enslaved people, and no women, children, or First Nations—participated in the first elections. Only a small portion of the whole population took part.

The assembly issued orders and adopted laws to govern the conduct of servants, control relations with First Nations, and regulate the increasingly important production of and trade in tobacco. It acted like a law-making body and referred to its enactments as laws, even though it also punished miscreants and issued orders of both an executive and judicial character. What was most important was that the men who governed Virginia also enforced the assembly's laws, and the other men and women who lived there obeyed them or suffered punishment as lawbreakers. Insofar as possible, members of the assembly followed the king's order that "laws, statutes, and pollicie" in the colony conform "as convenientlie maie be" to those of England.[16]

The surviving records of the Virginia Company and the journal of the 1619 General Assembly disclose that from pure necessity the company and its settlers had by then created several elements of a colonial government. The governor and council members exercised both executive and judicial powers, and the assembly exercised legislative powers. The first assembly endowed church wardens and ministers with specific responsibilities, directed ministers to conduct church services "according to the Ecclesiasticall lawes and orders of the churche of Englande," and in effect established the Church of England as the official church of the colony, which made it a part of the government in Virginia.[17]

Royal Colony

James I procured an order of court to give him justification to revoke the Virginia Company's charter on 24 May 1624 and thereby solve several problems that he then faced.[18] That left Virginia without any English legal authority to exist as a commercial enterprise or political entity and its residents without any legal sanction for the rudimentary political institutions and practices they had created. That also put private land titles at risk because the residents no longer had any legitimate administrative or judicial apparatus to protect their private property or their personal safety and no guarantee that the king would honor land titles the Virginia Company's governors had issued. Under English laws and practices, the company's land reverted to the king who had granted it to the company, and it became his to do with as he chose. Nobody who spoke English as a first language would have believed then that the land had reverted to or could revert to the members of First Nations tribes because under English property law and international law the First Nations had never legally owned it, either individually or collectively as tribes.

On 13 May 1625, scarcely two months after James I died, King Charles I proclaimed Virginia a royal colony, "to be a part of Our Royall Empire, descended upon Us and undoubtedly belonging and appertaining unto Us." After revocation of the Virginia Company's charter, the political legitimacy of the institutions of government rested entirely on the king, who might at any time change anything or everything. The king declared that he would appoint all government officers in Virginia and promised "that at Our owne charge we will maintaine those publique Officers and Ministers, and that strength of Men, Munition, and Fortification, as shall be fit and necessary for the defence of that Plantation." The king also promised to "settle and assure the particular rights and interests of every Planter and Adventurer . . . to give them full satisfaction for their quiet and assured enjoying thereof."[19] With those words, Charles I promised to protect residents of Virginia in the enjoyment of the rights of Englishmen that the charters James I had issued originally secured to them.

From the 1620s to the 1660s, some political leaders in Virginia repeatedly tried to revive the company or obtain a new royal charter to allow them and their London trading partners to dominate the increasingly lucrative tobacco trade. For more than a generation, old company men, various London mercantile leaders, and groups of Virginia tobacco planters and traders vied for control of the tobacco trade, but the king also wished to control the tobacco trade and extract revenue from it.

Uncertainty about the form of government in Virginia lasted for about fifteen years. Several times during those years the king implicitly recognized the legitimacy of the General Assembly when he required its assent to laws that governed the production of tobacco. The assembly and the other fledgling institutions of government in Virginia had no recorded explicit royal sanction until 1639. The detailed instructions that Charles I issued to Sir Francis Wyatt in that year for his second administration, and reissued in 1641 to Sir William Berkeley for his first, included specific directives for the functioning of the General Assembly, the Council of State, the courts that then existed in Virginia, the church, and the manner of making grants of land. The company and the colony's officers had created or modified institutions of government, the king had accepted them, and the residents of the colony obeyed them, which together made the institutions and practices legitimate in all eyes.[20]

Early in the 1670s, the General Assembly requested that King Charles II grant the colony a royal charter to protect the private property of Virginians and, in effect, protect the colony from further dismemberment after royal grants placed parts of Virginia in Maryland and North Carolina.[21] The king agreed to issue a charter that changed nothing and merely declared that the "colony and plantation of Virginia" remained in "immediate dependence on the Crown of England, under the Rule and Government of such Governour or Governours, as Wee, Our heirs or Successors shall, from time to time appoint in that behalfe and upon no other person or persons whatsoever." The draft charter also declared that "all lands now possessed by the several and respective planters or Inhabitants of Virginia are and shall be confirmed and establish'd to them and their heirs for ever, where the property of any particular man's interest in any lands there, shall not be altered or prejudiced by reason thereof."[22]

The draft charter did not go so far as the colony's agents requested to include declarations "That there shall bee noe Taxe or Imposition layd on the people of Virginia, but by theire owne consent, and that Express'd by the Representatives in Assembly, as formerly provided against by many Acts"; and that "The Authority of which Assembly Consisting of Governour Counsell and Burgeses, his Majesty is humbly desired to Confirme by his Royall Graunt."[23] Instead, the draft charter merely declared the existing reality to be a fact and altered nothing. In October 1676, at almost at the very last minute before the king signed the largely unsatisfactory charter, news of Bacon's Rebellion reached London, and the king and his ministers dropped the project to deal with the emergency. They never picked it back up after the collapse of the rebellion and reimposition of order in the colony. Political and economic conditions in Virginia after the rebellion prevented the General Assembly from ever again reviving the proposal.

Government of the Royal Colony

After James I revoked the charter of the Virginia Company in the spring of 1624, the Crown theoretically had several options from which to choose for governing the land and people that the company had formerly controlled. The king could issue a new charter to create a new commercial company, impose military rule on the colony, send over a civilian viceroy with plenipotentiary powers, or allow the political institutions already in place in the colony to remain in effect for the time being under his personal authority and direction. Charles I in effect chose the last option when he declared Virginia a royal colony in 1625 and, during the following decade, recognized the legitimacy of the existing political institutions and laws in the colony. In doing so, the king accepted the authority of the colonial assembly to create such laws as the

Crown approved for governing Virginia, laws that Parliament had no role in formulating.[24]

The men in Virginia who were in responsible positions when the Virginia Company ceased to exist in the spring of 1624 simply continued to administer day-to-day affairs as they had done before the king revoked the company's charter. With the sole exception of the king's decision personally to appoint the governor and the members of the Council of State, very little actually changed in Virginia's governmental institutions and practices immediately after the legal transition from company outpost to royal colony. During the following years and decades, the colonists developed the company's first institutions and practices into the more complex and sophisticated institutions that were in most respects fully functional by the middle of the seventeenth century and became elements of the colonial constitution. At each critical step, the Crown either imposed or accepted explicitly or implicitly each change to the structure and function of the colonial government.

A description of Virginia's governmental structure that the Governor Sir William Berkeley prepared for the information of the king's ministers in 1671 indicates that the principal institutions and practices of government were well established and legitimate by then. The royal government then and thereafter consisted of an executive authority composed of the royal governor and the Council of State, a system of royal courts, the General Assembly, county courts that functioned as county governments, and the parishes of the Church of England, which were for some purposes also units of local government.[25]

All the steps in the development of the institutions and practices were consequences of conscious decisions made in London or in Virginia, but they were not all parts of an overall plan. The changes accrued with time and necessity. Unfortunately for the student of those changes, the colony's records for the middle decades of the seventeenth century, when many of those changes occurred, do not survive in sufficient abundance to trace all the changes in detail or to ascertain some of the most important dates. The files of early seventeenth-century Virginia laws are incomplete. All of the early county court records do not survive, and even fewer of the early parish records still exist. Most of the original executive and many of the legislative records were lost during one of the British raids on Richmond during the American Revolution,[26] and a very large portion of the original records of the General Court perished when the state courthouse in Richmond burned at the end of the American Civil War in April 1865.[27]

Separation of executive, legislative, and judicial powers into discreet branches of the colonial government probably did not become complete until the fourth quarter of the seventeenth century.[28] The earliest surviving reasonably complete journal of proceedings of the House of Burgesses is for the session that began in March 1658/9, fifteen years after formation of the separate House of Burgesses.[29] The Virginia Historical Society preserves an original volume of General Court records from 15 April 1670 through 22 March 1676/7. Its contents disclose that by the 1670s, the council regarded its judicial work as separate from its executive and legislative work and had begun keeping its judicial records in separate record books.[30] The existence in the National Archives of Great Britain of separate legislative and executive journals for the Council of State beginning on 9 June 1680[31] and 11 June 1680,[32] respectively, was in part the consequence of an order of the king's Board of Trade that copies of executive and legislative records be sent to London and not prima facie evidence of a deliberate separation of powers commenced or completed in Virginia at that time.[33]

The king and his ministers did not require governors to send copies of Virginia's judicial records to London, so very few copies of the General Court's records survive in England. That made the loss of the unique original records of the court in 1865 an even greater loss than the destruction of most of the colonial executive and legislative archives in the 1780s because copies of many of the most important executive and legislative records dating from 1680 were preserved in London.

The Royal Governor and Council of State

The king of England was the sole source of political authority and legitimacy in colonial Virginia, even though he often took a hands-off attitude towards its government. The royal governor was the closest thing to the personal embodiment in the colony of the king himself. As such, the office of governor was, from the very beginning, the central political institution of the evolving colonial constitution. The king's formal commission to the governor bore the king's signature and the great seal of state, which invested that officer with viceregal authority. Every royal governor received a command from the Crown to assure that law and justice be administered in Virginia as it was in England, or as nearly as it could be, local circumstances permitting. These commissions required that the resident governor must sign the bills that the General Assembly passed before they could become laws, a process which bestowed royal authority on acts of assembly. Each time the king appointed a governor he also named members of a Council of State to serve with the governor, much as the Virginia Company had named a governor and council in the 1610s.³⁴ The commission was the sole written document of recognized constitutional status during the second quarter of the seventeenth century.

The formal instructions that officers of the Crown issued to the colony's governors in the king's name (or in the queen's name during the reign of Anne from 1702 to 1714) imposed many responsibilities on the colonial executive. Few of them, though, altered the formal political relationship between the Crown and the colony or between the governor and other elements of the constitution of Virginia.³⁵ The governor and Council of State exercised the executive functions of government without any other significant structural or constitutional changes being issued from London until the American Revolution. The increasingly long list of instructions that governors received required them to secure the rights and liberties of the people, to enact and enforce laws as consistently as possible with English laws and judicial proceedings, to protect the inhabitants from foreign or domestic dangers, and to guarantee that ministers of the Church of England carried the word of God to all the king's subjects in the colony.

In carrying out some of those responsibilities, governors acted on their own or with the advice of the Council of State to appoint proper persons to fill the necessary public offices. In carrying out other responsibilities, governors participated as part of the General Assembly or as presiding judge of the General Court in the enactment and enforcement of appropriate laws. Each governor, with the advice of the council, called the General Assembly into session annually until 1677 and thereafter, only when public business required the assembly to meet or the Crown so ordered. The governor signed commissions for county courts, militia officers, sheriffs, coroners, and other public officials in order to deputize them under the authority of the king. And the governor and the council members also had overall responsibility for supervising the work of most Crown officers and making grants of uninhabited land.³⁶

During the seventeenth century the Crown created the separate office of lieutenant governor and commissioned men to act as governor with that title whenever the royal governor was absent from Virginia. The office of lieutenant governor of the colony was not the direct predecessor of the later office of lieutenant governor of the state. In the seventeenth and eighteenth centuries, the word *lieutenant* meant deputy,³⁷ which lieutenant governors of the state have not been. Lieutenant governors of the colony held that title and executed the office of governor only in the absence of the royal governor. When lieutenant governors held office, they received a share of the governor's salary and fees through individual agreements each governor concluded with each lieutenant governor.[38] In 1702 the Crown issued an instruction to make formal the practice that had arisen in Virginia when both the governor and lieutenant governor were absent from the colony or had died. The Crown placed full executive responsibility on the Council of State and, five years later, specified that the senior member of the Council of State was to execute those duties. After 1728, that senior member held the formal title of president.[39]

Some of the men who held the office of royal governor remained in England and drew part of their salaries and fees without performing much or any of the work. From the death of Governor Edward Nott in August 1706 to the arrival of Governor Norborne Berkeley, baron de Botetourt, in October 1768, no royal governor ever served in or even set foot in Virginia. The chief executives of the colony during those decades were all lieutenant governors, and among them were some of the best known of the colonial executives: Alexander Spotswood, Sir William Gooch, Robert Dinwiddie, and Francis Fauquier. During intervals between their administrations, or on several occasions when lieutenant governors were temporarily absent, resident Virginians (all but two of them natives) served as acting governor with the title of president.

Law, tradition, precedent, and dictates of practical politics placed limits on the discretion that governors and lieutenant governors had in appointing provincial and county officials, and the Crown appointed many officers of the colonial government. Those limitations and appointments restricted the abilities of governors and lieutenant governors to form political alliances with members of the House of Burgesses and other influential Virginians in the interest of implementing royal directives. Other than the governor's power of persuasion and his right (seldom exercised) to withhold his signature from, and thereby veto, bills that the General Assembly had passed, governors had few tools with which to exercise much political influence.

In 1741, council member William Byrd (1674-1744) sent words of advice to a confidant of the absentee royal governor and urged the governor to limit his own role in the appointment of public officers so as to reserve for the lieutenant governor some formidable powers of political influence. The resident lieutenant governor, Byrd predicted, "will not have the least influence with our assemblys, if he cant make friends by the skillfull distribution of the few places that have always been in his gift. All other arts of perswasion are empty and vain, and my Lord may as well send over his picture as a lieutenant governor, who has it not in his power to gain over men of figure and interest in the country."[40]

As the king's personal deputy, the royal governor was also the nominal head of what might be termed the royal establishment. It consisted of officers who held royal appointments or appointments from the governor that empowered them to execute essential governmental functions under the authority of the Crown. The Crown's executive authority in the colony was fragment and not always under the supervision of the royal governor. The offices and officers of the royal establishment were essential parts of the imperial government in all the colonies. Numerous Virginians served in those offices and augmented their family wealth with income that they derived from them.

The governor's royal commission designated him military commander in chief of the colony and commander of naval forces with the title vice admiral. The organization of the militia and the terms under which militiamen were compensated for their time when called into the field were subject to conditions that the General Assembly (of which the governor, as representative of the Crown, was part) prescribed, yet the militia was entirely under the command of the governor. He appointed and commissioned a commanding officer of each county with the title county lieutenant and (usually following recommendations of the county courts) commissioned field officers and subalterns.[41]

The secretary of the colony was the official keeper of government records, including those of the land office. He was in charge of making certain that land grants, commissions, and other documents that the governor signed were all in proper order and that all the colony's laws and other official records were properly preserved. The secretary was a royal appointee with a commission from the Crown. For most of the colonial period, the secretary of the colony had authority to name county clerks, usually from a small cadre of young men who trained by working in the secretary's office without pay until they were appointed as a county clerk and who then returned a percentage of their fee income to the secretary by whose authority they held their appointments. Some of the secretaries of the colony were absentee officeholders like the governors and named deputies to run the office and collect the fees. The fees were very substantial, and the office of secretary was probably the most lucrative in the colony.[42]

Governor Sir William Berkeley appointed Richard Lee as attorney general in October 1643, the earliest surviving record of the office in the colony. The governor's commission empowered him in the king's name to appoint such essential officers as he deemed necessary.[43] Most of the attorneys general during the eighteenth century had read law in the Inns of Court in London and were able and skillful attorneys at law. They no doubt contributed to the increased professionalism of the bar in the colonial capital and perhaps elsewhere in the colony. Very few archival records concerning the work of the colony's attorneys general survive.

Records pertaining to the collection and handling of revenue during the first half of the seventeenth century contain few useful clues about who did the work and how well those officers managed that essential function of government. Parliament's acts of trade and navigation beginning in the 1660s generated customs revenue for the Crown. Consequently, the Crown created the office of receiver general to collect the revenue and the office of auditor general to oversee the accounts. As was the case with the office of secretary, the receiver and the auditor received royal appointments and, in some instances, remained in England and administered their offices through deputies who resided in Virginia. The patent holders as receiver general and auditor general received a percentage of the money that passed through their offices by way of salary and paid a portion of it to the deputies who did the work. Both offices were lucrative and desirable. Profitable too were the various offices that collected the customs and other duties, which members of politically influential Virginia families often secured. At each of the several ports of entry, a resident naval officer and a collector oversaw the record keeping and registration of trading vessels and collected the customs revenue. Governors usually appointed those officers and had some supervisory responsibilities over them, but those officials received their commissions from London.[44]

The Crown also had a resident escheator general in the colony to recover for the Crown land belonging to Virginians who died with no will and no heirs at law[45] and a surveyor general to oversee the work of local surveyors and men who surveyed unoccupied land on the western frontier. Appointments as a county surveyor allowed many Virginia men and their families to increase their wealth and landholdings substantially.[46]

Royal Courts

The creation of courts was one of the powers that the king exercised as part of his royal prerogative. During the final years of the Virginia Company's existence and during the first decades of royal government, the governor and the members of the Council of State nevertheless personally directed nearly all aspects of the administration of justice as well as of public administration. In 1621, the company instructed the governor and council to schedule quarterly court meeting dates in the capital for the convenience of people who required "justice or direction" of their personal affairs.[47] Incomplete surviving records of their proceedings between 4 February 1622/3 and 9 February 1632/3 preserve depositions, orders, judgments, and other records of both an administrative and judicial nature.[48] Because the records for most of the disputes that the council considered appear to be incomplete, it is not possible to ascertain how sophisticated the administration of justice was during the first decade of royal government.[49]

In exercising their responsibilities as judges, members of the council encountered enough variety and difficulty in their work that they soon realized they needed a law library to enable them to administer justice fairly and in keeping with English law and practice as the king required. George Thorpe wrote from Virginia to a company officer in London on 15 May 1621, "In the matter of our Government here wee are many times perplexed sometimes for lacke of Legal officers & some times for wante of books." He ordered an abridgment of the acts of Parliament, several standard manuals for administering estates and conducting proceedings in court, and "what other Lawe books" his correspondent "shall thinke fitt."[50] From that beginning the council assembled what, by the end of the colonial period, was an excellent, comprehensive library of English and colonial statutes, reference works, case reports, and learned treatises.[51]

The court was initially known as the Quarter Court because it met four times a year in Jamestown.[52] With the consent of the king expressed through the signature of the governors on the bills that the assembly passed, the legislature changed meeting dates, regulated procedures, and specified circumstances under which people could appeal a decision of a county court to the Quarter Court.[53] In 1684, the General Assembly required the court to hold only two meetings annually, in April and October.[54] Thereafter, the court was always denominated the General Court.

After governors began enforcing an order from the Crown early in the 1680s, no person could appeal a decision of the General Court to the General Assembly. Appeals could be heard only in the Privy Council in London.[55] The new order significantly increased the expense of pursuing an appeal and thereby probably reduced the number of appeals and as a consequence augmented the effective authority and the prestige of the General Court. None of the appeals to the Privy Council changed aspects of the colonial constitution.[56]

Beginning with the enactment in the 1660s of the English Navigation Acts to regulate and tax commerce between England and its colonies and overseas trading partners, the General Court conducted trials to enforce the trade and navigation acts in Virginia.[57] The General Court and the county courts had concurrent jurisdiction in cases involving the acts of trade and navigation and in some cases involving misdemeanors and minor civil actions, but the General Court usually left the latter to the county courts. The General Court tried most of the civil suits and chancery cases involving substantial amounts of property or money and all felony cases in which white people were defendants.

In 1707, the Crown instructed the governor to convene two additional courts each year so that white people accused of crimes not languish too long in jail awaiting their trials.[58] Called a Court of Oyer and Terminer (literally, courts to hear and determine a case), it met according to a law the General Assembly enacted midway between the semiannual meetings of the General Court. The Court of Oyer and Terminer was legally a separate court, but it had the same membership as the General Court and it conducted criminal trials under the same procedures as in the General Court. Residents of the colony, and students of the colony's legal history, generally regarded the Court of Oyer and Terminer as part of the General Court.[59]

In 1698, the Crown established a Court of Vice-Admiralty in Virginia for the more expeditious trial of cases that arose under the law of the sea, including condemnation of ships that privateers had captured. The Crown commissioned the court's principal officers (judge, advocate, register, and marshal), who in most instances already held prestigious posts in the government of the colony; but as with the other royal courts in Virginia, the General Assembly passed laws to regulate its proceedings.[60] Only a few records of the Virginia Court of Vice-Admiralty are extant, but they contain records of trials involving both piracy and infractions of the acts of navigation and trade.[61]

The General Assembly

Some of the Virginians' seventeenth-century innovations in their governmental institutions were quite significant. Perhaps the most important innovation followed the decision of Governor Sir William Berkeley in 1643—about a year after his arrival in Virginia—to allow or to encourage the elected burgesses to form their own separate house of the assembly. Members of the Council of State formed the other, or upper, house of the assembly, with the governor present through the session of May 1705; thereafter, council members sat alone during legislative sessions[62] except at the formal opening and closing ceremonies.

During the first half of the seventeenth century, burgesses represented the large class of middling tobacco planters who, for the most part, wished to be able to sell their tobacco in the high-priced markets of the Netherlands. The wealthiest planters with seats on the council had dominated the colony both politically and economically, and some of them, such as Samuel Mathews and William Claiborne, preferred to confine the colony's valuable tobacco trade to their politically powerful business partners in London. Berkeley, by allying himself with the burgesses and allowing them to meet as the separate House of Burgesses in 1643, created a bicameral legislature to counterbalance the influential councilors and not for the sake of bicameralism as the only appropriate structure for a legislature.[63]

The political legitimacy of the separate House of Burgesses quickly won widespread acceptance. This is strikingly evident from events less than a decade later. In 1652, Parliament sent a fleet of warships and soldiers to force the residents and governments of Virginia and Maryland to abandon their adherence to the monarchy and to submit to Oliver Cromwell's Puritan Commonwealth. Governor Berkeley and the General Assembly negotiated terms of surrender. From then until the restoration of the monarchy in 1660, the House of Burgesses assumed the role that the king had formerly held in Virginia and that the House of Commons had assumed in England. The burgesses appointed a Puritan as governor, and he, the council members, and the burgesses all agreed that "the right of election of all officers of this colony be and appertain to the Burgesses the representatives of the people." The elected burgesses repeated that assertion throughout the interregnum, the time between kings, when they annually appointed a governor and members of the Council of State.[64] Perhaps in part to avoid alienating the Cromwellians but also in shrewd, practical acknowledgment of the existence of a large population of Puritans in Virginia, the burgesses elected three Puritans in a row to serve as governor of the colony. The third of them was Samuel Mathews's namesake son,[65] but early in 1660, Governor Mathews died, and rumors reached Virginia that the Commonwealth was collapsing in England and that Charles II would soon take the throne. The House of Burgesses arranged for Berkeley to resume the governorship, and he, the members of the council, and the Burgesses soon thereafter proclaimed Charles II king.[66]

Until the 1680s, the General Assembly occasionally heard and decided appeals from the General Court.[67] Only a few of the judicial records of the assembly survive in the form of notes from the burgesses' Committee for Private Causes.[68] The General Assembly may have been prepared to act as a court of first resort in one vital religious matter. In 1641 and 1642/3 the assembly passed laws to prohibit Catholic priests from residing in Virginia and Catholics from holding public office. The laws imposed a fine of one 1,000 pounds of tobacco on any person "convicted before an Assembly" for violating the laws.[69] No records survive to indicate that the assembly ever conducted such a trial. The assembly was not prepared to act as a court of first resort in other instances. During the session of 1658/9, the assembly journal records "The widow Hudson extrajudicially bringing into the Assembly a petition against Collonel William Clayborne," the legislators required that she "take her course at comon lawe."[70]

During the seventeenth century, the General Assembly—especially the House of Burgesses—grew more and more to resemble the Parliament of England—especially the House of Commons—and began to operate with rules and procedures that resembled or derived from English parliamentary law and practice.[71] The earliest known rules of procedure for the House of Burgesses are found in one of the earliest extant journals, which is for the session that began in March 1658/9,[72] but the legislators had granted themselves some parliamentary privileges long before then. In the session of 1631/2, the General Assembly declared burgesses privileged from arrest during, going to, or returning from a session.[73]

Throughout the seventeenth century, members of the General Assembly passed laws of increasing sophistication as their colony grew in size and population.[74] In 1645, the assembly settled the number of members of the House of Burgesses at four per county,[75] then, during the session of 1660/1, reduced it to two.[76] The 1705 election law retained the two-burgesses-per-county rule, allowed one to the residents of Jamestown, and authorized the president and professors of the College of William and Mary to elect one burgess by virtue of their holding a royal charter, which they obtained possession of for electoral purposes in 1718.[77]

In 1653, shortly after the colony surrendered to Cromwell's Commonwealth, the assembly prohibited clergymen from serving as burgesses, a prohibition the members undoubtedly understood as corresponding to parliamentary practice. Virginia state constitutional conventions inserted similar prohibitions into the Constitutions of 1776, 1830, 1851, and 1864, and they remained part of the state's constitution until 1869.[78]

In 1646, the General Assembly required for the first time that men elect burgesses by voice vote.[79] Beginning in 1670, the assembly imposed restrictions on who could vote for members of the House of Burgesses. The 1670 law confined voting to "ffreeholders and housekeepers who only are answerable to the publique for the levies." The "usuall way of chuseing burgeses" by the votes of all free men, the legislators explained, had led to "tumults at the election to the disturbance of his majesties peace" rather than to the election of "persons fitly qualifyed."[80] In 1684, the assembly limited suffrage to "every person who holds lands, tenements or hereditaments for his owne life, for the life of his wife, or for the life of any other person or persons."[81] The assembly clarified the law in 1699 and declared "that no woman sole or covert, infants under the age of twenty one years, or recusant convict being freeholders shall be enabled to give a vote or have a voice in the election of burgesses."[82]

In 1736, the General Assembly revised the election law. The new law required that in order to vote, a man had to own one hundred acres of land or fifty acres of land and a house in order to vote in a county, or he had to own a house and lot in an incorporated municipality to vote there. It also allowed men to vote in any and all counties and cities where they owned land, and made them eligible to be elected in any of those cities or counties. (It was under this law that George Washington first won election to the House of Burgesses from Frederick County where he owned land, not from Fairfax County where he lived.) In what was probably a unique colonial legal provision, the law allowed men who jointly owned a tract of land of the required size to vote if they all agreed on which candidates were to receive their vote.[83]

In 1691, the General Assembly passed an act to appoint a treasurer to oversee the funds that the legislators raised by taxation or appropriated by statute.[84] Thereafter, at the conclusion of each assembly, the legislators renewed the law and elected a treasurer to handle what they regarded as their own money (and not the royal revenue that the king's receiver general collected and auditor general oversaw). On nearly every occasion until 1766, the assembly elected the Speaker of the House as treasurer and authorized him to retain a fixed proportion of the money that he collected or expended by way of salary and for the support of the dignity of the office of Speaker. In 1766, following a major financial scandal in the treasury, the assembly elected a treasurer and awarded the Speaker a salary, which separated the two offices as the Crown had wished for years.[85]

The General Assembly became a robust institution, and by the middle of the eighteenth century the House of Burgesses had become the dominant branch of the legislature. As happened elsewhere in the English North American colonies, the lower house came to represent the economic and social values of the colony's leadership class. In Virginia, that meant the large- and middle-scale planters of tobacco.[86]

The Crown issued orders from time to time that made important changes in the constitutional role of the General Assembly. A 1676 order reduced the frequency of meetings and empowered the governor and Council of State to determine when to hold elections for members of the House of Burgesses. For reasons that are not apparent, Governor Berkeley had issued no writs for general elections between 1660 and 1676. Virginians did not then regard frequent elections or elections at predictable intervals as essential components of their limited form of representative government. The surviving records from the time do not preserve complaints about the lack of a general election, but an absence of evidence on any subject from the seventeenth century (even more than for later centuries) does not constitute evidence of an absence.

In 1676, the Crown ordered that the assembly meet no more often than every second year unless "some emergent occasion shall make it necessary."[87] The order had little or nothing to do with the lack of elections during the previous sixteen years. It was one of many restrictions on colonial government institutions and practices that the Crown was then beginning to introduce. Another restriction was transferring from the burgesses to the governor the power to appoint the clerk of the House of Burgesses.[88] The order to reduce the frequency of legislative sessions did not require the governor to call an election before each meeting, or session. During the eighteenth century, general elections of burgesses took place at three- to five-year intervals except when vacancies occurred and voters in a county elected a replacement burgess in a special election.

About the same time that the Crown ordered the governor to send legislative and executive journals to London in 1679, the Crown ordered governors to send to London all bills that the assembly had passed for review before they could become law. Although the Crown did not renew the instruction in 1682,[89] that was the beginning of much closer royal oversight of the work of the General Assembly, comparable in some ways to Poyning's Law of 1494, which required English approval of acts of the Irish Parliament before they could take effect. Through instructions to Virginia's governors issued in 1707, 1710, 1717, 1720, 1728, 1738, and 1756, the Crown required the General Assembly to insert a clause to suspend the operations of any new statute that affected the royal prerogative or trade until the king and Privy Council allowed or disallowed it.[90] Other instructions issued in 1710, 1728, and 1738 included similar requirements for private acts, which usually dealt with people's estates.[91] Collectively, those orders severely restricted the ability of the General Assembly to legislate as its members saw fit. No new law and no law that amended an act that had previously received the royal assent could take effect in Virginia until after the king Crown and the Privy Council decided whether to allow or disallow it. That process could—and in more than a few instances did—take several years.[92] Sometimes, the Board of Trade or the Crown failed to act at all, which prevented bills from becoming laws.

Beginning with the 1619 General Assembly, governors possessed a "negative voyce," or authority to veto bills that the assembly passed by refusing to sign them.[93] Incomplete records of legislative proceedings for the seventeenth century render it impossible to know how many times governors refused to sign bills. Only one of the known refusals is recorded in a journal of the House of Burgesses. Most, though not all, of the known instances are recorded in the journals of the Council of State when it sat as the upper house of the General Assembly. Fewer than a dozen vetoes can be accounted for in the documentation, most of which occurred because a bill violated an explicit prohibition in the governor's royal instructions or did not contain a clause suspending its operation until the king could approve or disapprove it.[94]

County Government

Before the king made Virginia a royal colony in 1625, the company issued instructions for administering settlements outside the immediate vicinity of Jamestown.[95] As the number of settlers and settlements increased and spread up the rivers and along the shore of Chesapeake Bay, the governor and Council of State appointed men to take charge of local defense and authorized other men to keep the peace. Officials in Jamestown thus rid themselves of time-consuming and sometimes trivial work such as resolving disputes about ownership of livestock or whether some person's animals had done damage to another person's crops. An act of assembly adopted in the 1623/4 session ordered monthly courts to be held in the settlements then known as Charles City and Elizabeth City and later known as Charles City County and Elizabeth City County.[96] Later in the decade, Acting Governor John Pott issued orders to commanders of plantations to keep the peace and authorized appeals from rulings of the monthly court in Elizabeth City to the governor and Council of State in Jamestown.[97] In 1629, the assembly empowered local commanders to conscript men for defense,[98] and in 1631/2, it established monthly courts at five places and specified their jurisdiction.[99]

Through a long series of such delegations of responsibility to handle individual specific matters, the government of the colony created units of local government that thereafter evolved into full-fledged county governments. The earliest extant local court records for Virginia—for anywhere in North America—begin early in 1632/3 with regular meetings of the monthly court on the Eastern Shore, the peninsula between the Atlantic Ocean and Chesapeake Bay.[100] The devolution of some governmental responsibilities to the counties was a process, not an event, and may have continued for as long as fifteen or twenty years before county governments as later Virginians knew them had fully evolved. This process had proceeded far enough during the decade after the dissolution of the Virginia Company that an official record of 1634 refers to eight named "shires," or counties, in the colony.[101]

The governor issued a formal commission for each county in the king's name to invest local men with ample legal authority to govern their communities. Identified in the earliest records as commissioners of the peace, by 1662, the law designated them by the English title, justices of the peace.[102] During the 1645 and 1652 sessions of the assembly, the legislators granted county courts the authority to oversee the probate of estates, a responsibility that ecclesiastical courts, of which there were none in Virginia, exercised in England.[103]

With qualified sworn clerks, the courts became courts of record where people could have deeds, wills, and other important documents officially recorded, authenticated, and enforced. Although the county clerks were clerks of the county courts, the duties of the county clerks in Virginia evolved to be very different from the work of clerks of court in England. County clerks were among the most important officials in Virginia. During the eighteenth century, county clerks often took part in their offices, rather than in open court, in arranging settlements of debt collection suits, a process that ordinarily left no documentary record in county's record books.[104]

Justices of the peace gradually took over nearly all local governmental powers, and later acts of assembly enlarged and regulated their responsibilities.[105] Members of the county courts eventually gained almost complete control over who served in nearly every county office. In effect, the courts became self-perpetuating bodies by recommending men for the governor to appoint to fill vacant seats on the court. By the latter decades of the seventeenth century, governors routinely followed nearly all of those recommendations.

As the laws that the General Assembly enacted and the quality of arguments before the General Court both became more sophisticated during the seventeenth century, so did the operations of the county courts. In the early decades, lay justices of the peace settled disputes, punished petty infractions of the peace, and generally administered justice much more informally than their counterparts in England. Virginians streamlined and simplified procedures to allow them to avoid the complex legal language and technical matters that were associated with many standard English writs. For most purposes, the legal environment that they created suited the new world in which they lived and freed them from some constraints of English precedents and practices for which they had no need. By the middle of the eighteenth century, though, administration of justice at the local level had become much more sophisticated.[106]

The duties and legal responsibilities of justices of the peace, sheriffs, constables, and coroners as they had evolved by the early years of the eighteenth century are clearly described in George Webb's 1736 *Office and Authority of a Justice of Peace*. Webb's book was the first legal manual compiled and published in Virginia and that was intended specifically for the most important of all county officials—indeed, they were arguably the most important and influential public officials in the colony. The very necessity for a Virginian to compile and publish a manual for the colony's justices of the peace indicated how different the roles and responsibilities of those officers in Virginia had become from those of their counterparts in England, which rendered all the old English manuals largely irrelevant for Virginia's justices of the peace.[107]

Beginning in the 1660s, county courts shared concurrent jurisdiction with the General Court in the enforcement of the British acts of trade and navigation. The surviving records indicate that they did so competently and with recourse to the proper statutes and records.[108] The assembly's 1666 Act for the Supplie of Each Countie with Lawe Bookes required the county courts and the General Court to purchase the volumes of parliamentary statutes for enforcing the acts of trade and navigation and other parliamentary statutes and to acquire the standard reference works for justices of the peace for the probate of estates.[109]

In 1692, the General Assembly directed that when enslaved people were accused of crimes, the county sheriff should apply to the governor for a commission of oyer and terminer to empower justices of the peace named therein to hold a special court to try the accused "without the sollemnitie of a jury."[110] These courts had the same name as the Court of Oyer and Terminer that was formed in 1707 and that met twice a year in the capital, but the county courts of that name were not permanent courts but special courts that met only one time. For each trial, the governor issued a new commission to authorize justices of the peace whom he identified by name to try one accused person. Those courts did not afford defendants all the procedural protections of the common law, but this lapse from English legal customs that white Virginians prized for themselves evidently provoked no loud protests.

When the last of the Revolutionary conventions adopted a constitution for the new independent government of Virginia in 1776, the convention made only one change in the operations of the county courts. The new constitution empowered members of the courts to appoint new clerks when the clerks who were then in office died or relinquished their posts. The constitution specifically required the governor to appoint new justices of the peace from lists of names that the sitting justices submitted to him, which made permanent and inalterable the colonial practice that guaranteed to the justices of the peace their ability to control membership of the county courts.

Church Government

Development of institutions and practices of church government followed a trajectory similar to, but less well documented than, that of the county courts. Most of the English men and women who resided in Virginia were religious, and consequently, the institutions and practices of the Church of England were important to them.[111] The colony's religious institutions had origins in the beliefs and practices of the earliest settlers, and they and their successors developed their church into the stronghold of the Church of England in North America. Even after the General Assembly's adoption of the English Act of Toleration in 1699,[112] which in effect made the English act part of the constitution of the colony, a former Virginia clergyman wrote in 1724 that of all the colonies only Virginia "may be justly esteemed the happy Retreat of *true Britons* and *true Churchmen.*"[113]

The Virginia Company had laid the foundations for the church when it sent over a clergyman with the first shiploads of settlers. Before 1619, when the first General Assembly met, the company had required settlers to provide a glebe (a house and land) for the use and support of each clergyman.[114] Laws that the General Assembly enacted beginning in the 1640s provided for a uniform system of church governance throughout Virginia that probably incorporated existing institutions and practices.[115]

No bishop ever traveled to or exercised personal responsibility in Virginia, but the absence of a church hierarchy comparable to the elaborate organizational structure of the church in England did not indicate that religious beliefs and the church were not important. The absence of a hierarchy simply meant that institutions of church governance functioned differently in Virginia than in the old country. Laymen in Virginia had to improvise and take on responsibilities that in England only a bishop, church patron, or ecclesiastical court could do, such as allow vestrymen to select ministers and run the church and to empower justices of the peace to oversee probate of estates.

Without a bishop on hand to induct ministers into their cures, the governor initially either appointed or approved the selection and employment of ministers, but in 1643 (or perhaps even earlier), the General Assembly empowered vestries to appoint clergymen, a responsibility that lay parish officers in England never exercised.[116] That gave local laymen—vestrymen, churchwardens, and clerks of the vestry—almost complete control over the parish and the church. Vestrymen employed and dismissed ministers in ways with no counterparts in the ecclesiastical laws and practices of England. Late in the seventeenth century and early in the eighteenth century, that serious deviation from English ecclesiastical law and practice produced a long debate. The Board of Trade requested several formal advisory opinions from the king's attorney general and the counsel of the Board of Trade;[117] but neither the Privy Council nor the bishop of London tried to force changes in Virginians' long-established laws and practices, and resident lieutenant governors also refrained from trying—or were afraid to try—to make any changes.

Most seventeenth-century Virginia parishes were smaller than any county. Parishes were therefore the most local units of government in the colony. As in England, parishes had responsibilities that are now regarded in the United States as civil and not religious, such as maintaining roads until the 1650s; keeping official registers of births, marriages, and deaths; and sharing with county courts responsibility to identify and care for orphans and the destitute. Vestrymen and churchwardens also had legal responsibility as part of their official duties to report to the county court for prosecution of moral offences such as adultery, fornication, swearing, and nonattendance at church. In the early days, churches played a role in the punishment of some of those moral lapses by allowing accused or convicted people to cleanse themselves of guilt and to purge the community of wickedness by confessing in church in an old ecclesiastical ritual known as compurgation.[118] As an integral part of the colonial government, the church exercised that essential responsibility for protecting the moral and religious health of the community. Purging the community of wickedness was as important as, or more important than, cleansing the soul of a sinner.

So important were the parishes, both as communities of people and as governmental institutions, that from time to time in the 1650s and 1660s, some parish residents or vestries elected burgesses, and the other burgesses seated them alongside members elected from the counties.[119] Beginning in 1662, the General Assembly directed churchwardens to assemble the parish residents every fourth year to perambulate all property boundaries and renew boundary markers in order that all property be rendered secure and that disputes about property lines not disrupt the community. Beating the bounds, or processioning, as the practice was known, continued in many localities well into the nineteenth century.[120] Several times during the seventeenth century, and again in 1728, when the legislators tried to reduce tobacco production in order to raise the price per pound, they empowered churchwardens or vestrymen to enforce limits on the number of plants each laborer could tend.[121] That the legislature imposed those responsibilities on parish officials and not on justices of the peace, constables, or sheriffs indicates how important the parish communities and officials were. Eighteenth-century parishes generally imposed heavier taxes on the residents to pay for the civil and ecclesiastical responsibilities of the church than justices of the peace imposed to pay for operating the county governments and keeping the peace.[122]

Beginning in the latter years of the seventeenth century, bishops of London had nominal responsibility for managing the church in the colony, and they required that governors permit only men whom a bishop had ordained to serve as parish ministers. In 1684, the bishop appointed a commissary to serve as his personal representative in Virginia, but none of the commissaries supervised the colonial church with a firm hand—not even the most able and assertive commissary, James Blair, who served in that capacity from 1689 until his death in 1743.[123] However, the commissary almost always received a royal appointment to a seat on the prestigious and powerful Council of State by virtue of his being the bishop's personal deputy and thereby, after the governor, the highest ranking official of the Church of England in Virginia.

The Church of England in Virginia became a distinctive Church of Virginia during the seventeenth century, though without its own separate name. Until the disestablishment of the church in 1786, the organization and functioning of the church more nearly resembled the Church of Scotland or the congregational churches in New England than the Church of England in England.[124] On the eve of the American Revolution, Richard Bland, the keenest student of the colony's laws and history, concluded that in all the world, the Virginia church was "*sui generis:*" one of a kind.[125]

The Constitution of the Colony in Operation

The institutions and practices of Virginia's government that King Charles I explicitly recognized as legitimate in 1639 evolved in sophistication and complexity in the ensuing decades more under the superintending eyes of residents of the colony than of the Crown and its English bureaucracy. The governmental stability that the political leaders of the colony created served the colony well for the most part. It reduced the social instability that had marked the earliest years of settlement, and it gave the society and economy the opportunity to evolve as they did.[126]

The elements of the constitution of the colony that Virginians had created or shaped worked extremely well for the tobacco planters.[127] In each county a small, self-perpetuating group of justices of the peace that consisted almost entirely of planters ruled the community according to English and Virginia laws. They selected almost all the local functionaries of government. In most counties, some of the justices of the peace also served as members of the parish vestry. They too formed small, self-perpetuating local governments that ruled their parishes and governed the church according to Virginia laws and practices of their own devising. Together, justices of the peace and vestrymen—who were very often the same men—were the local governments in Virginia. In almost all respects, they were not answerable to any other authority except in extremely rare cases. The two eighteenth-century incorporated municipalities of Williamsburg and Norfolk had corresponding boards of aldermen who functioned in the same manner, although for the most part merchants and lawyers, not tobacco planters, held the offices.

Those few local government officials constituted the nucleus of each county's or city's body politic. In most instances the county's voters selected from among the justices of the peace and vestrymen and the members of the leading planter families when they gathered from time to time, at the governor's call, to elect burgesses to represent their counties in the General Assembly. A very large proportion of men elected to the House of Burgesses had served on the county court or a parish vestry or were members while serving in the assembly. In some decades, all or almost all the burgesses were or had been justices of the peace.[128] The virtual identities of interest among the small company of justices of the peace, vestrymen, and burgesses united them in enacting and enforcing laws to benefit their personal and collective interests as tobacco planters and social leaders. Government and politics were not in any modern respect democratic. In the limited sense that they were even representative, they guaranteed that men who held public office and shaped public policies represented the class of tobacco planters. Those men governed as if they believed that they were entitled to govern and, in fact, entitled to govern as they pleased. The colony's government at all levels was strictly hierarchical, which reflected the hierarchical social characteristics of the colony's population.

As the white population increased and spread westward during the eighteenth century, the General Assembly created new counties and parishes. The total number of Virginians who served on county courts and parish vestries and in the House of Burgesses significantly increased, but because of the larger increase in the whole population the proportion of the adult white male population who personally participated in government actually decreased. During the middle of the eighteenth century, about two-thirds to three-quarters of adult white males in Virginia may have owned enough land to qualify to vote for members of the House of Burgesses. At any given election, about half to three-quarters of qualified men actually voted.[129] The white men who voted constituted only a minority of all white men in Virginia, and that minority elected the members of the only elected governmental institution in the colony.

In Virginia, as elsewhere in the English colonies where slave labor became essential, legislators created a whole new body of statute law to regulate and govern the society that came to be based on slave labor, not only in tobacco fields but in virtually every other aspect of agriculture, commerce, and household management. The slave economy led the General Assembly to reverse two presumptions of the common law. In 1662, it declared that thereafter all children were to be considered born free or enslaved according to the condition of the mother rather than that of the father,[130] and in 1667, it passed a law to permit Virginians to purchase and hold Christians in lifetime slavery.[131] In 1705, when the rate of importation of African laborers was rapidly increasing, the General Assembly revised and reenacted all the laws relating to slavery to create Virginia's first comprehensive slave code.[132]

County courts also made new laws as a consequence of slavery. By the 1660s, the courts began reversing the common law doctrine of *caveat emptor*, let the buyer beware. The great demand for sound laborers in Virginia led the county courts to reverse that doctrine in transactions relating to indentured servants and enslaved people and to place on sellers a responsibility to disclose if a person was of unsound health or was pregnant. The alternative doctrine of *caveat venditor* became good law throughout Virginia without any legislative enactment. When the General Court heard arguments on the legality of *caveat venditor* in 1735, the judges affirmed it in *Waddill v. Chamberlayne* even after hearing a long, scholarly argument from the colony's very able and learned attorney general, Edward Barradall, that the common law required the judges to reinstate *caveat emptor*.[133]

From time to time, white men in Virginia who did not participate in governance objected to some features of the colonial constitution as it worked in the counties and parishes. The most abundant evidence of dissatisfaction can be found in the documentary record of Bacon's Rebellion of 1676.[134] It was the only large-scale, mass uprising of white men against the colony's public officials. In pleas to the General Assembly in June of that year and in complaints to royal commissioners of investigation early in 1677, white Virginians of the middling and lower classes enumerated some very serious grievances. They complained that burgesses assembled too often and voted themselves excessively large expense accounts that taxpayers had to pay. Legislators had raised taxes but left the frontiers defenseless against First Nations raiding parties. Justices of the peace taxed people by the head, or poll, and did not tax land, which placed a proportionally heavier tax burden on poor people and landless artisans than on owners of large plantations. Some county courts went into secret session to set the annual tax levy, and justices of the peace told men who complained about the practice that how the court did its work (the public's work) was none of their business. Men in several counties demanded that ordinary residents be permitted to take part in setting the county tax rates. Some county clerks refused to let men see or obtain copies of official county records. Some sheriffs contrived to retain their offices for several consecutive years, which enlarged their local political influence and also increased their income because they collected fees for performing some of their tasks and kept a percentage of the tax money that they collected in lieu of a salary. Other men complained that parish vestrymen were guilty of like abuses and asked that members of vestries be elected at regularly scheduled intervals. Still other men complained that when a war with neighboring First Nations tribes appeared imminent, militia officers called their men into the field to erect forts and other buildings on their own property at public expense. The conduct of haughty, overbearing, entrenched elites led to open revolt against some of the officials and practices of local institutions of the colonial government.

In May 1676, Governor Berkeley ordered a general election for members of the House of Burgesses and expressly declared that men who had been disfranchised since 1670 be permitted to vote. The new burgesses passed bills to redress most of the grievances, the Council of State also passed them, and the governor signed them. Because King Charles II incorrectly believed that the only reason the General Assembly had passed those laws was that Nathaniel Bacon, the rebel, had forced it to, he ignorantly ordered all the laws of that session of assembly repealed. In obedience to the king, the next assembly, which began in February 1676/7, reenacted none of the most important reforms. The rebellion failed to change any consequential portions of the colonial constitution. The colony's government continued to function with no major modifications for the next hundred years. During the American Revolution and in the nineteenth century, some of the same complaints again bubbled up and eventually led to some changes in the constitutions of the state or in its public policies, but the changes did not take place during the colonial era.

In almost every way, government under the constitution of the colony worked well for the men in charge. When Virginia men who had prospered under the colonial constitution wrote what they called a "Constitution or Form of Government" for their new independent state in June 1776, they eliminated many of the elements of the colonial constitution that the Crown had created, but they changed almost none of the institutions and practices that their ancestors had created.

The Constitution of the Colony Defended

During the decade before the American Revolution, Virginia's political and legal elite had to think deeply about how their constitution worked and the relationship between them and the king and Parliament in Great Britain. Three protracted controversies sharpened their thinking.

The first was the pistole fee controversy, which began in 1752.[135] Lieutenant Governor Robert Dinwiddie announced that he had permission from the Crown and approval of the Council of State to charge a new fee of one pistole (a Spanish coin then worth £1 2s 6d in the colonies) for affixing his signature to land grants. Members of the House of Burgesses objected strenuously that even with the approval of the Council of State, the lieutenant governor had no constitutional authority to create a new fee or tax, that only the representatives of the people in the General Assembly had that authority in Virginia. They cited as binding precedent an episode from the 1680s when the Crown had disallowed a governor's imposition of a new fee. For five years, the lieutenant governor and his legal support team in London waged a spirited contest with Virginians who complained to the king and Privy Council about an executive action that they said violated a precedent Charles II had established in the 1680s and that had thereby become part of the colonial constitution. The Privy Council allowed the governor to charge the fee but not for land grants already made out and ready for signing before the Council of State approved the fee.

The second controversy derived from the Crown's orders that the bills that the assembly passed contain clauses suspending their operation until the Crown decided whether to approve them. That severely restricted the ability of the General Assembly to respond to emergency situations as when, following tobacco crop failures in 1755 and 1758, the assembly passed short-term emergency laws to allow people who owed debts payable in tobacco to pay in money at a rate approximating two pennies per pound of tobacco.[136] The emergency measures, called Two-Penny Acts, contained no suspending clauses. The laws had the effect of significantly reducing the incomes of clergymen, who by law received sixteen thousand pounds of tobacco and cask annually. At two pennies per pound, they received a much smaller income in those years than they would have received had they been paid the legally established 16,000 pounds of high-priced tobacco. Several clergymen appealed to the king and Privy Council to disallow the 1758 law because its effect was to amend the long-established salary act without containing a suspending clause. The king sided with the clergymen and disallowed the law.

Richard Bland and other prominent Virginians argued in the assembly and in print—and who knows how many argued in taverns, parlors, churchyards, or at county court meetings—that the measures had been absolutely necessary, that the nature of the emergency did not permit the General Assembly to wait until the king could consider its proposed remedy, that the law applied to everybody and was not restricted in its operation to the clergy, and that therefore it was unjust for the Crown to disallow the law, which was, in any event, to be in effect for only one year.

Patrick Henry advanced the argument another important step. One of the clergymen sued to recover the difference between the amount of money he had been paid in 1758 under the Two-Penny Act and the value of the tobacco he stated that he was owed as a result of the king's disallowance of the law. After a jury determined in 1763 that he was entitled to damages, it had to set the amount. During that phase of the trial, Henry represented the vestry that had followed the dictates of the second Two-Penny Act. He argued that the General Assembly had every right to enact such laws during a temporary emergency. The jury awarded the clergyman one penny in damages, not the much larger sum that he claimed he was due. That verdict virtually nullified the king's nullification of the Two-Penny Act. The Parson's Cause, as it was popularly known, made Patrick Henry a hero, and it focused attention directly on the actions of the king. The ruling also gave credence to the belief that the king could not violate any part of the constitution of the colony that his predecessors and the people of Virginia had together created without forfeiting his claim to their allegiance.[137]

The third major controversy that led to further discussions of the nature of the constitution of the colony and the roles of Parliament and the Crown in it was the Stamp Act crisis.[138] Parliament announced in 1764 that to help pay the huge public debt incurred during the Seven Years' War (or French and Indian War) and to pay for keeping an army in North America it would impose a stamp duty in the colonies the following year. People would have to buy stamps from the government and affix them to legal documents, newspapers, playing cards, and numerous other important articles and services, much like the modern stamps on packets of cigarettes that signify payment of an excise tax. People in all the colonies objected for several reasons. For one, no Americans were represented in Parliament. For another, many Americans believed Parliament had no authority under the British Constitution to levy a tax outside the British Isles. And Parliament had not taxed residents of North America except in the regulation of trade, which colonists interpreted as effectively confirming that colonial assemblies alone could constitutionally tax residents of the colonies.

The General Assembly petitioned the king on 18 December 1764 not to sign the proposed law so as "to protect your People of this Colony in the Enjoyment of their ancient and inestimable Right of being governed by such Laws respecting their internal Polity and Taxation as are derived from the own Consent, with the Approbation of their Sovereign or his Substitute"—meaning the royal governor or lieutenant governor. The assembly defended that as a "Right which as Men, and Descendents of *Britons*, they have ever quietly possessed since first by Royal Permission and Encouragement they left the Mother Kingdom to extend its Commerce and Dominion." The two houses of assembly also sent separate addresses to the two houses of Parliament and repeated their assertion that only Virginians could constitutionally tax Virginians.[139]

After Parliament passed and the king signed the Stamp Act in 1765, justices of the peace in three Virginia counties resigned rather than require people to purchase stamps, conduct court business with stamped papers, or risk prosecution for failing to purchase and use stamps. In February 1766, justices of the peace in Northampton County "unanimously declared it to be their opinion that the said act did not bind, affect, or concern the inhabitants of this colony, inasmuch as they conceive the same to be unconstitutional,"[140] by which they meant a violation of the constitution of the colony. When the stamp distributor arrived in Williamsburg late in 1765, a large crowd of angry grandees forced him to resign.

That same year, Patrick Henry, who had recently been elected to the House of Burgesses for the first time, introduced and forced through very stern resolutions to condemn the law. Speaking in support of his resolutions, Henry denounced the king for conspiring with Parliament to violate the constitutional rights of American colonists when he signed the law. As the king was the ultimate source of constitutional legitimacy, the charge that he had acted unconstitutionally brought down on Henry cries of treason.[141]

In defending what they believed were their rights under the British Constitution, Virginians justified and explained those rights in terms of the constitution of the colony. Richard Bland published his *Inquiry into the Rights of the British Colonies* in 1766 and noted that "the civil Constitution of *England*" did not fix "the proper Connexion between the Colonies and the Mother Kingdom" or define "what their reciprocal Duties to each other are, and what Obedience is due from the Children to the Parent."[142] Bland referred to the cardinal features of the constitution of the colony and found his answers there. From the colonial constitution as it had evolved, he defined the nature of the relationship between the king and his Virginia subjects. Bland proved to his satisfaction that Parliament (king, lords, and commons all acting together) had no constitutional authority to legislate for or impose taxes on Virginians for any other purpose than to defend the empire and regulate trans-Atlantic trade.[143]

Bland was not stating new propositions so much as compiling systematic legal and historical arguments from precedents to explain the proper relationship of the people of Virginia to the king and Parliament, an argument that was widely understood and accepted in North America at that time.[144] Thomas Jefferson made the same point in his 1774 *Summary View of the Rights of British America* but found the origins farther back in a somewhat mythic Saxon past.[145]

In making an argument for the equality of colonial assemblies with Parliament, most Virginians and other colonial writers slighted the importance, or failed to understand the cardinal significance, of the seventeenth- and early eighteenth-century transformation of the constitutional roles of the Crown and Parliament as understood in Great Britain. In British eyes, Parliament had become superior to the Crown and therefore also superior to the colonies and their provincial legislatures.[146]

That is not how English-speaking residents of North America interpreted the authority of their colonial constitutions and charters within the larger constitutional network of the empire. Even while granting the superiority of Parliament over the Crown in Great Britain, and conceding to the king and Parliament the authority to regulate trade and imperial matters, residents of the colonies believed that their own separate constitutional relationships with the king made their provincial legislatures equal within their colonies to the authority of Parliament in Great Britain. In effect, but without using the explicit language, the king's North American subjects conceived of their colonies as parts of a larger, federal kingdom in which the king of Great Britain was king in the colonies by virtue of being the king of Great Britain. Americans believed that they and their assemblies had the same relation to the king as residents of Scotland and the Scotts Parliament had to the king between 1603 and 1707.

When, in 1766, Parliament repealed the Stamp Act of the previous year, it also passed, and the king signed, An Act for the Better Securing the Dependency of His Majesty's Dominions in America upon the Crown and Parliament of Great Britain. The Declaratory Act, as it was commonly known, stated flatly that Parliament "had hath, and of right ought to have, full power and authority to make laws and statutes of sufficient force and validity to bind the colonies and people of America, subjects of the Crown of Great Britain, in all cases whatsoever."[147]

Colonial rejoicing over repeal of the Stamp Act and other events caused Americans to miss the essential importance of the Declaratory Act. In the same year, 1766, when Bland published his *Inquiry* and Parliament passed the Declaratory Act, members of the General Court granted bail to John Chiswell, a well-connected man who had been charged with murder. Several men objected that Virginia law did not allow bail in such cases. In explaining the authority of the General Court judges, George Wythe, who was emerging as one of the legal luminaries of the colony, proclaimed, "The Court of King's Bench in England have power to admit all offenders whatsoever to bail, even those accused of high treason and murder. The origin of this power, which cannot be traced at this day, must be referred to the common law. . . . The General Court are, equally with the King's Bench, judges of all high offences." Wythe therefore concluded, "In short, it hath been agreed, and was never contested, as far as I have heard, that the powers of those Courts are the same within their respective jurisdictions." That is to say, in precisely the same way that Virginians regarded the General Assembly as the equivalent in Virginia of Parliament in England, at least some of them also perceived the General Court as the equivalent in the colony of the Court of King's Bench in the mother country. That relationship had been the case for so long that the "memory of man runneth not to the contrary" and was therefore constitutional according to the common law doctrine, or, as expressed in Wythe's words, as that "which cannot be traced at this day," and "it hath been agreed, and was never contested, as far as I have heard."[148]

People on both sides of the Atlantic Ocean used the same words and historical references to describe their increasingly different beliefs about their respective governments. In their debates about colonial charters and constitutions, Britons and Americans in effect talked past one another. That is especially obvious in their understandings about the nature of representation. Many Britons asserted that all the Crown's subjects were represented in Parliament by virtue of being the Crown's subjects—that is, they were virtually represented even if they had not voted, or if the men elected from their district did not live there. In theory, every member of the House of Commons represented the entire realm. North Americans by then had come to associate legitimate legislative representation with particular localities in which representatives had personal interests and about which they had personal knowledge—defined in Virginia law as men who owned land there. No member of Parliament could ever possess that knowledge or have that interest in any colony, and in fact many members of Parliament had little or no knowledge of or interest in their own constituencies. Colonial understandings derived as much from the historic relationships that their colonial assemblies had with the Crown as from the practical or theoretical reasons why residents of Great Britain could not properly represent the interests of residents of the colonies in Parliament.[149]

Until the 1760s, North Americans had few occasions to think deeply about the relationship between the constitution of Great Britain and their colonial charters and constitutions—whether, for instance, their colonial constitutions of government were parts of the British constitution or parallels of equal or nearly equal constitutional status. By the time of the American Revolution, Virginia's political leaders understood the colonial constitution as their own separate constitutional compact with the Crown. That is quite clear from the opening sentence of the Constitution or Form of Government that the Virginia Convention adopted in June 1776 when Virginians expelled the Crown from the government of Virginia. The first sentence referred to "George the third, king of *Great Britain* and *Ireland*, and elector of *Hanover*, heretofore intrusted with the exercise of the kingly office in this government." That declaration clearly stated the consensual, contractual, legal relationship they believed had obtained to that time between the king and his Virginia subjects.

The legislatures of the North American colonies took the lead in objecting to new taxes and regulations that the king and two houses of Parliament imposed on the residents of the colonies. In doing so, the assemblies—especially the lower houses—provoked the king into taking increasingly severe actions to crush the opposition. In 1768, King George III ordered that if the General Assembly of Virginia adopted any more resolutions that objected to the right of Parliament to tax or pass laws that imposed limitations on the colonists or on the colonial governments, the governor should dissolve the assembly and refuse to let it meet again without the king's express approval.[150]

The king's governors did exactly that. Governor Botetourt dissolved the General Assembly in the spring of 1769 after the House of Burgesses adopted spirited resolutions against acts of Parliament that levied taxes on the colonists.[151] So did Botetourt's successor in May 1774. Following the Boston Tea Party in December 1773, Parliament passed, and the king signed, what in Britain were called the Coercive Acts and in North America were called the Intolerable Acts. One of these acts replaced the governor and government under the royal charter of Massachusetts with a military governor; another closed the port of Boston to all commerce to punish the entire population of the city for the actions of the men who threw East India Company tea into the harbor.

The House of Burgesses passed strong resolutions against all the acts, and so under the king's instructions, Governor John Murray, fourth earl of Dunmore, dissolved the assembly.[152] That prevented the burgesses and council members from completing work on some essential bills, including the bill to renew the militia law, which expired that spring. Without a militia law, white Virginians were defenseless against First Nations on the frontier, enslaved people who might rise up anywhere, and British sailors or soldiers stationed on the coast near Williamsburg, Yorktown, and Norfolk.

Reduced to the status of private gentlemen, the burgesses extralegally reactivated a legislative committee of intercolonial correspondence and called for an extraconstitutional convention of men to select delegates to represent Virginia in the first Continental Congress to unite the colonies in defense of their constitutional rights as they perceived them under both the British and their colonial constitutions.[153]

The Future

All elements of the constitution of the colony of Virginia were firmly in place and functioning by the third quarter of the seventeenth century. The political leaders and legal elite of Virginia during the eighteenth century and the men who wrote the first constitution of the new independent state in 1776 knew no other system and were firmly committed to it and quite comfortable working within it because it suited them almost perfectly. Their understanding of representative government, their belief in the importance of the primacy of the elected branch of the legislature (in which the burgesses had represented their interests), their reliance on the undemocratic, self-perpetuating county courts (which they dominated), and their employment of their practical political skills that had been developed under that system in defense of colonial liberties and their common law rights expressed themselves powerfully in words and deeds at the time of the American Revolution. Their great practical political skill as well as their understandings of the workings of their version of early American statecraft provided Revolutionary Virginians opportunities to be influential in shaping the colonial response to British policies during the decade before the American Revolution. Those Virginians employed their talents to create and guide the government of the new nation during the Revolutionary War and to fashion the Constitution of the United States afterward.

What is most important here is that when the authors of the Virginia Constitution of 1776 abolished most of the royal parts of the colonial constitution, they changed very few of the elements of the old constitution that the colonists had created for themselves. The Constitution of 1776 guaranteed that most of the institutions and practices of the colonial constitution remained in place for fifty-four more years; and under the second state constitution, adopted in 1830, many of them continued in unchanged or modified form until 1851, a full seventy-five years after the end of royal government in Virginia. Some features of the colonial constitution endured even longer than that.

CHAPTER 2

The Constitution of 1776

"'Tis very much of the democratic kind," Richard Henry Lee wrote enthusiastically about the Virginia Constitution of 1776. He added that it was also "sufficiently guarded against the Monster Tyranny."[1] A few hours after Lee wrote his description of the "Constitution, or Form of Government," as the Virginia Convention of 1776 entitled it, the delegates unanimously adopted it and then elected Patrick Henry first governor of the independent Commonwealth of Virginia.

The constitution was not at all democratic according to the way in which Americans have understood the word since the early decades of the nineteenth century. It was in fact republican, or representative, in that it provided for a government without a king and, instead, with most of the powers of government lodged in the elected General Assembly. It was in that respect, with the locus of political power residing in the elected assembly, that Lee regarded it as "democratic," and in the absence of a king, "sufficiently guarded against the Monster Tyranny." The constitution provided for a republican government that represented the tobacco planters, whom the one elective branch of government under the colonial constitution—the House of Burgesses—had always represented.

Unlike the constitution of the colony, the new constitution for the independent Commonwealth of Virginia was a written document that defined and described Virginia's governmental institutions; but, understood in the same manner as people of the time regarded constitutions, the new constitution was also more than that one document. The convention had adopted a Declaration of Rights seventeen days before it adopted the constitution, and the convention silently or implicitly incorporated into the new government many of the institutions and practices that had become elements of the colonial constitution. Together, the Declaration of Rights, the Form of Government, and the colonial laws, institutions, and practices that were compatible with them became the new state's new constitution.

The Revolutionary Conventions

Revolutionary-era Americans created a revolutionary political institution, the constituent convention, to act for them when the regular constitutional institutions of royal government failed them.[2] In Virginia and elsewhere at the time, people referred to members of the conventions and of the Continental Congress as delegates. The noun *delegate* meant (and means) a person whom some other person or group has designated to act for them, has delegated authority to for some specific purpose. At that time and since in American language, the word has expressed the essence of the representative character of members of colonial, state, national, or political conventions in which elected people act for and on behalf of other people.[3]

The Virginia Convention of 1776 was the fifth in a series of extralegal conventions that met between August 1774 and July 1776. In 1774, members of the House of Burgesses acted on their own authority and outside the normal institutions and practices of the British or colonial constitutions. They issued a call for the first convention to devise a plan to protect planters' rights under the colonial constitution. During the summer, white men in all or nearly all Virginia counties endorsed the participation of their burgesses in the August convention, and in many or most counties, they also adopted instructions or recommendations to their representatives.[4] The widespread participation of the colony's voting men in 1774 when they adopted their resolutions gave a large measure of legitimacy to the actions of the men who attended the convention in August. The convention appointed men to represent Virginia in the First Continental Congress and adopted an association to prohibit importation of merchandise from Great Britain in hopes of pressuring British merchants to persuade Parliament to repeal or relax the Coercive Acts and other recent laws that taxed the colonists.[5]

In October 1774, the First Continental Congress appealed to the king, adopted a non-importation association very like the Virginia association, and recommended that residents of the colonies assemble and elect county and town committees to enforce the Continental Association.[6] During the following winter and spring men in all, or nearly all, Virginia counties and a few of the towns elected committees to enforce the two associations. Except for an occasional special election of vestrymen, it was the first time in Virginia that voters elected men to manage local affairs,[7] and, except in some incorporated towns and cities later, it was the last time before 1851.

The appeal that the First Continental Congress made to the king failed in its objectives, so Peyton Randolph, the Speaker of the House of Burgesses who had presided over the August 1774 convention and been president of the Congress, issued the call for the second Virginia Convention. It met in Richmond in March 1775 to elect delegates to represent the colony in the Second Continental Congress. At that convention, Patrick Henry made his famous Liberty or Death speech in support of a resolution to create a volunteer military force for the defense of Virginia.[8]

A third convention met in July and August 1775 and created a two-regiment army with Patrick Henry as commander in chief. It also authorized county committees to reconstitute the militia in each county, and it recruited a force of minutemen ready to march anywhere at a moment's notice. The convention issued paper money to pay for the military forces.[9] The convention also created a Committee of Safety that consisted of ten senior burgesses from different regions of Virginia and one young member of the Council of State to act as the executive arm of the unofficial, revolutionary government. The committee issued commissions to officers of the two regiments, the minutemen, and the militia, and it appointed contractors or hired men to supply provisions, horses, guns, and other military supplies.[10] The convention also adopted an ordinance—the conventions called their enactments ordinances, not laws, that being the proper style for an act of a convention—to authorize voters to elect new convention delegates for one-year terms in April 1776. The convention also directed the colony's treasurer to pay the delegates' travel expenses and per diem wages as if they were legally elected burgesses attending the General Assembly.[11] Except in the administration of justice, the conventions, the county committees, and Committee of Safety took over and exercised nearly all governmental responsibilities in Virginia from August 1775 to July 1776. The actions of Congress, the conventions, the county committees, the Committee of Safety, and the voters each gave legitimacy to the others.

The election ordinance was one of several clear evidences that people had realized that they were engaged in what could be an extended contest with royal authority. Military preparations and the coordinated actions of Congress and the colonial conventions so alarmed King George III that on 23 August 1775 he issued A Proclamation for Suppressing Rebellion and Sedition and called on all his subjects to take action against the "Treasonous and traitorous Conspiracies" in his North American colonies.[12] On 7 November, the royal governor of Virginia, John Murray, fourth earl of Dunmore, declared martial law and offered to free and arm enslaved Virginians who left their owners and volunteered to fight against the planters and for the king.[13] And on 23 December, the king signed an act of Parliament that declared the North American colonies to be in a state of rebellion and therefore no longer entitled to royal protection.[14]

The fourth of the Virginia conventions met in December 1775 and January 1776. Soon after the convention began its work, Virginia and British soldiers fought a bloody battle at the Great Bridge, near Norfolk, and on the first day of the new year, British warships shelled Norfolk. Virginia and North Carolina soldiers in the city then set fire to the residences and places of business of loyalists, and the flames spread and destroyed most of the city. The convention enlarged the colony's armed force from two to nine regiments, and it and the Committee of Safety took additional steps to cooperate more closely with the other colonies and the Continental Congress to defend Virginia against the forces of their king.[15]

By then, open warfare had made reconciliation practically impossible and therefore independence almost inevitable. If the colonies individually or collectively cast off their allegiance to their king, they had to form new governments. Indeed, as early as 4 December 1775, when Congress ordered reinforcements to Virginia in response to Dunmore's proclamation of martial law, it also recommended "that if the convention of Virginia shall find it necessary to establish a form of government," it should hold an election for a new convention to "establish such form of government as in their judgment will best produce the happiness of the people, and effectually secure peace and good order in the colony, during the continuation of the present dispute between Great Britain and these colonies."[16] And then, in two resolutions early in May, Congress ordered that "the exercise of every kind of authority" under the Crown "be totally suppressed" and recommended that all the colonies "adopt such government as shall, in the opinion of the representatives of the people, best conduce to the happiness and safety of their constituents in particular, and America in general."[17]

The different language of the congressional resolutions strikingly illustrates how much had changed between December 1775, when Congress defined the situation as a "dispute between Great Britain and these colonies," and May 1776, when it ordered suppression of royal government and the formation of new governments in North America.

Electing Delegates

Under the authority of the August 1775 ordinance, the election of convention delegates took place throughout April 1776 when qualified voters in each county or city assembled on the day that the local court met. Exactly as for the House of Burgesses, voters elected two delegates in each county, and voters in the city of Williamsburg and on the island of Jamestown elected one delegate each, as did the president and professors of the College of William and Mary. Voters in the burned-out port of Norfolk did not hold their election until May, and voters in King and Queen County also voted in May because on the appointed day in April, violent weather had prevented them from safely assembling. Voters in Williamsburg and in several counties also elected alternate delegates to serve while the regularly elected delegates were absent from the convention while representing Virginia in Congress.[18]

Of the 126 delegates and 6 alternates who had been eligible to attend the fourth convention, 88 won election to the fifth and last convention. The ordinance of elections included a provision lifted from the statute books that excluded clergymen from the convention, which disqualified two members of the fourth convention, and it also excluded army officers, sheriffs, and other men who held posts of profit, which disqualified ten other delegates. A few men chose not to stand for reelection, but a few who did lost their seats, and some who retained their seats won very close or heated contests. Edmund Pendleton, who had served as president of the Committee of Safety and of the fourth convention and was also to be president of the fifth, very narrowly won reelection; and George Mason, who prepared the drafts of both the Declaration of Rights and the Constitution or Form of Government, and who would become one of the most influential members, retained his convention seat but only with difficulty.[19]

Some of the men who replaced experienced delegates were also men of experience and had served in one or more of the first conventions or in the House of Burgesses previously. In some instances, local rivalries or other circumstances largely unrelated to the crisis within the empire brought about the defeat of sitting convention delegates. Nevertheless, a man who watched the same delegates that autumn when they returned to the Capitol as members of the first House of Delegates observed that the men were "not quite so well dressed, nor so politely Educated, nor so highly born" as the members of "some Assemblies have formerly been," but he believed that in carrying out their large and unprecedented responsibilities they were "full as honest, less intriguing, more sincere."[20]

The turnover in convention membership occurred simultaneously with the political ferment about whether to declare independence and reforming provincial governments in the spring. Some identifiable influential men remained opposed to declaring independence, as did an unknowable number of other men. The men who favored independence disagreed about the time and manner of taking the great step. Doubtless, some of the close contests and defeats of veteran convention delegates resulted from differences of opinion about how and with what to replace government under the king and the colonial constitution. For many men of the time, government without a king as the original source of authority was almost impossible to imagine. As Richard Henry Lee wrote to Patrick Henry midway through the elections, the December act of Parliament that declared the colonies out of the king's protection had "to every legal intent and purpose dissolved our government, uncommissioned every magistrate, and placed us in the high road to Anarchy. In Virginia we have certainly no Magistrate lawfully qualified to hang a murderer, or any other villain offending ever so atrociously against the state. We cannot be Rebels excluded from the King's protection and Magistrates acting under his authority at the same time. This proves the indispensable necessity of our taking up government immediately, for the preservation of Society."[21]

Thoughts on Government

John Page agreed with Richard Henry Lee. Page was a young member of the Council of State that had not met in nearly a year and was also a close friend of Thomas Jefferson. Page had served as vice president of the Virginia Committee of Safety since August 1775 and was a strong supporter of vigorous actions and of independence. In order "to prevent Disorders," four days before the voting concluded, Page wrote to Jefferson that "a Constitution should be formed as nearly resembling the old one as Circumstances, and the Merit of that Constitution will admit."[22] His friend Jefferson had probably already begun thinking about proposing some bold changes to the constitution of the colony. Jefferson later sent a draft for a constitution to the convention. In the meantime, Jefferson suggested that the convention recall its delegates to Congress so that they could take part in writing the new constitution. "It is a work of the most interesting nature," Jefferson continued, "and such as every individual would wish to have his voice in. In truth it is the whole object of the present controversy; for should a bad government be instituted for us in future it had been as well to have accepted at first the bad one offered to us from beyond the water without the risk and expence of contest."[23]

One handbill outline and two pamphlets that members of Congress published in Philadelphia for Virginia audiences framed the range of opinions about government that the colony's voters and convention delegates considered late in the spring and early in the summer of 1776.[24] Early in April, Richard Henry Lee published a skeletal outline for a state government. "LET the people choose as usual (where there is no good objection) a Representative body," he suggested, and "Let the Representatives appoint" a twenty-four-member second house of the legislature to serve seven-year terms. Let the two houses of the legislature annually elect a governor, who would be the third branch of the legislature (that is, have a right to refuse his assent to and thereby veto bills the other houses had passed), and also an advisory council of twelve men. The assembly should elect all judges to serve during "good behavior, with fixed, adequate, but not splendid salaries." The assembly should also elect a "Lieutenant-Governor, Secretary, Commissary, Attorney, and Solicitor-General" for seven-year terms and a treasurer annually. Lee suggested that the governor and council appoint justices of the peace, sheriffs, and other local officials "as usual, if no good objection," and that the governor "with advice of his Council of State" should exercise all executive powers and command the militia.[25]

Shortly after Lee published his outline, John Adams published *Thoughts on Government: Applicable to the Present State of the American Colonies, In a Letter from a Gentleman To his Friend*. The pamphlet was one of the most influential publications of the revolutionary year. Drawing on his wide reading and on his experience in local and provincial government in Massachusetts, Adams explained his recommendations. First, he argued, the representative assembly "should be in miniature, an exact portrait of the people at large. It should think, feel, reason, and act like them." Adams recommended that voters elect representatives annually and quoted an old maxim: "Where annual elections end, there slavery begins." The representatives should select an upper house of assembly consisting of a smaller number of men. The two houses together should annually elect a governor "who, after being stripped of most of those badges of domination called prerogatives, should have a free and independent exercise of his judgment, and be made also an integral part of the legislature." The assembly should also annually appoint all other state officers, and either the legislature or the governor and council should appoint judges, militia officers, and other necessary government officials. Adams recommended that judges be men learned in the law and that they should hold office for life or during good behavior. He also proposed that states provide for "the liberal education of youth" and suggested the propriety of sumptuary laws to discourage ostentatious inequalities. Under "such forms of government," Adams concluded, free Americans "would be unconquerable by all the Monarchies of Europe."[26]

The second important pamphlet was *An Address to the Convention of the Colony and Ancient Dominion of Virginia* and was in the form of a reply to Adams's *Thoughts on Government*. Its author was Carter Braxton, a Virginia delegate to Congress. The democratic elements of Adams's proposals disturbed Braxton, who could not understand how the more democratic political culture of Massachusetts could supply an appropriate model for the hierarchical, slave-holding political culture of Virginia. Braxton's plan deviated only a little from the constitution of the colony. He recommended election of legislative representatives every third year instead of annually and that the legislature should elect the governor and "Council of State" to serve for life or "during good behaviour." Members of the council, as under the constitution of the colony, should serve as the upper house of the assembly. The assembly should select most public officials, but the governor and council should appoint judges and militia officers. Other than council members serving as executive advisors to the governor and as members of the upper house of the assembly, no person should hold office in more than one branch of the government.[27]

Lee's handbill and Adams's pamphlet on the one hand and Braxton's pamphlet on the other appear to have set the outer boundaries for proposals for change and continuity. In a few surviving private letters and a small number of newspaper essays, other men also discussed how to structure a new government without a king. Most of their ideas fell between Adams's and Braxton's proposals on the spectrum of change and continuity. Patrick Henry praised Adams's *Thoughts on Government* and denounced Braxton's *Address* but without indicating which proposals in *Thoughts* most appealed to him or which in the *Address* he most opposed.[28] Some other commentators were similarly unspecific.

Several things appear to have been generally understood and not very controversial. Early in the convention, delegate John Augustine Washington perceived "no great difference of opinion" about the structure for the new government "among our best speakers." He named Patrick Henry, George Mason, James Mercer, Bartholomew Dandridge, Meriwether Smith, and, he was "apt to think," convention president Edmund Pendleton.[29] Delegates agreed for the most part that the legislature should be bicameral. The voters should elect the lower house. The legislature should elect the executive, which should be a weaker office than the royal governorship had been. And some degree of separation of powers between executive, legislative, and judicial responsibilities should be enforced. On those subjects, the authors of Virginia's Constitution or Form of Government were in general agreement with people elsewhere in the revolutionary colonies. But, as Page had suggested in his cautious recommendation for forming a new government, was it wise to contemplate significant modifications at so critical a moment as when changing a nearly 150-year-old form of government into something new at the beginning of, or in the middle of, a war?

The Convention of 1776

The Convention of 1776 met in the Capitol in Williamsburg from 6 May through 5 July and unanimously adopted its three momentous state papers: the instructions to the colony's delegates in Congress to move a resolution of independence, the Declaration of Rights, and the Constitution or Form of Government. The unanimous votes concealed many differences of opinion on matters of detail as well as of substance. Convention member Thomas Ludwell Lee distinguished for his brother Richard Henry Lee the presence in the convention of delegates who wished or were willing to make important changes from "a certain set of Aristocrates" who were not.[30] Only on the fundamental issue of the impossibility of continuing to live as subjects of the British king had the convention's members developed something approaching unanimity, and it was this conviction that led them to vote unanimously for the resolutions, the declaration, and the constitution despite their many disagreements.[31]

The delegates debated the main question of independence on 14 and 15 May. Thomas Nelson Jr. introduced a resolution, which Patrick Henry drafted, that recited colonial grievances against Great Britain and absolved Virginians of allegiance "to the crown of G. B." Bartholomew Dandridge proposed to declare on behalf of all the colonies, not just Virginia, "That the Union that has hitherto subsisted between Great Britain and the American Colonies is hereby totally dissolved, and that the Inhabitants of America are discharged from any Allegiance to the Crown of Great Britain." And Meriwether Smith introduced a resolution to declare "that the Government of this Colony as hitherto exercised under the Crown of Great-Britain be dissolved, and that a Committee be appointed to prepare a Declaration of Rights, and such a Plan of Government as shall be judged most proper to maintain Peace & Order in this Colony & secure substantial and equal Liberty to the people."[32] President Edmund Pendleton formed the three resolutions into one, beginning with Henry's recitation of grievances, revising the Smith and Dandridge proposals for independence into an instruction that the Virginia delegates in Congress introduce a resolution to declare all the colonies independent so that they could act in unity, and concluding with Smith's proposal for the preparation of a Declaration of Rights and "plan of government." On 15 May, the delegates unanimously adopted the composite resolution in spite of the objections from delegate and treasurer Robert Carter Nicholas that the step was premature because even though united, the colonies were yet too weak to succeed.[33]

Pendleton then appointed a twenty-eight-member committee to prepare the declaration and form of government. It included the most experienced delegates under the chairmanship of veteran legislator Archibald Cary. Pendleton included some promising young men, chief among them Edmund Randolph, who was an alternate delegate from Williamsburg sitting in for George Wythe (who was away representing the colony in Congress), and James Madison, making his political debut as a delegate from Orange County.[34] Pendleton appointed a few additional delegates to the committee later, the most important of them being George Mason, who arrived late and took his seat in the convention on 18 May.[35]

Convention delegates also did much more. For a majority of the time, they worked on draft resolutions and ordinances to control loyalists, enlarge the army, redeploy forces in response to movements of Governor Dunmore and British warships, procure supplies for the looming war, and issue orders for securing the western frontiers from anticipated First Nations tribes and loyalist assaults. So much did that work resemble the work of previous conventions or of a legislature that a few men, Thomas Jefferson chief among them, questioned several years later whether the Declaration of Rights and the Constitution or Form of Government that the convention adopted were genuine constitutional documents of superior moral and legal authority or mere ordinances of the convention that a later legislature might change.[36] By the nineteenth century, Americans understood their written state constitutions to be a higher law than mere legislation, as their colonial ancestors had understood the superior authority of their charters, institutions, and practices of the English constitution and their colonial governments. But in 1776 Americans faced a new challenge: how could the body politic create a new constitution of unassailable legitimacy and legal superiority?

The scanty surviving records do not disclose whether any delegates in Williamsburg raised Jefferson's later objection to the convention acting for the people without explicit authorization. In a history of Virginia that Edmund Randolph wrote thirty or more years after the fact, he declared that he recalled that convention delegates understood in 1776 that their constituents had fully empowered them to adopt a written constitution.[37] Historians have subsequently differed about when Americans as a whole came to believe that conventions elected for the sole and express purpose of writing constitutions were the only or most appropriate way to produce legitimate constitutions. The adoption of that understanding was one of the cardinal constitutional developments of the revolutionary generation regardless of whether, in 1776, some Virginians questioned whether their convention was justified in drafting a constitution.[38]

At the beginning of the nineteenth century, Virginia jurist and legal scholar St. George Tucker confirmed Randolph's understanding and concluded that the conditions under which men elected convention delegates in April 1776 clearly demonstrated that voters had empowered their representatives to take the obviously necessary steps to create a new government after the anticipated severing of the relationship between Virginians and their king.[39] Had Tucker known then about Jefferson's yet-unpublished letter suggesting that the convention recall the members of Congress to participate in reforming Virginia's constitution, he could have cited Jefferson's 1776 letter to refute Jefferson's 1780s objections.

The Declaration of Rights

Edmund Randolph explained years later the rationale as he understood it for the Declaration of Rights: "two objects were contemplated: one, that the legislature should not in their acts violate any of those canons; the other, that in all the revolutions of time, of human opinion, and of government, a perpetual standard should be erected, around which the people might rally and by a notorious record be forever admonished to be watchful, firm, and virtuous."[40]

George Mason introduced a draft for the Declaration of Rights to the committee before he introduced a draft for the Constitution or Form of Government. Committee members amended the draft and delegates amended it further during five days of debate in the Committee of the Whole. The convention approved amendments to the bill on 11 June and unanimously agreed to the final text on 12 June.[41]

The opening words of Section 1 of the declaration as the committee reported it to the floor on 27 May 1776 provoked debate. Mason had proposed, "THAT all men are born equally free and independent, and have certain inherent natural rights, of which they cannot, by any compact, deprive or divest their posterity; among which are, the enjoyment of life and liberty, with the means of acquiring and possessing property, and pursuing and obtaining happiness and safety." Robert Carter Nicholas objected that the language appeared to entitle enslaved Virginians to the same freedom that white Virginia men enjoyed; so after debate, the convention adopted revised language that Edmund Pendleton composed. The amended text declared "THAT all men are by nature equally free and independent, and have certain inherent rights, of which, when they enter into a state of society, they cannot, by any compact, deprive or divest their posterity; namely, the enjoyment of life and liberty, with the means of acquiring and possessing property, and pursuing and obtaining happiness and safety." Edmund Randolph later summarized the purpose of the changed language thus: "that slaves, not being constituent members of our society, could never pretend to any benefit from such a maxim."[42]

Sections 2, 3, and 4 as adopted expressed the delegates' understanding of representative government: "That all power is vested in, and consequently derived from, the people"; "That government is, or ought to be, instituted for the common benefit, protection, and security, of the people, nation, or community," and that the people retained the right to change their form of government; and "That no man, or set of men, are entitled to exclusive or separate emoluments or privileges from the community, but in consideration of publick services; which, not being descendible, neither ought the offices of magistrate, legislator, or judge, to be hereditary."

The first part of the Section 6 foreshadowed the Form of Government breaking up the executive, legislative, and judicial powers of the colonial Council of State by stating "That the legislative and executive powers of the state should be separate and distinct from the judiciary."

The remainder of Section 5 and Section 6 expressed the delegates' desire for frequent and regularly scheduled elections of legislators; the principle of "no taxation without representation"; and the first of five provisions derived from the English Bill of Rights, "That elections of members to serve as representatives of the people, in assembly, ought to be free; and that all men, having sufficient evidence of permanent common interest with, and attachment to, the community, have the right of suffrage."

Section 7 of the Declaration of Rights was added in committee and was derived from the Bill of Rights. It repudiated an ancient part of the royal prerogative: "That all power of suspending laws, or the execution of laws, by any authority without consent of the representatives of the people, is injurious to their rights, and ought not to be exercised." The new government of Virginia had no king, so the seventh section was not strictly necessary. However, the Declaration of Rights was both a statement of principles of government as well as a catalog of individual or collective rights. To this point, the declaration as adopted stated general principles of government.

The remaining sections of the declaration for the most part referred to essential rights of individual members of the community or of the body politic as a whole, expressed in hortatory or philosophical terms rather than as prohibitions or restrictions on governmental power.

Section 8 embodied principles of English law and guaranteed accused persons a right to a fair jury trial and a protection against compulsory self-incrimination. Section 9 was a verbatim extract from the English Bill of Rights. Mason included it in his draft, the committee adopted it, and the full convention passed it: "That excessive bail ought not to be required, nor excessive fines imposed, nor cruel and unusual punishments inflicted." The wording remained unchanged when it became the Eighth Amendment to the Constitution of the United States. The committee added a condemnation of general warrants as Section 10.

Section 11 was self-explanatory: "That in controversies respecting property, and in suits between man and man, the ancient trial by jury is preferable to any other, and ought to be held sacred." So was Section 12, "That the freedom of the press is one of the great bulwarks of liberty, and can never be restrained but by despotick governments." Section 13 derived from a long English distrust of a standing army that a king could employ to oppress the people. It declared "That a well regulated militia, composed of the body of the people, trained to arms, is the proper, natural, and safe defence of a free state; that standing armies, in time of peace, should be avoided, as dangerous to liberty; and that in all cases, the military should be under strict subordination to, and governed by, the civil power." That section, in some respects, also resembled part of the English Bill of Rights.

According to Edmund Randolph, when the declaration was under consideration in committee, Patrick Henry proposed what became Section 15:[43] "That no free government, or the blessing of liberty, can be preserved to any people but by a firm adherence to justice, moderation, temperance, frugality, and virtue, and by frequent recurrence to fundamental principles." The fifteenth section would have fit better with the first sections, which stated general principles, rather than as the next to the last that secured fundamental liberties of individuals and the community.

George Mason's draft language for the final section expressed the essence of the 1688 English Act of Toleration[44] but with a more latitudinarian language: "That religion, or the duty which we owe to our CREATOR, and manner of discharging it, can be directed only by reason and conviction, not by force or violence; and therefore, that all men should enjoy the fullest toleration in the exercise of religion, according to the dictates of conscience, unpunished and unrestrained by the magistrate, unless, under colour of religion, any man disturb the peace, the happiness, or safety of society. And that it is the mutual duty of all to practice Christian forbearance, love, and charity, towards each other."

That language generated a brief and intense debate that had its origins in very recent events in Virginia. The number of Baptists had rapidly increased in many parts of the colony. Most Baptist ministers often refused to abide by some of the terms of the Virginia law of 1699 that contained the essence of the English Act of Toleration. The ministers often failed to apply for official permission to preach, some of them held illegal night-time services, and some of them closed or locked doors to prevent magistrates from seeing their services.[45] Justices of the peace and sheriffs imprisoned Baptist ministers and persecuted members of their congregations.[46]

The persecution and imprisonments particularly disgusted freshmen convention delegate James Madison. He composed an amendment to the section on religion to make it state that "all men are equally entitled to the full and free exercise of it accord^g to the dictates of Conscience; and therefore that no man or class of men ought on account of religion to be invested with peculiar emoluments or privileges; nor subjected to any penalties or disabilities." He persuaded Patrick Henry, who had long championed the rights of Virginians who dissented from the official Church of England, to introduce the substitute language. Randolph recalled that as soon as Henry proposed Madison's amendment, suspicious delegates asked whether "it was designed as a prelude to an attack on the Established Church." Henry "disclaimed such an object," and Madison then persuaded Edmund Pendleton, a defender of the church, to introduce a revised amendment, which passed.[47]

As amended, the sixteenth and final section of the Declaration of Rights boldly and for the first time in North America affirmed the legal principle of full religious freedom but without necessarily jeopardizing the privileged status of the established church in Virginia: "That religion, or the duty which we owe to our CREATOR, and the manner of discharging it, can be directed only by reason and conviction, not by force or violence, and therefore all men are equally entitled to the free exercise of religion, according to the dictates of conscience; and that it is the mutual duty of all to practice Christian forbearance, love, and charity towards each other."

Adopted unanimously on 12 June 1776, the Declaration of Rights was the first document of its kind in the constitutional revolution that accompanied the American colonies' conversion into American states. So important was—and is—the Virginia Declaration of Rights that it deserves to be classed right alongside Thomas Paine's *Common Sense*, John Adams's *Thoughts on Government*, and Thomas Jefferson's Declaration of Independence, which are among the most important and influential state papers of the revolutionary year of 1776. The draft declaration and the declaration as adopted served as models or patterns for several other states. The Pennsylvania Constitution of 1776 included several clauses copied or adapted from the Virginia Declaration of Rights, and the North Carolina Constitution of 1776 derived much of its statement of rights directly from the Virginia text. Those and other early adaptations of provisions from the Virginia declaration retained the hortatory phrasing and were also often separate documents from the forms of government.[48] The very influential Massachusetts Constitution of 1780 was clearly derivative in several important parts although its text exhibited much revision of the wording. Because the Virginia Declaration of Rights was also translated into French and published and widely circulated in France, it also served as one of the sources from which revolutionaries there prepared the Declaration of the Rights of Man and Citizen in 1789. The Virginia Convention of 1788, which ratified the Constitution of the United States, also drew on the Virginia declaration to suggest amendments in the form of a bill of rights. James Madison employed those suggestions and recommendations from other ratification conventions the following year when he composed the first draft of what became the United States Bill of Rights.[49]

Central as the Declaration of Rights is in the intellectual and constitutional history of the American Revolution, it remained in several important particulars very much a document of a specific place and time. What the delegates included and what they did not include placed it clearly in the context of Virginia in the spring and summer of 1776. The delegates included provisions on topics that had recently been of large consequence in Virginia, such as freedom of the press, the tumultuous Baptist challenge to the Church of England, trial by jury in criminal and civil cases, and free and regular elections. Delegates did not include other jeopardized rights that the imperial crisis had made more important to residents of other colonies than to residents of Virginia. Twelve years later, when a Virginia convention ratified by a narrow margin the Constitution of the United States, its members recommended the addition of a bill of rights and enumerated the principles and rights in the Virginia Declaration of Rights, plus others, that were obviously of equal importance, such as guarantees of freedom of speech, the rights of petition and assembly, and against forced quartering of troops in private dwellings.[50]

The Commonwealth of Virginia

The convention replaced the common law constitution of the colony with a written Constitution or Form of Government for the independent Commonwealth of Virginia. George Mason prepared the first draft, which convention members acknowledged at the time, and introduced the word *commonwealth*.[51] Mason may have had in mind Oliver Cromwell's Puritan Commonwealth that had governed England without a king from 1649 to 1660, but he also may have selected the word as accurately descriptive or even looked back to the time of the founding of the colony when the word was widely understood to mean a lawful, righteous government that protected the legitimate rights of all parties.[52] The meaning might have been significant symbolically, even if the choice among titles was merely a distinction without any practical difference.

The Constitution of 1776

"*The* CONSTITUTION, *or* FORM *of* GOVERNMENT, *agreed to and resolved upon by the Delegates and Representatives of the several counties and corporations of* VIRGINIA," as the official printed text is headed, was the third state constitution of the revolutionary era, but the first two were provisional, or temporary. Men in New Hampshire had adopted a provisional constitution in January 1776, and men in South Carolina had adopted a provisional one in March. The delegates who adopted the Virginia constitution did not regard it as a provisional or temporary substitute for royal authority pending a settlement of differences with Great Britain because they had resolutely declared for independence. By 1780, when Massachusetts adopted a new constitution, the new American states had all completed the transfer of authority that royalty had imposed on the colonies to state governments based on the sovereignty of the people.[53]

The convention did not divide the first Constitution of Virginia into separate articles. The constitution consists instead of a sequence of paragraphs that treated related aspects of the new government. The Constitution of 1776 together with the Declaration of Rights was about 3,450 words long, approximately three-quarters the length of the Constitution of the United States before it was first amended. A week after President Edmund Pendleton appointed Mason to the drafting committee, the president noted with satisfaction that "The Political Cooks are busy preparing the dish, and as Colonel Mason seems to have the Ascendancy in the great work, I have sanguine hopes it will be framed so as to Answer it's end, Prosperity to the Community and Security to Individuals."[54] The often-grumpy Mason was not so optimistic and complained that "according to Custom" the committee was "overcharged with useless Members" and likely to be plagued with "a thousand ridiculous and impracticable proposals."[55] He seized the initiative as he had done with the Declaration of Rights and introduced a draft constitution for the committee to consider. As Edmund Randolph later recalled, Mason's draft "swallowed up all the rest by fixing the grounds and plan" for the new government.[56] The constitution as adopted closely resembled Mason's plan in many particulars, including the sequence of provisions and the substance and wording of many of them.

Members of the convention spent parts of only four days debating and amending the committee's draft—less time than they spent on the Declaration of Rights—before they unanimously adopted the constitution on 29 June.[57] Late in the deliberations in the Committee of the Whole, the delegates tacked onto the beginning of the constitution a long list of charges against the king from a draft constitution that Jefferson had sent from Philadelphia to Williamsburg. It is in the form of a preamble but not so named. Thus, the Constitution or Form of Government began, "WHEREAS George the third, king of *Great Britain* and *Ireland*, and elector of *Hanover*, heretofore intrusted with the exercise of the kingly office in this government, hath endeavoured to pervert the same into a detestable and insupportable tyranny," and concluded, "By which several acts of misrule the government of this country, as formerly exercised under the crown of *Great Britain*, is TOTALLY DISSOLVED." On behalf of the whole body politic, the "delegates and representatives of the good people of *Virginia* . . . do ordain and declare the future form of government of *Virginia* to be as followeth."

The first paragraph of the Form of Government repeated the essence of a clause in the Declaration of Rights and specified, "The legislative, executive, and judiciary departments, shall be separate and distinct, so that neither exercise the powers properly belonging to the other; nor shall any person exercise the powers of more than one of them at the same time, except that the justices of the county courts shall be eligible to either House of Assembly." In thus twice explicitly declaring the importance of separation of powers, the Virginia convention more emphatically proclaimed that principle than any other Revolutionary state convention, although other states also affirmed it, especially in separating legislative and judicial powers.[58] But the Virginia convention made an important exception by permitting justices of the peace to serve in the legislature, which preserved the ability of the established community of political leaders to continue their domination of both county government and the General Assembly. In transforming themselves from subjects of the king into citizens of an independent Virginia, the delegates inserted this and other provisions into their new constitution to preserve or augment the political influence and power that they had acquired under the practices and laws that they and their predecessors had devised under the colonial constitution.

SUFFRAGE

"The right of suffrage in the election of members for both Houses" of the General Assembly, the Form of Government decreed, "shall remain as exercised at present." That language thereby incorporated into the new constitution the 1736 election law (the statute that was in force "at present" in 1776), which restricted the vote to free adult men who owned or possessed a long-term lease on at least one hundred acres of land, or fifty acres and a house in the country, or a lot or part of a lot in Williamsburg or Norfolk. Even though the assembly had passed bills in 1762 and 1770 to reduce the freehold requirement to fifty acres, Crown authorities had never given assent to the bills, which therefore never took effect.[59] The 1736 law thereby appeared to become an unalterable part of the state constitution, but in 1785, the assembly reduced the freehold requirement from one hundred acres to fifty acres or to twenty-five acres and a house.[60] If anybody at the time objected that an effective change to the 1736 law violated the clear stipulation in the Constitution or Form of Government, he might have been answered with reference to the General Assembly having twice amended that law but that the king's bureaucracy had prevented the amendments from taking effect. Moreover, an ordinance that the convention adopted specifically declared that Virginia laws that were then in force and not contrary to the constitution remained in force but could be amended.[61]

The requirement that men own land in order to vote had been virtually universal in the colonies and most of the Revolutionary-era state constitutions retained this requirement. The property qualification remained in force in Virginia under the Constitution of 1776 and in revised form under the Constitution of 1830 until ratification of the Constitution of 1851, seventy-five years after Virginia ceased to be a colony. The property qualification was one of the most divisive topics in the two conventions that wrote new constitutions for Virginia between the American Revolution and the American Civil War. In 1776, though, it was not a hot topic of debate. Edmund Randolph later explained, "That the qualification of electors to the General Assembly should be restricted to freeholds was the natural effect of Virginia having been habituated to it for very many years, more than a century. The members of the Convention were themselves freeholders and from this circumstance felt a proud attachment to the country in which the ownership of the soil was a certain source of comfort. It is not recollected that a hint was uttered in contravention of this principle. There can be no doubt that if it had been, it would have soon perished under a discussion."[62]

Thomas Jefferson, who was more democratically minded than Randolph, retained the property qualification in his draft for a constitution, but he suggested reducing the minimum requisite for the suffrage from one hundred acres to fifty and, more importantly, provided for "an appropriation" of enough land to each free adult male to give each the minimum to become a qualified freeholder and voter.[63] Nobody, so far as the incomplete documentary record discloses, proposed to allow voters to elect any other public officials than the members of the two houses of the General Assembly.

THE GENERAL ASSEMBLY

The Form of Government provided that the legislature "shall be formed of two distinct branches, who, together, shall be a complete legislature. They shall meet once, or oftener, every year, and shall be called the GENERAL ASSEMBLY OF VIRGINIA." Only the first state constitutions of Pennsylvania and Georgia temporarily discarded the common bicameral structure of colonial legislatures,[64] but the paragraph in the Virginia constitution made three very important changes to colonial practices. By declaring the two houses of assembly "a complete legislature" it denied the executive any role in legislation. That provision abruptly terminated the authority that royal governors possessed to influence legislation under consideration or to refuse to sign and thereby veto bills that the two houses had passed. It also terminated executive authority to prevent the legislature from meeting, and it excluded members of the new Council of State from the legislature—one of three provisions in the new constitution that redistributed the combined administrative, legislative, and judicial roles of the colonial council and thereby destroyed it.

Whether executives should have a role in legislation was one of the matters on which convention members in Virginia and Americans elsewhere disagreed. Most of the first state constitutions prohibited gubernatorial vetoes,[65] but in April, Richard Henry Lee and John Adams had both proposed that the governor be part of the assembly, and during debate in the convention in June, Patrick Henry, according to the recollections of Edmund Randolph, argued "strenuously" for an executive veto. "Amongst other arguments" Randolph recalled that Henry made, "he averred that a governor would be a mere phantom . . . and that he would otherwise be ultimately a dependent instead of a coordinate branch of power."⁶⁶ The committee and the full convention retained Mason's language that declared the two houses "a complete legislature." The constitution also prohibited the executive from adjourning or dissolving the assembly "at any time." In thus weakening the office of governor, the convention strengthened the authority of the elected members of the assembly. In several other provisions, the delegates further weakened the office of governor and preserved or reinforced other colonial practices to limit executive influence.

Convention delegates changed the name of the lower house from its colonial title of the House of Burgesses to the House of Delegates rather than to the "Lower House of Assembly" as in Mason's draft. The constitution provided that members of the House of Delegates should be elected annually and no longer at the whim of the king, the royal governor, or even the governor of the commonwealth. The delegates placed in the new constitution the colonial laws and practices that had been in effect for more than a century that allowed two representatives from each county and, for almost half a century, one each for the city of Williamsburg and the Borough of Norfolk. The constitution endowed the assembly with the authority that it had asserted during the colonial period to grant separate representation to other cities and towns, which it did for the city of Richmond in 1789 and for the city of Petersburg in 1816.⁶⁷ By deliberately not including the almost depopulated island of Jamestown and the College of William and Mary in the composition of the General Assembly, the Constitution of 1776 silently deprived the few residents of the former and the president and half-dozen professors of the latter the right to their own representation in the General Assembly.

Another section in the constitution declared that "all ministers of the Gospel of every denomination, be incapable of being elected members of either House of Assembly, or the Privy Council." That later appeared to be a punitive innovation directed specifically at clergymen of the Church of England, some of whom opposed independence, but in fact it gave full constitutional status to a 1653 Virginia law,⁶⁸ which remained in the state's constitutions until 1869.⁶⁹

Mason's draft provided that the "Upper House of Assembly" consist of twenty-four members, the same number that Lee had suggested in his April outline. During debate on the floor, the delegates borrowed from Jefferson's draft the titles Senator and House of Senators for the upper house; but in the final discussions on 29 June, the delegates directed the secretary to erase "house of Senators" from the engrossed bill and insert "Senate,"⁷⁰ thus introducing into American legislative parlance the title of the ancient Roman institution.

The paragraph that created the state senate followed Lee's outline and Mason's draft and required that Virginia be subdivided into twenty-four districts, each entitled to one senator to serve a four-year term, and that one-fourth of the senators' terms should expire each year in order to create a rotation in membership. Also following Mason's draft, the Form of Government denied senators the right to introduce bills or to amend "money bills," meaning bills to raise money by taxation, but permitted them to amend other bills that the House of Delegates passed if the delegates consented. Also understood later as a restrictive innovation on senators, who in some states were regarded as special representatives of the society's elite,[71] the prohibition on the introduction of bills in the Senate of Virginia merely extended constitutional sanction to a practice in effect in Virginia since 1710. Records show that members of the colonial Council of State that were sitting as the upper house of the assembly never introduced bills after that date, although they probably suggested amendments to tax bills.[72]

Delegates had differing ideas about the upper house and certainly debated a variety of proposals about the Senate, but no records of the discussions during the convention survive. Before the convention met, some people, like John Adams and Richard Henry Lee, proposed that the lower house elect members of the upper house; and in an exchange of letters after the convention, Jefferson and Pendleton discussed whether the lower house or the voters could elect a wiser and more experienced group of senators.[73] Carter Braxton had wanted members of the Council of State, who served for life, to constitute the upper house. Richard Henry Lee had suggested seven-year terms for senators, but Mason had suggested four years. Mason had also proposed that voters choose electors to act for them and that the electors then elect members of the upper house, a filtering or refining process intended to allow voters to elect men whom they knew and trusted to act for them in extended districts that encompassed eligible men whom they did not personally know. Mason also suggested that senatorial electors possess property worth £500 and that no man be eligible for election to the upper house who did not own property worth at least £2,000 and be at least twenty-eight years old. He suggested a lesser minimum property ownership of £1,000 for members of the lower house.

The role and composition of the upper houses of assembly in the revolutionary states were subjects of revealing discussions throughout the country and throughout the period. Most commentators desired, like Mason, to create structures, procedures, or qualifications for office to ensure that upper houses consisted of wealthier, more prominent, or more experienced men than lower houses; but others wished for members of the two houses to represent different interests within the society.[74] Mason's draft incorporated features to achieve both objectives, but the convention's members replaced Mason's elaborate election procedure and restrictive qualifications with simpler ones. The new constitution authorized the same voters to elect members of both houses, and the only distinction it made between members of the two houses was that the minimum age for senators was to be twenty-five years and for delegates, twenty-one. The Senate of Virginia was therefore a more democratic body than most states' upper houses.

The Form of Government specifically granted to the General Assembly the exclusive authority that the king had formerly exercised to appoint the governor, members of the Council of State, secretary, attorney general, all other administrative officers, and state judges as well as the treasurer, whom the colonial assembly had named. It placed no time limits on their terms except that the assembly was to elect the governor and treasurer annually and the state's representatives in Congress for one-year terms. The convention and assembly created replacements for some of the royal officials such as a new office of auditor of public accounts. The office of secretary of the colony, shorn of its authority to appoint county clerks, became the office of the secretary of the commonwealth, a much less exalted, profitable, or politically influential position and one with largely clerical responsibilities. The constitution empowered the assembly to impeach the governor, administrative officers, and judges "offending against the state, either by mal-administration, corruption, or other means by which the safety of the state may be endangered." The constitution required that the General Court try cases of impeachment except that the Supreme Court of Appeals was to try cases of impeachment involving judges of the General Court.

By imposing no other limitations or grants of authority on the legislature, the new constitution implicitly vested in the General Assembly of the Commonwealth of Virginia all the legislative responsibilities and powers that the colonial assembly had exercised and, even without stating as much, also allowed the General Assembly to assume many of the powers of sovereignty that the Crown had exercised under the constitution of the colony. In effect, the legislatures of all the new states claimed or inherited much of the authority of the Crown. It is from that event and for that reason that legislators, jurists, and learned commentators have almost always interpreted state constitutions as permitting state legislatures to exercise any legislative power that their respective constitutions did not explicitly deny to them.[75] In 1918, the Virginia Supreme Court of Appeals affirmed, in *Strawberry Hill Land Co. v. Starbuck*, the long-accepted understanding that "the State Constitution is not a grant of power, but only the restriction of powers otherwise practically unlimited, that, except so far as restrained by the Constitution, the legislature has plenary power, and that every fair doubt must be resolved in favor of the constitutionality of an act of the General Assembly."[76]

By investing the General Assembly which consisted of two elected houses with so large a measure of governmental power—and without any of Mason's increased property qualifications for members or his indirect filtering method of electing senators—the convention's members gave Richard Henry Lee, on the morning they adopted the Form of Government, ample reason to describe it as "very much of the democratic kind."

THE EXECUTIVE

Richard Henry Lee regarded the radical reduction in the authority of the executive as a sufficient guard "against the Monster Tyranny." Convention members not only removed the executive from participation in, or control over, the assembly, they also denied the "Governour or chief magistrate" much other independent authority and transformed the executive into a weak branch of government largely subservient to the legislature.

Following Mason's draft very closely, the constitution decreed that the two houses of the General Assembly annually elect the governor and that no person could serve more than three consecutive one-year terms or be elected to office again after three terms until at least four years later (increased from Mason's three years). It also required the assembly to elect an eight-member advisory "Privy Council, or Council of State" with no legislative or judicial responsibilities at all. The constitution set no term limits on council members, but it required the assembly to remove two council members every third year and appoint replacements. The constitution authorized members of the council to select one of their number "as president, who, in case of the death, inability, or necessary absence of the Governour from the government, shall act as Lieutenant-Governour." That provision in effect abolished the colonial office of lieutenant governor and gave that title to the council member who in the colonial period had been styled president. The new constitution merely authorized a council member to act with the title lieutenant governor in the event of the governor's death or for the duration of the governor's incapacity or absence from the capital.

The convention elected several distinguished senior men (including four members of the royal Council of State) to the new council in June 1776, which indicated that the delegates intended the council to be a body of wise and experienced men to advise the governor. Three of the senior members declined,[77] and only John Page, who had served as vice president of the Virginia Committee of Safety since the summer of 1775, accepted. Within a few years, the Council of State had been so much transformed that membership on the council was no longer the capstone of a gentleman's successful career in public service but a stepping-stone for young men who wished to gain governmental experience accompanied by a salary.[78] James Madison, who served on the council for a time, later characterized it as "a grave of useful talents, as well as objectionable in point of expense."[79]

The constitution declared that the governor "shall with the advice of a Council of State, exercise the executive powers of government according to the laws of this commonwealth; and shall not, under any pretence, exercise any power or prerogative by virtue of any law, statute, or custom, of *England*." Because the assembly appointed the treasurer, secretary, and attorney general (and during the war created and named other officials, among them directors of a board of war and a naval office), the actual administration of government was very much fragmented, which further reduced the authority of the executive and augmented the potential for legislative management, for good or ill.

Except during the American Revolution and the War of 1812, when the responsibilities of governors often exceeded their constitutional or legal authority,[80] governors had little of consequence to do most of the time and could act both in important and routine matters only with the concurrence of a majority of council members. So inconsequential was the governorship that the state's newspapers only occasionally printed short notices after the assembly elected a new governor and seldom even reported on their taking office. No governor made an inaugural address before the American Civil War.[81] In 1810, Governor John Tyler (1747–1813) grumbled that his office was merely "a tedious insignificant one, and has but one good Trait in it, And that is this: it gives me not power enough to do mischief in any other way than by the Sin of Neglect."[82]

THE JUDICIARY

The convention completed breaking up the responsibilities of the colonial Council of State by redistributing its judicial responsibilities. The Form of Government authorized the two houses of assembly to "appoint Judges of the Supreme Court of Appeals, and General Court, Judges in Chancery, Judges of Admiralty," and an attorney general. The new Supreme Court of Appeals (which statutes and the court's own records often referred to merely as the Court of Appeals) succeeded to the appellate jurisdiction of the old General Court. A new General Court succeeded to the old General Court's criminal jurisdiction in cases involving white people, which thereby abolished the royal Court of Oyer and Terminer for criminal trials of white people. The constitution declared that judges hold office "during good behaviour" and made them subject to impeachment. It allowed the governor and council to make interim appointments to fill judicial vacancies but reserved to the General Assembly full authority to fill vacancies permanently. The constitution allowed judges "fixed and adequate salaries" and prohibited them from serving in the assembly.

The provisions for the judiciary indicate that a majority of the convention's members desired or anticipated some significant structural reforms in the administration of justice. Theretofore, justices of the peace in county courts and members of the Council of State sitting as members of the General Court had exercised both civil and criminal jurisdiction and also presided over proceedings in chancery, for which justices of the peace took a separate oath.[83] But the new constitution required the assembly to elect judges for separate courts of admiralty, "Judges in Chancery," members of the new General Court, and judges of a "Supreme Court of Appeals," which suggests an intention to separate some functions. The new court of admiralty that replaced the royal court of vice-admiralty lasted only until the ratification of the Constitution of the United States in 1788, which granted admiralty jurisdiction to the federal courts, after which the General Assembly abolished the Virginia court. Very few records of the Virginia Court of Admiralty survive.[84]

The Virginia constitution's provision for separate General Court and Chancery Court judges was the beginning of a long series of legislative and constitutional changes in court organization and distribution of jurisdictions that for a time separated equity proceedings from common law proceedings. The changes also eventually created a layered judicial system in which judges of the General Court and nineteenth-century judges of district courts shared concurrent jurisdiction with county courts (in some instances) and heard appeals from county courts.[85] By an ordinance that the convention adopted and statutes that the General Assembly later passed, county justices of the peace continued to preside over courts of oyer and terminer to try enslaved people accused of crimes. The General Assembly and the Constitutional Conventions of 1829–30 and of 1850–51 worked all that out during a long period of experience and experimentation.

COUNTY GOVERNMENT

Except for two or three references to justices of the peace and to reauthorizing the General Assembly to grant men in cities and towns the right to vote for their own representatives in the assembly, the Constitution of 1776 included nothing at all about local government. Other states' Revolutionary constitutions seldom mentioned local government institutions either. Historians and even legal scholars have often overlooked this absence or failed to perceive its consequences.[86] The silence in the Virginia constitution did not effectively abolish local government. By referring to four types of officers—justices of the peace, sheriffs, constables, and clerks—the convention in effect included their offices as they then existed in the form of government, each with the responsibility and authority under Virginia law as of 1776. The General Assembly had created county governments and established new counties as needed, which made county governments creatures and agents of the government of the colony.

In an undated draft opinion in *Case of the County Levy* that initially arose in 1789—a case that the records of the Supreme Court of Appeals do not indicate that the judges ever heard or decided—Edmund Pendleton, then president of the court, explained that an ordinance that the convention adopted after it approved the constitution to enable justices of the peace to continue in office had the intended effect of confirming all the laws and practices relating to county courts then in force. That included the authority that the assembly had granted them to lay and collect taxes to defray the costs of operating county government. If he was correct in so recollecting—and it is entirely possible that, as one of the best attorneys in the convention, he had suggested or drafted the ordinance—then he granted that ordinance quasi-constitutional status, which among other things authorized unelected justices of the peace to lay and collect taxes—taxation without representation—as well as made all the institutions and practices of the county courts part of the new state constitution.[87]

Justices of the peace in the county courts, St. George Tucker complained about a quarter of a century after the new constitution quietly authorized justices of the peace to continue to function almost exactly as before, "unite in their own persons such a variety of powers as appears perfectly incompatible with the principles of a democracy." Tucker was the most erudite legal scholar of late eighteenth- and early nineteenth-century Virginia and regarded and discussed county courts as parts of the government with full constitutional status when he enumerated and criticized their numerous powers. Justices of the peace "are judges in all cases of life and death where a slave is to be tried," he explained, because they continued to sit as judges of local courts of oyer and terminer without a jury to try enslaved persons accused of crimes as they had since 1692.[88] Justices of the peace were also judges at trials of all common law misdemeanors, and they constituted an examining court (preliminary to a grand jury hearing) with the authority to release a free person suspected of a felony. "They are judges without appeal," Tucker continued, "in all civil cases, where the matter in controversy is under ten dollars, and perhaps where it is under twenty dollars. They are also judges in all other civil cases arising within their county (whatever be the amount) both at common law, and in equity." Moreover, "They open roads, build bridges, erect courthouses and prisons, and levy the expense thereof on the county"—that is, the unelected justices of the peace taxed the county's residents. Tucker concluded, "So formidable an accumulation of powers in any one set of men, cannot fail, in process of time, of establishing an elective aristocracy in every county; a few generations, perhaps a few years, will convert it into an hereditary aristocracy.... This then may be regarded as one of those formidable evils in our present constitution, which no future conventions should permit to endanger the total subversion of the principles of our government."[89]

As well-informed as Tucker was about the county courts, he erred. Justices of the peace were not elected and therefore could not create "an elective aristocracy." In fact, a century or more before the Constitution of 1776, self-appointed justices of the peace had already created in each county "an hereditary aristocracy." The Convention of 1776 almost invisibly reauthorized and strengthened that local hierarchy. But of most importance here, Tucker referred to and treated the county governments as constitutional institutions despite the failure of the convention to mention them in the Form of Government.

CHURCH GOVERNMENT

As with the county courts, the Constitution of 1776 left the Church of England intact as a vital institution of local government even without mentioning it. Except in excluding clergymen from the General Assembly, the Constitution of 1776 contained not one syllable about religion or the parishes of the Church of England. That silence did not abolish the established church or the legal responsibilities of vestrymen, parish clerks, and ministers any more than other silences had abolished county courts. In both cases, the silences and ordinances of the convention left existing institutions and laws in place, though subject to later modification, such as transferring the responsibilities that parishes had exercised to care for orphans and the poor over to the counties and new boards of overseers of the poor late in the 1780s.

Circumstantial evidence strongly suggests that a large majority of the convention's members did not contemplate any change at all in the role that the Church of England had in the government of Virginia. Richard Henry Lee proposed in his April 1776 outline for a form of government that the assembly appoint the "Commissary." Until that time, the bishop of London, who had nominal responsibility for the colonial church, had appointed a commissary to be his personal representative in the colony. That Lee recommended transferring the appointment of a commissary from what was soon to be a foreign bishop to Virginia's legislators suggests that he expected the intimate old relationship between the church and the state, with their interlocking responsibilities, to continue. When Patrick Henry introduced James Madison's first amendment to the religion section of the Declaration of Rights, he immediately encountered resistance from convention members who feared the move was a threat to the establishment. Madison succeeded with his second amendment that he drafted because he engaged a well-known churchman to introduce it, and it did not even implicitly threaten the established church. And George Mason included nothing about the church in his draft constitution that could have stimulated debate.

Even more revealing, on the last day of the convention, delegates unilaterally amended the Book of Common Prayer, the Church of England's official form of worship that Parliament had first enacted in the sixteenth century. They ordered that the prayers for the king in the communion service and in the morning and evening services be deleted and prayers for "the Magistrates of this commonwealth" be substituted; and "In the 20th sentence of the litany use these Words That it may please thee to endue"—meaning to educate or instruct—"the Magistrates of this commonwealth with Grace Wisdom and Understanding."[90]

Actions of the convention members who attended the General Assembly that October as members of the House of Delegates also indicated that few of them were even willing to entertain proposals to modify the place of the church in Virginia's society and government. Thomas Jefferson returned to Virginia from Philadelphia for the autumn session of the assembly and introduced proposals to break the association of church and state. He later described the resistance he encountered from those delegates as producing one of the "severest contests" in which he was ever involved. He did manage to secure passage of a bill to exempt dissenters from paying taxes for the support of the Church of England and to stop the government from paying clergymen's salaries.[91]

Members of every General Assembly from then through the session in the winter of 1784–85 created a new parish coterminous with each new county they created. They preserved the established church and its place in Virginia's government for almost a full decade. Until January 1786, the Church of England remained part of the government of Virginia, and the government of Virginia remained part of the church in the new commonwealth.

Ordaining the Constitution

Members of the convention did not submit the constitution to the voters for approval or rejection but simply put it into operation. Whether they discussed the possibility of or necessity for a ratification referendum is not recorded. Jefferson had included a provision for popular ratification in the draft he sent down from Philadelphia, but it is unlikely that very many delegates were aware of his suggestion. Nor was it self-evident, to use a memorable phrase from 1776, that ratification by the voters in a referendum was then generally understood to be requisite to render a constitution legitimate. Nobody could cite a precedent because nobody had ever done anything remotely similar in the whole history of English-speaking people.[92] In the language of the final section of the preamble, the delegates did "ordain and declare the future form of government of *Virginia*."

Immediately after convention delegates unanimously adopted the Constitution or Form of Government on 29 June, they elected Patrick Henry governor, named the eight-member Privy Council, or Council of State, and appointed Edmund Randolph attorney general.[93] The convention left election of all other officials to the General Assembly that first met in October 1776.

The sequence of events during the final few days of the convention suggests that soon after adoption of the constitution, some members thought about essential matters that they should have included in it or that were clearly necessary to enable the new government to begin operation. They introduced resolutions on those topics, the president appointed select committees to draft the measures, the committees reported bills, and the delegates passed them.

Delegates adopted ordinances to create senatorial districts and set a date for election of the first state senators;[94] to authorize justices of the peace to remain in office and continue to administer justice;[95] to specify oaths of office[96] and an oath of allegiance to be imposed on suspected loyalists;[97] and to create a board of commissioners for the state's new, little navy.⁹⁸ They also passed the resolution to amended the Book of Common Prayer and another to adopt a device for the seal of state. The new seal depicted "Virtus the genius of the commonwealth dressed like an Amazon resting on a Spear with one hand and holding a Sword in the other and treading on Tyranny represented by a man prostrate a Crown fallen from his Head a broken chain in his left Hand and a Scourge in his right," with the new motto of the commonwealth, "Sic semper tyrannis," thus always to tyrants.⁹⁹ That seal visually completed the constitutional revolution of removing the king from the government of Virginia.

The convention included a provision of fundamental importance in the ordinance to enable magistrates to continue in office: "That the common law of England, all statutes or acts of parliament made in aid of the common law prior to the fourth year of the reign of king James the first"—that is, before the first settlement of Virginia in 1607—"and which are of a general nature, not local to that kingdom, together with the several acts of the general assembly of this colony now in force, so far as the same may consist with the several ordinances, declarations, and resolutions of the general convention, shall be the rule of decision, and shall be considered as in full force until the same be altered by the legislative power of the colony."¹⁰⁰ That provision effectively reenacted British statutes, parts of the common law of England, and the laws of the colony that were then in force in Virginia. That was the provision that Edmund Pendleton believed endowed unelected justices of the peace in the county courts with the power to tax.¹⁰¹ It also allowed slavery to continue to exist in Virginia under the authority, for the time being, of colonial laws.

The Constitution of 1776 in Operation

On the morning of 6 July 1776, Patrick Henry took the oath of office as the first governor of the independent Commonwealth of Virginia, which marks the effective beginning of government under the Constitution of 1776. It should have been an auspicious beginning, but it was not. Henry was so ill, probably from malaria, that people worried he might not live long enough that day to take the oath. With no quorum of members of the new Privy Council or Council of State in town to select a president, if Henry died the new government would begin with no executive officials at all, and it might in fact fail.¹⁰²

What members of the Convention of 1776 changed and what they did not change indicate that they had little or no intention of making a revolution in Virginia's government. The grandees were protecting the parts of the colonial constitution that they had created and the many rights and ample privileges that they claimed for themselves under it. That may not have been the case in every colony that became a state in 1776, but it was certainly the case in Virginia.[103]

The revolutionary language of liberty embodied in the Declaration of Rights and the Declaration of Independence provided other Virginians political leverage to advocate some revolutionary objectives and to make some other important reforms. During the war years, men and women began to petition the General Assembly on issues of public policy and insist on changes. Before the Revolution, petitions to the assembly concerned local or personal matters, such as proposals to relocate a courthouse, authorize a new ferry, establish a town, or provide a legal remedy for a personal or family problem, such as the distribution of an estate. But during and after the war years, men and women told their representatives what they thought about public policies and proposed changes in ways that they had not done before. They insisted on full religious freedom and the disestablishment of the Church of England, on revisions of tax policies, on changes to recruitment acts for the army, and on other issues that deeply concerned them. The petitioning gradually changed the relationship between legislators and their constituents. Unlike before the Revolution, candidates for the assembly made their views known to the voters and sought their votes based on important issues of public policy. To that extent, voters introduced a new democratic element into electoral politics in Virginia during the 1770s and 1780s.[104]

Thomas Jefferson took the lead in making other important changes. At the October 1776 session of the General Assembly, the House of Delegates created a select committee to revise all the laws of Virginia, in part to prune away vestiges of royal government and in part to adapt the laws of the commonwealth to its changed status. Jefferson, Pendleton, and Wythe did nearly all the work.[105]

The 1776 act for abolishing entail and the 1784 act for abolishing primogeniture were among the most influential and began a slow process of changing an important component of the social constitution of Virginia. The law of entail had allowed authors of wills and deeds to enter clauses to prohibit sale or subdivision of the property. Entails were permanent unless all the parties with claims on a property could agree to break the entail, and that required a long and expensive process of procuring a special act of the General Assembly for that express purpose. Abolition of entail prohibited people from creating new entails and also broke or abrogated all entails then in force.[106] By abolishing primogeniture, the assembly prohibited a related ancient legal practice that required that when a person died without leaving a will, the real estate automatically became the property of the eldest living son, or if there were no son, the law of primogeniture specified how the property was to descend so as to keep landed estates intact. Thereafter, when a person died intestate (without a will), all heirs received equal portions of the estate.[107] Together, entail and primogeniture had enabled Virginia's great landed families to amass and keep together the estates and to attain the social, economic, and political prominence that allowed them to dominate the political culture of the colony during the eighteenth century. Thereafter the number of great landed families and the influence of that class of Virginians very slowly declined, with important implications for the social, political, and constitutional development of the state.[108]

The final law to be enacted from the bills that the committee of revisers recommended removed the Church of England from the constitution and government of Virginia. During the decade after the adoption of the Constitution of 1776, brilliantly organized political pressure from Baptists, but also with important support from Presbyterians, deployed the language of the Declaration of Rights to bring about the most important revolution in revolutionary Virginia excepting perhaps only the act of declaring independence.[109] In January 1786, the assembly adopted Jefferson's Act for Establishing Religious Freedom, which denied any ecclesiastical authority any role in government and specifically declared that religious beliefs and practices were private, personal matters with which government had no legitimate concern. The law declared "that no man shall be compelled to frequent or support any religious worship, place, or ministry whatsoever, nor shall be enforced, restrained, molested, or burthened in his body or goods, nor shall otherwise suffer on account of his religious opinions or belief, but that all men shall be free to profess, and by argument to maintain, their opinions in matters of Religion, and that the same shall in no wise diminish, enlarge or affect their civil capacities."

The final provision of Jefferson's law gave it constitutional status insofar as possible: "And though we well know that this assembly elected by the people for the ordinary purposes of legislation only, have no power to restrain the acts of succeeding assemblies, constituted with powers equal to our own, and that therefore to declare this act irrevocable would be of no effect in law; yet we are free to declare, and do declare, that the rights hereby asserted are of the natural rights of mankind, and that if any act shall be hereafter passed to repeal the present, or to narrow its operation, such act will be an infringement of natural right."[110]

Without realizing it at the time, the legislators who adopted the Act for Establishing Religious Freedom also enabled the law of unintended consequences to operate along with it. The glebes of the parishes of the Church of England, property used for the support of clergymen that parishes acquired when they were parts of the colonial government, became a bone of legislative and legal contention after the disestablishment of the church. Members of other Protestant denominations demanded that the General Assembly strip the church of that property. They asserted that it belonged to the public and not to the congregations and that it therefore be devoted to purely secular purposes. During the two decades after the disestablishment, the legislature and the courts repeatedly involved themselves in settling questions of ownership of church buildings, cemeteries, and other property and in seizing abandoned glebe lands and converting them into resources for new boards of overseers of the poor in the counties.[111]

The largely unrestrained authority with which the constitution endowed the General Assembly permitted the assembly to take actions that prior to 1776 only the king could do, such as grant charters of incorporation for cities, educational institutions, and commercial and manufacturing corporations. Two of the first charters that the General Assembly granted incorporated Virginia's second and third institutions of higher learning, Liberty Hall Academy in 1782, a Presbyterian school founded in 1749, which evolved into Washington and Lee University; and Hampden-Sydney College in 1783, a Presbyterian school founded in the fall of 1776.[112]

Judicial Review

The Virginia Constitution of 1776 became, and was a legitimate constitution for, the commonwealth in the same way that the constitution of the colony had become, and been, legitimate before 1776 and in the same way that laws and court rulings were legitimate. Public officials accepted the old colonial constitution and laws, and most people swore allegiance to the new constitution and obeyed the new laws. The constitution and the laws functioned with few or no effective complaints that they lacked legal legitimacy. As General Court judge Spencer Roane wrote about the Constitution of 1776 in *Peter Kamper v. Mary Hawkins* in 1793, "This constitution is sanctioned by the consent and acquiescence of the people for seventeen years; and it is admitted by the almost universal opinion of the people, by the repeated adjudications of the courts of this commonwealth, and by very many declarations of the legislature itself, to be of superior authority to any opposing act of the legislature."[113]

The 1776 Constitution or Form of Government, the Declaration of Rights, the Act for Establishing Religious Freedom, and other documents of constitutional or quasi-constitutional status created new responsibilities for Virginia's judges; and new constitutions in other states and the Constitution of the United States had the same effect elsewhere. Understanding constitutions as laws of a superior force to legislative statutes, as Roane did, judges began to exercise responsibilities that legislators, essayists, and theorists had taken on themselves during the colonial period when questions arose whether public policies, laws, or public officials operated in a manner inconsistent with the constitution of England or the constitution of any one of the colonies. Published constitutions and other documents of constitutional status, not historical practices or political theories, became the lodestones for assessing the constitutional propriety of acts of legislatures and public officials.

George Wythe most forcefully asserted that judicial responsibility in his opinion in *Commonwealth v. Caton* in 1782 when a question arose whether a resolution of the House of Delegates was an impermissible act under the express language of the state constitution. Wythe wrote, "if the whole legislature, an event to be deprecated, should attempt to overleap the bounds, prescribed to them by the people, I, in administering the public justice of the country, will meet the united powers, at my seat in this tribunal; and, pointing to the constitution, will say, to them, here is the limit of your authority; and, hither, shall you go, but no further."[114] The other judges, except Edmund Pendleton who refrained from commenting on the subject, "were of opinion, that the court had power to declare any resolution or act of the legislature, or of either branch of it, to be unconstitutional and void"; but because "the resolution of the house of delegates, in this case, was inoperative, as the senate had not concurred in it," the court did not declare that the House of Delegates had acted unconstitutionally because that action was of no effect.[115] In the first court case in Virginia that raised the question whether a court had authority or responsibility to proclaim that another part of the government had violated the constitution, all but one of the state's appellate court judges explicitly asserted that the court had that responsibility to interpret and enforce the state's highest law, and that the state's constitution was, in fact, the supreme law in Virginia.[116]

Affirming an act as not contrary to the constitution is an act of judicial review just as much as declaring an action contrary to the constitution. That Pendleton in fact agreed with the other judges about their possessing a right to pass on the constitutionality of acts of government officials is evident in his draft opinion in *Case of the County Levy*. He wrote that the authority of unelected county courts to tax residents did not violate the assertion in the Declaration of Rights that people could not be taxed except by their elected representatives. And in that opinion, Pendleton also disclosed that he believed that the Declaration of Rights was of equal constitutional authority with the Constitution or Form of Government.[117]

When *Kamper v. Hawkins* reached the General Court in 1793, affording Roane his opportunity to affirm the legitimacy of the state constitution, the judges explained individually and at length that the very concept of the written constitution as a superior body of law required courts to review acts that might violate the constitution and to declare them unconstitutional and void if necessary. Several times during the life of the Constitution of 1776, the General Court and the Supreme Court of Appeals ruled that acts of the assembly did not violate the constitution, but each court ruled once that an act did violate the constitution.[118] The third state constitution, which was ratified in 1851, for the first time recognized the authority of judges of the Supreme Court of Appeals to exercise the power of judicial review, not by granting them that authority as if it were an innovation but simply by including cases involving "the constitutionality of a law" in a list of matters within the court's jurisdiction.[119]

The United States Constitutions

The Convention of 1776 included no provision in the Constitution or Form of Government by which to amend it, so it remained in effect without textual alteration until 1830 when voters ratified the second Constitution of the Commonwealth of Virginia which replaced it. That does not mean that the state constitution did not change. As one of the United States of America, the government of Virginia was also subject to the terms of the Articles of Confederation and then of the Constitution of the United States. The Articles and the federal Constitution imposed limitations on the governments of Virginia and the other states and also empowered their legislatures and executives to fulfill certain responsibilities that were not, in every instance, specified in their state constitutions.

The Constitution of the United States empowered state legislators to elect United States Senators and provide for the election of members of the House of Representatives and of presidential electors; to require that states give full faith and credit to the legal processes of other states; to empower them to return escaped fugitives from justice and people who had escaped from slavery; and to prohibit them from issuing paper money, separately waging war, or making laws repugnant to the federal constitution and laws.

Each of the obligations imposed on states enlarged the responsibilities of their public officers as prescribed in their respective state constitutions, and each of the guarantees placed corresponding limitations or prohibitions on state action. One of the most important and controversial changes that the federal constitution made granted Congress authority to tax inhabitants of the United States. Until then, Congress had requested that each state supply a certain portion of the necessary revenue, leaving it to each state legislature to determine what to tax and how to collect the tax. After ratification of the federal constitution, states no longer had a significant role in collecting national revenue.

More than a few influential people in Virginia and elsewhere feared that the new federal government would become too strong and would encroach on the rights of state governments or even reduce the states to political insignificance and endanger the rights of citizens. Congress therefore proposed amendments to the Constitution, and in December 1791, Virginia was the last state that ratified them and made the Bill of Rights part of the Constitution. The Ninth Amendment declared, "The enumeration in the Constitution of certain rights shall not be construed to deny or disparage others retained by the people"; and the Tenth Amendment declared, "The powers not delegated to the United States by the Constitution, nor prohibited by it to the States, are reserved to the States respectively, or to the people."[120]

The eight other amendments ratified at the same time prohibited Congress from infringing people's individual rights. At the time that the Bill of Rights was proposed and adopted, people interpreted the opening words of the First Amendment ("Congress shall make no law") as applying to the entire Bill of Rights. As Chief Justice John Marshall explained in *Barron v. Baltimore* in 1833, "In almost every convention by which the constitution was adopted, amendments to guard against the abuse of power were recommended. These amendments demanded security against the apprehended encroachments of the general Government—not against those of the local governments."[121] For the most part, Marshall's interpretation remained the case until the twentieth century.

Some other provisions of the federal constitution, such as those that granted Congress the power to regulate interstate and foreign commerce and to enact uniform rules of naturalization and bankruptcy, could be interpreted either as granting Congress exclusive powers, and therefore as additional limitations on the powers of state governments, or as creating concurrent powers with the states merely forbidden to pass or enforce laws that conflicted with the "supreme" laws of Congress. Litigation on those provisions that involved questions of whether congressional power was exclusive or concurrent have formed a large part of the evolving constitutional case law of the United States and in many ways have modified the explicit provisions of state constitutions.

Kentucky

Forty-five men elected from the nine westernmost Virginia counties met in convention in the town of Danville from 2 to 19 April 1792 to write a constitution for what on 1 June of that year became the fifteenth state in the union, the Commonwealth of Kentucky.[122] The differences between the Kentucky Constitution of 1792 and the Virginia Constitution of 1776 are more important and conspicuous than the similarities. A careful analysis of provisions in the Kentucky Constitution traced a majority of those provisions to the Pennsylvania Constitution of 1790,[123] but the wording of numerous provisions and the additions that members of the Kentucky convention made to the Virginia Declaration of Rights closely followed or actually repeated language from the new Constitution of the United States.

The first Kentucky constitution[124] was both more and less democratic than the first Virginia constitution. It abolished the property qualification for the suffrage, specified that all voting be by ballot, not by voice vote, and it allowed all adult white males to vote annually for members of the state's House of Representatives. The constitution apportioned members of the legislature on the relative populations of the counties, not two per county as in Virginia. But unlike in Virginia, it did not allow voters to elect state senators. Instead, it empowered the voters to elect a separate group of electors who in turn elected members of the state Senate and the governor for four-year terms. The constitution created a strong governor with no advisory council and gave the governor authority to veto bills the legislature passed but allowed the legislature to override a veto by a two-thirds vote of both houses. The wording of the veto section very closely followed the corresponding section in the Constitution of the United States.

Unlike the Virginia Constitution of 1776, which did not mention slavery at all, the Kentucky Constitution of 1792 explicitly made slavery constitutional and probably impossible to abolish by legislative action. The constitution prohibited the legislature from freeing any enslaved people without the consent of their owners. It also denied the assembly authority to forbid immigrants from bringing enslaved people into the state. Having explicitly protected the rights of some people to own other people, the constitution endowed the legislature with "full power to pass such laws as may be necessary to oblige the owners of slaves to treat them with humanity, to provide for them necessary clothing and provision, to abstain from all injuries to them extended to life or limb." Should owners fail in those responsibilities, the constitution authorized the state government to sell the enslaved victims to other owners, the proceeds from the sale nevertheless going to "their owner or owners," who, by ill treatment of human property, could thereby effectively lose nothing of value. (And the abused enslaved people did not necessarily gain anything unless a new owner happened to be less inhumane than the old.)

The Kentucky constitution also contained a provision that in 1799, voters could elect delegates to another convention to rewrite the constitution if changing conditions or experience living under the Constitution of 1792 warranted making revisions. And the Kentucky Convention of 1792 attached to the constitution a schedule, comparable to some of the ordinances that the Virginia Convention of 1776 adopted at the last minute, to enable government under the new constitution to go into effect smoothly. As had the Virginia Convention of 1776, the Convention of 1792 ordained the new constitution into effect without a ratification referendum. So too did the Kentucky Convention of 1799 after it drafted the second state constitution.[125]

In 1792, residents of western Virginia created a government quite different from the one under which they and all other Virginians had lived since 1776. Different conditions in the west contributed to some of the differences, but ideas and practices that men carried with them to western Virginia from other states contributed to some of the other differences. The most important constitutional innovation in 1792 was the article on slavery to protect that form of property from legislative or judicial interference or abolition. Its origins are to be found in the previous century and a half of American law and experience, particularly the law and experience of Virginia.

The Future

As the largest and most populous state in the new United States, Virginia—and Virginians—had an outsized influence on state constitution making and on other legal developments in the country late in the eighteenth century and early in the nineteenth. That was demonstrably the case with the Declaration of Rights.[126] Moreover, many young Virginia men moved to the west during the decades after the American Revolution began and took with them beliefs about law and society that they had learned in Virginia; and many of them took part in the preparation of state constitutions and legal codes in the new states they helped found. During the decades between the American Revolution and the American Civil War, for instance, more natives of Virginia than of any other state served in constitutional conventions in Ohio, Indiana, and Illinois.[127] On the other hand, natives of other states also influenced constitution making in Virginia, especially when western Virginians wrote a constitution for Kentucky in 1792, northwestern Virginians wrote a constitution for West Virginia in the winter of 1861–62, and Virginians who remained loyal to the United States wrote a new constitution in 1864 for the government of Virginia that remained one of the United States during the American Civil War.

CHAPTER 3

The Constitution of 1830

"There is no political maxim whose truth is more forcibly illustrated by experience than one contained in the declaration of rights of Virginia, 'That no free government, or the blessing of liberty, can be preserved to any people, but by a frequent recurrence to fundamental principles.'" That is the first sentence of an appeal that twenty-two white Virginia men published in June 1816 as part of a concerted campaign for major revisions of the state's 1776 constitution. The men condensed Patrick Henry's language of the fifteenth section of the Virginia Declaration of Rights but got its essence exactly right. "The entire neglect of this invaluable maxim," they went on, opening an incisive critique of the old constitution, had made "an absolute mockery of the principles of free government."[1] Fourteen years later, when the state got its second written constitution, most of the men who agitated for reform of the first constitution were badly disappointed.

Before the Movement for Constitutional Revision

Virginia changed in many important ways after the American Revolution. The most important changes were demographic and economic.[2] The western population grew, in some places very rapidly, but the population of most of the eastern counties, particularly the ones in the southeastern portion of the state, remained relatively stable or, in some instances, declined. The movement of people into the western portions was for the most part an immigration of white people, free people, and people whose families owned fewer enslaved laborers than in the older portions of Virginia. The movement of people out of the eastern portion was an emigration of both white and Black, free and enslaved, as white families with too many sons or too few acres of land migrated to the newly opened southwestern frontiers or into the Ohio Valley. The movement of peoples led to an increasing disproportion of white and Black residents in the various regions of Virginia. In some counties east of the fall line and south of the James River, white people became a minority, and among them, the large planters were an even smaller minority. To the immediate west, in the Blue Ridge and Shenandoah Valley, large plantations and enslaved people were becoming relatively more common, but in the Allegheny Mountains and the Ohio River Valley, large plantations and significant numbers of enslaved men, women, and children were scarce.[3]

Virginia became more diverse both demographically and economically. People from outside as well as inside Virginia settled in the west. Religious and cultural diversity as well as differences in agricultural production in different parts of Virginia gave the regions different political cultures. The farther west and northwest one went in Virginia, the less one saw plantations, tobacco cultivation, and wealthy families and their large mansions and the more one saw small farms and extractive industries such as timber cutting and mining. Large-scale wheat cultivation and flour milling were becoming the second-most-important agricultural and manufacturing enterprises in eastern Virginia after tobacco cultivation, and ironworks and many smaller-scale manufacturing establishments flourished along nearly all the major rivers in Virginia.

Enterprising Virginians worked on plans to connect the Atlantic Ocean with the interior of eastern North America all the way to the Ohio River. In 1816, the General Assembly created the Board of Public Works to direct and provide financing for those and other transportation projects. Through an innovative public-private partnership, the Board of Public Works purchased a significant portion of the initial stock offerings of canal and turnpike (and later railroad) companies, most of which were chartered for and constructed in the eastern portion of the state.[4] Because easterners dominated both houses of the assembly, which had exclusive authority to charter corporations, westerners had few chances to take an equal part and procure charters for transportation projects or banks in the west; but westerners had to pay a share of the taxes and eventually incurred a share of the public debt created to support construction of roads, canals, and railroads in the east.

Movement for Reform

In the western portions of Virginia as well as in some eastern neighborhoods, men desired changes in the state's constitution that had been written largely for the well-being of eighteenth-century tobacco planters and that continued to function for the benefit of eastern planters and entrepreneurs and to the disadvantage of western residents and other men who were not owners of enslaved people. The old constitution worked so well in support of the financial and political interests of political leaders in the east that those leaders resisted all proposals for change.

The other Virginians who published their condemnations of the Constitution of 1776 in June 1816 were by no means the first to find fault with the state's initial written constitution. As early as the autumn of 1776, some of Thomas Jefferson's Albemarle County constituents complained that the then-new constitution was defective. They wanted more democracy, including changes to allow voters to elect justices of the peace and sheriffs and to make it possible for citizens "to call to account" public officials who misused their powers. They also wanted limitations on the length of service of members of the General Assembly; prohibition of men voting in counties where they owned property but did not reside; allocation of representation in the House of Delegates based on "the number of Electors" in each county rather than by the rule of two delegates per county that the convention of 1776 had continued from colonial times; an opportunity for voters to pass on the propriety of bills that the assembly enacted; and abolition of the new Senate of Virginia as redundant inasmuch as the same voters selected delegates and senators. Jefferson's neighbors also demanded full religious liberty, abolition of primogeniture, and abolition of entail,[5] all three of which Jefferson helped them achieve, but their other proposals all failed; he did not even try to push them through.

Jefferson also favored changes in the 1776 Constitution or Form of Government but of a different kind. He and his most skilled legislative ally, James Madison, were unable in the 1780s to persuade the General Assembly to call a convention to consider his ideas. Jefferson's proposals, which reflected in part his frustrating experience as a wartime governor, included altering election schedules so that voters elected new members of the House of Delegates every third year rather than annually and elected senators every sixth year rather than every fourth. He proposed that the assembly elect governors for five-year terms with no eligibility for reelection. Jefferson also wanted all adult male freeholders or free white males who had lived in a county for one year to be able to vote, a significant relaxation of the old freehold requirement on the franchise; and he included a provision for the gradual abolition of slavery that would have all people born in the state after 31 December 1800 be free.[6]

Jefferson enumerated other criticisms of the state's constitution in his *Notes on the State of Virginia* later in the 1780s. He endorsed the 1776 proposal of his constituents that representation in the assembly be in proportion to the number of voters instead of two delegates per county. Jefferson contrasted Warwick County in the southeast, one of the smallest and probably the least-populous county, with the larger and much more populous counties and calculated that on election day "every man in Warwick has as much influence in the government as 17 men" in the Potomac Valley county of Loudoun. Collectively, Jefferson concluded, nineteen thousand men "living below the falls of the rivers, possess half the senate, and want four members only of possessing a majority of the house of delegates. . . . These nineteen thousand, therefore, living in one part of the country, give law to upwards of thirty thousand, living in another, and appoint all their chief officers executive and judiciary."[7] The numbers Jefferson cited were quite small, but he was writing about the minority of Virginians who voted, not the whole number of people who had to obey the laws that legislators passed and pay the taxes that lawmakers imposed on them.

Jefferson's complaint about the discrepancy between the effective political influence of voters in Warwick County and voters in more populous counties resonated powerfully in the 1810s when a new generation of Virginians deployed his reasoning and revived his comparison to argue that the undemocratic situation that he had described in the 1780s had grown worse. The men who published the call for action in June 1816 stated that "If representation were equalized and Warwick county were taken as the standard by which the number of representatives from all the other counties should be regulated," the counties of Loudoun and Frederick, to mention but two, "would be entitled to forty-five delegates each!" The men also pointed out that voters in the westernmost counties elected far fewer members of the Senate of Virginia than they would have been entitled to if seats in the two houses had been allocated solely according to population. "If it be asked," they concluded, "why so gross and flagrant an inequality of representation in the senate has been suffered to exist for so long—why a law has not been passed for new modeling the senatorial districts—the answer is an obvious one. The representatives of a minority of the people have the whole powers of government in their hands, and they will consent to no measure which has a tendency to transfer that power to its rightful owners, the majority. We say the rightful owners; for we presume it will not, and cannot, be denied, that it is a fundamental principle of our government, that the will of the majority should govern."[8]

The June 1816 newspaper article called on all Virginians to organize and propose a convention to rewrite the state's Revolutionary-era constitution. In August of that year, about seventy men from nearly forty Virginia counties (none of them in the east) met in the Shenandoah Valley town of Staunton and formally petitioned the General Assembly to pass a law to enable the people to vote for members of a convention to revise the state's constitution. "No doctrine has received a more universal assent," they declared, "than that in a republican government, the will of the majority should be the law of the land. And yet in a state, boasting of the pure republican character of its institutions, this first and fundamental principle of republicanism, does not exist."[9]

An appreciable number of members of the assembly already agreed. Early in 1816, the House of Delegates had almost passed a bill to call for a referendum on the question of summoning a convention, but on the third reading, the delegates adopted a "Ryder" not described in the journal and then defeated the bill by a vote of ninety to eighty-one.[10] The men who appealed to Virginians in June 1816 and the men who met in Staunton in August apparently believed that if they provided one more push the assembly would call a convention.

The push was not quite enough, but the following year, the legislators somewhat reduced the discrepancy between the eastern and western regions in the apportionment of seats in the Senate. The Convention of 1776 had apportioned seats in the Senate by an ordinance, not as part of the Constitution or Form of Government, and therefore the assembly retained constitutional authority to change the 1776 districts. In 1817 the assembly reapportioned senatorial seats and simultaneously revised the rate of taxation on real estate in different parts of the state. Legislators did both in one law, which indicates how intimate politicians regarded the relationship between property ownership and representation in the legislature, in much the same way that their early laws and their first constitution reflected an intimate relationship between property ownership and the suffrage. The new law made some alterations in the regions created in 1782 in response to complaints about inequitable taxation of land that roughly corresponded at that time with the distribution of wealth—that is, of large valuable plantations and slaveholding—in the state.[11]

The 1817 law created four regions that in general resembled the 1782 tax regions. The easternmost included all the region east of the fall line where shoal sections of the Potomac, Rappahannock, York, James, and Appomattox Rivers blocked navigation of deep-draft vessels, a line that ran roughly south from above Alexandria through Fredericksburg, Richmond, and Petersburg to the North Carolina border. That was then the heart of the slaveholding region of Virginia. The second region included all the area west of the fall line to the crest of the Blue Ridge Mountains. Ownership of enslaved people and the importance of slavery there had increased notably since the middle of the eighteenth century. The third embraced the relatively narrow valleys between the crest of the Blue Ridge and the crest of the Alleghany Mountains as far south as to include Lexington, a region where slavery was then of less consequence than in the eastern districts. Virginians have traditionally called that distinctive region the Valley, or the Valley of Virginia. The westernmost region encompassed all the land west of the crest of the Alleghany Mountains. In most of that region, slavery was of small consequence at that time.

In 1817, the assembly reduced the number of senators from the easternmost region from seven to five, increased the number from the westernmost region from two to five, and slightly increased the number of senators in the piedmont and Valley.[12] White residents of the mountains remained underrepresented in both houses of the General Assembly but to a somewhat lesser extent than they had been. White residents east of the Blue Ridge, where the largest numbers of enslaved Virginians resided, remained overrepresented in both the Senate and the House of Delegates.

Those few changes were all that the 1816 political agitation was able to achieve in the short term. One of the men who then supported constitutional revision, Samuel Kercheval, published under the pseudonym Henry Tompkinson a pamphlet entitled *Letters Addressed to the People of Virginia Showing the Necessity of Immediately Calling a Convention for the Revision and Amendment of our State Constitution*. No copy of it is known to survive, but the copy he sent to Thomas Jefferson brought from the former governor and president a very long and detailed letter on the subject of the state's constitution. In spite of Jefferson's repeated requests to keep the letter private, Kercheval showed it to many of his friends in the northern counties of the Shenandoah Valley, and shortly after Jefferson's death ten years later, he published it in several newspapers.[13] Delegates to the Virginia Convention of 1829–30 referred to it, quoted it, praised it, or condemned it several times and also referred to or quoted Jefferson's *Notes on the State of Virginia*. As a consequence, Jefferson, though by then dead, may have had a larger influence in that convention than he had had in the Convention of 1776, to which he had sent a draft for the state's first constitution.

Jefferson began his letter to Kercheval by recalling that in 1776, "the abuses of monarchy had so much filled all the space of political contemplation that we imagined every thing republican which was not monarchy." By "republican" Jefferson meant a government that represented the people, or voters, and one without a formidable executive. The "inequality of representation, in both houses of our legislature," Jefferson admitted, "is not the only republican heresy in this first essay of our revolutionary patriots at forming a constitution." He criticized the old scheme of apportion of assembly seats, and he condemned the structure of the executive department, in which "the Governor is entirely independant of the choice of the people, & of their controul; his Council equally so, and at best but a fifth wheel to a waggon." Appellate court judges whom the assembly elected to serve during good behavior "are dependant on none but themselves." And worst of all, justices of the peace on the county courts "are self-chosen, are for life, and perpetuate their own body in succession forever, so that a faction once possessing itself of the bench of a county can never be broken up, but hold their county in chains, forever indissoluble."[14]

Jefferson's 1816 proposals were more democratic than his 1780s critique. He proposed that members of the assembly be apportioned among the counties and cities on the basis of population and that judges, justices of the peace, sheriffs, and juries be popularly elected. He went further and suggested dividing the counties into small wards, rather like the New England townships which he admired, to allow the residents of each to elect their own justices of the peace, constables, militia officers, juries, and supervisors of schools and roads. Jefferson also recommended that the state hold a convention every generation for "periodical amendment of the Constitution." He defined a generation as encompassing nineteen years, corresponding to eighteenth-century European mortality rates which indicated that half a population alive in a given year would be dead nineteen years later. Every generation, the body politic was new and should be entitled to rewrite its constitution of government.[15]

By 1816, when Jefferson wrote his long letter to Kercheval, most new states in the west had done away with property ownership as a prerequisite for the suffrage. What later Americans referred to as Jacksonian Democracy had yet to emerge as the dominant ideology of American politics; but it was then emerging, and most Americans increasingly came to believe that all adult white men should have the right to vote and that all men were equally entitled to run for, or even equally qualified to serve in, public office.

Virginians who debated whether to undertake constitutional revision made frequent references to the ideals of the American Revolution and contrasted those ideals with the actual functioning of the state's government under its first constitution. What they seldom did—and what other people might logically have expected them to do—was employ the writings and speeches of Virginia men who had gained national reputations with theoretical or polemical essays and speeches about republican government in the United States. Many men engaged in such writing such as Judge Spencer Roane of the Supreme Court of Appeals, Congressman John Randolph of Roanoke, the agrarian John Taylor of Caroline, and several other lesser-known men. They formed the basis of a political faction that came to be known as the Tertium Quids—third things—who were neither Federalists nor Jeffersonian Republicans (the first two national political organizations). Those writers and speakers opposed energetic use of the powers of the national government to drive or direct national economic growth and the expansive interpretation of the Constitution of the United States required to give such proposals constitutional sanction.

Quids based their objections on an interpretation of the federal Constitution that required it to be read and applied as a restrictive straightjacket on the federal government. They wrote and spoke as advocates of representative, or republican, government and might therefore have been the logical exponents of political theories on which to base a revisal of the state constitution. But reformers and opponents of reform seldom referred to those men or their writings because the theorists and polemicists had actually been expounding a theory of federalism—what was proper and what was improper for the federal government to do based on the preexisting rights of the states—and not a political theory about representative government as it functioned, or should function, within the states, particularly in Virginia, where a small minority of adult white men voted, and where the General Assembly created a massive and expensive public works program not unlike that which the Quids condemned the federal government for even considering.[16]

Public discussions about amending or replacing the old constitution repeatedly focused attention on important issues of state politics. During the decades prior to the Convention of 1829–30, at least fifty-five groups of people from different portions of the state, mostly in the west, petitioned the assembly to call a convention for that purpose.[17] Scores of men made speeches, published essays, or contributed to the discussions[18] and revealed in nearly every instance that the people of the state were divided between prosperous easterners who disproportionately benefitted from the existing constitution and everyone else, mostly westerners, who believed themselves correspondingly aggrieved. Somewhat less evident in the beginning was a closely related division between slaveholders and nonslaveholders. Men who owned more than a few people were fearful that if the suffrage were extended to all white men or to westerners with little stake in the slave economy, those men would place higher taxes on slave property or threaten the institution. Men with little or no slave property were displeased at how often the interests of eastern slaveholders thwarted the aspirations of men who did not own land or enslaved people by denying them the vote or a proportionate share of influence in the state government.[19]

Discussion of these important and divisive topics in Virginia during the 1810s and 1820s was but one of many episodes in a very long and wide-ranging national discussion about the fundamentals of representative, or republican, government. Who should be allowed to vote and who not? Why? Who or what did the legislators whom they elected represent—the voters who elected them; the whole population of the county, city, town, or legislative district; the free white population only; or counties or cities as legal jurisdictions and subordinate local agencies of state government?[20]

If ownership of land indicated that adult white men had "sufficient evidence of permanent common interest with, and attachment to, the community"— in the words of the Virginia Declaration of Rights—to qualify them to vote, did the representatives whom they elected to the legislature also represent that property as the source and guarantor of political rights? If so, should property in the form of land continue to be the only property taken into account in defining representation? Ownership of slaves as well as ownership of land conferred prestige and social stature on a person or family in post-Revolutionary Virginia. Owners of enslaved people had a conspicuous stake in the prosperity and stability of the state—in the status quo, in fact. Should men who owned enslaved laborers be allowed to vote even if they owned little or no land?

Land and slaves were not the only valuable property. As the state's economy changed and developed, people created large-scale business enterprises such as canals, banks, mills, and foundries. Those businesses and a diversifying commercial agriculture relied on the institutions and practices of finance capitalism. Should ownership of shares of stock in those enterprises or of a store, shop, factory, or mill not also be satisfactory evidence of an adequate share of "permanent common interest with, and attachment to, the community"? All these and other considerations rolled into one very big and important question: what was the proper structure for representative government in the nineteenth century— particularly in a nineteenth-century southern and border slave state? Men of the Revolutionary generation had debated but not answered those questions.

The discussions continued for generations without a clear consensus emerging in the country or in Virginia. All the questions remained unanswered in the state for decades and even remained so after the Constitutional Convention of 1850–51. The continuing debates involved matters of personal or regional interest, abstract political theories, and practices of government that affected people differently in the different regions of the state.

The longest and most powerful of the appeals for democratic reforms came from men in the capital city who called themselves *the Non-Freeholders of the City of Richmond*. They quoted from the Virginia Declaration of Rights and referred to the writings of Thomas Jefferson to argue for removing what the petitioners called distinctions "between the privileged and the proscribed classes" in Virginia, between freeholders who could vote and the majority of white Virginia men who could not. "Experience has but too clearly evinced," their long plea began, "what, indeed, reason had always foretold, by how frail a tenure they hold every other right, who are denied this, the highest prerogative of freemen. . . . Comprising a very large part, probably a majority of male citizens of mature age, they have been passed by, like aliens or slaves, as if destitute of interest, or unworthy of a voice, in measures involving their future political destiny: whilst the freeholders, sole possessors, under the existing Constitution, of the elective franchise, have, upon the strength of that possession alone, asserted and maintained in themselves the exclusive power of new-modelling the fundamental laws of the State: in other words, have seized upon the sovereign authority."[21]

The *Non-Freeholders* were correct. The 1830 census disclosed that 150,050 adult white men then resided in Virginia,[22] but in the 1828 presidential election and the 1828 referendum on whether to hold a convention, between 38,500 and 39,000 men voted.[23] And because in 1830 a majority of adult white men lived east of the Blue Ridge,[24] *Non-Freeholders* in the east had every bit as much reason to complain as white men farther west.

VIRGINIA FREEWOMAN complained, too, and published a long essay a few days after the *Non-Freeholders* presented their petition to the convention. The author demanded that women also be allowed to vote or that if the freehold requirement be retained women who owned land should have the same political right to vote as men who owned land. Her reasoning was identical to that of the men. She too had material interests in the welfare of the commonwealth. Why is it, she asked, that "*one half of the Society* is to be cut off, at one blow, from all share in the administration of government?" Concluding with evidence that she not only owned land and knew what she was talking about but that she also knew her Shakespeare (she quoted from *The Merchant of Venice*), VIRGINIA FREEWOMAN asked, "Why are we proscribed? Why are we denied the privilege of voting? Why are we eternally to be kept in the bondage of a despotic government? 'Have *we* not eyes? have *we* not hands, organs, dimensions, senses, affections, passions? fed with the same food, hurt with the same weapons,—subject to the same diseases, healed by the same means, warmed and cooled by the same winter and summer as a *man* is? if you prick us, do we not bleed? if you tickle us, do we not laugh? if you poison us, do we not die? and if you wrong us,' shall we, (no, not revenge!) but assert our rights, and expose your gross injustice?" White men who owned too little property to vote and enslaved people could have made exactly the same complaint that VIRGINIA FREEWOMAN made on behalf of white women.[25]

88 CHAPTER THREE

Electing Delegates

Early in 1825 by a vote of 105 to 98 the House of Delegates passed a bill "concerning a Convention" to provide for a referendum on whether to hold a constitutional convention, but after amending it, the Senate defeated it on an unrecorded voice vote.[26] Late in July, another convention, attended by a larger number of men than in 1816, from mountain and western counties met in Staunton and renewed the plea for a convention to revise the constitution. Its formal address to the General Assembly was not so eloquent as the one the convention of 1816 adopted, but it contained precisely the same complaints about inadequate representation in the General Assembly for the western region and objections to the freehold requirement.[27]

The members of the General Assembly were almost evenly divided about whether to call a constitutional convention, which suggests that proposals for reform probably had support from a majority of the voting-age population—perhaps even of the voters—but failed to achieve success in the assembly because of the disproportionate representation. On 25 January 1827, the House of Delegates narrowly defeated yet another bill to hold a referendum on a convention. The vote was 107 to 103.[28]

Hard as the able representatives of the privileged eastern counties fought against it, eventually the increasing numbers of eastern and western men wielding the powerful language of liberty from the American Revolution forced a bill through the General Assembly. In December 1827, the House of Delegates passed A Bill Concerning a Convention by a vote of 114 to 86, and on the last day of January 1828 the Senate passed it 14 to 10.[29] The law directed that because "a portion of the good people of this Commonwealth are desirous of amending the Constitution of this State," the voters should assemble on their respective county court days in April of that year and vote on the question, "Shall there be a Convention to amend the Constitution of this Commonwealth?"[30]

The result was 21,896 for a convention and 16,637 against. Not surprisingly, voters in the mountains and in western Virginia overwhelmingly voted in favor of a convention. Voters in the valleys and piedmont as well as in some counties along the Potomac River also favored a convention but not by so large a margin. Most voters east of the Blue Ridge and south of the Rappahannock River voted against the convention. Variations existed within regions, as in the two counties on the Eastern Shore; in the northern county of Accomack, 78.8 percent of the voters favored the convention, but in the southern county of Northampton, 50.5 percent voted in favor.[31]

At the next session of assembly, the legislators passed the necessary enabling act. The law authorized the election in May 1829 of four delegates from each of the twenty-four senatorial districts, which gave eastern voters the opportunity to elect a substantial majority of delegates. Eastern domination of the assembly, and especially of the Senate, enabled the legislators to give a strong advantage to opponents of change. The law required that the convention submit its proposed new constitution to the voters for ratification or rejection,[32] which the Convention of 1776 had not done.

Ninety-six men won election to the convention, but one delegate-elect died and another resigned before the convention met. Seven other men resigned during the convention, but their successors all attended. Scores of delegates had been or were justices of the peace, many had been or were members of the General Assembly, and several were, had been, or were to be judges of the Virginia Supreme Court of Appeals. Thirty-one of them were, had been, or would be members of the House of Representatives, and eight were, had been, or would be members of the United States Senate. The then governor and four former or future governors were delegates. Two former attorneys general of Virginia, Chief Justice John Marshall, and a future associate justice of the Supreme Court were delegates. Many of them had held multiple distinguished offices. The delegates included three secretaries of state, two secretaries of the navy, one secretary of war, former presidents James Madison and James Monroe, and future president John Tyler (1790–1862).[33]

Delegates from eastern Virginia were more than twice as likely to have attended or graduated from college as delegates from other regions; 73 percent of eastern delegates were planters, lawyers, or both; 65 percent of them were Episcopalians; and a large majority were of English ancestry. From other regions of the state, few of the delegates were Episcopalians, more were of Scottish or Scots-Irish ancestry, and fewer were planters or lawyers. From the piedmont, 48 percent were planters, lawyers, or both; from the Valley region between the Blue Ridge and crest of the Alleghany Mountains, only 14.5 percent were planters or planter-lawyers, but 15 percent were engaged in manufacturing. A full 28 percent of western delegates were merchants or engaged in commerce as distinguished from a mere 4 percent of eastern delegates who were in the same profession. Western delegates were more likely than eastern delegates to have been born in some other state. Reflecting the uneven distribution of enslaved people in the state, more eastern delegates than western delegates owned enslaved people; among delegates who did own enslaved people, easterners on average owned larger numbers than westerners. Educational, ethnic, cultural, religious, and professional differences reflected the large regional diversity within the large and increasingly diverse Commonwealth of Virginia.[34]

The Convention of 1829–30

The convention met in Richmond from 5 October 1829 to 15 January 1830. It has been referred to as one of the most distinguished assemblages of Virginia men anywhere, anytime. It has also been somewhat inaccurately described, perhaps with pardonable exaggeration, as the last of the great constituent assemblies in the United States and as an unequalled theater of debate.[35] It was an unusually fine theater for learned, eloquent, and especially for long-winded debate.[36] The first half of the nineteenth century was an age of oratory, at which Virginia political leaders often excelled; and those who did not excel tried anyway. Well-known artist George Catlin painted the scene in the chamber of the House of Delegates with all the delegates in attendance and was able to paint their faces from life.

The Virginia Convention of 1829–30 was probably the best-documented American convention to that time. The convention's secretary kept and published a full journal of the convention's actions and all of its committee reports.[37] Most of the petitions and other documents submitted to the convention survive in manuscript form in the state's archives.[38] A stenographic reporter recorded all the debates and published them in a volume of almost nine hundred pages of small, dense type.[39] Newspapers reported on some of the convention's proceedings, and several observers and participants left or later compiled descriptions of the delegates and their work.[40]

The convention met in the chamber of the House of Delegates in the Capitol until 7 December, when the General Assembly resumed its sessions, and the delegates moved to the nearby First Baptist Church. On the first day, former president James Madison, who was probably the last surviving member of the Convention of 1776, nominated former president James Monroe for president of the convention. The delegates unanimously elected Monroe, then Madison and the chief justice of the United States, John Marshall, escorted him to the speaker's chair where he assumed his office and briefly addressed the convention.[41] Because of Monroe's age and poor health, he resigned from the convention on 12 December, and the delegates unanimously elected Philip Pendleton Barbour to succeed him. A former Speaker of the House of Representatives, Barbour later served as a federal judge and an associate justice of the Supreme Court of the United States.

On the convention's fifth day it created four committees to report on what changes might be desirable in the Declaration of Rights, the legislative department, the executive department, and the judiciary. The delegates also ordered the auditor of public accounts to compile data on the state's population and taxes. One report was to list the numbers of white, free Black, and enslaved people in each county and city as recorded in the 1790, 1800, 1810, and 1820 federal census returns. Other reports were to show the number of acres of land in each county, city, and town; the amount of land in each jurisdiction that was subject to taxation; the amount of taxes collected on that land in each; the amount of taxes collected on items of personal property (including property in the form of enslaved people) in each; the number of taxable people in each; and an estimate derived from tax returns of the number of white, free Black, and enslaved people in each county and city as of that date. The auditor reported from 1828 tax data as the 1829 reports were not yet complete. The delegates also instructed the auditor to tabulate and report all the data for each of the four regions into which seats in the state senate had been assigned since 1817 and from which the convention delegates had been elected in 1829.[42]

Members of the convention were closely divided on the most important and controversial issues with which they grappled. "Besides the ordinary conflicts of opinions concerning the structure of Gov^t," Madison wrote shortly after the convention adjourned, "the peculiarity of local interests real or supposed, and above all the case of our coloured population which happens to be confined to a geographical half of the State, and to have been a disproportionate object of taxation, were sources of jealousy & collisions, which infected the proceedings throughout."[43] Madison was not surprised. He had noted almost forty years earlier that slavery dictated the nature of Virginia's government. "In proportion as slavery prevails in a State," he had written in the 1790s, "the Government, however democratic in name, must be aristocratic in fact. The power lies in a part instead of the whole; in the hands of property, not numbers. . . . In Virginia the aristocratic character is increased by the rule of suffrage, which requiring a freehold in land excludes nearly half the free inhabitants, and must exclude a greater proportion, as the population increases."[44]

Madison was certainly correct that the uneven distribution of slavery throughout Virginia was one of the root causes of differences of opinion about the suffrage, representation, and taxation, which were all inseparably entangled. As a result, members of the convention from the southeastern portion of the state generally feared that an extension of the franchise to more white men who had little or no interest in slavery would be dangerous to their economic and social structures that were based on slavery. They relied, as did opponents of change in some other states, on restrictive rules for representation and apportionment every bit as much as restrictions on the franchise.[45]

The different regions with different political cultures inclined convention members toward different beliefs about what Madison called "the structure of Gov!."[46] The most adamant opponents of change, probably from a mixture of philosophical reasons and self-interest, rejected the proposition that men had any natural rights at all. They argued that men existed only in a state of society, that they had not derived any natural rights from a state of nature, and that such rights as they possessed or should possess derived from the structure of the society in which they lived. Abel P. Upshur, from the Eastern Shore, advanced that argument at the greatest length.[47] Benjamin Watkins Leigh, the most formidable and brilliant of the opponents of reform, eventually lost patience with what he thought were naive and theoretical reformers and denounced them and their ideals. "We are employed," he sneered at them, "in forming a Government for civilized men, not for a horde of savages just emerging from an imaginary state of nature."[48]

As the debates continued into the winter, tempers flared, and the divisions among the delegates made it difficult for them to make important decisions and stick to them. By close margins, the convention made and unmade decisions on some of the most important topics, such as how far to enlarge the suffrage, how much to revise legislative apportionment, whether to allow voters to elect more public officials, including the governor, or to retain or abolish the "fifth wheel" Council of State, which had been an aggravation to governors and council members alike.[49] Delegates discussed slavery less than they might have, but it appears that most of them believed with Madison that slavery influenced all the important decisions. He and many of the men from the piedmont and Valley regions ultimately or reluctantly sided with the easterners. Enslaved people were property, slavery involved rights of property ownership, and with property being one of the most important objects of legislation and of taxation, they were extremely reluctant to jeopardize it by granting the reformers all that they desired. And the reformers, although not arguing against slavery, deeply resented how the demands of the easterners served to deny westerners and other Virginians what they regarded as their natural right to an equal part in their own government. By narrow margins, the opponents of reform emerged victorious on virtually every issue. They successfully opposed democratic reform to preserve slavery.[50]

The delegates also rejected one novel proposal. It came from Alexander Campbell, the only clergyman in the convention. He proposed that "it shall always be the duty of the Legislature of this Commonwealth to patronize and encourage such a system of education, or such common schools and seminaries of learning, as will in their wisdom be deemed to be most conducive to secure to the youth of this Commonwealth, such an education as may most promote the public good." Campbell's proposal to establish the first public school system in a southern state, which would have been one of the first in the nation, died in convention without a single word of discussion.[51]

The Constitution of 1830

Convention members wrote a new constitution that was about 6,100 words long, about 60 percent longer than the state's first constitution. The detailed new section on suffrage, the long lists of counties in the apportionment of seats in the General Assembly, and the new section that prescribed qualifications of delegates and senators together account for much of the additional length. The convention formally divided the new constitution into articles and sections, as in the Constitution of the United States.

THE DECLARATION OF RIGHTS AND PREAMBLE

Article I of the new constitution stated, "The Declaration of Rights made on the 12th June, 1776 . . . requiring in the opinion of this Convention no amendment, shall be prefixed to this Constitution, and have the same relation thereto as it had to the former Constitution of this Commonwealth." The convention did not, however, state precisely what that relation had been or was to be. The authenticated enrolled text in the state's archives has the Declaration of Rights on a separate sheet of parchment from the other sheets that contain the text of the constitution.

To the preamble for the Constitution of 1776 that the delegates retained for the new constitution, the convention added a paragraph that recited that the General Assembly had authorized a referendum on whether to hold a convention, the voters had approved, the assembly had passed the authorizing statute, and the voters had elected delegates to draft a new constitution "to be submitted to the people and to be by them ratified or rejected."

Article II of the new constitution repeated verbatim the short sentence in the Constitution of 1776 that required separation of the legislative, executive, and judicial branches of government and prohibited any person from serving simultaneously in more than one of them with the exception that county justices of the peace remained eligible to serve in the two houses of the General Assembly.

SUFFRAGE AND REPRESENTATION

Article III was by far the longest and most important in the new constitution. As in the Constitution of 1776, the new constitution treated legislation, representation, and the suffrage together. The members of the General Assembly were the only elected officials in the state, other than members of a few city and town councils, members of the United States House of Representatives, and presidential electors who acted for only one day every fourth year.

The first words of Section 14 confined the suffrage to "Every white male citizen of the Commonwealth, resident therein, aged twenty one years and upwards." The word *white* was new to Virginia's constitutional law. The General Assembly had confined the suffrage to adult males since 1699[52] and to "Every male citizen (other than free negroes or mulattoes)" since 1785.[53] The word *freeholder* and other terms used to describe eligible voters before that time commonly had both white and male connotations.

A majority of convention delegates refused to abolish the requirement that adult white men own or hold a long-term lease on property in order to be able to vote. They made an important change, however. The new constitution required voters to own or hold a long-term lease on land worth $25 or "for twelve months next preceding" the date of an election be "a house-keeper and head of a family within the county, city, town, borough or election district . . . and shall have been assessed with a part of the revenue of the Commonwealth within the preceding year, and actually paid the same."

Benjamin Watkins Leigh, the most determined and formidable opponent of democratic reforms in the convention, proposed the change, which reflected a new, more commercial understanding of the importance of property. If, as before, ownership of land remained prima facie evidence of what the Declaration of Rights denominated "evidence of permanent common interest with, and attachment to, the community," then the value, rather than the size, of the property and payment of taxes on it became the new measures of the owner's right to take part in government.[54] And because the state imposed taxes on personal property in the form of slaves, owners of enslaved people who owned little or no land could therefore claim the right of suffrage. Other forms of untaxed property, such as ownership of a shop or business enterprise, shares of stock in a bank, canal company, or toll road, did not automatically confer the right to vote.

Section 14 added new restrictions on the suffrage and declared, "That the Right of Suffrage shall not be exercised by any person of unsound mind, or who shall be a pauper, or a non-commissioned officer, soldier, seaman or marine, in the service of the United States, or by any person convicted of any infamous offence." Section 15 retained another colonial Virginia practice introduced in 1646[55] that was then beginning to fall out of favor elsewhere in the United States. It declared, "In all elections in this Commonwealth, to any office or place of trust, honour or profit, the votes shall be given openly, or *viva voce*, and not by ballot."

The convention scrapped the two delegates per county apportionment of the House of Delegates that was established in 1661,[56] but it did not significantly reduce the influence of the eastern counties or allocate seats in the assembly by population. By what can only be described accurately as the Great Gerrymander,[57] the new constitution specified that the lower house consist of 134 delegates (reduced from 213 in the assembly session of 1828–29) elected annually from districts distributed within the geographical zones that the 1817 reapportionment of the Senate created. The constitution enlarged the Senate from 24 to 32 members, "of whom thirteen shall be chosen for and by the counties lying West of the Blue Ridge of mountains, and nineteen for and by the counties, cities, towns and boroughs lying East thereof." That increased the number of members of both houses to be chosen from west of the Blue Ridge, but it left electors east of the Blue Ridge permanently able to elect majorities in both houses even though the demographic data that the auditor of public accounts compiled for the convention's members suggested that within a decade or two, a majority of white Virginians would reside west of the Blue Ridge.

The constitution required that the General Assembly reapportion both houses of the assembly every tenth year beginning in 1841, but it prohibited the assembly from altering the number of senators and delegates in any of the regions to preserve the permanent majorities east of the Blue Ridge. The constitution did not require that any scheme of apportionment or redistricting provide for substantial equality of population or of the number of voters in each district or region.

Section 4 granted the assembly authority to permit qualified residents of newly formed counties or cities to elect their own separate members of the assembly but only so far that "the number of Delegates shall not at any time exceed 150, nor of Senators 36." The section reinforced the permanent constitutional status of the Great Gerrymander and reiterated, "the number of Delegates from the aforesaid great districts, and the number of Senators from the aforesaid two great divisions, respectively, shall neither be increased nor diminished by such re-apportionment."

THE GENERAL ASSEMBLY

As in the Constitution of 1776, the House of Delegates and Senate of together constituted "a complete Legislature." The governor received no new authority to veto bills or otherwise take part in the legislative process. The constitution empowered the General Assembly to elect most executive and judicial officers. Article III, Section 8, repeated in almost the same words as in the Constitution of 1776 the assembly's authority to appoint an attorney general to serve at the pleasure of the legislature, and the one-sentence Article VI that authorized it to appoint a treasurer annually. It required for the first time in Virginia that candidates for the assembly be actual residents of the county or district and not merely own property there. It also set new the minimum age for service in the House of Delegates at twenty-five and for service in the Senate at thirty. Section 10 repeated the 1776 prohibition on members of the Senate introducing bills, but it omitted the prohibition on senators proposing amendments to "money bills," which levied taxes. Other sections of the new constitution retained the provision in the Constitution of 1776 that made clergymen ineligible for service in the assembly. The new constitution also authorized (but did not require) legislators to bar from public office men who had participated in a duel.

The new Article III, Section 6, borrowed language from the Constitution of the United States and endowed the assembly with authority to create districts for the election of members of the House of Representatives: "The whole number of members to which the State may at any time be entitled in the House of Representatives of the United States, shall be apportioned as nearly as may be, amongst the several counties, cities, boroughs and towns of the State, according to their respective numbers, which shall be determined by adding to the whole number of free persons, including those bound to service for a term of years and excluding indians not taxed, three-fifths of all other persons."

Insertion of the so-called three-fifths clause into the new constitution was the first, even though oblique, recognition of slavery in a Virginia state constitution. The clause dated back to the 1780s when Congress and the Constitutional Convention of 1787 had adopted compromises on issues relating to taxation and representation and devised the formula of "three-fifths of all other persons," meaning enslaved persons. Because the fraction allowed representation to embrace both numbers of people and valuable property, the three-fifths clause—"federal numbers," as delegates to the Convention of 1829–30 called the concept—had strong appeal to delegates from the slaveholding areas of the state.

The new constitution included the substantive part of the 1786 Act for Establishing Religious Freedom[58] and gave that legislative enactment, theretofore generally treated as of constitutional consequence, explicit constitutional status. The convention went further and added new language: "And the Legislature shall not prescribe any religious test whatever; nor confer any peculiar privileges or advantages on any one sect or denomination; nor pass any law requiring or authorising any religious society, or the people of any district within the Commonwealth, to levy on themselves or others, any tax for the erection or repair of any house for public worship, or for the support of any church or ministry; but it shall be left free to every person to select his religious instructor, and to make for his support such private contract as he shall please."

THE EXECUTIVE

As with the provisions in the Constitution of 1776 concerning the executive department, Article IV of the new constitution was brief, and the office of governor remained weak. The suspicion of royalty and strong executive authority that had animated authors of all the Revolutionary-era state constitutions still influenced convention members in Virginia more than half a century later. The new constitution raised the minimum age for the governor from twenty-five to thirty years and borrowed from and adapted language in the Constitution of the United States to require that in order to be eligible for election as governor a man must be "a native citizen of the United States, or shall have been a citizen thereof at the adoption of the Federal Constitution, and shall have been a citizen of this Commonwealth for five years next preceding his election." The constitution authorized the General Assembly to elect a governor for a three-year term instead of a one-year term as under the Constitution of 1776 and with no eligibility for immediate reelection.

The constitution retained the much-criticized Council of State but reduced it from eight members to three and required the General Assembly to elect members for staggered three-year terms. The constitution authorized the senior member to act as governor with the title lieutenant governor "in case of the death, resignation, inability or absence of the Governor from the seat of Government."

THE JUDICIARY

Article V concerning the judiciary was also brief and in effect enlarged the assembly's discretion to establish courts and define their jurisdiction by omitting a requirement that the assembly appoint separate judges for the General Court and Court of Chancery. It added, "The Legislature may also vest such jurisdiction as shall be deemed necessary in Corporation Courts, and in the Magistrates who may belong to the corporate body. The jurisdiction of these tribunals, and of the Judges thereof, shall be regulated by law." Section 6 of the article empowered the General Assembly to remove any judge from office "by a concurrent vote of both Houses of the General Assembly; but two thirds of the members present must concur in such vote, and the cause of removal shall be entered on the journals of each."

Proposals for change often met resistance. For example, by law, people had a right of appeal from lower courts to the Supreme Court of Appeals and need not appeal solely on the basis of an alleged judicial error or a controverted point of law. Court of Appeals judge St. George Tucker had complained in 1807 that the consequence was a clogged appellate court docket impossible to clear and consisting too often of cases in which appellants merely asked the judges to retry the merits of the case. The General Assembly refused to act on Tucker's proposal to limit appeals, perhaps because it would have reduced the ability of lawyers and clients to protract debt cases and postpone or avoid payment.[59] Moreover, the judges often issued opinions in the most important cases seriatim, each judge writing an opinion on every case, as had traditionally been the practice in English courts.[60] That added significantly to the amount of work each judge had to do during each session. The new constitution included no provisions to remedy the condition or clear the court's docket. In 1848, Judge John Coalter noted in passing in *Crenshaw and Crenshaw v. Slate River Company* that the court was "Borne down . . . by the great mass of business on the docket."[61]

The constitution did not mention judicial review, a responsibility of judges that by 1830 had become widely accepted in Virginia and elsewhere in the United States.[62]

LOCAL GOVERNMENT

During debate on the judicial article, a delegate moved to strike the reference to county courts. The new language authorized the assembly to provide for and define the jurisdiction of those courts in the same manner as it would "ordain and establish" all other courts. John Marshall successfully argued against deleting reference to the county courts. "We must have a County Court of some kind," he told the other members; "its abolition will affect our whole internal police. I am not in the habit of bestowing extravagant eulogies upon my countrymen. I would rather hear them pronounced by others: but it is a truth, that no State in the Union, has hitherto enjoyed more complete internal quiet than Virginia. There is no part of America, where less disquiet and less of ill-feeling between man and man is to be found than in this Commonwealth, and I believe most firmly that this state of things is mainly to be ascribed to the practical operation of our County Courts. The magistrates who compose those courts, consist in general of the best men in their respective counties.

They act in the spirit of peace-makers, and allay, rather than excite the small disputes and differences which will sometimes arise among neighbours. It is certainly much owing to this, that so much harmony prevails amongst us."[63]

By referring to the "internal police" of Virginia, Marshall may have had in mind some of the many local governmental functions that justices of the peace and county courts exercised in addition to their judicial responsibilities, such as taxing residents to pay for local government expenses, compelling people to work on the public roads, and the like. Marshall had the colonial grandees' faith in Virginia's "best men." He evaded the issue of the unelected, undemocratic character of the county courts that Thomas Jefferson and St. George Tucker had complained about[64] and that members of the convention had also pointed out in the winter of 1829–30. Their decision to change nothing about the county courts and, as in 1776, to require that the governor appoint justices of the peace only from lists of names that county courts submitted, allowed those courts to continue functioning with implied but not explicit constitutional status very much as they had functioned for almost two hundred years.

The provisions for appointment of justices of the peace seemed quite clear, but two episodes in the 1840s disclosed some unanticipated problems. Late in 1846, justices of the peace in Frederick County sent to the governor the names of twenty-two men for appointment to the county court, but the governor issued commissions for only twelve of them. A majority of the justices of the peace declared that the governor did not have constitutional discretion to commission only some but not all of the men whom the county court had recommended. In 1848, in *Frederick Justices v. Bruce et al.*, the Supreme Court of Appeals affirmed a circuit court order that only directed the county court to seat the men the governor had commissioned. The court did not issue an opinion in the case, which left unanswered the question whether the governor had constitutional discretion to decline to commission some of the men whom the county court had recommended.[65] The other episode occurred in 1848 in Ritchie County, where the number of qualified justices of the peace had fallen so low that members of the county court could no longer summon a quorum to recommend names to the governor to fill the vacancies. For a time, the court ceased to function.[66]

Members of the convention scarcely discussed the topic of local government at all and thereby let things remain as they were.[67] The two references to county courts and justices of the peace in the article on the judiciary, together with a few references to municipal magistrates in towns, were the only words concerning local government in the new constitution. As in 1776, the Convention of 1829–30 made no changes and silently permitted the local institutions and practices in place since the colonial period to remain and continue to function as before.

Ratification

One of the last decisions that members of the convention made before they voted on the new constitution was to reject 68 to 25 a motion to include a process for amending it.[68] On 14 January 1830, the convention adopted the constitution by a vote of 55 to 44.[69] Almost all the eastern delegates voted in favor of the constitution, and almost all the western delegates voted against it. The convention adopted the constitution because many piedmont and Valley delegates voted in favor of it. The accompanying schedule requested the General Assembly to provide for a ratification referendum at the next April elections. The schedule did not specify the date on which the Constitution of 1830, if ratified, superseded the Constitution of 1776.

The convention was an almost complete victory for eastern defenders of the status quo, for the owners of slave property, in the diverse and divided state. The sole important changes were to write into the unamendable constitution a detailed and extremely rigid method of apportioning seats in the General Assembly favorable to the eastern slaveholding region and to change how the property qualification for the suffrage should be calculated. The new constitution did not permit any extension of democracy as constitutional reformers in some other states were beginning to implement, such as authorizing voters to elect state or local officials in addition to members of the General Assembly.

James Madison, somewhat sadly, voted for the new constitution and therefore voted against the interests of the majority of white Virginia men. He mistakenly regarded it as a satisfactory sop to "the ultramontane part of the State, the part which had called loudest for & contributed most to the experiment for amending the Constitution." The new constitution, he concluded incorrectly, "alleviates greatly where it does not remove the objections, which had been urged & justly urged by that part, whilst the other part of the State, which was most opposed to any changes, will regard the result as an obstacle to another Convention, which might bring about greater & more obnoxious innovations."[70]

Madison completely misjudged how "ultramontane" Virginians would react, though, as well as the long-term consequences of the constitution. The eccentric John Randolph of Roanoke also voted for the new constitution, even though he had vehemently opposed all changes to the state's first constitution.

He, better than Madison, foresaw the consequences of the new constitution and predicted that it would not last more than twenty years.[71]

Many other eastern opponents of change were disappointed that the convention made any changes at all to the old order, but they apparently agreed with Madison that if they failed to accept the new constitution and left the old one in force, a much more formidable democratic reform impulse would overwhelm them with "greater & more obnoxious innovations" sooner rather than later. Those conflicting and strongly held opinions appeared clearly in the weeks between the adjournment of the convention and the ratification referendum, particularly in the west. The disappointment of western reformers and eastern men who were not freeholders became obvious immediately.

Western men campaigned to defeat ratification as energetically as they had worked to bring about the convention. In several western counties, men assembled and adopted resolutions that condemned the undemocratic new constitution. Files of newspapers from western and northwestern Virginia are incomplete, which leaves the extent of the organized campaign against ratification difficult to assess. The *Wheeling Compiler* for 10 March 1830, to cite one surviving copy, published resolutions adopted in several counties and a long essay signed JUSTICE that condemned the constitution and urged western men to vote against ratification. In that same issue, the *Wheeling Compiler* printed the congressional exchange between Daniel Webster and Robert Y. Hayne about the nature of the union and the meaning of the Constitution of the United States, which presented a parallel argument about unity and sectional divisions within the nation.

Former delegate Alexander Campbell condemned the work of the convention in a long series of articles for the *Wellsburg Gazette* (which does not survive). The *Wheeling Gazette* (which does survive) and perhaps other northwestern newspapers reprinted the articles. Campbell recounted the debates in detail to expose what he believed were the constitution's most egregious affronts to free white Virginia men who were not landowners or slaveholders. Among his numerous criticisms was that in the provision for drawing districts for the state's representatives in Congress, the convention had borrowed the three-fifths clause—federal numbers—from the Constitution of the United States and thereby inserted the detestable institution of slavery into the Constitution of Virginia. "This is the secret of the whole matter," Campbell wrote in his fifth essay. Eastern Virginians had treated western Virginians as "demi-slaves, or an Irish peasantry.... Why, in the name of the five senses, should we be subjected to perpetual servitude if this be not the principle"—protection of slavery—on which the new constitution was based?[72]

The official published vote in the April 1830 ratification referendum was 26,055 for ratification and 15,536 against. Westerners who had overwhelmingly voted in favor of holding the convention voted overwhelmingly against the constitution that the convention produced. Eastern voters who had overwhelmingly opposed holding a convention at all voted even more overwhelmingly in favor of the constitution. And as in the 1828 referendum, voters in the piedmont, the valleys, and in some Potomac River counties were divided in opinion about the constitution. More than enough of them, though, voted with easterners in favor of the constitution to ratify it.[73] The reaction in the west suggests that westerners were even angrier at easterners after the convention than they had been before.[74]

The Constitution of 1830 in Operation

The Constitution of 1830 governed Virginia for twenty-one years and perpetuated numerous important constitutional institutions and practices that had arisen in the seventeenth and eighteenth centuries or had been devised in 1776. The new provision that awarded the vote to men who owned real property worth $25 or paid state taxes enfranchised a number of Virginians, but the exact number is not entirely clear. The 1830 census, which had not been taken at the time the convention adjourned, counted 150,050 white male adult Virginians.[75] In 1829, the auditor of public accounts estimated that 92,856 white men owned enough land to vote—about two and a half times the number who had voted in the 1828 presidential election and the 1828 referendum.[76]

In the 1828 referendum on whether to hold a convention, 35,533 men were reported as voting, and in the 1830 ratification referendum, 41,618 men were reported as voting,[77] an increase of 16.1 percent. That may or may not be an accurate measure of the increase in the number of Virginia men able to vote. In many eastern counties, the number of men who voted for the constitution in 1830 exceeded the number who voted against the convention in 1828 by large margins, in some counties by more than 40 percent. It is not possible to calculate how far short the 1828 referendum tally was of the whole number of eligible voters; nor is it clear how much the increase in 1830 reflected increased eastern fears about western pressures for more democratic reforms.

The 1828 referendum and the 1828 presidential election returns reported very similar numbers of voters: 38,533 in the referendum and 38,831 in the election. A careful analysis of the two votes disclosed no meaningful relationship between the vote for president, which turned on issues of national politics and partisan identification of voters, and the vote on whether to hold a convention, which turned almost entirely on regional differences within Virginia.[78] Because of uncertainties and the unique peculiarities of the two referenda, it may be that the only statewide election returns by which to compare the numbers of voters prior to and subsequent to the adoption of the new constitution are the presidential elections of 1828 and 1832, but those numbers are not so reliable an indication as they at first appear. Returns from three counties were missing or incomplete in 1832. Some large unexplained increases reported from some counties between 1828 and 1832 and some other large unexplained decreases in others suggest that at least some of the county returns for each election may not have been complete at the time of tabulation. The creation during the interim of four new western counties from parts of ten others makes it virtually impossible accurately to evaluate some local or regional changes.

The best available data indicate that 38,831 men voted in 1828, and 45,667 voted in 1832.[79] If the variables more or less cancel each other out, perhaps the 17.6 percent increase in the number of reported votes from the 1828 to the 1832 presidential election is a rough approximation of the consequence of the new constitution. That change is not much different from the 16.1 percent increase calculated from the two referenda of 1828 and 1830. These numbers suggest a rise in the proportion of adult white male Virginians who voted or were eligible to vote from about 25.8 percent in 1828 to about 30.4 percent in 1832.

Other changes in the constitution were all comparatively minor. The reduction, rather than the elimination, of the Council of State from eight members to three proved to be a mistake for the "grave of useful talents," as Madison had described it, or the "fifth wheel to a waggon," as Jefferson had called it.[80] Until the Constitution of 1851 abolished the council, it continued to be of no use as a source of experienced wisdom to advise the governor as the members of the Convention of 1776 had originally intended.[81] The council's journal shows that for much of that period, the members often rotated their attendance so that only one or two members attended[82]— just enough to give legality to executive actions.

And some days not even one was present. The requirement that the governor act only with the consent of the council could prevent the governor from acting at all. Whether the executive could act sometimes literally became a matter of life and death. In the autumn of 1831, a court of oyer and terminer in Southampton County sentenced to death several of Nat Turner's associates in the rebellion against slavery that he had led in August of that year. The judges recommended that the governor offer clemency to some of the convicted people who had been less active than others or had been compelled to join Turner and were therefore technically guilty but in the opinions of the judges did not deserve to be hanged. Governor John Floyd, with advice of the council, had authority to commute such death sentences to sale and transportation out of the country, but when the judges' pleas for clemency reached the governor's desk not a single member of the council was in town. The governor therefore could not act to grant or deny clemency. Not acting was effective denial, and one man and one woman were consequently hanged in Southampton County.[83]

In January 1832, five months after Nat Turner's Rebellion, members of the House of Delegates debated the future of slavery in Virginia. Several members from the piedmont, valleys, and western Virginia sought a practical means of ridding Virginia of slavery. One of them was Thomas Jefferson Randolph, grandson of Thomas Jefferson. Still harboring doubts about the morality of slavery and its compatibility with evangelical Protestant Christianity, as well as fears about its unwholesome effects on free representative government, the delegates opened the debate. They failed to offer acceptable proposals for abolishing slavery without compensating owners of slave property, which would be prohibitively expensive, nor could they agree among themselves or persuade other legislators that free white and free Black Virginians could live together safely. Other delegates argued strenuously that a properly regulated system of slavery was not inherently immoral or dangerous; that justice to Virginians who owned other Virginians required legislators to protect rather than to threaten their right to own other human beings; and that all proposals for reducing or eliminating slavery in Virginia were impractical or even dangerous.[84]

Legislators eventually stopped the debate and postponed the question indefinitely so as to draw no more attention to any problems that slavery posed and to avoid providing publicity for antislavery ideas that might promote unrest among the enslaved population. In 1904, Thomas Nelson Page inaccurately wrote in his influential *The Negro: The Southerner's Problem* that "a bill to abolish slavery in Virginia had failed in her General Assembly" in January 1832 "by only one vote and that vote the casting vote of the speaker."[85] Nothing even remotely comparable occurred. Antislavery attitudes were not then that widespread. In fact, the assembly tightened the laws of slavery and subjected free Black Virginians to some of the laws that governed slaves. In 1832, the legislature ordered that criminal trials of "free persons of color," as the laws generally describe them then, be conducted before local courts of oyer and terminer without juries, precisely as for enslaved people since 1692, and prohibited Black men from preaching even in their own churches.[86] In 1833, the assembly created a fund to pay for the exportation of free Black Virginians.[87] In 1848, the assembly made it a criminal offence for any "free person" to speak, write, or otherwise maintain "that owners have not right of property in their slaves," or to "write, print, or cause to be written or printed, any book, pamphlet, or other writing" that denied "the rights of masters to property in their slaves." The law also made it illegal for federal postmasters to allow such printed materials to pass through the mail in the state. The same law also made it illegal for enslavers to allow the enslaved people whom they owned to live as if free.[88]

By then, ideas about slavery had begun to change, and that change, together with the spread of the ideas and ideals of Jacksonian Democracy and a large increase in the population of Virginia in the west, were in large part responsible for the very important wholesale revision of the Virginia constitution in 1851.

The Future

The divisive Convention of 1829–30, the bloody events of Nat Turner's Rebellion in 1831, and the brief legislative debate about slavery early in 1832 did not separately or even together constitute a major turning point in Virginia's history. If anything, they demonstrated how little changed as a consequence of any or all of these events. The new constitution changed very little in the manner in which state and local governments functioned and therefore made little difference in how people lived, but Virginia continued to change demographically, socially, economically, and politically. When another constitutional convention assembled twenty years later, the consequences of those changes for Virginia's government became evident. In the meantime, the divisions between eastern and western Virginia grew in intensity. As early as 1832, an eastern member of the General Assembly, reflecting on the constitutional convention and the legislative debate about slavery, sadly made a prediction. "Eastern and Western People were not all the same people," the governor recorded him as saying, "that they were essentially a different people, that they did not think alike, feel alike, and had no interests in common, that a separation of the State must ensue."[89]

CHAPTER 4

The Constitution of 1851

In April 1850, exactly twenty years after voters ratified the Commonwealth of Virginia's second state constitution, another generation of voters passed a referendum to hold a convention to rewrite the constitution. The interval between the votes corresponded closely to Thomas Jefferson's belief that every nineteen years—every generation—the people were entitled to rewrite the fundamental document of their social contract. He understood a generation to encompass nineteen years based on eighteenth-century European mortality schedules that indicated that half the people alive in a given year would be dead nineteen years later. Every nineteen years the body politic was new.[1]

With respect to the political leadership of Virginia, that was almost literally true. Hugh Blair Grigsby wrote in his history of the Convention of 1829–30, of which he had been a member, about how speedily death removed the delegates to that convention from public life, especially its most influential and senior members.[2] And very few of the members who survived to 1850 won election to the convention that year.

The nineteenth-century world changed fast. Steam engines, for instance, rapidly transformed the movement of people, agricultural commodities, merchandise, and information of all kinds. In October 1832, steam locomotives began running up and down the first thirty miles of track south of Petersburg toward Weldon, North Carolina, and sustained the remarkably high speed of eighteen to twenty miles per hour.[3] It was the first operation of a steam railroad in Virginia and one of the first in the South. In May 1835, a Norfolk newspaper reported under the breathless headline *Something Extraordinary* that the steamboat *Thomas Jefferson* had left Norfolk "on Monday morning at six o'clock, for Richmond, with passengers, and returned in season to leave here again next morning (yesterday) at the same hour! This is the first demonstration that has been given of the practicability of going from Norfolk to Richmond and returning on the same day. . . . The distance between Norfolk and Richmond, by water, is computed at 150 miles, and as the Thomas Jefferson stopped six hours in the 24 which intervened between her time of leaving here on Monday and Tuesday mornings, she run 300 miles in 18 hours; very nearly equal to 17 miles an hour."[4]

Virginians who lived their adult lives entirely in the rapidly changing nineteenth century had significantly different experiences, ideas, and interests than the Revolutionary-era founders. At the same time, the nineteenth-century men fulfilled some of the ideals of the founders. Seventy-five years after George Mason and Thomas Jefferson had declared that all men were created equal, the Virginia Constitution of 1851 finally made all adult white men in Virginia substantially equal politically.

The New Politics of Virginia

Virginians of the mid-nineteenth century lived in a different politically partisan world than the men who attended the Convention of 1829–30. Shortly after that convention completed its controversial work, which aggravated sectional divisions within the state,[5] national political changes created a new partisan politics in Virginia that divided the politically active part of the population in other ways. Virginians, along with other Americans, coalesced into two new political parties: Democrats and Whigs.[6]

The two parties transformed Virginia politics. Campaigns for national office and for the General Assembly grew increasingly exciting, and the number of Virginia men who voted increased under the slightly relaxed qualifications in the Constitution of 1830. During the 1840s, leaders of both parties endorsed abolition of the old property qualification for the suffrage. In part, that was a simple quest for additional voters and votes, but it also reflected the popular new mood in the country. Most Americans were coming to believe that their political legacy expressed in the language of liberty from the American Revolution was a democratic politics in which all adult white men had an equal stake in the country and an equal right to participate in its government. The concept came to be known as Jacksonian Democracy. It fatally undermined the centuries-old belief that only men who literally owned part of the country were fully entitled to have any part in governing it.

The continuing increase in the population of white people in the western part of the state and the increase of public participation in the political process worked together to amplify sectional divisions. When the Convention of 1829–30 completed its work, which guaranteed white voters east of the Blue Ridge permanent majorities in both houses of the General Assembly, white residents east of the Blue Ridge outnumbered white residents west of it by about 57,000. The 1840 census showed 2,000 more white people west of the Blue Ridge than east of it; and the 1850 census showed 90,000 more white people in the west than in the east.[7]

And despite annual sales of perhaps eight to ten thousand Virginia men, women, and children to slave markets in the lower Mississippi River region during the four or five decades before the American Civil War[8] and the migration out of the state of thousands of white families and their numerous enslaved laborers, the population of enslaved Virginians remained high. In the southeastern quarter of the state, the proportion of the population trapped in slavery increased, but it also increased west of the Blue Ridge as a result of economic transformations including railroad construction. Owners of enslaved people remained worried that an increase of political power in the west posed serious economic threats to their ability to profit from slavery. For decades prior to the American Civil War, Virginians who owned few or no enslaved people often expressed resentment about tax policies that directly benefitted owners of enslaved men, women, and children. The protection of slave property had many, often divisive, repercussions throughout the state's (and the nation's) political economy.[9]

A major sea change was in process at midcentury, though, which may not have been so conspicuous at the time as it soon became (and is) in hindsight. With the disappearance of the generations of Virginia men and women who personally recalled the Revolutionary language of liberty in the eighteenth century, so disappeared most of the antislavery sentiment that had been embedded in that language. During the 1840s and 1850s, a majority of white men and women in Virginia gradually accepted a proslavery ideology, an accompanying proslavery theology, and a racist belief in the permanent, unalterable inferiority of people of African birth or ancestry. Lamentations about slavery as a necessary evil or an unfortunate inheritance from the past that could not safely be got rid of gradually gave way to open endorsements of slavery as good for everybody, even including enslaved people themselves. Some individual men and women remained opposed to slavery, but their opposition had become politically inconsequential by 1850, and it virtually disappeared from public discourse by 1860.[10]

Politicians who accommodated themselves to or came late to embrace slavery marched along with majority opinion on the subject. For example, as Congressman John Letcher prepared to run for governor in 1859, he had to dispel an old charge that he doubted the propriety of slavery. In a public declaration, he stated that he was "the owner of slave property, by purchase, and not by inheritance." He had not, like many Virginia politicians, merely inherited slave property and become an owner without having to take any positive action. Letcher won the election and was governor during the secession crisis and the first two years of the Civil War.[11]

One very important implication of that change of attitude about slavery that some political leaders recognized by midcentury was that they may have had less occasion to entertain the fears that had animated many eastern members of the Convention of 1829–30. Proslavery ideas permeated the culture by 1850, and many or most white Virginians adopted those ideas. Ownership of slave property, like ownership of land, was a mark of economic success and social status. Many families hired enslaved people to work for them because they could not, or not yet, afford to purchase laborers.[12] In short, as had the political partisanship of the second party system, widespread public acceptance of slavery seriously reduced the importance of another of the principal objections to universal white manhood suffrage. People who did not own enslaved laborers posed little danger to the institution.

Virginians apparently came late to adopting the political implications of white supremacy and white solidarity that the acceptance of slavery as a positive good made possible. Well before the middle of the nineteenth century, white people in the lower South had recognized, and in their politics implemented, those beliefs. Slavery made universal white manhood suffrage safe and acceptable, and universal white manhood suffrage and white supremacy made slavery safe.[13] Virginia's people and its political leaders were still thinking through the implications in 1850 when voters elected delegates for the state's third constitutional convention.

Sectional Divisions

The economic and demographic changes that had generated sectional discord during the first quarter of the nineteenth century accelerated during the second quarter and intensified the conspicuous divisions within Virginia.[14] As Charles Henry Ambler, the first historian of sectionalism in the state, wrote early in the twentieth century, antebellum Virginia could be viewed as consisting of two large, unequal inclined planes that sloped away from the mountains in the center, one toward the Atlantic Ocean, the other toward the Ohio River.[15] That clear mental image rested directly on the geography of Virginia and reflected Virginians' nineteenth-century perceptions. Those perceptions are easily seen in the division of the state into four taxation districts in 1817, with two east of the Blue Ridge Mountains and two west. That same division dictated the distribution of seats in the Convention of 1829–30 and in the General Assembly after that convention created the Great Gerrymander.[16]

The division of Virginia into two states in 1863 seemed to prove that the mountains had always divided the people of the state into two distinct populations, but the political reality was more complex than Ambler's simple geometric representation of economic and political geography suggests. By 1850, it was the crest of the Alleghany Mountains, not the crest of the Blue Ridge, that separated east from west.[17]

Northwestern Virginians who lived near the Ohio River shared a landscape, an economy, and, in many instances, views on slavery with residents of the free states of Pennsylvania and Ohio. Most qualified men west of the mountains voted for Democratic Party candidates, but in some of the more diversified industrial regions around Charleston in the Kanawha River Valley and in Wheeling in the panhandle, Whig Party candidates often won election to the General Assembly and to Congress.

Virginians in the sparsely populated counties on the western slope of the Alleghany Mountains lived in a very different world. Slavery was of little consequence there, but like a majority of other western Virginia men, they also tended to vote Democratic.

The counties in the upper watershed of the Tennessee River, where rivers and streams flowed southward out of Virginia into Tennessee, were part of a larger economic and cultural region that was in the midst of major changes in the middle of the nineteenth century. Reliance on slave labor and the population of enslaved people increased dramatically at midcentury. The consequences became very conspicuous during the 1850s and during and after the secession crisis.

In eastern Virginia, the landscape took its shape and character from the great bay of Chesapeake and its tributaries. The density of the enslaved population was greater throughout the region than farther west, and although most voters supported the Democratic Party, Whigs were relatively strong in many areas, especially in towns and cities. The rural counties of eastern and southeastern Virginia more nearly resembled the lower South than did any other parts of the state. At midcentury, more than 40 percent of Virginians in almost every county east of the Blue Ridge and south of the Rappahannock River lived in slavery. In eighteen of the fifty-six counties, more than 50 percent of the population was enslaved in 1860; in another twelve counties, more than 60 percent; and in two others, more than 70 percent. The white farmers and planters in the vast rural parts of southern and southeastern Virginia consequently more often identified their interests with those of cotton planters in the lower South than with the values of other Virginians elsewhere. When voting, they usually favored Democrats who during the 1840s and 1850s were more forceful defenders of slavery and of the interests of owners of slaves than the more accommodating Whigs, who feared alienating antislavery northern Whigs.

Between the eastward-flowing rivers and the westward-flowing rivers was the northward-flowing Shenandoah River, which squeezed itself between the Blue Ridge Mountains to the east and the Alleghany Mountains to the west. The North and South Branches of the Potomac River drained the eastern slope of the Alleghany Mountains immediately to the west of the counties in the Shenandoah Valley. That area was at the northern end of what Virginians called the Valley of Virginia, a region so distinctive and important they gave it capital letters. Slavery had always been of somewhat less importance to residents in the Shenandoah Valley than to residents to the east of the Blue Ridge but of more importance to Valley residents than to those to the west. By midcentury, however, residents of the Shenandoah Valley had become more and more dependent on slavery, and slavery became more important there, just as in southwestern Virginia. The Whig Party thrived in the Valley. What might be regarded as the capital of the Valley, the town of Staunton, was the county seat of Augusta County—which was, on election days, one of the most reliable Whig counties in the state.

Early nineteenth-century Virginians often spoke of a divided Virginia with the Blue Ridge Mountains separating east from west. By 1850, though, the real line of demarcation between east and west, as Ambler had written and as maps printed after 1863 show, was the crest of the Alleghany Mountains, not the Blue Ridge.

The complex regional diversity that had prevented delegates to the Convention of 1829–30 from contriving a new constitution satisfactory to very many voters increased after the convention and exploded again into political bitterness within a few years. Some of the political issues that produced political discord were closely linked to national partisan politics and divided Whigs from Democrats. Issues that involved matters of state government policy also sometimes divided Whigs from Democrats, but others divided people by region. Other than slavery, almost all the regional divisions arose from the disproportionate representation in the General Assembly that the state's first two constitutions required.[18]

Public works policy was one of the most evident divisions because only the General Assembly could charter a company to sell stock and raise money to construct a canal, toll road, or railroad. The state's Board of Public Works, established by law in 1816 and given constitutional status in 1830,[19] and the General Assembly had favored Virginians east of the Alleghany Mountains in chartering banks and companies to construct and operate canals, turnpikes, and railroads—what people at the time called internal improvements. Because easterners held comfortable, unassailable majorities in both houses of the assembly, construction of new transportation arteries proceeded much more rapidly and successfully east of the Blue Ridge and in the Valley than anywhere else. The state government subsidized construction of more than fifteen hundred miles of railroad track before 1861, almost all of it east of the mountains. Some lines ran north and south through eastern Virginia, but none of the east–west lines crossed the mountains. Westerners were less able to procure legislative charters for corporations to do business in their region. In particular, the lack of banks in the mountains of Virginia and in the Ohio Valley seriously hampered business and commercial enterprises. The limitations became a major grievance in western Virginia.[20]

As in the 1820s, in the 1840s, some eastern Virginians sympathized with the desire of western Virginians for constitutional change. In the southeastern city of Norfolk, civic and business leaders complained about how the General Assembly had favored railroad interests in Richmond and elsewhere in central Virginia at the expense of Norfolk. Some of them even suggested that the city detach itself from Virginia and join North Carolina where it might, as the major seaport for much of that state, receive more favorable treatment.[21]

Electing Delegates

The old western grievance about malapportionment of representation in the two houses of the General Assembly erupted again after legislators refused in 1841 to obey the mandate of the Constitution of 1830 that the assembly reapportion house and senate seats within the four regions prescribed for the House of Delegates and the two prescribed for the Senate. Angry men in several western counties and cities assembled and petitioned the General Assembly to call another constitutional convention.[22] More than fifty men gathered in Lewisburg, in Greenbrier County, in August 1842 and complained about the "grievances under which the people of Virginia labour, from the unequal, arbitrary and geographical basis upon which the representation of the state is founded." The men signed a petition to the General Assembly to demand the reapportionment that the state's constitution required. They then went much further and declared that they could not "sanction any apportionment of representation, which is not based on white population or its equivalent," but they did not clearly explain what an equivalent could be.[23]

Legislators failed for the remainder of the decade to act on reapportionment or to call a convention.[24] The reason was that the eastern majority insisted on apportioning seats in the convention on a combination of population and the value of taxable property. With the looming prospect of universal white manhood suffrage, men in the slavery-rich eastern portion of the state realized that they had to rely even more than in the past on a scheme of representation that protected their peculiar sectional interests.[25]

In March 1850, the assembly finally passed a law to hold a referendum in April on whether to call a convention. The law provided that if the vote was in favor of holding a convention an election of delegates would take place on the fourth Thursday in August, and the convention would meet in October. Easterners passed the bill over westerners' objections to the advantage easterners gave themselves by its provisions. The convention law created thirty-seven electoral districts for the election of 135 delegates. As in 1829, the election scheme favored the east. It was not based explicitly on the geography of the Great Gerrymander but on a combination of population and tax data that worked the same way.

The General Assembly ascertained the size of each district and the number of delegates for each by adding to the population of white people in each city and county the number of dollars the residents paid in taxes on their personal property. Personal property included enslaved people with a value greater than all other classes of property except land combined, which strongly tipped the weight of regional representation in favor of the east. Delegates represented both white people and their property, so voters in regions with more valuable taxable property—more slaves—in effect had more influential votes than voters in regions with a lesser amount of taxable property.[26]

The House of Delegates passed the bill on 16 February 1850 by a margin of 78 to 42. On 2 March the Senate amended it to change the boundaries of two western districts and passed the bill 17 to 11. Two days later, by an unrecorded voice vote, the House of Delegates accepted the Senate amendment. At the same time, the delegates defeated by a vote of 76 to 35 a motion that the whole subject be "indefinitely postponed."[27] That vote and the margins by which the two houses passed the bill suggest that about two of every five legislators opposed holding a convention at all or preferred no convention to one in which seats were allocated in such a discriminatory sectional manner.

The incomplete file of original election returns from the April referendum record a vote in favor of a convention of 46,327 to 20,668, with more eastern voters in favor and many western voters opposed for the same reasons eastern and western legislators had differed earlier in the spring.[28] On 22 August, voters elected delegates whom contemporaries and some later writers believed were on the whole inferior in talent and experience to the distinguished membership of the Convention of 1829–30[29]—as if that remarkable company of overage overachievers was what Virginians could always expect and were entitled to. Delegates elected in 1850 were on average younger than delegates elected two decades earlier, but they were not untalented. Voters elected six former or future members of the United States Senate, twenty-three former or future members of the United States House of Representatives, three future members of the Confederate States House of Representatives, several former or future cabinet members, one future state attorney general, three future governors, and several future gubernatorial candidates. The delegates included seventy-seven or seventy-eight Democrats and fifty-eight or fifty-seven Whigs, depending on who did the counting. The number of delegates who owned enslaved people fell from 90 percent of the whole number in 1829–30 to 60 percent in 1850–51. Of the 135 delegates, 97 were lawyers.[30] Excepting slave ownership, the composition of the constitutional convention was very like the composition of any other state convention anywhere else in the country in the middle of the nineteenth century.

The August election occurred against a backdrop of dramatic congressional debates and maneuvering that in September produced the Compromise of 1850. Much as the uneven distribution of slavery in the state divided Virginians geographically, political issues arising from slavery also divided the people of the nation geographically. No politically aware Virginian could have missed the importance of slavery in national and state politics in the summer of 1850. Few or none could have failed to understand that slavery was at the root of many of the issues that the convention members considered beginning in October.

The Convention of 1850–51

The state's third constitutional convention met in Richmond in two sessions, from 14 October to 4 November 1850 and from 6 January to 1 August 1851. The break between the short first session and the long second session allowed the delegates to obtain and use data from the 1850 census, which was not yet available when the delegates first assembled.[31]

The convention's secretary kept a thorough journal of the proceedings, which the convention published, along with most of the committee reports and other documents,[32] and the original manuscripts and working papers are preserved in the state's archives.[33] Private letters from some convention delegates and observers illuminate portions of the convention's work.[34] The convention authorized men to publish the debates as supplements to Richmond's major newspapers for statewide distribution and afterward in book form. The published debates are incomplete, though. Members of the convention grumbled about the tardy publication of unsatisfactory newspaper supplements and threatened not to pay for any more. The newspaper printers ceased work in the spring.[35] The resulting 504-page book edition of delegates' speeches covers only the dates 6 January through 6 March 1851,[36] and the extant supplements are also incomplete, even with collating surviving copies in the library of the College of William and Mary and in the Library of Virginia.[37]

On the first day and by a large majority, the delegates elected John Young Mason, of the southeastern county of Greensville, president.[38] He was one of the very few delegates who had been a member of the Convention of 1829–30 and also one of the older delegates. He was born in 1799 and had served in both houses of the General Assembly during the 1820s, for three terms in the House of Representatives in the 1830s, as a federal judge from 1841 to 1844, as attorney general and secretary of the navy during the 1840s, and later was United States minister to France from 1853 until his death in Paris in 1859.[39]

Mason made a short address to the delegates after being elected president and made another on the final day a few minutes before the convention adjourned. When he spoke on the last day, Mason complimented the delegates on measuring up to the very high standard of the famed 1829–30 convention. "The Convention of 1829," he recollected, "bore on its rolls those sons of Virginia, however advanced in life, who had earned public confidence by serving their country in her places of highest trust. It was an august assemblage" that had included James Madison, James Monroe, and John Marshall. The midcentury convention included able men, also. "You are generally young men," Mason continued; "you cannot point to such a long career of public service. But in talent, cultivation, enlightened patriotism, in those elements which qualify for public usefulness, I am proud to say that this Convention shews, that the sons of Virginia have not degenerated."[40] (It is unclear whether the secretary used the antique Elizabethan spelling *shews*, which legislative clerks still sometimes employed, or copied it from a text that the president prepared and provided him.)

Mason was correct. A careful study of the available debates in the Virginia convention and comparison with other contemporary state constitutional conventions disclosed that members of the Convention of 1850–51 were every bit as capable and learned as the more celebrated members of the Convention of 1829–30 and that on the whole the level of discourse in both was above the standards of other antebellum state constitutional conventions.[41] Advocates of democratic reforms in 1850 and 1851 still cast their arguments in the context of rights and liberties earned during the American Revolution, but more than in 1829–30, they also grounded their arguments in practical political language of causes and consequences. So did the opponents of proposed reforms. The debates often resembled the give-and-take in a legislature as much as a discussion of principles and constitutional proprieties. Perhaps the partisan politics of the second quarter of the nineteenth century had changed both the context and the character of political discourse.

The convention attracted large crowds of spectators eager to see and hear some of the state's ablest orators. Political oratory retained the popularity that it had enjoyed at the time of the previous convention, and the delegates did not disappoint. Men and women crowded in to witness displays of learned and sometimes witty debate. The members were as long-winded as in 1829–30, some of them even more so. When Henry A. Wise, for instance, spoke about representation late in April, he talked for five full days to say all that he thought was important to say. A former congressman and future governor, Wise was only one of the members who spoke at great length and drew large crowds. He was a brilliant and riveting speaker, and in this instance, he outdrew North America's most distinguished tragedian, Junius Brutus Boothe, who was then playing the lead in *Hamlet* in one of Richmond's theaters.[42]

The loss of transcriptions of the debates for more than half the convention's duration leaves historians without a full record of the members' discussions about some of the most important democratic reforms. The long months of debate about numerous proposals for settling the basis for representation in the General Assembly seriously divided the members and angered western men because eastern men insisted that property, by one mechanism or another, must form at least part of the scheme. Members from both regions mentioned slavery much more openly and often than in the Convention of 1829–30 as men discussed whether or how to secure it against a too-high rate of taxation or the potential threat that an ever-increasing population of white men who owned no enslaved people might pose to the institution.[43]

The members' decisions to introduce almost universal white manhood suffrage and to allow popular election of most public officials, including trial and appellate court judges, produced a remarkably different constitution for the state and were the first major reforms of government institutions and the suffrage since the American Revolution. And at that time, the Virginia Constitution of 1776 had continued in place many important institutions and practices that in most instances originated in the seventeenth century. In 1776, the Virginians who adopted the Declaration of Rights along with the state's first written constitution had been among the most innovative creators of constitutions in the new United States. By 1830, Virginians had fallen behind the other states in adapting to the emerging democratic culture. In 1850, when the third state convention began its work, they were almost literally bringing up the rear.

The Constitution of 1851

In 1851, the convention adopted a constitution that in almost every respect, excepting its origins in a slaveholding state, was very like other state constitutions throughout the United States. As with the Constitution of 1776, the attested enrolled parchments of the Declaration of Rights and the constitution are missing from the state's archives. The texts printed as separately paginated appendices to the convention's official journal are therefore the only authorized and most authentic texts. The constitution and Declaration of Rights together contain about 11,550 words, almost twice the length of the Constitution of 1830. It included long new sections on suffrage, a much longer new section on representation in the General Assembly, long lists of counties assigned to legislative and judicial districts, and more detail in many other provisions, including several long paragraphs relating to taxation and the public debt and several more on the Board of Public Works. In that, too, the Constitution of 1851 resembled mid-nineteenth-century state constitutions in other regions of the country where conventions placed new restrictions on legislatures, in some places enlarged powers of the executive, and placed in their constitutions additional protections for individual and community rights.

THE DECLARATION OF RIGHTS AND THE PREAMBLE

The convention members' decision to increase the number of elected officials in the state required them to make minor changes to the wording of two sections in the Declaration of Rights. They added one word and deleted eleven to change the opening language of Section 6 from, "That elections of members to serve as representatives of the people in Assembly, ought to be free" to, "That all elections ought to be free." They also changed the meaning of Sections 8 and 11 that guaranteed the right of jury trials in criminal and civil cases by inserting after each mention of an "impartial jury" the words, "of twelve men."

The only substantive change members made to the preamble was to insert a paragraph reciting that in March 1850, the General Assembly had authorized the April referendum, the August election of delegates, and the meeting of the convention in October, and that, by a law the assembly adopted in March 1851 while the convention was still in session, the assembly "did further provide for submitting the same to the people for ratification or rejection."

SUFFRAGE AND REPRESENTATION

Convention members discarded centuries of English and Virginia belief and practice when they abolished ownership of property or payment of taxes as a prerequisite for the suffrage and brought Virginia into line with practices in most other states.[44] They adopted universal white manhood suffrage with a few stated exceptions carried over from the Constitution of 1830. The delegates condensed the final sentence of the old suffrage article to, "And no person shall have a right to vote, who is of unsound mind, or a pauper, or a noncommissioned officer, soldier, seaman or marine in the service of the United States, or who has been convicted of bribery in an election, or any infamous offence." Section 4 repeated the old constitution's requirement for voice voting and prohibited voting by ballot[45] but added, "dumb persons entitled to suffrage may vote by ballot."

Universal white manhood suffrage was one of the most important and conspicuous reforms embodied in the new state constitution. By far the most difficult task that the members faced was settling on a broadly acceptable basis for apportioning seats in the General Assembly, a problem that their predecessors had not been able to resolve satisfactorily. Convention members argued about that subject for months at the beginning of 1851, and they, too, failed. They reached no consensus on what legislators should represent— people, voters, regions, property, or particular interests such as ownership of slave property.[46]

The convention redesigned and disguised the Great Gerrymander. It omitted reference to the 1830 constitution's four regions for election of delegates and two for election of senators. The new apportionment, though, was also based on sectional considerations and was almost as injurious to the west as the old. The new constitution created districts for the election of delegates and senators that strongly favored the eastern portion of the state where a large majority of enslaved people and owners of enslaved people lived. Depending on how some counties along the Blue Ridge are counted, the apportionment granted voters west of the Blue Ridge, where about 55 percent of the state's white population lived, a slim 4 or 5 vote majority in the 152-member House of Delegates but granted the 45 percent minority of white voters who lived east of the Blue Ridge a whopping 30 to 20 majority in the 50-member Senate. If the crest of the Alleghany Mountains rather than the crest of the Blue Ridge is considered the real dividing line between east and west, as it was in reality in 1850, the west fared almost as badly, with more than a third of all the state's white people allotted 49 of 152 delegates but only 11 of 50 senators.[47]

Convention members made that distribution of seats in the assembly temporary because they could not agree on a satisfactory permanent basis for representation. Virginians and their representatives in convention had not yet agreed on how to answer the question dating back to before the American Revolution of who or what their representatives should represent. In six paragraphs of more than eight hundred words, Article IV, Sections 5 and 6, required the General Assembly to settle on a principle of representation in 1865 and in that year and every tenth year thereafter reapportion both houses of the assembly in accordance therewith. If the assembly could not then agree, the new constitution required voters to select one from among four options.

One option was to apportion seats in both houses on the number of voters in each county and city, called the "suffrage basis," the number of adult white men who actually voted. Representatives would represent voters. That option appeared to favor the western portion of the state at that time, and if the demographic trends evident during the first half of the century continued would probably be the basis voters would select in 1865 if the assembly with its eastern-dominated Senate did not first impose another.

The second option was to apportion the two houses on what the new constitution called a "Mixed Basis," that is, "according to the number of white inhabitants contained, and the amount of all state taxes paid, in the several counties, cities and towns." Representatives and senators would represent white people and their property. That was how representation in the convention was apportioned. It favored residents of the east over residents of the west, and because of the very valuable taxable slave property would almost certainly continue to do so.

The third option was to apportion the House of Delegates on the suffrage basis and the Senate on the amount of taxes paid. Delegates would represent voters, and senators would represent property. That would likely result in prolonging regional antagonism or even create political paralysis on such profoundly important subjects as taxation because owners of slave property could retain a larger representation in the assembly than their numbers otherwise allowed.

The fourth option was to apportion the House of Delegates on the suffrage basis (voters) and the Senate on the mixed basis (white people and their property). That, too, could prolong regional conflicts.

None of the options allowed white, male voters to select either the white or total population as the foundation of legislative representation. The constitution restricted voters to those four options in 1865 but only if the General Assembly did not agree on a basis for representation. The wording of Section 5 did not explicitly restrict the assembly to those four options. The assembly could, for instance, choose to apportion either or both houses on the basis of the white population, which no doubt would have been welcomed in the west. The assembly could also settle on what convention delegates in 1830 had called "federal numbers" based on the three-fifth clause of the Constitution of the United States. Representation would then be determined "by adding to the whole number of free persons, including those bound to service for a term of years, and excluding Indians not taxed, three-fifths of all other persons," as the Constitutions of 1830 and 1851 and the federal Constitution all required for congressional districts.[48]

Convention members in 1850–51 came from very different regions where residents had widely varying opinions about slavery and the economics of slavery. But as under the Great Gerrymander of 1830, under the Constitution of 1851 and the options available to voters in 1865, the Senate of Virginia became the impregnable fortress for the protection of slavery.

THE GENERAL ASSEMBLY

The convention revised constitutional provisions respecting the General Assembly in accord with trends observable in many other states at midcentury. Commentators at the time, and students later, interpreted those trends as evidence of an increasing distrust of uncontrolled legislatures, not unlike the fears of uncontrolled executive power that had strongly influenced the writers of Revolutionary-era state constitutions.[49] The distrust is evident in constitutional provisions of many states to reduce the frequency of meetings from annual to biennial and to limit the length of sessions. Article IV, Section 8, of the new Virginia constitution did both.

To match the new biennial schedule for assembly sessions, the convention extended the terms of office for the 152 members of the House of Delegates (increased from the maximum of 150 that the Constitution of 1830 imposed) from one year to two. It left the terms of the 50 senators (increased from the maximum of 36) at four years but altered the rotation of members to require that one-half the senators be elected every second year rather than one-fourth every year. The constitution removed all remaining restrictions on members of the Senate introducing bills. The constitution created the new office of lieutenant governor to be the presiding officer of the Senate but gave the lieutenant governor no vote on any question, even in the event of a tie vote of senators.

In addition to retaining the provision from previous constitutions that excluded clergymen from the assembly,[50] Section 7 also declared that "no salaried officer of any banking corporation or company, and no attorney for the commonwealth" be eligible to serve in the legislature. Perhaps the first portion of that provision reflected unease with the political reality that corporate entities, which were rapidly becoming much more numerous and important in Virginia and elsewhere in the country, derived their legal existence from acts of the legislature, which created a potential for corruption, improper personal gain, or excessive commercial influence in the legislature.[51]

Article IV specifically mentioned slavery for the first time in any Virginia constitution. It included a provision that had been in the statute books since 1806, that "Slaves hereafter emancipated shall forfeit their freedom by remaining in the commonwealth more than twelve months after they become actually free, and shall be reduced to slavery under such regulations as may be prescribed by law." It also empowered the General Assembly to impose restrictions "on the power of slave owners to emancipate their slaves; and may pass laws for the relief of the commonwealth from the free negro population, by removal or otherwise"; prohibited the General Assembly from "emancipating any slave, or the descendant of any slave, either before or after the birth of such descendant"; and placed a limit of $300 on the market value of enslaved men and women older than twelve subject to the personal property tax. That provision also protected slavery by making it impossible for the General Assembly, even without intending to undermine slavery, to ruin slave owners financially by taxing slave property at so high a rate as to make it unprofitable or a financially insupportable burden on owners. After all, the power to tax, as Chief Justice John Marshall had famously written in 1819 in *McCulloch v. Maryland*, "involves the power to destroy."[52]

The General Assembly had begun selling bonds backed by the taxing authority of the state so that the Board of Public Works would have the resources to purchase shares of stock in canal, toll road, and railroad companies to stimulate rapid capital accumulation and construction.[53] The new constitution placed the first limits on the assembly's authority to borrow money and on the resultant liabilities that the state incurred. After 1851, the assembly could issue no bonds that matured more than thirty-four years after the date of issue or that paid a higher rate of interest than 6 percent per annum, which was a fairly standard rate for government bonds at the time.[54] It required the state to establish a sinking fund and annually deposit into it sufficient money to retire the principal at the bonds' maturity.

Sections 32 through 38, entitled General Provisions, placed other responsibilities and limitations on the General Assembly. Section 32 appended to the excerpt from the 1786 Act for Establishing Religious Freedom that the Convention of 1830 had inserted into the Constitution of 1830, "The General Assembly shall not grant a charter of incorporation to any church or religious denomination, but may secure the title to church property to an extent to be limited by law." Acts of incorporation as issued since the American Revolution allowed the General Assembly to name the first corporate officers, provide for naming their successors, and specify modes of operation. In the event of a divided congregation or denomination, the assembly might attempt to take a side in a dispute about matters of doctrine. Hence, members of the convention denied the assembly constitutional authority to charter a church congregation or denomination.[55] In spite of attempts made in 1902 and 1969 to delete the provision, every subsequent Virginia constitution, right through the one ratified in 1971, included it.[56]

THE EXECUTIVE

Article V, on the executive department, also contained changes, but it was brief, as articles on the executive had been in the first two state constitutions. In 1851, the Virginia convention placed new restrictions on state legislatures but did not, at the same time, increase the powers of the office of governor as new constitutions in some other states did. The convention did abolish the expensive and useless three-member Council of State, which no delegate even bothered to defend.[57] The article provided for the popular election every fourth year for the governor and for a lieutenant governor to preside over the Senate and become governor in the event of a vacancy in the governor's office. The new constitution prohibited men from serving consecutive terms as governor, another indication that convention delegates in Virginia, unlike delegates to some other state constitutional conventions, remained unwilling to enlarge the political influence of the state's governor.

The constitution empowered the General Assembly to elect a treasurer and auditor of public accounts, as it had done since 1776, for two-year terms and left the definition of their authorities to the legislature. It required the assembly to create three districts in the state for the popular election of three members of the Board of Public Works, each member to serve a six-year term, the terms staggered so that one member would be elected every second year. The constitution left it to the assembly to define the authority of the board. The article on the judiciary authorized the voters to elect the attorney general for a four-year term.

It is easy to look back and interpret the election in the autumn of 1851 of the first governor from west of the Alleghany Mountains (and, as events would have it, also the last) as a victory for western Virginians that the suffrage provisions of the new constitution made possible. Democrat Joseph Johnson, of Harrison County, defeated Whig George William Summers, of Kanawha County, by a vote of 65,895 to 57,260 in the first popular election of a governor of Virginia.[58] Both men were from the west, where a majority of white Virginians lived; but both men were also prominent leaders of their respective political parties; and it is almost always overlooked that while the constitutional convention was still early in its arguments about the basis of representation in March 1851, the General Assembly, acting under the Constitution of 1830, which was still in effect, elected Johnson as governor for the term to begin 1 January 1852. The vote was 92 for Johnson and a total of 54 for about a dozen other men. The distant runner-up was the western Whig, George William Summers.[59]

THE JUDICIARY

Article VI of the new constitution authorized voters to elect all the state's judges from justices of the peace up to and including judges of the Supreme Court of Appeals. Regarded at the time as a democratic reform, election of judges was a popular feature of many mid-nineteenth-century state constitutions, which made more public officials, including judges, responsive and accountable to the people.[60] In 1831, the General Assembly had already made the Supreme Court of Appeals more readily accessible to western Virginians by requiring the court to hold one session annually in Lewisburg in the western mountain county of Greenbrier.[61]

The new constitution again revamped the organizational structure of the state's courts but left the assembly wide discretion in making changes in their respective jurisdictions. The constitution abolished the old General Court and divided the state into twenty-one judicial circuits, into ten districts each consisting of two or more circuits, and into five sections each consisting of two districts. It empowered voters in each circuit to elect a judge for an eight-year term and in each section to elect a member of the Supreme Court of Appeals for a twelve-year term.

Article IV, Section 38, concerning elections and powers of the General Assembly, specified that "special elections to fill vacancies in the office of Judge of any court shall be for a full term," not merely to complete the unexpired term. That provision allowed terms of office for judges to become staggered, so that the terms of all the judges who were to be elected at the same time following ratification of the constitution would not thereafter always begin and expire simultaneously.

Article VI was more specific than either of the previous constitutions about the jurisdiction of the Supreme Court of Appeals. With a few exceptions, it confined the court to appellate jurisdiction only. The article for the first time constitutionally recognized judicial review as a legitimate responsibility of courts, not by authorizing judges of the Supreme Court of Appeals to exercise it but by referring to it as if it were an accepted, existing responsibility of courts, which by then it was.[62]

Section 12 gave constitutional status to Special Courts of Appeal, which the assembly had created from time to time since the end of the eighteenth century to decide cases in the event one or more judges of the Supreme Court of Appeals had to recuse himself because he was an interested party in a suit.[63] The section allowed the assembly to create "Special Courts of Appeals, to consist of not less than three nor more than five Judges," of the Supreme Court of Appeals and of the Circuit Courts "to try any cases remaining on the dockets of the present Court of Appeals when the Judges thereof cease to hold their offices"—that is, when judges in office under the Constitution of 1830 vacated their seats after ratification of the new constitution.

Convention members knew that the number of those cases was large. The General Assembly had established a new Special Court of Appeals in 1848[64] because the Supreme Court of Appeals had for several decades been unable to clear its docket. "For many years," the court's reporter wrote in 1849, "the number of causes pending in the Supreme Court of Appeals at *Richmond* had continued to increase, so that in the winter of 1847–8 they amounted to five hundred and sixty four; and except such cases as were entitled to precedence, the delay in the decision of a cause in the Court was about eight years. The number of cases decided annually was scarce equal to the appeals allowed; and there was, therefore, no hope that under the then existing system the evil of the delay of justice would ever be relieved."[65]

The long delay was a major failure of the state's judicial system. The law of 1848 established a new Special Court of Appeals that consisted of some members of the Supreme Court of Appeals, the General Court, or Circuit Courts to decide cases that had been stranded too long on the appellate court's clogged docket. Several lower court judges immediately challenged the constitutionality of the law. In *Sharpe v. Robertson* in January 1849, judges of the Supreme Court of Appeals ruled four to one (as in the past on many important cases, they rendered their opinions seriatim) in favor of the constitutionality of the Special Court of Appeals. The four judges stated that the 1848 law merely regulated the jurisdiction of the Supreme Court of Appeals and did not create a second, equal court, which would be in violation of the constitution's creation of "a Supreme Court of Appeals" that permitted no more than one.[66]

The Constitution of 1851 did nothing to prevent cases from accumulating on the docket faster than the judges of the court could decide them. In the winter of 1861–62, when northwestern Virginians wrote a constitution for the new state of West Virginia, some of them complained that judges of the Virginia Supreme Court of Appeals had frequently indulged themselves in writing long essays on points of law that were not always necessary to the decision of the case and that they neglected to consider fully some important arguments of counsel. The judges therefore produced long and complex decisions that did not always adequately settle all the legal questions. That may also have protracted the judges' work and been one of the reasons why they had been chronically unable to clear their clogged docket. The new West Virginia constitution included a revised version of the old Virginia language that specified that "every point made and distinctly stated in writing in the cause, and fairly arising upon the record of the case, shall be considered and decided, and the reasons therefor shall be concisely and briefly stated in writing, and preserved with the records of the case."[67]

LOCAL GOVERNMENT

As had their predecessors in 1776 and 1829–30, members of the Convention of 1850–51 made no separate provisions for local government and thereby left it to the General Assembly to make such changes as time and experience made necessary. They placed a few references to county and city officers, some of whom were not judicial, in Article VI on the judiciary.

Article VI, Section 27, terminated the ability of justices of the peace to fill vacancies on the county courts and empowered voters to elect justices of the peace. That change ended a two-hundred-year, uninterrupted process by which county courts operated as self-perpetuating local oligarchies.[68] Four other sections of Article VI authorized voters in each county to elect the clerk of court, county surveyor, commonwealth's attorney, sheriff, "and so many Commissioners of the Revenue as may be authorised by law." Section 31 placed limits on the tenures of sheriffs: "No person elected for two successive terms to the office of Sheriff, shall be re-eligible to the same office for the next succeeding term; nor shall he, during his term of service, or within one year thereafter, be eligible to any political office." The section also authorized voters to elect as many constables and overseers of the poor "as may be prescribed by law" for each county.

Two sections concerned the administration of justice in incorporated towns and cities. Section 33 empowered the General Assembly to "vest such jurisdiction as shall be deemed necessary in Corporation Courts, and in the Magistrates who may belong to the corporate body." Section 34 stated, "All officers appertaining to the cities and other municipal corporations, shall be elected by the qualified voters, or appointed by the constituted authorities of such cities or corporations, as may be prescribed by law." In some cities, voters elected magistrates, but in others, municipal officials appointed them. In some cities, mayors held their own courts for petty breaches of the peace, and aldermen with powers comparable to those of justices of the peace issued licenses, recorded the free papers of Black people, and registered deeds and oversaw probate of estates.

The new constitution made explicit what legislators and convention members had theretofore always understood: that county and city governments and government officials were subordinate agencies to, and agents of, the state government. The constitution reserved to the General Assembly almost plenary authority to specify or alter the jurisdiction of all courts as well as the structure of municipal governments, with the result that considerable variety obtained throughout the state.

The provisions for the popular election of county and municipal government officers may not have worked a speedy change in the functioning of the administration of justice at the local level.[69] They did, however, work a revolution in local politics by giving voters in counties and some cities the chance for the first time to select their own judges, sheriffs, and other local officers. And by making those offices elective, the provisions promised to make those officers beholden to their constituents, not to the justices of the peace who up until then had selected most of them, including themselves.

Ratification

On 31 July 1851, the day before the convention adjourned, its members approved the new constitution by a vote of 75 to 33 and submitted it to the voters for ratification.[70] The schedule that the delegates adopted at the same time authorized a ratification referendum on the fourth Thursday in October 1851 and granted "all persons qualified under the existing or amended Constitution" the right to vote in the referendum. The schedule specified that at the same time, voters also elect members of both houses of the General Assembly and a new governor, lieutenant governor, and attorney general. It directed that the new members of the assembly and state officers take office on the second Monday in January 1852 and it declared vacant, as of that date, all legislative and executive offices men selected under the Constitution of 1830 then filled. The new constitution therefore became fully effective on 12 January 1852.

Unlike in 1830, most leaders of both political parties in all regions of the state announced support for the new constitution.[71] The complex undemocratic section on representation went down better in the east than in the west, as the vote for the adoption of the constitution in the convention and the ratification referendum both indicate, but the democratic reforms of universal white manhood suffrage and popular election of most public officials were generally popular throughout the state.[72] Voters, including many adult white men who had never voted before, ratified the constitution on 23 October 1851 by an overwhelming vote of 75,748 to 11,863.[73]

The Constitution of 1851 in Operation

As a consequence of ratification of the new constitution, the number of Virginia voters significantly increased. Incomplete election returns indicate that more than 67,000 men voted in the May 1850 referendum on whether to hold a convention. The October 1851 ratification referendum conducted under universal white manhood suffrage (and with fewer incomplete returns) indicate that about 81,000 men voted,[74] an increase of about 21 percent. Considering how many returns from counties in the 1850 referendum were incomplete, the difference between the numbers of recorded votes in 1850 and 1851 is not a reliable indication of the effect of the suffrage provisions of the new constitution. In the gubernatorial election held that same day in October 1851, more than 123,000 men voted, nearly double the number who voted in the 1850 referendum.[75]

Perhaps, as with the relaxed property qualification introduced in 1830, the better measuring stick is the increase in voting between the presidential elections held before and after the convention. In the presidential election of 1848, about 92,000 men (47 percent of eligible men) had voted; in 1852, more than 132,000 (63 percent of eligible men) voted, an increase of more than 43 percent,[76] which, all other things being accounted for, may be a more accurate short-term reflection of the consequence of introducing universal white manhood suffrage in Virginia in 1851.

Thereafter, the number of men who voted in Virginia continued to increase, as did the percentage of qualified men who actually voted. The intense partisanship of the 1850s was largely responsible. About 71.5 percent of adult white men in Virginia voted in the presidential election of 1860.[77] For Virginia's white men, the assertion in the Declaration of Independence that "all men are created equal" came close to a political reality on election day for the first time in 1851. The revised and disguised Great Gerrymander, however, made some white men more equal, as George Orwell's pigs would have said, than others.

The First Amendment

Like the Constitutions of 1776 and 1830, the Constitution of 1851 contained no provision for amending it, but in May 1861, voters ratified an amendment to it. Not surprisingly the amendment arose from regional differences about slavery, about what many Virginians, mostly but not all in the west, considered an unfair advantage that the state constitution gave to owners of slave property. The provision of the constitution that fed the grievance was the one that eastern and slave-owning delegates had placed in the constitution in 1851 to limit taxation of slave property and prevent slavery from becoming economically unsustainable. Article IV, Sections 23 and 24, stated that "Taxation shall be equal and uniform throughout the commonwealth, and all property other than slaves shall be taxed in proportion to its value," but that enslaved people older than twelve could not be taxed on more than $300 of their value.

During the decade after ratification of the new constitution, the market price of slave laborers rose drastically as a consequence of a brisk demand in the lower Mississippi River Valley. Virginia enslavers in the eastern part of the state annually sold thousands of men, women, and children to the southwest. The increasing difference between the market value and the taxable value of Virginia's most valuable personal property exacerbated resentment among people who did not own slave property and believed that they paid higher taxes as a consequence and that owners of slave property paid less than their fair share.[78]

Western members of the Virginia Convention of 1861, who were elected to recommend a course of action for Virginia during the secession crisis, demanded that it submit to the voters an amendment to the state constitution to require that all personal property without exception be taxed at its market value. Some of the men who heard the demand may have understood it as a quid pro quo for western support of secession, which was much more popular in the southeastern portion of the state than anywhere else; but most of the delegates who demanded equalization of taxation of all personal property regarded it not as a tradeoff for their support of secession but as a redress of a serious grievance.[79]

Members of the Convention of 1861 who opposed the amendment objected that the constitution did not allow for amendments and that the convention had been called for the specific and sole purpose of recommending a course of action for Virginia during the secession crisis. Eventually, however, after the convention voted for secession and in hope that bowing to the western demand for equalizing personal property taxes would bring reluctant westerners to support secession, the delegates submitted a constitutional amendment to the voters. Acting as the immediate representatives of the people, not as mere legislators, the delegates decided that they were fully within their competence to submit a constitutional amendment to the voters who in their sovereign capacity could ratify it or reject it.[80]

The text of the amendment was simple: "Strike out the 22d and 23d Sections of the 4th Article of the present Constitution and Insert the Following in Lieu Thereof.

"Taxation shall be equal and uniform throughout the Commonwealth, and all property shall be taxed in proportion to its value, which shall be ascertained in such manner as may be prescribed by law; but any property may be exempted from taxation by the vote of a majority of the whole number of members elected to each house of the General Assembly."[81]

On 23 May, when voters ratified the ordinance of secession, they also ratified the amendment. Official returns from 126 of the state's 154 counties and cities showed a vote of 111,854 for the amendment and 95,109 against. The vote in the west was overwhelmingly in favor among the counties that opened polls or reported, but in the east, a very large proportion of voters opposed it.[82]

The Failed Constitutional Revision of 1861–62

Most of the members of the Convention of 1861 returned for a short second session in June and for a longer third session in November and December. The convention in effect governed the state with the assistance of the governor, who did not summon the General Assembly into session during the first eight months of the Civil War.[83]

By a vote of 74 to 10 on 5 December 1861,[84] the delegates submitted a revised constitution to the voters for ratification or rejection in a referendum scheduled for 13 March 1862. On 2 May 1862, the governor announced that 13,233 men had voted for the revised constitution and 13,911 against it, which defeated ratification by a very slim margin. In a second vote on that day, 16,518 men had voted for, and 9,201 men had voted against, a section that would have restricted the suffrage to men who owned property or paid taxes,[85] much as the Constitution of 1830 had required.

That little more than 27,000 men voted in the wartime referendum makes it difficult to ascertain the larger public's opinion about the revised constitution. That nearly two-thirds of men who voted favored restricting the vote to taxpaying adult white men suggests that a substantial portion of the population in the Commonwealth of Virginia that was one of the Confederate States of America, may have disagreed with some of the democratic reforms embedded in the Constitution of 1851.

The revision not only would have restricted the suffrage; it restored annual sessions of the General Assembly, took away voters' ability to elect judges and some local officials, and augmented the sections that protected slavery by explicitly forbidding the legislature from emancipating any enslaved men, women, or children. Comparison of the provisions of the failed revision of 1861–62 with the provisions of the constitution that northwestern Virginians wrote for the new state of West Virginia at almost the same time discloses that northwestern men entertained more democratic ideas about government and politics than political leaders in the part of Virginia that was one of the Confederate States of America from 1861 to 1865.[86]

The Constitution of West Virginia

Immediately after the convention in Richmond voted to secede from the United States on 17 April 1861, several uncompromising opponents of secession from northwestern counties returned home and began the process of restoring Virginia to the Union. That was the first of several steps necessary for separating the loyal part and people of Virginia from the disloyal part and people of Virginia. Insofar as was possible under the unprecedented conditions that then existed, the men who created West Virginia acted with scrupulous attention to legal and constitutional forms; and in a series of referenda at each step they sought and received authorization from the voters.[87] The last in a series of conventions that met in Wheeling for that purpose in the summer of 1861 called for election of delegates to a convention to write a constitution for the proposed new state of West Virginia.[88] The convention met from 26 November 1861 to 18 February 1862 and prepared a constitution that voters overwhelmingly ratified in April.[89]

The West Virginia Constitution of 1863 was more democratic in several respects than the government of Virginia had ever been under any of its constitutions—certainly much more democratic than it would have been under the constitutional revision that the Richmond convention proposed in December 1861. The first constitution of the new state granted equal representation in the legislature to all voters and required equal populations in all legislative districts. It required that voting be by ballot, not by voice vote, as had been the case in Virginia since 1646. The constitution abolished the county courts and created a statewide system of courts as well as elective county boards of supervisors for counties. It was the first state constitution south of the Mason-Dixon line and the Ohio River to require the legislature to create a state system of free public schools. It required that all taxes be based on the fair market value of property. It also acknowledged the responsibility of the new state to pay a fair portion of the public debt of old Virginia. And at the insistence of Congress, it included a provision for the gradual abolition of slavery that would nevertheless leave some enslaved adults in slavery well into the twentieth century.[90]

The Future

The Constitution of 1851 as amended in May 1861 remained in full effect until April 1865 in the Virginia that was one of the Confederate States of America. At the time of the surrender of the Confederate armies, officials of that state government abandoned their offices, ceased officiating, and let government under the Constitution of 1851 die. That constitution was one of the last casualties of the Civil War.

The generation after ratification of the Constitution of 1851—that is to say, the nineteen-year Jeffersonian generation—was the most profoundly important epoch of constitutional change in Virginia's long history. Beginning with white manhood suffrage and popular election of most public officials in 1851, the period concluded following the secession of more than fifty northwestern counties, the abolition of slavery that transformed nearly half a million enslaved people into American citizens, the enfranchisement of Black men and even more thorough democratic reform of local government, creation of the state's first system of free public schools, and changes in the Constitution of the United States that transformed the relationship between the national government and the governments of the states. And an unbelievably bloody and destructive Civil War. No generation of Virginians before or since ever experienced such drastic changes in their lives or in their relationships to their governments. The Constitution of 1851 was the first act in that revolution, although it was not in any sense the cause of it.

CHAPTER 5

The Constitution of 1864

The Constitution of 1864 had the shortest life of any Virginia constitution, scarcely more than five years. Most political histories that focus on the period refer to the constitution and the convention that created it in passing, but three of the four modern, full-length narrative histories of Virginia do not mention the constitution at all.[1] It is the least studied and least understood of all the state's constitutions, and the convention that created it is the least well documented. To date, the 1864 convention and constitution are the subject of only one brief scholarly analysis.[2]

The Constitution of 1864 came into existence under unprecedented circumstances following the equally unprecedented acts of secession, formation of the Restored Government, and creation of West Virginia. Myths and misunderstandings surround the circumstances under which the Convention of 1864 created the constitution. Some historians have referred to the constitution and the Restored Government dismissively with quotation marks around the words or a deprecatory *so-called*, as if they were not to be taken seriously. Those forms of aspersion originated during the short life of the constitution. Confederate Virginians never acknowledged the moral or legal legitimacy of the new state of West Virginia or of the government of Virginia that loyal men restored to the United States in June 1861.[3] Some Virginians questioned the legitimacy of the Constitution of 1864 because only a small number of men elected from a small number of counties and cities drafted it. Other Virginians dismissed it because the convention that wrote it promulgated it without a ratification referendum, even though the Convention of 1776 had done just that with the state's first constitution. And some others challenged its legitimacy because they mistakenly believed that only a few hundred Virginians had voted to ratify it and that therefore the large majority of white Virginians had not given—or even had a chance to give—their assent to it.[4]

Incorrect phrases like "military rule," "military reconstruction," and the like also placed a stain of illegitimacy on the Constitution of 1864. From late in the nineteenth century into the early decades of the twenty-first, people who were not specialists on the period appear to have concluded or unthinkingly assumed that because the United States Army oversaw the state government from the spring of 1867 until January 1870, the constitution was therefore not really an operating constitution. However, political officials and judges in Virginia accepted the de jure and de facto legitimacy of the Constitution of 1864 for the whole state after government under the Constitution of 1851 ceased to function in April 1865 when officials of the Confederate state government dispersed and left it unenforced thereafter.

The Restored Government of Virginia

The three conventions that met in Wheeling in May and June 1861 to begin the formation of West Virginia first took steps to restore the loyal parts of Virginia to the Union. On 11 June, about one hundred men from thirty-five western counties and two each from the eastern counties of Fairfax and Alexandria (which until 1846 had been part of the District of Columbia), including almost forty duly elected members of the General Assembly, met in Wheeling and began a revolution as important as the revolutionary act of secession that the delegates had adopted in Richmond. The delegates in Wheeling declared that all Virginia officials who adhered to the Confederacy had forfeited their offices by supporting the rebellion against the legitimate government of the United States. On their own authority as elected representatives of the people, the delegates in Wheeling then elected a new governor, lieutenant governor, and attorney general.[5]

On 20 June, their loyal governor, Francis Harrison Pierpont (or Pierpoint, he changed the spelling of his name about that time), appeared before the convention, took the oath of office, and delivered the first inaugural address that any governor of Virginia ever made.[6] He then summoned a special session of the General Assembly of Virginia to meet in Wheeling on 1 July, and he also appealed to the president and the secretary of war in Washington for protection from armed secessionists and for official recognition as the legitimate government of the loyal people of Virginia.[7]

President Abraham Lincoln complied on 4 July. The disloyal people of Virginia, he explained in a message to Congress, had "allowed this great insurrection to make its nest within her borders; and this Government has no choice left but to deal with it where it finds it. And it has the less regret, as the loyal citizens have in due form claimed its protection. These loyal citizens this Government is bound to recognize and protect as being Virginia."[8] Lincoln's recognition of the legitimacy of the actions of loyal Virginians in June 1861 was his first experiment in devising means of reconstructing the union of states.[9]

Pierpont had a new die struck for the seal of Virginia so that he and the secretary of the commonwealth could properly authenticate public documents. He had the engraver add to the design (which was first created in 1776) words from Daniel Webster's famous toast, "Liberty and Union," as an explicit visual repudiation of secessionist assertions that liberty for Southern white people was no longer possible in the United States.[10]

In the summer of 1863, after the admission to the United States of the new slave state of West Virginia, Pierpont moved the Restored Government from Wheeling to Alexandria, across the Potomac River from Washington, DC. The Virginia over which he presided shrank considerably in size and population with the creation of West Virginia. It is likely that even within some of the counties and cities from which members arrived to serve in its General Assembly the authority of his government was imperfectly enforced. Unfortunately, we have no analyses of the functioning of the Restored Government or of the operations of government in the localities it purported to encompass.[11]

The small size of the area of Virginia that Pierpont tried to govern after the summer of 1863 appeared to give credence to charges that his was merely an inconsequential rump government for an insignificantly small part of the state. If the counties and cities represented in the Constitutional Convention of 1864 had been a separate state in 1860, however, it would have been larger than two states and more populous than three. Its 3,200 square miles was more than two and a half times the size of Rhode Island and more than one and a half times the size of Delaware. The population of the Virginia counties and cities together exceeded the populations of each of the states of Oregon, Florida, and Delaware and of Kansas which became a state early in 1861. The white population of 87,633 in 1860 was greater than the white population of Florida and greater than the entire population of Oregon. The 44,840 enslaved Virginians who lived in those counties and cities constituted almost 10 percent of all enslaved Virginians.[12]

Events of the secession crisis and Civil War not only created but also changed the Restored Government. The war made many loyal Americans think seriously about some fundamentally important matters, such as the nature of the Union, the purposes of the war, and especially the future of slavery.

The abolition of slavery in the 1860s was the one most profound revolutionary change during any correspondingly short time in North American history. Considering how long slavery had existed and how firmly it was embedded in the society, economy, and law, its abolition, if viewed from a historical perspective, actually occurred quite rapidly. The momentous revolution was not an event but a process that took place at different times in different places and under different circumstances between the abolition of slavery in the District of Columbia by congressional action in April 1862 and ratification of the Thirteenth Amendment in December 1865. In reality, the legal end of slavery in any one of those places may not have coincided in time with the actual end of enslavement.

Changing circumstances forced Governor Pierpont and other loyal Virginians to change their ideas about slavery. By 1863, Pierpont realized that for several reasons, including slavery, his state needed a new constitution. So many counties that were part of Virginia when the Constitution of 1851 was adopted were no longer part of Virginia that the districts defined in that constitution for the election of legislators and judges were obsolete, and the old constitution contained no provision for amending it to realign them. Pierpont also concluded that his government of Virginia could not function as a slave state. The Emancipation Proclamation did not apply to some parts of the Restored Government. The governor and the United States Army were therefore under conflicting legal responsibilities concerning the many thousands of resident enslaved men, women, and children and the additional thousands who escaped from slavery and were within their overlapping jurisdictions. Moreover, the Constitution of 1851 under which the Restored Government operated did not permit legislative abolition of slavery.[13]

On 7 December 1863, Pierpont recommended that the General Assembly summon a constitutional convention to abolish slavery in Virginia. He had been a strong western critic of the overbearing political power that slave owners in eastern Virginia had exercised before the Civil War, but he had been no abolitionist, and he never became an egalitarian.[14] Events of the war had convinced him, as he explained to the assembly, that "There can never be any peace and unity among the people so long as this institution exists." So profoundly had circumstances and his beliefs changed that he even declared, "Immediate emancipation is God's plan." Pierpont recommended that the convention abolish slavery in Virginia and request the federal government to compensate owners for the value of their property that they were to lose.[15]

The Convention of 1864

On 18 December 1863, the General Assembly passed a law to authorize voters "in all the counties and districts of this Commonwealth" (in practice meaning in the loyal/liberated/occupied parts of Virginia) to elect convention delegates on 21 January 1864.[16] Almost no records pertaining to the election survive, and the number of voters is not known nor the number of candidates. At least two people ran for the Fairfax County seat, and at least three for the two seats to represent the district of Norfolk County and the town of Portsmouth. Stray newspaper reports indicate that 127 men voted in the city of Alexandria and 208 in the county of Fairfax.[17] (In the 1860 presidential election, 1,594 men had voted in the district comprising the city of Alexandria and Alexandria County, and 1,467 men had voted in Fairfax County.[18] The steep decline in the number of voters resulted from the absence of men in both contending armies and the refusal of supporters of the Confederacy to vote in Restored Government elections.) Voters elected a total of seventeen delegates from the counties of Loudoun and Fairfax and the city of Alexandria in northern Virginia; the counties of Northampton and Accomack on the Eastern Shore; and the cities of Williamsburg, Portsmouth, and Norfolk and the counties of Warwick, Princess Anne, Norfolk, New Kent, James City, Elizabeth City, and Charles City, all in southeastern Virginia.[19]

Four of the seventeen delegates were not native Virginians (one each from Pennsylvania, Massachusetts, New York, and Connecticut), a higher proportion than in any previous Virginia convention, but two of them had lived in Virginia for a decade or more before the Civil War.[20] Only one was a practicing attorney, the all-time low number and percentage of lawyers in a Virginia constitutional convention. Among the other delegates were four farmers, two physicians, the owner of a mill and lumber yard, a merchant, a naval contractor, a saddler, a cooper, a machinist, and a harbor pilot. Most of the delegates belonged to what later generations called the working class or the professional middle class. At least four delegates owned or had owned enslaved people, though none more than a few. John Hawxhurst, who represented Fairfax County, had been born a Quaker in New York and, with his brother Job, moved to Virginia about 1850. Both were antislavery, and Job was an active abolitionist and won election to the House of Delegates under the Constitution of 1864.

The seventeen delegates met in the United States Courthouse in Alexandria from 13 February through 11 April 1864. They elected LeRoy Griffin Edwards, clerk of the Norfolk city council, as president. William J. Cowling, a native midwesterner and publisher of the *Virginia State Journal*, a Republican newspaper in Alexandria, became secretary. Cowling reported some of the convention's debates in his paper, but only one copy survives for the weeks that the convention met, and even though a few excerpts from the *Virginia State Journal*'s reports appeared in the *Alexandria Gazette*, no useful record of the convention's deliberations survives.[21] Cowling published the journal and the constitution in separate booklets shortly after the convention adjourned.[22] His manuscript journal is preserved in the state archives in the Library of Virginia,[23] but for reasons that are not now known, the enrolled parchment of the Virginia Constitution of 1864 somehow got into the collections of the Virginia Historical Society, a private not public institution, probably before the end of the nineteenth century, as if it were not an official government document.[24]

The Constitution of 1864

The members of the convention were all loyal Union men, and most were willing or eager to abolish slavery under the conditions that had arisen since the beginning of the Civil War. Except in the abolition of slavery, the constitution they wrote in 1864 was a much less significant reform than the constitution northwestern Virginians wrote in Wheeling for West Virginia in the winter of 1861–62. The men in Alexandria even rolled back two democratic reforms embodied in the Constitution of 1851. The Constitution of 1864 included large blocks of the Constitution of 1851 without alteration or significant change, and like the state's three previous constitutions it contained no provisions for amendment. The constitution was almost ten thousand words long, about 10 percent shorter than the Constitution of 1851.

The most important reform was the abolition of slavery in the state. The convention's members omitted all references to slavery and the three sections that protected it in the Constitution of 1851. On 10 March they voted 15 to 1, with one delegate absent or not voting, to adopt Sections 19, 20, and 21 of Article IV. The first declared, "Slavery and involuntary servitude (except for crime) is hereby abolished and prohibited in the State forever," and the third that "The general assembly shall make no law establishing slavery or recognizing property in human beings." People rang the city's church bells in celebration and fired a hundred guns in honor of the event. The *New York Times* and other newspapers in the United States reported the vote and saluted the Virginia delegates.[25]

Section 20, the second of the constitution's three provisions respecting the abolition of slavery, extended to children of freed or poor Blacks the right to an apprenticeship that had theretofore been available for the most part only to the children or orphans of poor white people. That was the extent of the new constitution's provisions for the people it freed. That left it to later legislatures and the Convention of 1867–68 to change the state's marriage and inheritance laws to legalize marriages that had never had legal status and to allow children, who had theretofore been legally classified as illegitimate property, to inherit property from their parents.[26] That apprenticeship system often resulted in overseers of the poor taking the children of poor freed people away from their families to learn a craft or be raised as servants in the households of strangers.[27]

Because the federal government took no action to compensate owners of the enslaved people thus freed—or to compensate any other owners in any other state—those owners suffered severe financial losses as a consequence of the abolition of slavery in Virginia. No useful scholarship documents what, if anything, state and local officers of the Restored Government did to enforce the constitutional abolition of slavery or whether or how people within its jurisdiction freed enslaved men, women, and children during the twelve months between the end of the convention and the end of the Civil War.

SUFFRAGE AND REPRESENTATION

To the suffrage provisions in Article II, the convention made both minor and very significant changes. A minor change altered the requirement for residence in the state from two years to one. Either by design or as an unanticipated consequence, that permitted a substantial number of men who served in the United States Army to remain in Virginia and take part in politics soon after the war and in a few instances even before that. The first major change restored one of the requirements in the Constitution of 1830 that in order to vote, an adult white man must have "paid all taxes assessed to him, after the adoption of this Constitution."[28] That limited the grant of universal white manhood suffrage introduced in the Constitution of 1851[29] and closely resembled the corresponding provision in the draft constitution that the Convention of 1861 unsuccessfully proposed for ratification.

The second important change abolished voice voting and required that all men vote by ballot. Virginia was one of the last states that still required voice voting. The third important change required that men who wished to vote swear an oath disavowing secession and the national and state governments of the Confederacy and an oath of loyalty to the Constitutions of the United States and of the Restored Government of Virginia. Section 7 declared, "no person shall vote, or hold office, under this Constitution who has held office under the so called confederate government, or under any rebellious State government, or who has been a member of the so called confederate Congress, or a member of any State legislature in rebellion against the authority of the United States, excepting therefrom county officers."

Section 6 omitted the complex apportionment provisions that the Convention of 1850–51 had added to the constitution as part of the revised and disguised Great Gerrymander.[30] Not unlike a provision in the new Constitution of West Virginia, the new constitution required "the General Assembly, in the year one thousand eight hundred and seventy, and in every tenth year thereafter, to re-apportion representation in the Senate and House of Delegates ... from an enumeration of the inhabitants of the State." Interestingly, the section made no distinction between white and Black "inhabitants of the State"; and slavery being abolished, convention members had no occasion to debate whether to retain the "three-fifths of all other persons" language that the previous two state constitutions included for drawing boundaries of congressional districts.[31] The new Virginia constitution did not, however, go so far as West Virginia's and require that the state's legislative districts, like its congressional districts, be compact and composed of contiguous counties containing as nearly as practicable equal populations. For the first time, though, the Constitution of the Commonwealth of Virginia required that members of the legislature represent the people in each of the counties and cities, not any local or regional interest or any property.

THE GENERAL ASSEMBLY

Most of Article IV on the General Assembly repeated the provisions of Article IV in the Constitution of 1851. Section 2, though, acknowledged the legal existence of the state of West Virginia by omitting in the enumeration of counties and cities that were allowed representation in the assembly all the counties then included in the new state. It also permitted the assembly to change the number of members of the two houses of the General Assembly. "The House of Delegates shall consist of not less than eighty and of not more than one hundred and four members," it declared, and "The Senate shall never be less than one-fourth nor more than one-third the number of the House of Delegates." The new constitution retained the provision in the Constitution of 1851 for two-year terms for delegates and four-year terms for senators. It did not require staggered terms for senators as in 1851, but the schedule that the convention adopted allowed the Senate to authorize the election of half the senators every second year. The constitution restored annual meetings of the assembly in place of the biennial meetings first required in 1851. It also reduced the maximum length of legislative sessions first imposed in 1851 from ninety days to sixty days.[32]

Section 27 also acknowledged the existence of West Virginia in a long paragraph that provided for payment of Virginia's antebellum public debt. Virginia authorities later relied on that section and its successor section in the Constitution of 1869 during the long legal process to force West Virginia to pay a portion of the old state's antebellum public debt.[33] The section also prohibited the General Assembly from allowing or providing for "the payment of any debt or obligation created in the name of the State of Virginia by the usurped and pretended state authorities at Richmond" and prohibited cities and counties from levying taxes "for the payment of any debt created for the purpose of aiding any rebellion against the State or the United States." That imposed limits on the government of Virginia in 1864 that were similar to limits that Section 4 of the Fourteenth Amendment to the Constitution of the United States imposed on all states when it was ratified in 1868.

Section 29 prohibited the government from creating any new public debt "except to meet casual deficits in the revenue, to redeem a previous liability of the state, or to suppress insurrection, repel invasion, or defend the State in time of war." That permanently terminated the state's antebellum policy of borrowing money to purchase shares of stock in corporations to enable them to raise capital speedily for the construction of roads, railroads, and canals.[34]

THE EXECUTIVE

Article V of the Constitution of 1864 on the executive department made only a very few inconsequential linguistic changes to Article V of the Constitution of 1851. The only important change was in Article VI Section 1, on the judiciary which authorized the governor to nominate judges but left their election to the General Assembly.

THE JUDICIARY

Convention members made some other important changes in Article VI on the judiciary and eliminated mention of all West Virginia counties in the creation of judicial circuits. They reduced the number of judges of the Supreme Court of Appeals from five to three. More importantly, in 1864 the convention members scrapped the popular election of all judges which was introduced in 1851. Section 1 specified that judges "shall be chosen by the joint vote of the two houses of the general assembly, from persons nominated by the governor." That section was a retreat from the democratic elections first required in 1851; but unlike the proposed revision of 1861 that would have also restored election of judges to the assembly, the 1864 constitution gave the governor, for the first time, an important role in appointing judges when the assembly was in session. Before the Convention of 1864, the General Assembly of the Restored Government had not displaced or sought to replace any of the five elected judges of the Supreme Court of Appeals, and the assembly did not exercise its authority under the Constitution of 1864 to appoint three judges until early in 1866.

LOCAL GOVERNMENT

Like the three Virginia constitutions before it, the Constitution of 1864 had no separate section on local government. Article VI Sections 18 and 24 through 33 merely repeated without significant modification the provisions for county and municipal courts and offices from the Constitution of 1851.

PROCLAIMING THE CONSTITUTION IN EFFECT

On 4 April 1864, following debates for which no records survive, members of the convention voted 10 to 7 against submitting the new constitution to the voters for ratification or rejection.[35] The final words of the preamble echoed the words of the Constitution of 1776 and referred to the December 1863 law under which the delegates were elected: "We therefore, the delegates of the good people of Virginia, elected and in convention assembled, in pursuance of said Act, have adopted the following constitution and form of government for this commonwealth."

Three days later, on 7 April, the delegates adopted the new constitution by a vote of 13 to 4. The four men who voted against it probably did so because they had favored submitting the constitution to the voters for ratification.[36] The next day the delegates passed an ordinance to put the new constitution into effect on the day the convention adjourned,[37] which was on 11 April 1864. Thirteen of the seventeen delegates then signed the official enrolled parchment. It is possible that the two delegates from the Eastern Shore left town to return home before the signing ceremony, but the delegates from Alexandria and Norfolk, who both were still in town, did not sign.[38]

The schedule that the convention adopted at the same time for smoothing the transition from government under the old constitution to government under the new declared that "The Senate may so fix the term of members first elected thereto from districts not now represented"—that is, from counties and cities then in the Confederate part of Virginia—"that one-half the number of Senators (or as near that number as may be) shall be elected every two years"; and that "The General Assembly shall pass all laws necessary for carrying this Constitution into full force and effect."

Immediately before the convention adjourned on 11 April, the convention's president, LeRoy G. Edwards, addressed the delegates who remained in the city. "I came to this Convention," he began, "with very humble aspirations, but with a sincere desire to do something towards restoring to our distressed and ruined people a civil government under which they might be free from oppression and wrong.... I have grieved to see devastation and wretchedness around me, and wept to witness the want and humiliation which our once free and happy people have been compelled to bear. If all these could have fallen on the guilty only I would not complain, although my sympathies might have been pained; but the innocent and helpless suffer, as must always be the case in a war like the present, and how to relieve their distress, or at least to ameliorate their condition, is the great desideratum with me, as I believe it is with every one of you."

Edwards went on to recall that he had grown up in the Northern Neck "among those who had been the immediate associates of Washington, and helped to raise the mighty fabric of government which has given refuge and protection to so many of the oppressed of the earth." As a young man he had served in the field with his militia unit during the War of 1812, which he remembered as "our second war of independence." Edwards then rhetorically asked, "Can it be wondered, then, that I am strongly attached to the Union as it was, and as I hope it may again be? Yes sirs," he continued in the same spirit of pathos that enveloped his entire speech, "a hope lingers that we shall yet have that Union restored, and that we may be able to leave to our children what our fathers left us as a legacy—the best government on this earth."[39]

Legitimacy of the Constitution of 1864

Throughout the war the federal government recognized the Restored Government as the legitimate government of the loyal people of Virginia. Because of some irregularities in elections for members of the House of Representatives that were conducted under the authority of the Restored Government, Congress did not seat any of the men elected to the lower house of Congress after 1863.[40] The General Assembly elected federal judge John C. Underwood to the United States Senate on 9 December 1864, but he never took his seat,[41] and for some unrecorded reason, the assembly did not elect a successor to Senator Lemuel J. Bowden, who died on 2 December 1864, so Virginia was not represented in Congress at all after that date. Probably because of difficulties during the war, loyal Virginians did not vote in the presidential election of 1864,[42] but that did not necessarily demonstrate that Congress no longer regarded the Restored Government as legitimate. The administration certainly continued to treat it as legitimate. The president nominated, and the Senate confirmed, appointments of postmasters, collectors of revenue, federal attorneys, and judges and other officers of federal courts in Virginia. On 8 February 1865, the Senate of the Restored Government ratified the Thirteenth Amendment to abolish slavery in the United States, and the following day, the House of Delegates ratified it. Secretary of State William H. Seward certified the actions of Virginia's assembly as the twelfth of the requisite twenty-seven legislative ratifications necessary for placing the amendment in the Constitution of the United States.[43]

Insofar as is known, no significant doubt arose about the legitimacy of the Constitution of 1864 as the only constitution for the whole state after the collapse of the government of the Confederate state of Virginia in April 1865 and the consequent extinction of the Constitution of 1851. However, John Minor Botts cast aspersions on the Constitution of 1864 that many years later created doubts about its legitimacy. A June 1865 newspaper reported him as saying "that he could not approve the manner in which the Alexandria Constitution was forced upon the people of Virginia, it having been framed by eleven men and adopted by four or five hundred voters." He cited no source for the incorrect number of delegates or for the number voters.[44]

Botts did not usually get his facts wrong, but he did on that occasion, both as to the number of members of the convention and his statement that "four or five hundred voters" ratified the constitution in a referendum that was not in fact ever authorized or held. Botts's reputation gave his assertion some credibility. A Whig congressman in the 1840s, a member of the Convention of 1850–51, and a noted long-winded orator with strong opinions, Botts had been an unsuccessful candidate for the Virginia Convention of 1861 in opposition to secession. He remained steadfastly loyal to the United States during the Civil War and even spent time in prison as a result. He entitled his long 1866 autobiography *The Great Rebellion: Its Secret History, Rise, Progress, and Disastrous Failure*. In 1865 and 1866 Botts helped organize the moderate wing of the state's Republican Party.[45] His disparaging comment about the constitution that other loyal Virginians wrote in 1864 consequently carried weight.

A careless historian early in the twentieth century transformed Botts's comment into a durable misstatement of fact. Botts had said that he did not approve the manner of forming the constitution, but he clearly stated that he admitted the legal authority of the constitution and also the legitimacy of the Restored Government and of the government of West Virginia.[46] In 1904, Hamilton J. Eckenrode repeated in his *Political History of Virginia during*

Reconstruction Botts's statement that "four or five hundred voters" was how many—that is to say, how insignificantly few—Virginians ratified the Constitution of 1864 even though in fact, it was not ratified. Eckenrode's *History* thus incorrectly impugned the constitution's legitimacy.[47]

Eckenrode was not alone in his opinion. Four years earlier, in William A. Anderson's 1900 presidential address to the Virginia State Bar Association, Anderson had condemned the Constitution of 1864 and the convention that prepared it as without any moral or legal legitimacy. A Confederate veteran, Anderson was elected to the first of two four-year terms as attorney general the following year, and his opinion also carried weight.[48] Two decades later, historian Ralph C. McDanel made an even greater blunder when he wrote that the "Alexandria Constitution of 1864" had "never been recognized as valid."[49]

Historians and legal scholars have unsuspectingly relied on or repeated that misinformation into the twenty-first century and thereby perpetuated a false impression that only a few voters ratified the constitution and that it was therefore of questionable legitimacy or that it even functioned as the state's fundamental law at all.[50]

In fact, the Constitution of 1864 was in full force without recorded dispute throughout Virginia following the collapse of the Confederacy and of the government of the Confederate state of Virginia. Governor Pierpont, the attorney general, the secretary of the commonwealth, and other officers of the Restored Government moved from Alexandria to Richmond and administered government under the authority of the Constitution of 1864 without legal challenge. They met some political resistance, to be sure, but in the immediate aftermath of the war and the loss of the Confederate cause, most white Virginians evidently resigned themselves to the end of slavery and to the authority of the liberating/occupying military force of the United States that stood behind the Restored Government. Insofar as is known, no one ever made a serious political charge about, or filed a legal challenge to, the shift of government from the authority of the Constitution of 1851 to the authority of the Constitution of 1864 for all of what was then Virginia. In fact, three contemporary Virginia legal authorities of unimpeachable qualifications clearly affirmed the de jure and de facto authority of the constitution.

The earliest is an unpublished legal brief filed in the case of *Elijah R. Walker v. William H. Loving*, argued in the court of Nelson County. The case concerned a bargain concluded in that county on 11 March 1865. Among the several issues in the suit was the validity of the transfer of ownership of an enslaved woman in partial satisfaction of an obligation. Was the transaction legal inasmuch as it took place more than twenty-six months after the Emancipation Proclamation declared free the enslaved people who resided in areas that were then in rebellion against the United States and eleven months after the Constitution of 1864 abolished slavery in the state? Nelson County was in the central Blue Ridge, well within the region Lincoln regarded as "in rebellion" but far from the region where the admittedly weak arms of the Restored Government could reach.

The undated legal brief (a reference to the pending Fourteenth Amendment indicates that it was composed sometime between the middle of 1866 and early in 1868) which was filed with the court and preserved in the suit papers came from the pen of John White Brockenbrough. He had compiled and published an edition of John Marshall's federal district court decisions, was a former judge of the federal court for the Western District of Virginia, a former member of the Provisional Congress of the Confederate States of America, a former judge of the Confederate States court for the Western District of Virginia, and one of the founders of what became the law school at Washington and Lee University.[51] Any Virginian would have been hard pressed to find a finer lawyer or more skilled judge to assess a Virginia law or constitution—or one more unsympathetic toward the authors of the Constitution of 1864.

Brockenbrough ably analyzed all the substantive and procedural legal issues that the case raised, including the important question of whether or when the Constitution of 1864 was the de jure and de facto constitution of Virginia and whether, when, or where it thereby abolished slavery in the state. The former judge carefully dissected the Emancipation Proclamation and the presidential authority on which Lincoln based it (which, somewhat surprisingly, he fully endorsed as a lawful wartime act) to buttress his original statement that the proclamation had no effect anywhere in Virginia until the United States Army arrived to enforce it. After more than fifteen hundred words, Brockenbrough concluded that "slavery continued to flourish in full vigor in V^a, & throughout the Confederate States, so far as they were within the lines of our armies, as an institution organized, protected & regulated by law, untill the final collapse & overthrow of the cause of the C.S: that untill that event the C.S. were a de facto Sovereign & independent Government." The portion of Virginia in which Nelson County was located was therefore within the bounds of the Confederate state of Virginia.

Brockenbrough wrote more than 750 more words on the legal authority of the Constitution of 1864. He argued that the constitution that the "(miscalled) Convention of V^a at Alexandria" adopted that abolished slavery in Virginia "was wholly inoperative within the lines of the C.S. armies: & that if the said Constitution, with its abolition of slavery, is now of binding force & obligation every where in V^a, (which is not denied but on the contrary fully conceded,) it has become so by Conquest and prospectively, from the 10th of April 1865," the day after the Confederate army surrendered at Appomattox Court House. Brockenbrough concluded that the constitution originally "had no existence in V^a except the little strip of territory covered by the arms of the U.S. It was not the Constitution of V^a till was made so by conquest on the 10th of April 1865," a month after the transaction that led to the lawsuit.

Following his long discussion of the Constitution of 1864, Brockenbrough added an extremely important bit of information. "I have not cited any decisions of our courts in support of the construction contended for," he explained, "because I was not aware that any such decision had been pronounced." As if taking judicial notice of the fact, he reported as part of the history of his time that the Constitution of 1864 became the legitimate, acknowledged, legal constitution of all Virginia in April 1865, which he and no other person had denied "but on the contrary fully conceded."[52]

The second legal commentator was former secretary of the commonwealth George Wythe Munford, who had compiled the Code of 1860. In the "Historical Synopsis," or introduction, to his *Third Edition of the Code of Virginia*, also known as the Code of 1873, he related the intervening political and legal upheavals and treated the Constitution of 1864 as "the organic law for the state" even though only a few delegates "from an inappreciable number of counties" had drafted and proclaimed it in effect without a ratification referendum. He expressed no doubts or hesitation about its legal legitimacy.[53] The third authority was John B. Minor, a distinguished law professor at the University of Virginia. In describing the end of slavery in the 1882 edition of his *Institutes of Common and Statute Law*, he explicitly accepted the legal authority and legitimacy of the Constitution of 1864.[54] The three authorities agreed that the arbitrament of war effectively settled the legal status of the Constitutions of 1851 and 1864 in postwar Virginia.

The Constitution of 1864 in Operation

By the time Pierpont moved the sole surviving government of Virginia to Richmond late in the spring of 1865, he had decided on a policy of speedy reconciliation of former Confederates with loyal Virginians. He supplied scores, perhaps hundreds, of endorsements for prominent Virginia men who had supported the Confederacy, took oaths of allegiance to the United States, and applied for presidential pardons under the lenient terms that President Andrew Johnson offered.[55] Pierpont also called a special session of the General

Assembly, which met in the Capitol in Richmond for a week beginning on 19 June 1865, to remove some of the disabilities on other adherents of the Confederacy so that they and all other otherwise qualified white men throughout the state could vote in elections for legislators, local officials, and members of Congress.

Article III, Section 1, of the Constitution of 1864 disfranchised men who had supported the Confederacy or "held office under the so called confederate government, or under any rebellious State government," but it also granted the General Assembly "power to pass an Act or Acts prescribing means by which persons who have been disfranchised by this provision shall or may be restored to the rights of voters." The legislators passed a law on 22 June to allow men disqualified under that provision of the constitution to vote if they took the oath of allegiance to the United States that President Andrew Johnson published on 29 May and also an oath "to uphold and defend the Government of Virginia, restored by the Convention which assembled at Wheeling on the eleventh of June, eighteen hundred and sixty-one."[56] At the same time, the assembly scheduled elections for members of Congress and the assembly for October.[57]

The General Assembly also took an unprecedent step in order to remove more barriers to the abilities of former Confederates and supporters of the Confederacy to vote and hold office. It ordered that at the October general election, a referendum item be on the ballot: "Shall the next general assembly be clothed with power to alter or amend the third article of the constitution?"[58] Lacking any constitutional authority to propose amendments, the legislators appealed to the superior political sovereignty of the voters to empower members to be elected in October to change that one article without stating or limiting how the assembly might amend it.

Under the relaxed suffrage provisions of the law of June 1865, many thousands of Virginia men voted that autumn who would not have been eligible otherwise. Republican leaders in Congress, though, refused to seat any of the nine men elected to the House of Representatives from Virginia at that time or any from the other states of the former Confederacy or any senators that their legislatures appointed.[59]

The General Assembly that met from 4 December 1865 through 3 March 1866 and in two sessions between 3 December 1866 and 29 April 1867 included senators and delegates from all the counties and cities that remained in Virginia. A large number of them had actively supported the Confederacy or passively accepted its authority, and many of them had political experience or had held public office before the war or even during it. The membership of the assembly reassured Virginians who feared the consequences of federal control of the state after the war and probably alarmed freed people and advocates of serious reforms. The assembly's members on the whole represented the values and political leadership of old Virginia more than that of the new Virginia without slavery. The legislators took maximum advantage of the opportunity and extended as far as they could Pierpont's plan for quickly reconciling former Confederates with loyal Virginians—but not necessarily for reconciling loyal Virginians with former Confederates.

On 12 October 1865, voters approved the proposal that the assembly submitted in June to allow legislators to amend Article III. By what Pierpont described in December 1865 as "a large majority," the incomplete returns he had received by then indicated that voters approved.[60] Legislators adopted two amendments in different forms, which suggests that at least some of them may have been unsure how to proceed in the utterly unprecedented business of legislative amendment of the constitution or precisely what they intended to change.

By statute on 5 December 1865, the General Assembly deleted the paragraph that required voters and office holders to take an oath that they had never supported the Confederacy or held office "under the so-called confederate government, or under any rebellious state government."[61] On 24 February 1866, the assembly by what it identified as an ordinance, not a statute, replaced the entire suffrage article with language very similar to that in Article III, Section 1, of the Constitution of 1830. The amendment required voters to have paid all their state taxes and reinstated the two-year residency requirement, which the Constitution of 1864 had reduced to one year, and reinstated the requirement in the Constitution of 1851 that "In all elections votes shall be given openly or viva voce, and not by ballot."[62] As the unpredictable events of the postwar months and years fell out, Virginians did not again elect state officers or legislators in accordance with the Constitution of 1864, so the portion of the amendment that abolished the ballot and restored voice voting applied only in local elections held in 1866 and 1867.

The 1865–66 session of the General Assembly repealed the laws relating to slavery[63] and passed some new laws that the abolition of slavery had made necessary, but for the most part, legislators in 1865 and 1866 did very little to change the political economy or society of old Virginia.[64] They even tried to turn the clock back to 1861 in one respect and repealed the laws that give Virginia's assent to the admission of West Virginia as a separate state and that also authorized referenda in Jefferson and Berkeley Counties, among others, to allow residents of those counties to decide whether to remain part of Virginia or become part of West Virginia.⁶⁵ Under instructions from the assembly, the attorney general later sued the state of West Virginia to prohibit it from collecting taxes in Jefferson and Berkeley Counties until the Supreme Court of the United States could decide whether the counties were legally part of the new state. Early in 1871, the Supreme Court ruled in *Virginia v. West Virginia* that the actions of the constituent conventions that met in Wheeling, the acts of the General Assembly of the Restored Government that gave its consent to the creation of the new state, and the law of Congress that admitted West Virginia to statehood together constituted a valid compact that made West Virginia a state and also made Jefferson and Berkeley Counties part of that state. Supreme Court justices did not bother to point out the obvious fact that by suing West Virginia, Virginia in effect acknowledged the new state's legal existence. The Supreme Court thereby recognized the Restored Government as the legal government of Virginia as of June 1861, as the president and Congress had done from the beginning.⁶⁶

The General Assembly's election of three members of the Supreme Court of Appeals as provided for in the Constitution of 1864 further reassured white Virginians who worried about the future. Pierpont nominated, and on 22 February 1866 the legislators elected, Richard Cassius Lee Moncure, of Stafford County, who had served on the court since April 1851; William Thomas Joynes, a prominent Petersburg attorney; and Lucas Powell Thompson, an accomplished lawyer from Staunton who for many years had conducted a private law school there.⁶⁷ Thompson died soon after being elected and never took office. After the assembly adjourned, the governor appointed Alexander Rives to take his place and the following December nominated him, and the assembly formally elected him.⁶⁸ Rives was a very able lawyer from Charlottesville and a future federal judge.

In the winter 1865–66 session of the General Assembly, the governor and legislators took steps to resume payments on the antebellum state debt, which pleased business leaders and the legal community. In the session the following winter, the legislature promised to pay the full principal and interest, including interest that accrued during the war when neither the Restored Government nor the Confederate state government paid interest on the debt.⁶⁹

Some laws that legislators adopted during the winter of 1865–66 looked forward to a new Virginia without slavery. Some of these laws definitely benefitted freed people. The 27 February 1866 law popularly known as the Cohabitation Act, for instance, permitted formerly enslaved people who had regarded themselves as married to register and legalize their marriages. They could also legitimize their children and thereby allow them to inherit property from their parents. The law also required county and city officials to create and maintain separate public registers of marriages of Black men and women as they had done for white people since the Constitution of 1851 first required them to do so.[70] Pierpont had recommended something similar in his first message to the assembly after the new constitution abolished slavery, but the assembly had not then acted.[71] Freed people took maximum advantage of the opportunity to legalize and protect their families, as is evident in the three dozen or more surviving cohabitation registers, as they were called, that are in the collections of the Library of Virginia and in county courthouses.[72] The Convention of 1867–68 added a clause to the state constitution to secure those rights.[73]

Many laws left over from slavery times still operated, including the then current version of a law that dated back to the seventeenth century that prohibited all Black people and members of First Nations tribes from testifying against any white people in court.[74] Pierpont believed that in the new free labor economy Black people needed the right to testify in court in order to enforce terms of labor contracts and to protect their freedom, rights, and property. He had recommended repeal of that law back in Alexandria in December 1864, but the assembly then did nothing.[75] Those and other restrictions on Black Virginians remained on the books in the months after the end of slavery and provoked anger among the freed people. Legislators did not always react sympathetically to pleas to ameliorate the effects of those old laws, and it enacted some other restrictive laws.[76]

The new vagrancy act that the General Assembly passed in January 1866 was the best known of these restrictive laws. It looked backward rather than forward and brought an angry reaction from the commanding officer of the United States Army in Virginia. The preamble of the law stated that "there hath lately been a great increase of idle and disorderly persons in some parts of this commonwealth." That was a clear reference to unemployed freed people, many of whom had gone in search of family members from whom the domestic slave trade and the hiring out of enslaved laborers had separated them. Nothing comparable to the departure of freed men, women, and children from the farms and town houses of their former masters or mistresses had happened to any appreciable number of white Virginians, which indicated that the law was intended to apply mainly to freed people. The preamble declared that if the assembly did not act, the state would "be overrun with dissolute and abandoned characters."

The law authorized justices of the peace and overseers of the poor to arrest unemployed people and hire them out "for any term not exceeding three months" and "for the best wages that can be procured," the money to be "for the use of any of the vagrant or his family." If any people so employed should run away "without sufficient cause," the act authorized law enforcement officers to return runaways to their employers, for whom they would work for free for an extra month wearing a ball and chain. If the employer refused to take them back the law required them to work on the public roads or other projects, also for free and also wearing a ball and chain. Absent any suitable public projects, unemployed and homeless men were to be confined to jail and fed bread and water only. None of the state's previous vagrancy laws had authorized officials to hobble people with a ball and chain. The new law treated vagrants—specifically those who had fled forced labor and been recaptured—like convicted felons. The way in which the law authorized white men to hire out mostly Black people to private employers almost certainly reminded freed people and others of slavery days, when counties and cities could require free Black men and women who owed back taxes to be hired out as if they were enslaved or even to be reenslaved.[77]

Because employers could set prevailing wages so low that people could not subsist on them, workers would therefore become wage slaves. Ten days after the assembly passed the vagrancy act, the army's commanding officer in Virginia issued an order to prohibit its enforcement. General Alfred H. Terry damned the law in an overstatement as reducing freed people "to a condition of servitude worse than that from which they have been emancipated—a condition which will be slavery in all but its name." Nevertheless, the law remained in force with some modifications until the end of the nineteenth century.[78]

On 9 January 1867, both houses of the General Assembly by large margins and with indignant language refused to ratify the proposed Fourteenth Amendment to the Constitution of the United States.[79] The new radical Republican majority in Congress had decided to put a stop to the processes by which former Confederates in Virginia and elsewhere sought to reconstruct the United States and their states on their own terms and with as little change as possible.[80] As an important part of those Republicans' reform agenda, they submitted the Fourteenth Amendment to the states for ratification in the summer of 1866. It declared that all persons born or naturalized in the United States were thereby citizens of the nation and of the state where they resided. It prohibited states from abridging the "privileges and immunities of citizens of the United States; nor shall any State deprive any person of life, liberty, or property, without due process of law; nor deny to any person within its jurisdiction the equal protection of the laws." If any state denied any part of its adult male citizens the right to vote, the amendment empowered Congress to reduce the state's representation in Congress proportionately. It declared all public debts incurred in support of the rebellion void and authorized Congress to enforce all parts of the amendment "by appropriate legislation." Because Congress later required each of the states of the former Confederacy to ratify the amendment prior to admitting senators and representatives to their seats in Congress, the refusal of the General Assembly to ratify the amendment early in 1867 prolonged the period during which Virginians were unrepresented in Congress.

First Military District

What at the time was often incorrectly called "military rule" or "military government" in Virginia lasted from the spring of 1867 to January 1870, almost half the total life of the Constitution of 1864. The phrases erroneously suggested to ill-informed citizens or to careless historians that the United States Army ran the government or actually was the government.

The Act to Provide for the More Efficient Government of the Rebel States, sometimes referred to as the First Reconstruction Act, which Congress passed over the president's veto on 2 March 1867, created military districts throughout the states of the former Confederacy and authorized the commanding general of each to supervise the actions of state and local government officials. The law declared Virginia to be the First Military District.[81] The generals and their subordinate military officers did what they could—which was sometimes not nearly enough—to protect the rights of the newly freed people. From time to time, the generals dismissed some state or local officials and appointed successors, but in Virginia and elsewhere, state constitutions and state laws remained in force, and public officials in those states remained in office and acted under the authority of, and in accord with, their states' constitutions and laws when possible.[82] Agents of the army's Bureau of Refugees, Freedmen, and Abandoned Lands possessed the authority and sometimes acted to remove legal disputes from local or state courts to bureau tribunals to protect the safety of vulnerable freed people or to adjudicate disputes about labor contracts between freed people and their employers, neither of whom had much or any prior experience living and working in a free labor market.[83]

The Supreme Court of the United States, in the 1868 case *Texas v. White*, declared that the unprecedented federal supervision of state governments was clearly constitutional. In the majority opinion of Chief Justice Salmon P. Chase, he fully vindicated the authority of the president as commander in chief of the armed forces to employ the army to suppress the rebellion and later, under acts of Congress, to oversee the governments in what the law of 2 March 1867 described as "the Rebel States," as if the rebellion were not yet fully quashed. Congress, Chase explained, properly exercised its authority to provide oversight for civil government in the states in which government officials had formerly waged treasonous war against the United States. Chase and the other justices of the Supreme Court did not distinguish Virginia, Louisiana, and Arkansas from the other states of the former Confederacy, even though their governments then functioned under constitutions that loyal men wrote during the war for governments then under the protection of the United States Army.

Chase further asserted that secession was not constitutional because "The Constitution, in all its provisions, looks to an indestructible Union composed of indestructible States." Therefore, none of the states that had tried to secede had ever been out of the United States as Confederates had maintained. The governments of those states had merely been out of their proper relationship to the United States government while some of their residents and public officials acted unconstitutionally and made war against the United States. The federal government had the responsibility, Chase went on, under Article IV, Section 4, of the Constitution of the United States and in keeping with the Supreme Court's 1849 ruling in *Luther v. Borden*,[84] to secure to the people of every state a republican form of government. Because those states were in an anomalous condition as a result of what happened during and immediately after the war, temporary federal supervision of government in those states was therefore constitutionally acceptable. That did not destroy the states or the state governments any more than ordinances of secession had destroyed the United States; but until the governments of the states of the former Confederacy and their officials functioned in a constitutional manner, the federal government had a constitutional responsibility to the residents of those states to provide proper civil governments. Hence, regardless of whether state and local officials were duly elected according to state laws or had been appointed under the authority of acts of Congress, they were to be regarded as lawful provisional governments and provisional officials until such time as Congress decided individually that each state was fully eligible to be restored to its proper relationship to the other states—that is, entitled to representation in both houses of Congress and no longer requiring federal oversight.[85]

Before the Supreme Court of the United States ruled in *Texas v. White*, the Virginia Supreme Court of Appeals issued a ruling that was entirely compatible with it. Governor Pierpont, with the approval of the commanding general, continued to act as provisional governor after the term to which he was elected in 1863 expired at the end of December 1867. One of Pierpont's first official actions after that date produced a lawsuit that tested the legality of his continuing to act after the expiration of his elective term. Pierpont pardoned James L. Lawhorne, who had been convicted of a crime, but the jailer refused to release him on the grounds that a private citizen named Pierpont had no authority to issue a lawful pardon. Lawhorne petitioned the Supreme Court of Appeals for a writ of habeas corpus as the state's constitutions had allowed since 1851.[86] In *Ex Parte Lawhorne* on 13 January 1868, the state's judges accepted without question the lawful authority of the president and general to recognize Pierpont as provisional governor after 1 January 1868 and for him to continue to exercise all the lawful authority of the governor's office as provisional governor by military appointment. The most important thing here is that none of the judges thought it necessary even to pause to question or affirm the authority or legality of the so-called First Reconstruction Act or of the Constitution of 1864. They implicitly accepted the lawful authority of both.[87]

Another case arose after the commanding general, under orders to replace all former Confederates and men who had held office under the Confederacy, dismissed the three judges of the Virginia Supreme Court of Appeals in June 1869 and appointed three men who all were or had been lawyers in the United States Army. Then and thereafter, lawyers, judges, politicians, journalists, and historians almost always wrongly referred to the court during the brief terms of those judges as the Military Court of Appeals, as if it were a species of court-martial improperly imposed on the civilian people of Virginia. Peachy R. Grattan, the court's official reporter, was partly or solely responsible for that disparaging and wholly incorrect characterization. In the nineteenth volume of the decisions of the Supreme Court of Appeals that Grattan published, he segregated the decisions of those judges from the decisions of their predecessors and successors and distinguished the court on every page with the running head "MILITARY COURT OF APPEALS" in place of the standard and correct "COURT OF APPEALS OF VIRGINIA" that he printed on every other page.[88]

The elected members of the General Assembly and the judges of the Supreme Court of Appeals appointed under the Constitution of 1869 both fully recognized the lawful authority of that court. In November 1870, the judges decided a case concerning the date on which the authority of the judges that the general had appointed ended—on 26 January 1870, when the act of Congress in effect terminated the authority of the general; on 25 February, when the judges concluded a session begun early in January; or when their successors qualified under provisions of the Constitution of 1869, which the 5 March 1870 law commonly known as the Enabling Act specified.[89] The General Assembly had by then removed the president of the court from office because he still held his commission in the army, which Article IV, Section 26, of the then new Constitution of 1869 prohibited.[90]

Section 2 of the Enabling Act declared, "All official acts heretofore done by any such officers" both state and local, both executive and judicial, "and otherwise lawful, are hereby declared as legal and binding as if they had been done by officers duly elected and qualified under the constitution of this state."[91] That clearly made rulings of the three judges of the Supreme Court of Appeals valid and final; but Section 2 contained an exception that allowed parties to suits that the two remaining judges of the court had decided between 26 January and 25 February to petition the new five-member Supreme Court of Appeals to rehear their cases. The new judges ruled by a vote of 3 to 2 in the combined cases *Griffin's Executor v. Cunningham* and *Washington, Alexandria & Georgetown R.R. Co. v. Alexandria & Washington R.R. Co., et al.* that the portion of the Enabling Act that authorized the court to rehear the cases was not a proper legislative act. The court ruled that it was an unconstitutional judicial act that violated the requirement for separation of powers that had been in every state constitution since 1776. What is most important here is that the Enabling Act confirmed the lawful finality of court judgements prior to 26 January 1870. Neither of the two judges who wrote the separate opinions in November 1870 that declared a portion of the act unconstitutional, nor either of the two who separately dissented, even questioned the legality or competence of the military appointees of the court, of the legality of their appointments, or the full legal authority of their decisions; nor did the fifth judge who then voted with the majority and who, in March 1871, wrote an opinion to deny a motion for a rehearing of the case.[92] They all thereby joined the members of the General Assembly in fully accepting the lawful authority of all federal appointees under the congressional act of 2 March 1867.

The Future

Virginia was a very different state after the Civil War than before. The abolition of slavery changed almost all social, economic, and political relationships between white people and Black people, between people who owned property and people who did not, and between people who worked for themselves and people who worked for others. Virginia became a smaller and less-populous state. With the loss of about three-eighths of its land area to West Virginia, it was no longer so large a state or in any way an Ohio Valley state. With the loss to West Virginia of a large part of Virginia's white population and a small part of its Black population, Virginia was also a blacker state after the Civil War. At the time of the 1860 census, Virginia's population was 34.4 percent Black; in 1870 it was 41.9 percent Black.[93] Together, those changes made Virginia less of a border or mid-Atlantic state than it had formerly been and more of a Southern state. Those changes had large implications for Virginia's political and constitutional future as well as its economic and social future.

The second half of the 1860s, when the Constitution of 1864 was in effect, was as dramatic and important politically as the first half had been militarily. Much of that drama is properly part of the history of the Convention of 1867–68 and the constitution that it produced. Some of the drama had origins in acts of Congress, but most of it was in the profound transformations Virginia had undergone since 1860.

CHAPTER 6

The Constitution of 1869

Virginia's first post–Civil War constitution has been known by several names. In common parlance since the final decades of the nineteenth century and in much of the state's historical literature it was and has been called by the informal name the Underwood Constitution, after federal judge John C. Underwood, the radical Republican president of the convention (also sometimes called the Underwood Convention) that wrote it. It has been called the Constitution of 1868 because the Convention of 1867–68 adopted it on 17 April 1868 and planned to submit it to the voters for ratification that June. The records of the convention in the state's archives at the Library of Virginia identify the authenticated enrolled constitution by the date that it bears as the Constitution of 1868.[1] It has also been referred to as the Constitution of 1869 because voters finally ratified it on 6 July 1869, and the General Assembly elected at the same time first met under its authority in October 1869. In legal scholarship and most twentieth- and twenty-first-century reference works it has been referred to without any reasons adduced as the Constitution of 1870, probably following Armistead R. Long's 1901 book, *The Constitution of Virginia: An Annotated Edition*, in which he incorrectly stated without citing any evidence or reason why he believed that "government went into operation under the new Constitution on the 26th of January, 1870."[2]

Federal oversight of the state government effectively ended in Virginia on that date when the president signed an act of Congress that approved the ratified constitution and allowed the seating of senators and representatives elected from Virginia. Even though the law clearly referred to the October 1869 actions of the General Assembly "elected under said constitution,"[3] the law left an incorrect impression that the constitution first went into effect or finally became fully effective on 26 January 1870. The act of Congress did not specify a date on which the constitution should take effect, nor did any proclamation by the governor, nor any declaration of the commanding general of the First Military District, nor the 5 March 1870 act of General Assembly. The 5 March 1870 act was commonly referred to then as the Enabling Act which established dates by which some of the officials that were elected or appointed to office under the old constitution or by the general vacated their offices.[4]

Ratification of the constitution by popular referendum on 6 July 1869 without a specified date for it to supersede the Constitution of 1864 might be understood as being immediately self-activating and not requiring any other action to put it into full effect. Officials of the legislative, executive, and judicial branches of the state government as well as county and city officers evidently began governing under and in accordance with the new constitution at different times, introducing it incrementally beginning in the summer of 1869 rather than all at once. The ratification date of 6 July 1869, the election of statewide officers and members of the General Assembly on that same day, and the first meeting and actions of the assembly in October of that year argue strongly for identifying it as the Constitution of 1869.

Constructing a New Virginia

For Black Virginians, most of whom had recently been enslaved, the second half of the 1860s appeared to usher in the best times that they could have ever imagined. For supporters of the former Confederacy and many other white Virginians, those years seemed to portend the worst times that they had ever feared. Virginians in the 1860s who thought they had everything before them in their spring of hope differed radically in their thinking from Virginians who feared in their winter of despair that they had nothing before them.

The abolition of slavery in Virginia changed the status of every person with African ancestry, even if some or most of a person's ancestry was also European or First Nations. That included many Virginians whom the laws had formerly identified as "free persons of color." They were all then free, but the abolition of slavery did not indicate what their new status would be. It is likely that many of the state's white people, especially those who had formerly owned Black people, assumed or hoped that after April 1865 those Black people would become what "free persons of color" had formerly been: entitled to some rights as human beings but not to all the valuable rights of citizenship that white Virginia men had possessed or incrementally acquired since the first immigration of Englishmen in 1607.

Most Black Virginians in the new environment eagerly seized opportunities for themselves and their families. Even before the Civil War ended, some Black men began organizing to take part in politics. The quickness with which they organized and the insistence with which they demanded what they believed were all their rights as free American citizens undoubtedly astonished and frightened many white Virginians.

In February 1865, when loyal white residents of Norfolk proposed to replace the local military authority with civilian municipal government, Black men insisted that the president and the commanding officer of the United States Army in the district permit civilian government only on a "loyal and equal basis."[5] On 4 April 1865—the day after the liberating/occupying United States Army entered Richmond and the authority of the Constitution of 1851 began quickly to erode away to nothing—members of the Colored Monitor Union Club met in Norfolk. They insisted on all the rights of citizenship, including "the right *of universal* suffrage to *all* loyal men, without distinction of color" and voted "to memorialize the Congress of the United States to allow the *colored* citizens the *equal* right of franchise with other citizens."[6] The men met again later in April, and in May, more than a thousand of them attempted to vote but without success.[7]

Members of the Colored Monitor Union Club reassembled again on 5 June and adopted a long "Address From the Colored Citizens of Norfolk, Va., to the People of the United States." They claimed citizenship without reserve in the address and in the pamphlet that they had printed that autumn with an account of the formation of the club and the attempt of the men to vote in May. The long and impassioned address to their *Fellow Citizens* began, "We do not come before the people of the United States asking an impossibility; we simply ask that a Christian and enlightened people shall, at once, concede to us the full enjoyment of those privileges of full citizenship, which, not only, are our undoubted right, but are indispensable to that elevation and prosperity of our people, which must be the desire of every patriot."[8]

In the spring and summer of 1865, Black men also founded political organizations in Williamsburg, Richmond, Hampton, and perhaps in other Virginia cities and insisted that the state and federal governments protect their new rights as free citizens.[9] In Richmond early in June, for instance, a very large public meeting drew up a long resolution and appended to it evidence of abuse Blacks had suffered since April, some of it at the hands of United States Army officers and soldiers. The meeting appointed a committee to present the address and complaints to the president of the United States. He received the men politely in Washington but did little or nothing to ameliorate their situation.[10]

The few well-documented local political organizations of Black men were certainly not the only political groups freed people founded during the weeks and months after the end of slavery. Otherwise, it would have been difficult or impossible for them to organize and convene more than sixty men from throughout Virginia in the Colored State Convention in Alexandria early in August. It was the first statewide convention of Black Virginians ever. "We claim, then, as citizens of this State," one of their several declarations insisted, that "the laws of the Commonwealth shall give to all men equal protection; that each and every man may appeal to the law for his equal rights without regard to the color of his skin; and we believe this can only be done by extending to us the elective franchise, which we believe to be our inalienable right as freemen.... We claim the right of suffrage."[11]

The wordings of Black Virginians' demands for the right to vote immediately after the Civil War were almost eerily reminiscent of the words that were used in the plea some white Virginia men made to the Constitutional Convention in the autumn of 1829 in support of universal white manhood suffrage. "Experience has but too clearly evinced," their petition had begun, "what, indeed, reason had always foretold, by how frail a tenure they hold every other right, who are denied this, the highest prerogative of freemen."[12] Those beliefs about the suffrage as the foundational basis of citizenship appealed strongly to men of all races throughout the country and throughout the century, including enslaved and recently enslaved men.

If the demands of the Colored State Convention for the suffrage were not enough to give backward-looking white Virginians reasons to worry, some forward-looking white Virginians endorsed the call for Black men to be enfranchised. Some of those men were native Virginians who had remained loyal to the United States during the war. Backward-looking men called them by the insulting name scalawags. Other forward-looking white men from outside Virginia had settled in cities of the Restored Government before the end of the war and sought their postwar futures in Virginia. Backward-looking men called them by the insulting name carpetbaggers. The forward-looking white men embraced to greater or lesser degrees the opportunity that the end of slavery offered to replace Virginia's old hierarchical white political culture with a new politics compatible with radical Republican thinking and incorporating freed people into the new democratic system. Those loyal white Virginians joined the Union Party (the old Republican Party) during the Civil War.

After the war, many of them joined the radical wing of the new Republican Party of Virginia.[13]

Radical white Republicans were alarmed at the ease with which supporters of the former Confederacy won endorsements from Governor Francis H. Pierpont and pardons from President Andrew Johnson.[14] The pardons allowed former Confederates to return to politics in 1865 and in effect put back in authority many of the political leaders of Virginia who had governed the slave state of Virginia before the Civil War and the Confederate state of Virginia during the war.[15] Radical white Republicans understood that they would remain a permanent minority party if they did not enfranchise Black men and make a political alliance with them.[16] The white men formed the Virginia Union Association late in June 1865 to "secure the elective franchise to our colored population, as soon as it can be safely done."[17]

The prospect of Black men voting worried most supporters of the former Confederacy as well as some good Union men and moderate Republicans. Among them was Pierpont, who had serious doubts about the wisdom of what radical Republicans proposed, especially granting the vote to freed people, most of whom could not read.[18] On that issue and many others during the second half of the 1860s, politically alert white Virginians differed among themselves on some very important matters of public policy that had serious implications for the state's constitutional future. Backward-looking men and moderate Republicans became more alarmed and more insistent after Congress imposed military supervision on the government of Virginia and nine other states of the former Confederacy. It began with the Act to Provide for the More Efficient Government of the Rebel States, sometimes referred to as the First Reconstruction Act, which Congress passed over the president's veto on 2 March 1867. The act created military districts throughout the former Confederacy and authorized the commanding general of each district to supervise the actions of state and local government officials. The law designated Virginia as the First Military District.[19]

White Virginians who opposed the reforms that the radicals in Congress advocated differed among themselves about how much of the reforms traditional Virginia political leaders could or should tolerate in the new Virginia. Adamant opponents of the proposed changes founded the Conservative Party of Virginia at the end of 1867. Its leadership and membership indicated that a large number of experienced and able white Virginia political leaders were eager to maintain control of the political process and government for themselves and to exclude from public office, and if possible from the suffrage, all radical reformers—especially Black ones.[20]

Electing Delegates

Leaders and supporters of the Conservative Party had good reasons to be fearful. Congress required ten of the states of the former Confederacy to adopt new constitutions, even Virginia, which was then functioning under the constitution loyal men had written in Alexandria in 1864. Congress ordered the army to conduct elections for constitutional convention delegates and directed the commanding generals to allow Black men to vote and be eligible to be elected and to serve in the conventions.[21]

During the registration of voters that army officers conducted prior to the election, 105,832 Black Viriginians registered, not far short of the 120,101 white men who registered.[22] Many white men who opposed what Congress proposed decided not to register, and others, because of their Confederate pasts, were legally unable to register and vote.

On 22 October 1867, Black Virginians voted for the very first time and had their votes counted and reported, albeit the army officers at each of the polls required voters to deposit their ballots in separate boxes for Black and white voters and recorded votes of Black men and white men on separate tally sheets. Voters cast ballots rather than voted orally as the amended Constitution of 1864 then required because the election took place under the authority of acts of Congress and not of the constitution or laws of Virginia. Voters cast two ballots that day: on the question whether to hold the convention and for candidates who wished to serve in the convention if the voters authorized it. Having voters approve the convention (as voters had approved proposals for constitutional conventions in 1829 and 1850 and to amend the Constitution of 1864)[23] gave the convention a legitimacy based on the votes of Virginians in addition to the authority of the acts of Congress.

A significant number of registered white voters refused to take part, and Black men actually cast more votes than white men. The vote broke sharply along racial lines, with 92,507 Black voters providing a large portion of the 107,342 votes for holding the convention and white voters casting all but 638 of the 61,887 votes against. Moreover, almost all Black men voted for candidates who favored radical reforms, and most white voters opposed those candidates.[24]

Men who supported radical reforms won a majority of seats in the convention. Among them were twenty-four Black Virginians, about half of whom had lived in slavery until the spring of 1865. The voluminous though incomplete records of the 1867 election in the Library of Virginia include numerous poll lists indicating who voted for whom as well as original ballots from a large number of polling places in a large number of cities and counties.[25]

Only one of the 104 men who attended the convention had ever been a delegate to a Virginia constitutional convention. John Hawxhurst, who represented the city of Alexandria, had represented Fairfax County in the Convention of 1864. White Virginia men with significant prior political experience were poorly represented because many of them had not registered to vote or sought election to the convention. White Virginia men with more-or-less radical views included some who were very well-known because of their prewar antislavery work, their wartime loyalty to the United States, or their postwar involvement in radical Republican politics. The two most famous were John C. Underwood and James W. Hunnicutt. Underwood was then the judge of the federal court for the district of Virginia. A native of New York and active abolitionist, he had moved to Virginia early in the 1850s but had to flee the state before the Civil War because of his antislavery actions. He had returned to Virginia before the war ended and become a champion of the civil and political rights of Black men. Although a resident of Alexandria in 1867, he won election as a delegate from Richmond largely because of his popularity among Black men in the capital city.[26] Hunnicutt, originally from upcountry South Carolina, had attended Randolph-Macon College in Virginia and become a Methodist minister. He had antagonized traditional white Virginians for years because he was loyal to the United States during the Civil War and became a supporter of Black people's rights afterward. At the time of the convention, he was editor of the radical Republicans' Richmond newspaper, aptly titled *The New Nation*.[27]

The delegates were the most diverse by occupation, background, class, and race of any Virginia convention before or since. The members included a dozen natives of New York, four natives of Great Britain, one of Canada, and half a dozen or more natives of other states, an unprecedented number and percentage of delegates who had not been born in Virginia. Notes on each of the delegates that Major General John McAllister Schofield compiled about the delegates were very brief and not in every instance accurate. He described some delegates misleadingly as "Adventurers," as if they had moved to Virginia in stereotypical carpetbagger fashion to take personal economic advantage of the postwar circumstances.

Schofield counted nearly two dozen lawyers, eight physicians or dentists, six clergymen, and two newspaper editors. At least seven men had served in the United States Army or Navy during the Civil War, and three others had held federal government offices. Five were or had been county sheriffs, clerks of court, or magistrates, and three were schoolteachers. Seven delegates engaged in commerce in one fashion or another, and one operated a distillery.

Artisans and manual laborers included four shoemakers, one stonemason, a tailor, and three men Schofield identified as laborers and two as mechanics. He labeled nineteen men as farmers, but that definition was very vague. Some recently freed men worked the land but did not own their own farms. Among the farmers, Schofield listed Luther Lee, a former captain in the 20th New York Cavalry who during the war was stationed in Norfolk County "where he married a widow with a farm." Somewhat typical of Schofield's notes on radical delegates was a dismissive appraisal of Richmond delegate James Morrissey, "an Irishman, who keeps a whiskey shop in the city frequented principally by negroes. *Radical.*"[28]

The Convention of 1867–68

The convention met in the chamber of the House of Delegates in the state Capitol from 3 December 1867 through 17 April 1868. Radical members elected Underwood as president by a vote of 64 to 33 over Norvell Wilson.[29] The delegates' voting records on critical issues indicate that the margin of Underwood's victory is a good indication of the relative strength of the radical delegates in the convention.

Black men and women crowded into the galleries in the Capitol day after day to watch the first African American officeholders in the state's history participate in writing a new constitution.[30] The twenty-four Black delegates were the first and almost the only Black Virginians ever to take part in writing a constitution for Virginia. A century later, Richmond civil rights attorney Oliver W. Hill was a member of an advisory commission that the governor appointed in 1968 to suggest changes to the Constitution of 1902;[31] and William Ferguson Reid, a Richmond-area dentist, was a member of the House of Delegates in the 1969 and 1970 sessions that prepared a revised constitution that voters ratified.[32] Several Black legislators who served in the General Assembly in the 1870s and 1880s and after Reid in the twentieth and twenty-first centuries took part in proposing constitutional amendments, but the twenty-four Black members of the Convention of 1867–68, Hill, and Reid are the only Black people who have ever had a role in writing a constitution for Virginia.

About half the African American delegates had been enslaved as recently as two and a half years earlier. Four or five had escaped slavery and gained better educations in the North than they could have obtained in Virginia. Schofield noted that fifteen of the twenty-four delegates were not literate,[33] but in the instances of at least of six of them, he was demonstrably incorrect.[34]

Curious journalists focused their attentions on those two dozen men. Newspapers included numerous reports of the convention's work, but many of the articles that white men wrote included so many derisive comments that it is not possible to know in some instances what parts of what they printed about Black delegates or white radicals were accurate. White journalists lampooned some of the active Black delegates with crude language and unflattering line drawings. Racist writers for the Richmond newspaper *Southern Opinion* were especially nasty.[35] Most of the Black delegates engaged in the debates only rarely, leaving them vulnerable to charges that they were ignorant and did not know what they were doing. Sometimes, though, even when belittling those delegates, journalists inadvertently disclosed that they did know what they were doing. About David Canada, of Halifax County, a writer for the *Southern Opinion* described him sitting silently like a sphynx as if oblivious to what was going on around him. Canada "never speaks," the reporter concluded, "though his nod is radical," which indicated that Canada knew the nature and importance of the subjects being discussed and on which he voted.[36]

Richmond's other daily newspapers also treated the convention contemptuously. Ten days after the Constitutional Convention first met, the city hosted the founding meeting of the Conservative Party of Virginia to make certain that Virginia "is, and ever shall be, *a white man's government.*"[37] The editor of the Richmond *Daily Examiner and Inquirer* contrasted the two conventions. "A Convention will organize in this city to-day," he explained, "having for its object the preservation of that magnificent fabric of Caucasian civilization which for two centuries has kept Virginia in the front rank of modern States." On the next day, the editor resumed: "The silent contempt with which eight hundred Virginia gentlemen treated the vile rabble called a 'Constitutional Convention,' which is performing in the Capitol, was especially worthy of commendation."[38] The word *performing* suggested a circus or freak show. The editor of the Richmond *Daily Dispatch* was scarcely less rude.[39]

The political bias in the journalistic reports of the convention is only one of the reasons why the work of the convention is inadequately documented, though the convention probably could be evaluated more thoroughly than it has been. William H. Samuel published the convention's journal and a volume of its committee reports, working papers, resolutions and amendments, and other documents and data that the convention compiled.[40] He charged the convention more than most delegates were willing to pay for printing and stopped publishing a record of the debates as of 29 January 1868. The 750-page volume recording the debates through that date leaves much of the delegates' discussions unreported.[41] The Richmond *Enquirer and Daily Examiner* and the Richmond *Daily Dispatch* reported on the debates selectively, usually in a racist and partisan manner, and did not reproduce speeches verbatim.

The convention met in the second half of the 1860s after the Civil War had generated fresh thinking about freedom and slavery, the purposes of the union of states, and the nature of representative democracy. The immense steps that the conventions in Virginia and the other states of the former Confederacy took during those years embodied the most important transformations that that people of those states had ever experienced in so short a time.[42] How far could change go? If formerly enslaved Black men, who had become citizens according to the Civil Rights Act of 1866[43] and the Fourteenth Amendment, could suddenly be empowered to vote, why not women? Some women insisted that the words of the Fourteenth Amendment applied to them and made them citizens as well. Advocates of woman suffrage increased their energetic campaign for the vote.[44]

Anna Whitehead Bodeker was one of them. On 6 May 1870 she became the founding president of the Virginia State Woman Suffrage Association. Among its members were John C. Underwood and his wife. The association eventually collapsed for want of enough supporters, but in November 1871, Bodeker went to a polling place in Richmond to vote. When denied the right to place her ballot in the box, she placed in it instead a note that declared that according to the Fourteenth Amendment she was an American citizen and therefore had a constitutional right to vote.[45]

What has that to do with the Convention of 1867–68? Two things. First, it illustrates the truly revolutionary nature of some of the proposals that people made during the volatile 1860s. Nobody had previously organized an association for promoting woman suffrage in Virginia. And second, Judge Underwood, who joined Bodeker's association in 1870, actually proposed votes for "our female citizens" in an unusual 16 January 1868 speech from the floor of the convention when he was its president. He acknowledged that "such is the prejudice of our people, and so little are we yet advanced beyond that savage state of society which makes conscientious and heaven-inspired woman the drudge or toy of her stronger and coarser companion, that I despair at this time of securing so desirable a progress."[46] No member put Underwood's recommendation into a formal motion, but that was the first time so far as is known that any public official in Virginia proposed to enfranchise women.

The formal journal and the published record of Underwood's speech do not indicate how Black women in the gallery reacted to his proposal. They had often attended meetings when men discussed politics, and they sometimes made their opinions known. They had been conspicuously present in the gallery at the First African Baptist Church in Richmond when the 1867 Republican Party state convention met there and loudly let their opinions of the proceedings be heard. Votes for women had even been a topic of discussion in some local meetings. Even without the vote, women wielded political influence through suasion in their families just as white women had since the 1840s or earlier.[47]

None of the state's previous constitutions had mentioned women at all. Delegates to the Convention of 1867–68 also left women out of the constitution that they wrote and almost entirely out of their discussions about the legal and political rights of men. Insofar as extant records show, they did not seriously consider an important reform some other states had already made or were then making in the aftermath of the war, to bestow on women full rights to acquire, own, and dispose of real estate.[48] Virginia statutes and court precedents preserved the essence of English common law that required that when women married or remarried all their property thereby became the property of their husbands.[49] In the tough times after the Civil War, some governments in states of the former Confederacy reversed that old rule and granted women full rights to own and control property however obtained, joining other states that did so even before the war. As a delegate to the South Carolina Constitutional Convention declared, even while the Virginia convention was in session, unscrupulous men had already appropriated to themselves or squandered the property that families had intended for the benefit of their children. He charged that those fortune hunters intended to "marry a plantation and take the woman as an incumbrance."[50]

In Virginia, though, convention delegates declined to make or even seriously consider such an important modification in legal practices, gender relations, or family law that had obtained in Virginia from the beginning of English settlement. Not until 1877 did the General Assembly adopt a married women's property act. Virginia was the last of the then existing states to allow women equal rights with men in the ownership of real property.[51]

That Underwood proposed votes for women is a good indication of how much the desire for radical changes animated some members of the convention even if they declined to consider making any changes about the rights of women while they made major changes about the rights of men. The radicals were determined to destroy the hierarchical white political culture that had created slavery and betrayed the nation during the Civil War. That culture was already endangered. Economic, demographic, and political changes underway since the American Revolution and the democratic reforms embodied in the Constitution of 1851 had undermined but not destroyed the state's old politics.[52] As white opponents of fundamental change feared, the Convention of 1867–68 very nearly did destroy it.

The Constitution of 1869

The constitution that the biracial convention created between December 1867 and April 1868 was in several respects an even more radical reform document than the Constitution of 1851, which had instituted universal white manhood suffrage and for the first time allowed voters to elect most public officials, including judges. The Convention of 1867–68 included in the new constitution some standard provisions from the Constitution of 1864 and its predecessors, but it modified some, radically rewrote others, deleted still others, and added very important new provisions. The delegates amended the Declaration of Rights and for the first time inserted it into the body of the constitution as Article I with the title of Bill of Rights that the Convention of 1864 had given it. The delegates also reversed the sequence of the articles on the executive and the General Assembly.

The unamended constitution was the longest Virginia constitution yet written, about 13,175 words, approximately a one-fourth longer than the Constitution of 1851 and one-third longer than the Constitution of 1864. The official authenticated enrolled constitution is in the archives at the Library of Virginia. Its twenty-nine sheets (leaves five and six in reverse sequence) are ceremoniously tied together with multi-colored tape, some of it red. It is a beautiful example of elegant penmanship, but it contains erasures, corrections, numerous misspellings of county names, inconsistencies of capitalization and punctuation, and several scribal errors. The clerk who inscribed it omitted some words, and he or the convention's printer erroneously transposed words in Article VIII, Section 5, which authorized the General Assembly to establish "such agricultural schools and grades of schools" (as in the manuscript) or "such grades of schools and agricultural schools" (as in the printed text) "as shall be for the public good." The text of the constitution as the convention had it printed in the spring of 1868 is more accurate in some but not all respects than the imperfect enrolled parchment, which for all its many minor errors is nevertheless the official text of record.[53]

PREAMBLE

The delegates retained the cumulative preamble of the Constitution of 1864 which recited the authorities under which the Conventions of 1776, 1829–30, 1850–51, and 1864 had written new constitutions for Virginia, and they added to it a short paragraph reciting their own authority under the 2 March 1867 act of Congress and the referendum in July of that year.

THE BILL OF RIGHTS

As western Virginians had done for the Kentucky Constitution of 1792 and northwestern Virginians had done for the West Virginia Constitution of 1863, members of the Convention of 1867–68 incorporated the Declaration, or Bill, of Rights into the body of the Constitution of Virginia for the first time as Article I. Delegates removed requirements added to Sections 8 and 11 in 1851 that juries in civil and criminal trials must consist of twelve members and no other number. To Section 14 on freedom of the press they added a freedom of speech provision, that "any citizen may speak, write and publish his sentiments on all subjects, being responsible for the abuse of that liberty." The insertion preserved the General Assembly's authority to enact laws to allow people to sue if they believed themselves victims of slander or libel, which was consistent with centuries of English and American law.

The other additions to the Bill of Rights were the most important changes made to the document since the Convention of 1776 adopted the first such declaration in American history. Delegates added a new Section 2 that condemned secession and the Confederacy. It declared, "That this State shall ever remain a member of the United States of America, and that the people thereof are part of the American Nation, and that all attempts, from whatever sources or upon whatever pretext, to dissolve said Union or to sever said nation, are unauthorized and ought to be resisted with the whole power of the State." The new Section 3 resembled a provision in the West Virginia Constitution of 1863 and the Virginia Constitution of 1864 and read, "That the Constitution of the United States, and the laws of Congress passed in pursuance thereof, constitute the supreme law of the land, to which paramount allegiance and obedience are due from every citizen, anything in the constitution, ordinances or laws of any State to the contrary notwithstanding." Those sections were definitely, and perhaps intentionally, insulting to supporters of the former Confederacy who had regarded themselves as Virginia patriots who had sought to restore the Union that the founders had created with the sword during the American Revolution and with the pen by the adoption of the Constitution of the United States.[54]

Delegates rewrote and transferred the prohibitions on slavery from Article IV, Sections 19 and 21, in the body of the Constitution of 1864 to a new Section 19 of the Bill of Rights: "That neither slavery nor involuntary servitude, except as lawful imprisonment may constitute such, shall exist within this State." They added a very important new Section 20, "That all citizens of the State are hereby declared to possess equal civil and political rights and public privileges." And a new Section 21 paraphrased the Ninth Amendment to the Constitution of the United States to declare "That rights enumerated in this bill of Rights shall not be construed to limit other rights of the people not herein expressed. The declaration of the political rights and privileges of the inhabitants of this State is hereby declared to be a part of the Constitution of this Commonwealth, and shall not be violated on any pretence whatever."

SEPARATION OF POWERS

The new constitution's brief Article II reiterated the requirement for separation or "Division of Powers" that was in all the state's previous constitutions. It replaced the old exception that justices of the peace could serve in the General Assembly with, "nor shall any person exercise the power of more than one of them at the same time, except as hereinafter provided."

SUFFRAGE

The new Article III, Section 1, enfranchised "Every male citizen of the United States, twenty-one years old, who shall have been a resident of this State twelve months, and of the county, city or town in which he shall offer to vote three months next preceding any election." It then severely limited the franchise with a very long enumeration of exceptions: "Every person who has been a senator or representative in Congress, or elector of President or Vice-President, or who held any office, civil or military under the United States, or under any State" and had "given aid or comfort to the enemies thereof." The list enumerated virtually every public office from the most exalted down to and including "Inspectors of Tobacco, Flour, &c." The section nevertheless "Provided, That the Legislature may, by a vote of three-fifths of both Houses, remove the disabilities incurred by this clause from any person included therein, by a separate vote in each case."

Section 7 also required men elected or appointed to public office to swear allegiance to the Constitutions of the United States and of Virginia and to "recognize and accept the civil and political equality of all men before the laws"—to accept the fact and finality of the abolition of slavery and the citizenship of Black Virginians—of Black Americans. Section 7 also required every person elected or appointed to any public office to swear that he had never voluntarily supported the Confederacy.

Those proscriptions on voting and holding office were capital victories for the most radical men in the convention and were much more restrictive than the provisions in the Constitution of 1864 that the constitutional amendments of 1865 and 1866 had first relaxed and then deleted. Section 2 restored voting by ballot, and Section 3, for the first time in a Virginia constitution, established a qualification for jury service and linked it to suffrage and thereby made unrepentant Confederates ineligible. Article III, in short, banned all active and most passive supporters of the Confederacy from the ballot box and public office unless they renounced or disavowed their past allegiance to the Confederacy.

The delegates revised and added to the few other restrictions on the franchise in former constitutions. The new constitution disfranchised "Idiots and lunatics" who in previous constitutions had been defined as "persons of unsound mind." People who had been "convicted of bribery in any election" had been disfranchised since the Constitution of 1830,[55] but delegates added to that limitation men who had been convicted of "embezzlement of public funds, treason or felony." And the delegates replaced the authorization in previous constitutions for the assembly to disfranchise people who participated in duels with a blanket disqualification to vote or hold office of all Virginians who participated in a duel.

Because of the restrictions on former Confederates, Article III was the source of considerable controversy from the very beginning, which delayed ratification of the new constitution for more than a year.

THE GENERAL ASSEMBLY

Article V on the General Assembly made only a few changes to Article IV in the Constitution of 1864 and retained nearly all the authorizations and limitations imposed on the assembly in the state's second, third, and fourth constitutions. The new constitution specified that the House of Delegates be composed of 138 members elected from ninety-six districts and the Senate of Virginia consist of 43 members elected from not more than forty districts. To the opening words of Section 14, which read, "The privilege of the writ of *habeas corpus* shall not in any case be suspended," the delegates added, "unless when, in cases of invasion or rebellion, the public safety may require it." Section 6 required the assembly to meet annually in sessions not to exceed ninety days (as in the Constitution of 1851,[56] which the Constitution of 1864 had reduced to sixty days[57]) without approval of three-fifths of the members of each house, then not to continue longer than thirty more days. Sections 2 and 3 retained the two-year terms for members of the House of Delegates, introduced in 1851, and four-year terms for members of the Senate, in effect since 1776, with half the senators' terms expiring every second year as the Constitution of 1851 had required and the Constitution of 1864 had permitted.

Section 4 required the assembly to redraw districts for both houses after each federal census as required in the Constitution of 1864.[58] The article omitted the prohibition on clergymen serving in the assembly, which had been in all of the state's previous constitutions and was derived from a colonial law of 1653.[59] President John C. Underwood recommended removal of that prohibition at the beginning of his long speech on 16 January 1868.[60] The delegates also omitted the prohibition on legislative service of bankers and commonwealth's attorneys that was first introduced in 1851 and for the first time allowed the lieutenant governor, when serving as president of the Senate, to vote in the event of a tie. The new Section 11 for the first time inserted into the state constitution the parliamentary privileges for legislators that had been in the Constitution of the United States since it was ratified in 1788.

The specific authorizations to the assembly to act on particular subjects in this and other articles of the new constitution did not fundamentally alter the well-recognized understanding that state legislatures inherently possessed all powers that their state constitutions did not clearly prohibit them from exercising. In fact, Thomas M. Cooley published the first edition of his influential *Treatise on the Constitutional Limitations Which Rest Upon the Legislative Power of the States of the American Union* in 1868, the very year that the convention completed work on the new Virginia constitution, and based his main thesis on that widespread understanding.[61] By including specific authorizations in the constitution, the delegates elevated their innovations to constitutional status and immunized them from judicial or legislative alteration.

THE EXECUTIVE

Article IV on the executive department retained most of the provisions concerning the governor, lieutenant governor, secretary of the commonwealth, treasurer, auditor of public accounts, and the Board of Public Works from Article V of the Constitution of 1864, which differed only a little from Article V in the Constitution of 1851, but the new article included a few important innovations. The most important was a new Section 8 which authorized governors to veto bills that the two houses of the General Assembly had passed. The two houses could override a veto by a two-thirds vote in each house with the names of senators and delegates who voted for and against published in the legislative journals. That new section for the first time gave governors a formal role in the legislative process and, together with popular election of the governor beginning in 1851, was the most important nineteenth-century change to the executive department, even more important than the abolition of the old Council of State in 1851. The veto brought the authority of Virginia's executive into line with a majority of other states that had increased the powers of their governors during the nineteenth century when they placed limitations on their legislatures.

Section 15 permitted the assembly to establish in the office of the secretary of the commonwealth "a Bureau of Statistics and a Bureau of Agricultural Chemistry and Geology." Section 16 allowed for creation of "a Bureau of Agriculture and Immigration under such regulations as may be prescribed by law," as if poor white and Black Virginians might not be adequate to the tasks of rebuilding and refashioning the state's ruined economy or to compensate for emigration or wartime deaths. And Section 17 changed the membership of the Board of Public Works from three popularly elected men from different districts in the state to the governor, auditor of public accounts, and state treasurer. Those provisions allowed the executive department under the general direction of the governor to take the lead in stimulating economic development and commerce through coordination of public works projects, acquisition and publication of scientific information about agriculture and the state's natural resources, as well as to attract immigrants with needed job skills or who would work for low pay.

As in all the state's previous constitutions, the Constitution of 1869 made the governor commander in chief of the military forces of the state. However, the new constitution defined the militia as consisting "of all able bodied male persons between the ages of eighteen and forty-five years" without reference to race, which for the first time allowed and required African American participation. The article exempted from service men "who belong to religious societies whose tenets forbid them to carry arms" if they paid for a substitute. It also required the assembly to provide "for the encouragement of volunteer corps of the several arms of the service, which shall be classed as the active militia; and all other militia shall be classified as the reserve militia, and shall not be required to muster in time of peace." Members of the volunteer militia units during the remainder of the nineteenth century were always all white.[62]

THE JUDICIARY

Article VI on the judiciary made some very important changes. It provided for a state court system that consisted of a five-member Supreme Court of Appeals, sixteen Circuit Courts with one judge each, and a County Court with one judge for each county. A new Article VII on county government created new executive and legislative structures for county governments. Together, the two articles abolished the old county court system that had been in effect since the second quarter of the seventeenth century. The new constitution restored full authority to the General Assembly to elect judges of the Circuit Courts and Supreme Court of Appeals, with no nomination by the governor being required or allowed when the assembly was in session, as under the Constitution of 1864.[63] For the first time, the constitution specified qualifications of office for judges of the Supreme Court of Appeals and of Circuit Courts who "shall, when chosen, have held a judicial station in the United States, or shall have practiced law in this or some other State for five years." It required all of them to be "learned in the laws of the State." Until that time, justices of the peace in the counties as well as aldermen or judges of hustings or corporation courts in the cities had often been laymen without formal legal training. The Constitution of 1869 very nearly completed the slow process that was under way since the American Revolution to provide Virginians with a thoroughly professional judicial system from bottom to top.

Section 2 concerning the Supreme Court of Appeals required that "the assent of a majority of the judges elected to the court"—not a mere majority of judges present—"shall be required, in order to declare any law null and void by reason of its repugnance to the Federal Constitution, or to the Constitution of this State." That was a more powerful constitutional authorization for the state's highest appellate court to exercise judicial review than in the Constitutions of 1851 or 1864.[64]

Section 3 preserved the assembly's authority to create Special Courts of Appeal to dispose of cases in which judges of the Supreme Court of Appeals had to recuse themselves as interested parties or "to try any cases on the said docket which cannot be otherwise disposed of with convenient dispatch." The court's docket had remained clogged, and the lawyers in the convention feared that antebellum problems would continue because the five judges would remain unable to decide all the cases that came before them. During the first two and a half years that the new constitution was in force, the Special Court of Appeals heard and decided more than 125 cases,[65] but that merely reduced rather than solved the basic problem. As late as 1886, the editor of the *Virginia Law Journal* was still predicting that the Special Court of Appeals would clear the remaining backlog of the Supreme Court of Appeals' docket, which he estimated would be down to about 130 cases later that year.[66] The chair of the Virginia State Bar Association's Committee on the Judiciary System of the State reported in 1897 that "the present Court of Appeals has showed so much industry in getting rid of cases on the docket that they are rapidly catching up, and I am told that they will soon be right up with their docket."[67] The judges finally cleared the docket not long before the Constitutional Convention of 1901–2 met,[68] more than thirty years after constitutional convention delegates for the third time provided for Special Courts of Appeal to do just that.

Convention members omitted the clauses that had appeared in the Constitutions of 1851 and 1864 that stipulated that when a vacancy occurred on the Supreme Court of Appeals, the replacement judge serve a full twelve-year term from the date of taking office.[69] Over time, that would have created staggered terms of service so that the terms of all five judges of the Supreme Court of Appeals would not, after their initial appointments, begin and end simultaneously.

That omission led to an interesting court case, *Burks v. Hinton*. The terms of four of the five judges of the Supreme Court of Appeals whom the General Assembly elected in 1870 expired at the end of 1882. In the meantime, the fifth judge had died, and the assembly had elected Edward Calohill Burks to fill the vacancy. In 1882, when a biracial coalition of members of the Republicans and Readjusters held majorities in both houses of the General Assembly, the legislators elected five Readjusters to replace the sitting members of the court. The new judges had to decide, immediately after they took office, a controversy that arose from the convention's decision to omit the language that would have gradually created staggered terms for members of the court. Burks believed that the language of the constitution gave him the right to serve a full twelve years from the time of his taking his seat; but Drury A. Hinton, one of the new judges elected in 1882, believed that he was entitled to Burks's seat on 1 January 1883. Hinton properly took no part in deciding the case. The other four new judges ruled 3 to 1 that the constitution's omission of provisions that required judges elected to fill vacancies to serve full terms entitled Hinton to the seat.[70]

The Readjuster judges all served their full terms. Early in 1894, eleven months before their terms expired, Democrats in the General Assembly elected five Democrats to replace them. Both in 1882 and 1894, assembly members acted exactly in accordance with the state constitution, even though, to some observers, the replacement of all judges of the state's highest court on both occasions looked like partisan interference with the independence of the judiciary.[71] Had the constitution provided for staggered judicial terms, partisanship might have had a lesser impact on the membership of the Supreme Court of Appeals, and those interpretive misunderstandings probably would not have occurred.[72] The Constitutional Convention of 1901–2 required judicial terms to be staggered from the time of the first judges' appointments.[73]

LOCAL GOVERNMENT

Article VII on "County Organizations" was the first ever constitutional provision for government of Virginia's counties. Together with Sections 14 through 21 of Article VI, which mostly concerned courts in cities and towns, the Constitution of 1869 was the first to prescribe institutions of local government in detail. The new constitution gave county and municipal courts full equal constitutional standing for the first time. City charters, which differed in their provisions, allowed voters in some cities, or city councils in some others, to elect a mayor who could hold a mayor's court for minor offences.

Article VII created a new administrative structure for counties and, even without mentioning the old county courts, effectively abolished the courts on which since the second quarter of the seventeenth century justices of the peace had served, largely without legal training, to exercise executive and legislative powers in their counties and sit en banc as the local court of first resort. After 1869, justices of the peace, who still often had little or no formal legal education, became petty local magistrates with limited authority, and their courts were no longer courts of record.[74]

Section 2 required the assembly to divide each county into three or more townships (much as Thomas Jefferson had proposed in the 1810s[75]) and authorized voters in each annually to elect a supervisor, a township clerk, a tax assessor, a tax collector, a commissioner of roads, an overseer of the poor, and one of three constables and three justices of the peace, who served for staggered three-year terms. The section also required all the supervisors in each county to meet annually at the courthouse on the first Monday in December "and proceed to audit the accounts of said county, examine the books of the Assessors, regulate and equalize the valuation of property, fix the county levies for the ensuing year, apportion the same among the various townships, and perform such other duties as shall be prescribed by law."

Article VII created the basic form of county government that persisted in modified form to this present writing. It greatly extended local democracy in Virginia by creating numerous township and county officials and allowing voters to elect them. It is almost certain that the extension of local democracy allowed a large number of middle- and lower-class men of both races to serve in public office for the first time. That was an equally profound political revolution as that of 1851 which for the first time allowed voters to elect some local officials.[76] Little scholarly research has been done to document how many Black men won election to local offices, but the number was probably large, as evidenced in part by how critical white supremacists later were about the effects of the Constitution of 1869.[77]

The Constitution of 1869 did not include comparable detailed specifications for the government of cities and towns. Aside from Sections 15 through 21 of Article VI concerning municipal courts, the state's fifth constitution remained almost as silent about cities and towns as the first four had been about them and counties as well.

The General Assembly continued, as in the past, to limit actions of county governments on many subjects and to authorize county governments to take specific actions in many other matters. During the final three decades of the nineteenth century, the assembly, by one count, passed at least 2,346 special local laws to enable or prohibit individual counties or groups of counties to act on particular matters. Of those laws, 527 concerned roads, 446 revenue, 366 wildlife and domestic livestock, 185 schools, 168 fences, and 158 local borrowing.[78] The structure of local government appeared to be democratic, but in action it remained severely restrained by centuries of legislative and constitutional tradition that accorded local governments very little autonomy. A tabulation of comparable special local acts of assembly that affected cities and towns would almost certainly be similar.

EDUCATION

Article VIII was entirely new. It required the General Assembly at its first session after ratification to establish a "uniform system of public free schools, and for its gradual, equal and full introduction into all the counties of the State, by the year 1876, or as much earlier as practicable." Statistics demonstrated the need for education among the people of the state. About 44 percent of all people in Virginia older than ten could not read. One of every four white Virginians older than ten, and nine of ten Black Virginians older than ten, could not write. The state then had 2,024 schools (many of them private academies) but only about seven public schools that offered education above the elementary level. Fewer than sixty thousand white people and only about eleven thousand Black people had attended any school in 1869 when the Freedmen's Bureau closed its schools.[79]

The new constitution created a new State Board of Education consisting of the governor, attorney general, and state superintendent of public instruction with authority to appoint "subject to confirmation by the Senate" a superintendent of schools for each county. Sections 7 and 8 devoted to the public schools the interest the state earned from its old Literary Fund, mostly money the state received in fines. Section 8 also authorized the assembly to levy an ad valorem property tax of "not less than one mill nor more than five mills, on the dollar" for public education and permitted county referenda to authorize additional local taxes to supplement state revenue. Section 8 also contained a provision that the state provide money "to supply children attending the public free schools with necessary text-books, in cases where the parent or guardian is unable, by reason of poverty, to furnish them." Section 12 empowered the General Assembly to "fix the salaries and prescribe the duties of all school officials" and "make all needful laws and regulations to carry into effect the public free school system."

During the convention's debate on the education article, Thomas Bayne, a Black delegate from Norfolk and a former member of the Colored Monitor Union Club there, proposed an amendment to require that schools be "free to all classes, and no child, pupil or scholar shall be ejected from said schools on account of race, color, or any invidious distinction." A majority of the delegates were white, and they defeated Bayne's motion 56 to 15.[80] Rejection of the amendment left the question of racial segregation legally unsettled, but in practical terms, it meant that unless the General Assembly directed otherwise, the schools were certain to be segregated. In 1870 when the General Assembly debated the bill to create the public schools, Black members of both houses unsuccessfully introduced amendments to prohibit racial segregation. Most of the Black members of the House of Delegates then symbolically voted against the important bill that they favored as their only means of objecting to what they regarded as an insulting discrimination arising from racial prejudice.[81]

Early in 1870, the General Assembly appointed a Presbyterian minister, William Henry Ruffner, as superintendent of public instruction. He and University of Virginia law professor John B. Minor drafted the law to implement the constitutional requirement.[82] Ruffner presided over the school system for twelve years and has been dubbed the Horace Mann of Virginia, after the famed founder of the first comprehensive public school systems in New England before the Civil War.[83]

TAXATION AND FINANCE

Article X on taxation and finance was new. It included the few provisions on those subjects from the article on the General Assembly in the Constitutions of 1851 and 1864 and several important additions. Section 1 prohibited taxation of Virginia citizens for "taking or catching oysters from their natural beds with tongs," but it allowed taxation of the sale of those oysters the same as taxation of sales of other goods or services. Section 3 allowed the assembly to exempt from taxation "property used exclusively for State, County, municipal, benevolent, charitable, educational and religious purposes." Section 4 authorized the assembly to tax "incomes in excess of six-hundred dollars ($600) per annum" and to levy taxes on the sale of a long list of enumerated items of merchandise.

Section 10 amplified the prohibition in the Constitution of 1864 on paying public debts incurred in support of the rebellion. Its language was no doubt offensive—perhaps intentionally offensive—to supporters of the former Confederacy. It stated, "no appropriation shall ever be made for the payment of any debt or obligation created in the name of the State of Virginia; by the usurped and pretended State authorities assembled at Richmond during the late war; and no county, city, or corporation shall levy or collect any tax for the payment of any debt created for the purpose of aiding any rebellion against the State, or against the United States."

Section 19 revised the language of the Constitution of 1864 concerning the antebellum state debt: "The General Assembly shall provide by law for adjusting with the State of West Virginia the proportion of the public debt of Virginia, proper to be borne by the State of Virginia and West Virginia, and shall provide that such sum as shall be received from West Virginia shall be applied to the payment of the public debt of the State." Immediately following the war, Governor Pierpont and the General Assembly had attempted to negotiate with the government of West Virginia to obtain at least a partial payment of what Virginians believed West Virginians should pay of that debt, but for a variety of reasons, the negotiations failed. In 1906, the attorney general of Virginia filed suit in the Supreme Court of the United States to force West Virginia to pay. Following an extremely long and complex legal contest, the West Virginia Legislature finally agreed in 1919, after the Supreme Court ruled in a series of suits all styled *Virginia v. West Virginia*, that it was liable for payment of a portion of the antebellum debt. West Virginians paid taxes until 1939 and Virginians until 1944 to retire all the pre-1861 debt.[84]

The final, unnumbered, section in Article X entitled "Usury" allowed a maximum annual interest rate of 12 percent if "agreed upon by the parties and be specified in the bond, note, or other writing evidencing the debt. When there is no such agreement, the rate of interest shall be six per centum per annum."

MISCELLANEOUS PROVISIONS

Article XI entitled "Miscellaneous Provisions" dealt largely with property and, as with some of the tax sections, reflected new economic conditions after the

Civil War. Under the generic heading "Homestead and Other Exemptions" the sections allowed the General Assembly to provide legal means by which people could protect their residences and some business property to a maximum amount of $2,000 from seizure through a court process for debt. Virginia was one of the last states to afford that protection to its residents either by statute or constitutional provision, and by 1868, most states had placed homestead exemptions into their constitutions.[85]

Section 4 prohibited the General Assembly from passing "any law staying the collection of debts, commonly known as 'stay-laws.'" Section 6 "abrogated" a stay law that the assembly adopted on 2 March 1866[86] and An Act to Exempt the Homesteads of Families from Forced Sales adopted on 29 April 1867.[87] Section 7 declared, "The provisions of this article shall be construed liberally, to the end that all the intents thereof may be fully and perfectly carried out."

On 13 June 1872, the Supreme Court of Appeals in three cases combined under the style *The Homestead Cases* ruled unanimously that Article XI, Section 1, and the provisions of the homestead act that the General Assembly passed in June 1870[88] "so far as they apply to contracts entered into or debts contracted before their adoption, are in violation of the constitution of the United States and, therefore, void." Article I, Section 10, of the Constitution of the United States prohibited state governments from abridging obligation of contracts, as did Article V, Section 14, of the Constitution of 1869. Debt agreements entered into before ratification of the new constitution were contracts. Unless those contracts had expressly excluded the forms of property that were itemized in the new constitution from liability to seizure, the new provision in the Virginia constitution unconstitutionally invalidated parts of those old contracts.[89] For all agreements entered into after adoption of the new state constitution, the homestead provision and laws enacted under its authority remained valid.[90]

Another unnumbered paragraph in Article XI entitled "Church Property" declared that no events of "the late civil war" could alter ownership of church property. It also prohibited the General Assembly from passing any law that allowed or required any person or group other than original owner (or owners) "or the legal assignees of such original parties" to obtain ownership. Several large religious denominations, including Presbyterians, Methodists, Episcopalians, and Baptists, had splintered into northern and southern factions before or during the war. Questions therefore arose about who owned buildings, burial grounds, parsonages, church schools, or other property after those events. In February 1867, the assembly had adopted a law to create a legal process for members of divided congregations to decide who should own the congregation's property.⁹¹ Congregations split in many communities after the war when African Americans withdrew from, or were excluded from, churches that had formerly been racially integrated. Members of the convention may have inserted the new provision into the constitution to secure titles to church properties in those circumstances, but the best study of racial division of postwar churches found no instances of lawsuits that the constitutional provision governed.⁹²

The final, also unnumbered, section of Article XI entitled "Hiership of Property" amplified and placed in the constitution the essence of part of the Cohabitation Act of 1866.⁹³ It read in full, "The children of parents, one or both of whom were slaves at and during the period of cohabitation and who were recognized by the father as his children and whose mother was recognized by such father as his wife, and was cohabited with as such, shall be as capable of inheriting any estate whereof such father may have died seized or possessed, as though they had been born in lawful wedlock." That section empowered the man to acknowledge who his wife was and who were his children, but it reinforced traditional patriarchal perceptions of gender roles and did not allow the woman to acknowledge who her husband was or who her children were.

AMENDMENTS AND CONVENTIONS

Article XII empowered the General Assembly by majority votes of each house before and after an election of members of the House of Delegates to propose amendments to the constitution, which the voters by a majority vote could ratify or reject. The article also required that at twenty-year intervals beginning in 1888 voters decide the question, "shall there be a Convention to revise the Constitution and amend the same?" No doubt fearing that if the reforming impulse of the 1860s dissipated, the convention inserted an important limitation, "Provided, that no amendment or revision shall be made which shall deny or in any way impair the right of suffrage or any civil or political right as conferred by this Constitution except for causes which apply to all persons and classes without distinction."

Delayed Ratification

On 17 April 1868, the convention adopted the new constitution by a vote of 51 to 26.⁹⁴ President John C. Underwood was extremely pleased that the convention concluded its work and enabled him to sign the official enrolled constitution on 17 April 1868, seven years to the day after the Convention of 1861 had voted in the very same room to secede from the United States.[95] Few things gave the high-tempered, openly partisan judge more pleasure than belittling or insulting secessionists and former Confederates. He even displayed on the wall of his Alexandria law office one of the original signed copies of the Virginia Ordinance of Secession by way of keeping everyone's mind focused on the wickedness of slave owners and traitors.[96]

The constitution produced a radical and democratic reformation in governmental structures and responsibilities and in the state's political culture. In addition to granting Black men the right to vote and creating a public school system for children of all races, it required public officials to acknowledge the equal citizenship rights of all people irrespective of race. In all those respects, the new constitution was more or less offensive to white Virginians who had been accustomed to public life as it had existed before the Civil War. Moreover, the new constitution gratuitously scorned Confederate Virginia. It required officeholders to "recognize and accept the civil and political equality of all men before the laws," and it referred to "the usurped and pretended State authorities assembled at Richmond during the late war."

Convention delegates adopted an ordinance to create new districts for the election of members of the House of Representatives[97] and another to require a referendum on 2 June 1868 by which voters could ratify or reject the constitution and on the same date elect members of the General Assembly, all state officers, and members of the House of Representatives. The ordinance ordered that the General Assembly thus elected meet on 24 June 1868, and it "requested" the commanding general of the First Military District "to enforce this ordinance."[98]

General Schofield did not. He had supervised the state government with a rather mild hand since March 1867 and believed in leniency toward former Confederates who took the required oaths and peaceably accepted the new realities of life in postwar, postslavery Virginia. In that and in other respects, he and Governor Pierpont entertained similar views looking toward a speedy reconciliation after the war.[99] Schofield believed that the harsh disfranchisement provisions defeated that purpose, and he told the delegates as much in a blunt speech to the convention on its final day. He also feared that with so many educated white men disqualified and so few experienced Virginians available to serve in public office, the new constitution could not properly function. Under the pretense that the convention had spent all the money appropriated for it, he never directed the army to conduct the ratification referendum.[100]

Schofield soon thereafter and somewhat surprisingly replaced Pierpont as provisional governor with Henry Horatio Wells, a New York native and radical Republican resident of Alexandria. Republicans nominated Wells for governor in anticipation of the summer election, and Conservatives nominated a candidate to oppose him, but the postponement of the ratification referendum meant that the election of a new governor and members of the General Assembly and of Congress scheduled at the same time did not take place.[101] The unintended consequences were numerous and significant: no ratified constitution as Congress required; no election of state or local government officers; no elected legislators to meet in the General Assembly and elect judges and revise the laws to comport with the new constitution; no meetings of the assembly at all between April 1867 and October 1869; no assembly ratification of the Fourteenth and Fifteenth Amendments as Congress required; no quick end to military oversight of the state's government; and no state or congressional authority for Virginians to vote in the presidential election of 1868.

Those serious consequences eventually convinced some reluctant Conservative Party leaders to seek a solution to the long political stalemate. They swallowed their disgust and persuaded the party to empower a select committee to work out a compromise to save what they could after suffering what they believed was a terrible political defeat. In January 1869, members of the committee of nine, as they soon came to be called, traveled to Washington and negotiated an agreement with President-elect Ulysses S. Grant and Republican leaders of Congress. They agreed to hold the required ratification referendum in the summer and at that time allow voters to vote separately on the two sections of Article III that disfranchised and barred from public office supporters of the former Confederacy. The price Conservatives had to pay was to accept suffrage and full and equal political rights for Black Virginians.[102]

Under authority of a special act of Congress and a presidential proclamation to implement the agreement,[103] on 6 July 1869 voters defeated the clause that disfranchised former office holders 124,360 to 84,410 and the section that barred them from office 124,715 to 83,458. Eligible voters ratified the new constitution by an overwhelming vote of 210,585 to 9,136.[104]

Voters also elected members of both houses of the General Assembly, members of the House of Representatives, and a moderate Republican slate of candidates for governor, lieutenant governor, and attorney general. On 21 September 1869, Brigadier General Edward Richard Sprigg Canby, who was then commander of the First Military District, replaced Wells as provisional governor after Wells lost the election for governor. The new provisional governor was another New York native, Gilbert Carlton Walker, who had defeated Wells by running as a moderate Republican with strong Conservative support.[105]

Walker called the General Assembly into session, and on 8 October 1869, the newly elected members of both houses ratified the Fourteenth and Fifteenth Amendments as Congress required. The vote in the Senate on the Fourteenth Amendment was 36 to 4 and in the House of Delegates 126 to 6. The vote in the Senate on the Fifteenth Amendment was 40 to 2 and in the House 132 to 0.[106]

On 26 January 1870, the president signed An Act to Admit the State of Virginia to Representation in the Congress of the United States. The preamble stated that because "the people of Virginia have framed and adopted a constitution of State government which is republican; and whereas the legislature of Virginia elected under said constitution have ratified the fourteenth and fifteenth amendments to the Constitution of the United States; and whereas the performance of these several acts in good faith was a condition precedent to the representation of the State in Congress," it authorized senators and representatives from Virginia to take their seats.[107]

The act of Congress did not, as some former Confederates believed and some careless historians have repeated, readmit Virginia to the United States. As Chief Justice Samuel P. Chase had explained in *Texas v. White* in 1868, none of the states of the former Confederacy had ever been out of the United States, only out of their proper relationship to it.[108] On 26 January 1870, Congress simply declared, as the title of the law indicated, that Virginia had met all the requirements for having its senators and representatives seated in Congress. The law did not as of that date or any other breathe first life into the new constitution that voters ratified in July 1869.

The act of Congress required public officials in Virginia to take an oath of loyalty to the United States and either swear that they had never voluntarily taken part in the rebellion or that they had had their legal disabilities as a consequence of doing so removed. Moreover, the law prohibited any changes to the new state constitution "to deprive any citizen or class of citizens of the United States of the right to vote who are entitled to vote by the Constitution"; to deny any person the right to hold office "on account of race, color, or previous condition of servitude"; or "to deprive any citizen or class of citizens of the United States of the school rights and privileges secured by the constitution of said State."[109]

The Constitution of 1869 in Operation

Early the next day, on 27 January 1870, Governor Walker took the oaths of office as the elected governor of Virginia, no longer the provisional governor. He immediately called the General Assembly into special session,[110] and General Canby issued orders that terminated all military supervision of civilian government in Virginia.[111]

On 5 March, the governor signed a law with a fine descriptive title, An Act to Enable Officers Now Holding Office in Virginia by Military Appointment, or Otherwise, to Hold Over Until Their Successors are Elected or Appointed and Have Duly Qualified; to Ratify and Confirm the Official Acts of All Such Officers, and to Provide for Filling Vacancies in the Offices of Justices and Constables. It was known at the time as the Enabling Act, and it settled what the General Assembly, in the preamble to the law, described as "grave doubts ... as to the right of the civil officers of this commonwealth to continue to hold their offices and to exercise the powers, perform the duties, and enjoy the privileges and emoluments appertaining to the same." The law affirmed the legal status of all public officials however appointed or elected before 26 January and declared legal their official actions taken before passage of the act. The law also made specific provisions for filling vacancies in some offices after passage of the law and before the appointment or election of successors under provisions of the new state constitution.[112]

The General Assembly that adopted the Enabling Act met in four sessions between the first week of October 1869 and the end of March 1871. With thirty Black legislators in attendance, the assembly was as remarkable in its membership as the constitutional convention had been. The law that they passed in the summer of 1870 to create the state's first system of free public schools was perhaps the most important piece of postwar legislation. Another law that they passed in March 1871 to pay the antebellum public debt was of comparable importance because it committed the state to paying the whole $45.6 million principal at 6 percent annual interest.[113] It seemed like good business sense at the time to restore the public credit, and most of the Black legislators in both houses of the assembly voted for it.[114] At the same time, legislators also voted to sell almost all the state's stock in railroads at what critics believed were scandalously low prices. Some people charged that bond speculators and railroad attorneys purchased the votes of assembly members with money, alcohol, and women.[115]

The General Assembly of 1869–71 set the stage for the main political dramas of the remainder of the century.[116] Very soon after legislators passed what was generally referred to as the Funding Act of 1871, it became clear that paying interest on the debt would virtually bankrupt the state and starve the treasury of money needed to pay for the new school system. Questions of how to pay interest on the debt and properly support the new school system dominated state politics for more than a decade. Black men and white men, some of them non-elite white men, came together in a new political alliance. Questions involving the debt, the schools, and race quickly became entangled in ways that could not be disentangled. Because the new constitution granted the governor authority to veto bills that the General Assembly had passed, the governor became a major actor in those political dramas. Some of the first and most important vetoes governors handed down during the 1870s involved paying interest on the debt and paying for the schools with money that some legislators tried to divert from debt service.

With restrictions on supporters of the former Confederacy removed from Virginia's constitution and laws, the Conservative Party won majorities in both houses of the General Assembly in 1869 and elected all statewide officers from that year through 1877. Most African Americans evidently voted for Republican candidates until Conservatives split into two factions, Funders who insisted on paying all the principal and interest on the debt, and Readjusters who proposed to adjust, or readjust, the rate of interest downward and to do the same with the amount of principal to be paid so that the assembly could increase appropriations for the schools.

Some Funders embraced reduction of the interest rate as early as 1872 when the General Assembly passed and the governor vetoed the first of several bills for that purpose. The same year, the assembly overrode a veto to prevent people from paying taxes with the interest-bearing coupons on the bonds with which the state refinanced the debt; but later that year, the Supreme Court of Appeals, in *Antoni v. Wright*, declared that law unconstitutional.[117] Coupons piled up in the state treasury and were utterly useless to the state in meeting its many obligations. Some Funders later joined the Readjusters when it became clear that voters of both races wanted adequate appropriations for the schools. By the end of the 1870s, Readjusters shrewdly made their public appeals for votes by informing voters that their choice was to send their tax money to northern and European bond speculators or to spend it for the benefit of Virginia's children. Readjusters won majorities in both houses of the assembly in 1879, and in 1881 they retained their majorities and also elected a governor, lieutenant governor, and attorney general.

The General Assembly session of 1881–82 enacted more reform legislation than any other assembly of the nineteenth century. It was one of the most reform-minded sessions ever. It reduced the interest rate again, slashed the amount of principal to be paid, and diverted large sums of tax money from debt service to the public schools. The assembly also reduced taxes on farmers and raised taxes on railroads and other corporations. Within two years the Readjusters converted a Funder treasury deficit into a surplus and at the same time significantly increased appropriations for the public schools. Readjusters replaced almost all the school superintendents in the state with men committed to good education for all children, including Black children, and overhauled the administrations of the state's colleges. Legislators founded both a mental hospital for African Americans, what later became Central State Hospital, and a college for Black men and women, what later became Virginia State University. They also abolished use of the whipping post for punishing Black people, a painful and humiliating legacy of slavery days. That assembly's reforms were the second serious attempt to construct a new Virginia politics, an attempt that the Constitution of 1869 made possible for the first time.

In 1883 the state's Conservative Party, which had disintegrated as an organized, effective political party, reorganized as the Democratic Party. Its leaders rather cynically jettisoned their Funder past and endorsed the Readjusters' refinancing of the debt in order to be able to appeal to white voters on a white supremacy platform that included support for public education. Democrats took control of state government in the general election that year and held on with increasing majorities in both houses of the General Assembly through the remainder of the nineteenth century and until the fourth quarter of the twentieth century.[118]

The Politics of Constitutional Amendment

The Constitution of 1869 made amendments possible for the first time. Some readily available texts of the Constitution of 1869 omit the amendments, and the few references to them are either erroneous or misleading. Jacob Brenaman in his little 1902 reference book, *A History of Virginia Conventions*, listed eight amendments even though the number was actually seven. He chose to distinguish two parts of an amendment ratified in 1876 as if they were separate but nevertheless printed identical figures for ratification votes, which he derived from one return for the one amendment that had several parts and purposes. His descriptions of the amendments were also very incomplete and seriously misleadingly.[119]

The first and last three of the seven amendments were largely unrelated to the extremely important substance of the other three, which were entangled in the contentious politics of the time. The first amendment, ratified in May 1872, repealed Article X on usury to allow the General Assembly to amend the existing statutes and specify that borrowers and lenders could negotiate interest at any rate up to a maximum of 8 percent per annum but left all other loans at 6 percent.[120]

The fifth of the amendments, ratified in November 1894, added a clause to Section 10 of the Bill of Rights to permit the General Assembly to provide "for the trial otherwise than by a jury of a man accused of a criminal offence not punishable by death or confinement in the penitentiary" to allow judges to hear and decide minor criminal cases without a jury if the defendant did not insist on a jury trial.

The sixth of the amendments, ratified in November 1901, repealed Article X, Section 2, which exempted oystermen from being taxed on the oysters they harvested with tongs from "natural beds," that is, from naturally occurring oyster beds and not from artificial shoals they created and seeded with oyster spat. And the seventh of the amendments, also ratified in November 1901 changed the date for holding elections of county officers from May to November.

The second, third, and fourth amendments were more controversial and more important to more people. In 1874, the General Assembly submitted and voters ratified an amendment to modify Article VII on county government. It changed the names of townships to magisterial districts (the word *township* was too redolent of New England democracy), eliminated several elected township officers, and authorized the election of one county surveyor and one county tax commissioner rather than several separate tax assessors and collectors in each township. The amendment streamlined the structure of county government and reduced the expense to taxpayers by reducing the number of elected officials in each county. By reducing the number of public offices that Black men and ordinary white men might hope to hold, the amendment may be understood as restricting local democracy.[121]

In 1876, the assembly submitted and voters ratified an amendment that made several major changes. It inserted a provision into Article III, Section 1, to require that voters "shall have paid to the State, before the day of election, the capitation tax required by law, for the preceding year," and it also disfranchised every person convicted of "petit larceny." The capitation tax—poll tax—placed a new financial burden on the franchise with the deliberate intention of making it too expensive for some Black men to vote. What was called the "chicken-thief" amendment was based on a racist assumption that Black people were inherently more dishonest than white people and that they often stole things like chickens that had almost no monetary value in the same way that owners of enslaved people had believed that enslaved people had often taken foodstuffs from their owners.[122]

The amendment had the desired effect. The number of voters declined by about 10 percent and no doubt contributed to a reduction in the number of Black Virginian men able to win election to the General Assembly. Thirty Black men won election to the assembly in 1869, and between eighteen and twenty won in each of the elections of 1871, 1873, and 1875; but only eight were able to win in 1877. A corresponding decline in the number of Black men elected to local offices was almost certainly another consequence of the amendment, which was adopted only two years after the constitutional amendment that reduced the number of elective local offices.[123]

The 1876 amendment also made important changes to Article V on the General Assembly, some ostensibly to save money. It allowed the assembly to create districts for the election of not fewer than 90 nor more than 100 delegates (reduced from 138) and from 33 to 40 senators (reduced from 43). It restored biennial sessions that were originally established in 1851 but had been changed to annual sessions in 1864 and 1869.[124] The amendment also added two new sections to Article V to authorize the assembly "to provide for the government of cities and towns and to establish such courts therein as may be necessary for the administration of justice." That affirmed and gave explicit constitutional protection to the assembly's inherent authority to create municipal governments and provide for their form and function.

The amendment also added a new section that granted the assembly "power, by two-thirds vote, to remove disabilities incurred under clause third, section one, article third of this constitution, with reference to duelling."

In spite of the obstacles that the 1876 amendment deliberately placed on voting by Black men, the strong appeal of the Readjusters brought Black men back into politics in alliance with white men who favored supporting the public schools adequately. That enabled Readjusters to win majorities in both houses of the General Assembly in 1879, and they proposed their own amendment to the constitution to repeal the poll tax as a prerequisite for voting. In November 1882, voters ratified it, but it left in place the petty larceny provision. Black voting and office holding never again reached the levels that they had attained immediately after ratification of the Constitution of 1869, but throughout the remainder of the 1880s and into the 1890s, African Americans provided enough votes for Republican Party candidates that Democrats believed themselves to be constantly under threat of another biracial agrarian and working-class coalition that might succeed permanently at what the Readjusters had succeeded only temporarily.[125]

In 1884 after Democrats won majorities in both houses, the General Assembly passed—over the governor's veto—a new election law usually referred to as the Anderson-McCormick Act. It created three-member electoral boards for each county and city and authorized the assembly to elect all the board members.[126] The law gave the Democratic Party majority in the assembly monopoly control over who registered voters and conducted elections, and they used it to their partisan advantage.

The law fostered new forms of political corruption. The requirement for voting by ballot instead of by voice vote had not insulated voters from intimidation or guaranteed fairness at polling places. Candidates printed ballots with their own names on them, or political parties printed ballots with the names of all party nominees on them and provided voters with ballots. Candidates or parties often printed ballots on different sizes or colors of paper. Voters either deposited ballots in the ballot box or handed them to an officer of election who placed them in the box. Everyone could see how every voter voted or intended to vote, but if an officer of election took a ballot from a voter to place in the ballot box, the voter had no guarantee that the officer would not switch ballots or fold his together with other ballots to alter the outcome. If at the end of the day a ballot box contained more ballots than the number of voters who had been to the poll, Democratic officers of election could either throw out the results if a Republican victory might result or reach into the ballot box and blindly grope around for what felt like Republican ballots and remove enough of them to equalize the numbers of voters and ballots before beginning the count.

In 1894, the General Assembly passed a new voting law, the Walton Act, which introduced the secret, or Australian, ballot. The state printed ballots with all the names of all the candidates for every office, and voters marked them at the polling place. That meant, without specifically requiring as much, that voters must be literate. The new voting system was secret, but like the old, it was also susceptible to corruption. The law required each voter to draw a line through "three-fourths of the length of the name" of every candidate he wished to vote against.[127] That provided Democratic vote counters ample leeway to decide that a Republican voter had not quite drawn a legal line through enough of a Democratic candidate's name, which disqualified the ballot; or that a Democratic voter had just barely drawn a legal line through a Republican candidate's name, which allowed the ballot to count and be counted for the Democratic candidate.

Throughout the thirty-three years that the Constitution of 1869 was in force, officials who conducted elections employed many means to influence the outcome of elections. Some required that Black men or known Republicans stand in separate lines from white Democrats, allowed all the Democrats to vote first, or made certain that lines of Black men moved so slowly that many men were unable to vote before the poll closed. Counters of votes also sometimes cheated, altered official returns, destroyed ballots, or stuffed ballot boxes. Party workers of both parties sometimes resorted to public intimidation of voters, bribery, or violence to win elections. Some politicians bragged about the effectiveness of their nefarious techniques for guaranteeing that election returns reported what they wanted. Some other Virginia political leaders were embarrassed that their electoral practices had become as notoriously corrupt as in some other parts of the country. All of which led to the Convention of 1901–2, the principal purpose of which was to install constitutional barriers against Black men voting so that Democrats did not have to cheat in order to win elections.[128]

The Constitution of the United States

The federal government's suppression of the rebellion during the first half of the 1860s and its unprecedented supervision of state governments during the second half were together at least as important constitutional revolutions as the constitutional revolution in each of the states of the former Confederacy. The potential vast extension of the power of the federal government incorporated into the three amendments made to the Constitution of the United States between 1865 and 1870 created the potential for a profound upheaval in relationships between the national government and the governments of the states.

The Thirteenth Amendment ratified late in 1865 permanently abolished slavery in the United States. That meant that even if Virginians repealed the prohibition on slavery in the new state constitution, they could not reestablish slavery. Therefore, in 1902, when the next state convention eliminated the 1860s prohibition of slavery and several of the other innovative 1860s provisions from the state's constitution, it made no difference.

The Fourteenth Amendment ratified in 1868 granted citizenship to all people "born or naturalized in the United States," which effectively overturned Chief Justice Roger B. Taney's 1857 ruling in *Dred Scott v. Sandford* that under no circumstance could people of African descent be citizens of the United States.[129] The amendment also declared those citizens to be citizens of the states where they resided and prohibited states from denying any of them "the privileges or immunities of citizens of the United States"; depriving "any person"—not merely any citizen—"of life, liberty, or property, without due process of law"; or denying "any person within its jurisdiction the equal protection of the laws." The amendment empowered Congress to reduce representation in Congress for any state that deprived a portion of its male citizens of the right to vote; and it prohibited state and local governments from paying any public debts "incurred in aid of insurrection or rebellion against the United States."

The Fifteenth Amendment, ratified in 1870, declared, "The Right of citizens of the United States to vote shall not be denied or abridged by the United States or by any State on account of race, color, or previous condition of servitude." Later in the century and early in the next, when some white men in Virginia and white people in other states of the former Confederacy desired to disfranchise Black men, they had to resort to poll taxes, literacy tests, and other contrivances that did not appear to violate the race-explicit wording of the amendment, however much they violated its evident spirit.

All three amendments empowered Congress to enforce their terms by "appropriate legislation." Congress used the authority of the amendments to pass several civil rights acts during the 1860s and 1870s to prohibit people and states from denying African Americans their rights as citizens and voters. The amendments and the civil rights acts all tipped the balance of governmental power in favor of the national government as never before and correspondingly restricted the political and legal independence of state governments in ways and to an extent that not even the most adamant antebellum apostles of states' rights had dreaded.[130]

The Future

The twenty years—approximately a Jeffersonian generation[131]—between the election of members of the Convention of 1850–51 and 1870 produced the most important and thorough constitutional revolution in Virginia's history. Virginians thereafter lived in a completely reformed political system that was adapted to their newly constructed social and economic systems. Slavery was abolished, and nearly half a million Virginians became citizens, although women did not obtain all the rights of citizenship. All adult men—not merely white men who owned land—gained a constitutionally protected right to vote and hold public office. Voting by ballot replaced voice voting. Legislators represented their constituents, not a vested property interest. Popularly elected local governments replaced the old undemocratic county court system that tobacco planters and slave drivers had created in the seventeenth century. All the state's courts, for the first time, were supposed to have judges with proper legal training. Governors became important political leaders and exercised influence with the legislature for the first time. Elections of governors became one of the central events of partisan politics. Private enterprise would have to develop a transportation infrastructure for the state without public financial assistance, or the state would have to do that work itself. All citizens could hope to send their children to a free public school. The federal government became empowered to guarantee equal citizenship rights and voting rights, anything in state constitutions and laws to the contrary notwithstanding.

In short, the elite white male oligarchic government of Virginia that was formed in the early decades of the seventeenth century was entirely swept away in the 1850s and 1860s. In its place, men of all races and classes had equal opportunities to participate in politics and government (for the first time), and the creation of a public school system promised that in the future, a broadly educated electorate would (also for the first time) determine who served in that government. The constitutional revolution appeared to be complete and secure.

The Constitution of 1869 suited people who initially opposed it better than they anticipated. A Conservative Party member admitted privately early in the thirty-three-year life of the constitution that it was actually a pretty good constitution in spite of the radical political motives of its Republican authors.[132] The editor of the *Virginia Law Journal* wrote early in 1886 that "we have lived without serious inconvenience" under the Constitution of 1869.[133] And in 1888, when the constitution required voters to determine whether to hold a convention to revise it, they overwhelmingly defeated it 63,125 to 3,698,[134] a nearly 17 to 1 margin; and voters defeated another proposal for a convention in 1897 by a vote of 83,453 to 38,326,[135] more than 2 to 1. Not until 1900, in response to new demands from white supremacists in the state's Democratic Party and advocates of regulation of railroads, did voters authorize a convention, and then only by a margin of 77,362 to 60,375.[136]

Nevertheless, in political discourse late in the nineteenth century and early in the twentieth, as well as in much of the literature of Virginia's political history, people almost always employed unflattering adjectives when they referred to the constitution that granted the suffrage to Black Virginians and in so doing, enabled the Readjusters to challenge aspects of elite white political dominance in Virginia. It was then that the Convention of 1867–68 and the Constitution of 1869 became known as the Underwood Convention and the Underwood Constitution. The unpopular and excessively partisan judge became one of the symbols of biracial, democratic reform. Coupling his name with the convention and constitution damned them both and concealed or devalued the many contributions of the convention's delegates, including two dozen Black members, as well as obscured the other important democratic reforms embodied in it.

The reason for prolonged, even unthinking, condemnations of the Constitution of 1869 was not that it was a bad constitution but that from its origins under the auspices of radical Republicans in Congress in the 1860s through the end of the nineteenth century, it enfranchised and gave political influence to Black men. That change uprooted and overturned centuries of governmental institutions and political practices that had enabled elite white male political domination of Virginia and its government. The Constitution of 1869 gave Virginia its first public schools. It gave thousands of its new Black citizens the right to vote. It allowed Black and white voters to work together to refinance the public debt and increase appropriations to the schools for the benefit of all their children. The Readjusters showed that under that constitution, biracial politics in a Southern state was possible and that nonelite white people could also have an influential voice in Virginia politics. The Readjuster movement provided one of the first examples of how a state of the former Confederacy could construct a new government and new society.[137]

The Democrats' speedy destruction of much of that new Virginia in the 1880s also demonstrated how difficult constructing a new, biracial politics and society would be anywhere in the states of the former Confederacy. The Virginia experience late in the 1870s and early in the 1880s undoubtedly explains why in the 1890s, the People's Party—the biracial agrarian reform movement called the Populist movement—had such a minor influence on the state's politics. Virginia's dominant Democrats had made certain when they destroyed the Readjusters that nothing comparable would again be possible in Virginia—that Black men, Republicans, and nonelite white voters could not cooperate politically to the disadvantage of elite white Virginians.[138] It was then that convention president John C. Underwood and Readjuster Party leader William Mahone became the most hated white men in Virginia, and they remained so well into the twentieth century, long after both men were dead.

CHAPTER 7

The Constitution of 1902

"During the dark days of reconstruction, before the passions engendered by the war had cooled," John Goode recalled on 12 June 1901 in his address to the opening session of the Convention of 1901–2, of which he had just been unanimously elected president, "another convention assembled in this city and framed a constitution under which we now live—with some modifications. That convention was composed of aliens to the Commonwealth, and newly emancipated slaves. Virginians to the manner born"—a common alternative for "to the manor born" that Goode used or the stenographer wrote when he reported the speech—"who owned the property and paid the taxes, and who represented the virtue and intelligence of the Commonwealth, were placed under the ban of proscription and excluded from its halls."[1]

Goode was not correct. Congress had not excluded all white Virginia men who owned property or paid taxes from eligibility to win election to the Convention of 1867–68. Congress had disfranchised only men who refused to take an oath of allegiance to the United States and disavow their Confederate pasts. Unwilling to do that, many Virginia men voluntarily declined to register, vote, or seek election to the convention. Their actions had given radical reformers, including both white and Black natives of Virginia, a majority in the convention that produced the most democratic constitution that any Virginians had yet written.

Goode was the most senior of the few men with long experience in public life who won election to the constitutional convention in 1901. He had been a prominent lawyer and political leader for half a century since his first election to the House of Delegates in 1851. From 1875 to 1881, he had served three terms in the House of Representatives; for fifteen months during the first administration of President Grover Cleveland, he had been solicitor general of the United States; and in 1898, he was elected president of the prestigious Virginia State Bar Association. Before that, Goode had also won election to the Confederate House of Representatives, and he was the only member of the Convention of 1901 who had served in the Convention of 1861, in which he had supported secession.[2]

Goode's 1901 speech accepting the presidency of the convention summed up the attitudes of a majority of what he called "our people"—elite white men and women—at the beginning of the twentieth century, both toward their past and their future, as well as toward "the members of the colored race." Like most white Virginians of the time, Goode believed that the "all powerful Creator" had made persons with African ancestry "inferior to the white man, and ever since the dawn of history, as the pictured monuments of Egypt attest, he had occupied a position of inferiority. In the language of an eminent Virginian, on another occasion, he had founded no empire, he had built no towered city, invented no art, discovered no truth, bequeathed no everlasting possession to the future through law-giver, hero, bard, benefactor of mankind."[3] Beginning with the words "he had founded no empire" and to the end of the sentence, Goode quoted University of Virginia law professor James F. Holcombe's 1858 address that was published under the title "Is Slavery Consistent with Natural Law?"[4] Holcombe had believed that it was. He had served with Goode as a secessionist in the Convention of 1861 to preserve in Virginia the enslavement of what they both believed then, and Goode still believed later, was an inferior race of people. Goode quoting Holcombe explicitly linked the beliefs and motivations of advocates of secession and defenders of slavery with the men who proposed to disfranchise Black voters forty years later.

Goode approvingly detailed for his fellow delegates the steps that some states of the former Confederacy had recently taken to evade the mandate of the Fifteenth Amendment in order to deny the vote to Black men for reasons other than "race, color, or previous condition of servitude." He listed literacy tests, poll taxes, grandfather clauses, and other measures that deprived men of the ability to vote for reasons other than race. Goode did not recommend that Virginians should necessarily copy what other southern white men had done but contrive their own means of excluding Black men from politics and government. "We are here as Virginians," he told them, "to make a Constitution for Virginia, and Virginia heretofore has been accustomed to lead and not to follow. . . . Allow me to express the hope that as a beneficent result of whatever plan of suffrage you may adopt politics in Virginia may be so purified that in all the years to come her escutcheon shall not be stained by any act of fraud, bribery, corruption, false registration, false counting, or any debauching methods in the conduct of the elections." The published record of Goode's speech indicates that at that point the delegates erupted in "Great applause."[5]

What Goode said and meant and what the other delegates heard and applauded was simply this: exclude Black people from politics, and decent white Democrats would therefore no longer have to cheat to win elections against Republicans, white or Black. That is what they meant by purifying politics. Remove the temptation from white men to cheat by depriving Black men of the right to vote. Punish the victims.

Just as Goode's historical context for the Convention of 1867–68 was flawed, his assertion that the convention over which he was to preside was to lead the way in disfranchising Black Americans was also incorrect. In fact, the Virginia Convention of 1901–2 was the last of what are called disfranchisement constitutional conventions in the states of the former Confederacy.[6]

People who paid attention to public discussions on the subject were well aware of what was at stake. John Mitchell Jr., publisher and editor of the *Richmond Planet*, the state's most influential Black newspaper, repeatedly reminded his readers (very few of whom were white, apparently) of what advocates of constitutional disfranchisement were doing. He denounced the convention that met in June 1901 as the "unconstitutional 'Constitutional' Convention" because the stated purpose of a large majority of the delegates who won election to the convention was in plain violation of the purpose of the Fifteenth Amendment and also of the January 1870 act of Congress that affirmed the Virginia Constitution of 1869 and readmitted senators and representatives from the state to their seats in Congress.[7] That law had prohibited any changes to that constitution "to deprive any citizen or class of citizens of the United States of the right to vote who are entitled to vote by the Constitution"; to deny any person the right to hold office "on account of race, color, or previous condition of servitude"; or "to deprive any citizen or class of citizens of the United States of the school rights and privileges secured by the constitution of said State."[8]

Calling the Convention

The number of Virginians who voted during the 1890s had steadily declined—white voters and Black, Democratic voters and Republican. That decline—even as the population increased—is imperfectly understood. It is probable that the widespread corruption at polling places that was well established and well-known, together with the predictable results that corrupted electoral processes produced, may have worked to reduce the number of Virginia men who thought it worth their bother to go to the poll and vote.[9]

The Anderson-McCormick election law of 1884, which gave Democrats control of the conduct of elections, and the Walton Act of 1894, which required voters to be literate and to mark ballots in a very precise manner,[10] had allowed politicians to corrupt the voting process. That made it increasingly difficult for Republican candidates to win elections anywhere east of the mountains by the 1890s and for Black men to win elections anywhere, even where they were in the majority. Democrats stuffed ballot boxes, intimidated or bribed voters, and threatened or assaulted them to influence the outcomes of elections. In at least one instance, they printed ballots in German Fraktur, which almost nobody could read, and then privately instructed local Democrats how to mark the ballot. In self-defense, Republicans fought fraud with fraud. After almost every congressional election during the 1880s and 1890s, at least one defeated candidate filed a formal challenge against the victor. The House of Representatives published several large volumes of investigative hearings and testimony that fully documented the corrupt practices of both political parties.[11]

Those corrupt practices clashed conspicuously with the democratic rhetoric of the age. However much men, like convention president John Goode in his acceptance speech to the convention, might extoll the purity of the democratic election process, they simultaneously, like he, also advocated the undemocratic disfranchisement of Black Americans. Race and politics became entangled in a tight knot that influenced everything else in Virginia politics during the final decades of the nineteenth century. In pursuit of some objectives, most especially white supremacy and restoring government to elite, white, male control, some politicians sacrificed or trampled on some of their democratic ideals.[12]

The leadership of the state's dominant Democratic Party was of divided opinion on whether revision of the constitution was necessary to preserve white supremacy and Democratic Party dominance. In fact, the party's leaders, the two United States senators, Thomas Staples Martin and John Warwick Daniel, were of divided opinion on many of the most urgent political issues of the 1890s.

The agrarian reform movement known as Populism was the most obvious recent source of division. Secretive railroad lawyer Thomas Martin, whom railroad interests probably helped elect to the United States Senate during the

1893–94 legislative session, opposed all the economic reforms and regulation of banks and railroads that the Populists advocated.[13] Martin also did not believe that white supremacy and the dominance of his part of the party were any longer in genuine danger. He did not publicly support, and probably privately discouraged, the movement for a constitutional convention, especially if regulation of railroads should be an objective of its members and provoke more divisions within the party. "I remember Senator Martin's saying to me once," and admirer recalled many years later, "that in politics a man should never look for a fight."[14]

Some Democrats agreed with Martin that the election laws that they had enacted since the overthrow of the Readjusters worked well enough to ensure white supremacy and Democratic Party dominance, and they tolerated the corrupted electoral processes that those laws allowed. Some of them were publicly quite pleased at the effectiveness of the corruption that they had created for that purpose. Other Democrats, either more firmly opposed to Black participation in public life at all or perhaps more apprehensive about another biracial coalition of farmers and working-class men, wanted to drive them out of public life entirely and permanently and clean up the electoral process. They disagreed with Martin on the urgency of the need for disfranchisement.

John W. ("I am a Democrat because I am a white man and a Virginian") Daniel,[15] the unsuccessful Funder candidate for governor in 1881 and a popular Lost Cause speaker, became the most prominent Virginia Democrat who supported a disfranchisement constitutional convention, even as Martin opposed it. Martin was extremely unpopular among Democrats who expressed disgust at the political corruption on which his dominant position in one faction of the party was based.[16] Daniel and like-minded Democrats described themselves as reformers intent on saving democracy, but to do that they proposed to deny the suffrage to men who threatened white supremacy and to drive them out of public life forever.

They were strongest in what people of the time called the Black Belt, the region south of the James River, east of the foothills of the Blue Ridge, and west of Norfolk and Portsmouth. It had been the heartland of slavery before the Civil War and of secessionist sentiment in 1861. It still had the largest numbers of Black people—hence, "Black"—in the state and by far the largest percentages in most counties. Taking heart from successful constitutional disfranchisement conventions in several other states of the former Confederacy, white supremacist Democrats in that region argued for and created a convention to disfranchise Black voters. Hardly anybody doubted those Democrats' motives at the time. Before and during the convention, Democrats from elsewhere in the state often referred to the special requirements of white men in the Black Belt, clearly understood their motivations, and usually tried to accommodate their demands.[17]

Black Belt legislators with Daniel's support persuaded the General Assembly to pass a law in March 1900 to hold a referendum late in May on the question of calling a constitutional convention.[18] At the Democratic Party state convention in Norfolk at the beginning of May, Daniel and other supporters of rewriting the constitution succeeded in getting the party to endorse the constitutional convention. The wording of the resolution of endorsement is revealing. It began with an assertion that "it is the evident desire of the white people of Virginia to amend and revise the present Constitution." That was true only in that none but white Virginians so desired—almost certainly not a majority of them, probably not even a majority of Democrats, yet, and definitely not very many or any white Republicans. The Democratic convention presumed to speak for all white, adult, male Virginians—"our people," the only ones who mattered to them—and made the referendum on the constitutional convention a party question. In effect, it required Democrats to vote for holding a constitutional convention in the referendum scheduled for three weeks later.[19]

The endorsement resolution contained a promise that the revised constitution would not "disfranchise any citizen of Virginia who had a right to vote prior to 1861, nor the descendant of any such person." Some states of the former Confederacy had incorporated just such provisions, the so-called grandfather clauses, into the new state constitutions that they wrote to prevent the disfranchisement of white men—the only class of men who voted in 1861—under other provisions designed to disfranchise Black men.

And finally, the resolution pledged "that when such Constitution shall have been framed it shall be submitted to a vote of the people for ratification or rejection." Members of the Democratic convention knew that proposals for a disfranchisement convention had generated fears that the proposed convention might ordain a new constitution into effect without submitting it to the voters, and those fears threatened approval of the referendum. After all, if a constitution were submitted to the electorate in order to disfranchise some or many of the men who were then able to vote, it would almost certainly not be ratified. Elsewhere, in order to achieve disfranchisement by state constitutional revision, conventions wrote new constitutions and proclaimed them in effect without ratification referenda in Mississippi in 1890, in South Carolina in 1895, and in Louisiana in 1898. A convention did likewise in Alabama in 1901.[20] So as not to risk their cause, Black Belt advocates of disfranchisement necessarily deferred to widely held convictions that popular ratification referenda were essential to the creation of legitimate state constitutions.

The March 1900 law scheduled the referendum for the fourth Thursday in May. That was the day for electing county officers and was traditionally the election with the lowest voter participation. The law required that voters deposit in the ballot box a ballot with the printed words "for constitutional convention" if they wished to vote for the convention. If they wished to vote against the convention, the law required them to erase or strike out the words before they placed the ballot in the box.[21] That was how elections had been conducted in Virginia since passage of the Walton Act in 1894, which required voters to draw a line through the name of every candidate they wanted to vote against. If a voter cast a ballot in the referendum but did not indicate on it in the correct manner that he opposed, the ballot would probably be counted in favor; or if a voter did not know what to do when handed an affirmative ballot and did not know that there was no negative ballot, then he may have lost an opportunity to register a negative vote.

The 24 May 1900 vote on the referendum passed by a margin of 77,362 to 60,375.[22] Only 30.1 percent of the 447,815 adult men in Virginia[23] voted that day, about half the number who voted in that autumn's presidential election.[24] A small minority of adult men in Virginia, 17.2 percent of them, actually voted the convention into being. If adult women were added to the calculus, then about 8.5 percent of adult Virginians called the convention.

The vote did not break down cleanly by geographical region (or probably even by political party) as the following year's election of convention delegates, for the most part, did. A great many Democrats evidently voted against calling a convention. The referendum passed by a majority of about 7,000 in the Black Belt, but the vote for the convention was not uniformly distributed throughout the region. In some counties, Republicans may have turned out to vote against the proposal in greater proportions than in others, or local Democrats remained opposed. A majority of voters in the southwestern part of Virginia—south of the latitude and west of the longitude of Roanoke—voted against the convention by a margin of almost 5,000 votes. Voters in the state's eighteen incorporated cities together cast a 16,987-vote majority for the convention, very close to the statewide margin that approved the referendum.

Other than majorities in all the cities, and close contests in counties with Republican majorities or large Republican minorities, there was almost no statewide pattern to the vote that explained the outcome. Close votes in twelve counties east of the mountains where Republicans were probably less numerous than farther west may possibly be explained by local political circumstances peculiar to each, but the most likely explanation for most of them is that all Democrats were not yet convinced.

All things considered, Republican convention delegate Abraham L. Pedigo had some plausible grounds for his complaint to the convention in May 1902. "We were elected by the people to represent them in a Convention they neither called nor wanted," he charged in the most damning language he could muster. The convention was "illegitimate," he began. It "was conceived in fraud and iniquity; the Legislature that initiated it well knew that the people of the State did not want a Constitutional Convention." Members of the General Assembly, Pedigo went on, "knew that the only way they could succeed was by fraud and chicanery." They "fixed the election at a time when only a few people attended elections, and they provided a shamelessly fraudulent ballot, which was deliberately intended to swindle the illiterate negroes of the eastern counties into voting for the calling of a Convention, the avowed object of which was to disfranchise them.... The act of the Legislature was most disgraceful."[25]

Electing Delegates

Early in 1901 the General Assembly enacted a law to provide for the election of one hundred delegates from eighty-two House of Delegates districts on 23 May of that year—local election day, again.[26]

Disfranchisement of Black voters was the most important issue in the calling of the convention and the election of delegates, but it was not in every jurisdiction the only one. Comments that members made during the convention suggest that a desire for some form of additional regulation of corporations—railroads, in particular—may have persuaded some of them to become candidates or enticed other men to vote for them. Suspicion of, or animosity toward, corporations appears to have been widespread in the state. A few delegates likened the actions of corporations to extortion or highway robbery. Others complained that railroads and other corporations exercised too much influence during sessions of the General Assembly, particularly in preventing the passage of an employers' liability act to require railroads to compensate families of employees who were injured or killed on the job. Daniel C. O'Flaherty, who represented Warren and Clarke Counties in the northern Blue Ridge, remarked that he had heard some people predict that "the Constitution will be defeated by the corporations" in a ratification referendum if it included provisions that railroad men regarded as unfavorable. He, too, was worried,

"But further," he went on, "if the corporations of Virginia own the people of Virginia, I want to know it. I want to make the battle right now, and fight it out to the finish, and if they have their hands upon the throats of the people of this Commonwealth, let us find it out, and, so far as I am individually concerned, if they win out, I can walk out of the State."[27]

Even Eppa Hunton, who had recently relinquished the position of general counsel of the Southern Railroad, admitted that "the effect of the participation of the corporations of Virginia in the personal politics of Virginia has been demoralizing and debauching, second only to the presence of the negro vote in the electorate. I know that one of the strongest incentives to me to come to this body, next to that of trying to free us from the horrors of the Fifteenth Amendment, was to do all in my power to keep the railroads of Virginia out of the politics of Virginia."[28] Convention members' strong words and support for regulation of railroads indicate that the issue played a more important role in the election of delegates than has been appreciated. Residents of Virginia may have been more in tune with Americans than we have believed on an issue that Populists had advocated and that was dear also to progressive reformers.[29]

Such qualified men as voted in May 1901 elected eighty-eight Democrats and twelve Republicans (or eleven Republicans and one independent, depending on who did the counting) to serve in the convention.[30] Sixty of the Democrats from districts that included 64 of the state's 118 jurisdictions won without any opposition or with only token votes for other men. Only one of the Republicans was so fortunate. That nearly two-thirds of the Democratic candidates ran without Republican opposition strongly suggests that in the counties and cities of their districts, Republicans sat out, or boycotted, the election. That does not explain all the electoral results, though, nor could the reverse circumstance in Tazewell County explain the uncontested election of Republican Albert P. Gillespie. Perhaps in some jurisdictions, the most obvious candidate (Senator John Warwick Daniel in Campbell County, for one) appeared impossible to beat. That may explain the unopposed candidacy of former Democratic attorney general Rufus Adolphus Ayers in the southwestern legislative district of Wise, Dickenson, and Buchanan Counties, part of the Ninth Congressional District, where the Republican Party was strong and gaining strength. Beginning in 1902, Republican candidates won ten consecutive congressional elections there.[31]

Eight of the twelve Republicans were from the western mountain and valley counties. Three were from the piedmont immediately east of the Blue Ridge. A Republican won a three-way race in Orange County with a 42 percent plurality, and Republicans won close elections in Franklin County, south of Roanoke, and in Henry County, a Blue Ridge county on the North Carolina border, where Pedigo won by a close vote of 1,084 to 1,068. Only Joseph Allen Bristow, of Middlesex County, was from the east. He was a Confederate veteran, businessman-planter, and former supporter of the Readjusters who had received a patent for a deepwater oyster tong that he designed. He narrowly won election in the district of Middlesex and Essex Counties because some of the district's Democrats refused to vote for their party's nominee who had supported the radical economic agenda of the Populists in the 1890s.[32]

About half the men elected in May 1901 had no prior experience in state government, and the names of an even larger number of them never made it into the history books.[33] John Goode was the only one who had ever taken part in writing a state constitution. He served in the third session of the Convention of 1861 that rewrote the Constitution of 1851 to eliminate several important democratic reforms that it had introduced. Voters did not ratify that constitution. With the exception of two or three men who were born in neighboring North Carolina, the delegates were all native Virginians, the highest proportion of state natives of any Virginia convention. Former Readjuster governor William E. Cameron, fully reconciled to the Democratic Party of white supremacy, represented his native city of Petersburg. John Garland Pollard, from Richmond, and Henry Carter Stuart, from Russell County in southwestern Virginia, later served as governor. About thirty current or former members of the General Assembly and seven current or former members of the House of Representatives won election to the convention. Senator Daniel had served in the Senate of Virginia and was the unsuccessful candidate for governor against Cameron in 1881. Eight members of the convention later served in the House of Representatives, and one of them was also to be in the United States Senate.

In addition to Bristow and Daniel, at least fourteen other delegates were also Confederate veterans, and a larger number were sons of Confederate veterans. Four delegates were former or current superintendents of schools, two were journalists, and two were clergymen. Richard McIlwaine was a Presbyterian minister and president at the time of Hampden-Sydney College. Baptist minister Wayland F. Dunaway was also a lawyer. Between ten and fifteen men each derived most or all of their incomes, as Bristow did, from agriculture or as businessmen.

At least sixty-two members of the convention were or had been lawyers, approximately the same proportions as in the Conventions of 1850–51 and 1861. Attorney William Alexander Anderson, another Confederate veteran and coauthor of the Anderson-McCormick election law of 1884, was elected attorney general in November 1901 while the convention was in session, and John Garland Pollard was elected to the same office in 1913. Anderson, President John Goode, and William B. Pettit were all former presidents of the Virginia State Bar Association. The unsuccessful 1901 Republican candidate for lieutenant governor, convention member Robert William Blair, who had very narrowly defeated a Democratic judge in Wythe County, was also a lawyer and the son of former Readjuster attorney general Frank S. Blair, whom Rufus Ayers defeated when Blair ran for reelection in 1885.

Twenty-two judges or former judges won election to the convention. Several other members later served on the bench, including Preston W. Campbell, who was a justice of the Supreme Court of Appeals from 1924 to 1946 and chief justice for almost fifteen years of that time. The number of judges in the convention and the proportion of delegates who were judges or had been judges was larger than in any previous convention. Otherwise, as had been the case in all the state's previous constitutional conventions, except that of 1867–68, the members were all white and male, and most were social, economic, and political leaders in their communities.

The Convention of 1901–2

The Convention of 1901–2 was the last elected convention that wrote a constitution for Virginia. The General Assembly proposed an extensive revision in 1928 and a whole new constitution in 1970, both in the form known in parliamentary procedure as an amendment in the form of a substitute. Voters ratified them both.

The convention's members elected John Goode president, but many observers had expected that Senator Daniel, the foremost advocate of the convention, would be elected president. However, he may have feared that his partisan past might provoke some Republicans or even some Democrats to vote against him, which inclined him to agree to serve as president only if the delegates unanimously elected him. Uncertain about the outcome, he declined to be a candidate, and the convention elected Goode.[34] The president appointed Daniel chair of the critical Committee on the Elective Franchise, Qualifications for Office, Basis of Representation and Apportionment, and on Elections.[35]

On the first day when members began to organize their work, Allen Caperton Braxton, a Staunton lawyer, objected to a seemingly routine motion that the delegates take the usual oaths as officers of state government. In a well-informed, logical, and apparently extemporaneous argument, Braxton maintained that the convention's members had been elected to replace the existing state constitution and that they should not begin their work by swearing to uphold and defend it. He clearly impressed the other delegates, who postponed deciding the question, reargued it again, and eventually tabled the motion.[36]

For a large majority of the delegates, that was their introduction to Braxton, who was to be one of the most influential members of the convention. He had no prior legislative or public service experience of any kind, but he may have been the best prepared member of the convention. He conducted an extensive correspondence with advocates of disfranchisement in states of the former Confederacy and with experts on the constitutional law that was involved. His personal papers in the library of the University of Virginia preserve a large body of correspondence with experts throughout the nation on disfranchisement and corporate regulation. Braxton's careful and thorough preparation showed right from the very beginning in the discussion about the oath of office.

Some of the lawyers in the convention either already knew him or knew who he was. About the time convention members first took their seats, Braxton's two-part essay, "Powers of Conventions," appeared in the *Virginia Law Register*, the state's professional legal journal.[37] The occasion for the article was to try to settle an important political and legal question: did members of the constitutional convention, as the direct representatives of the people, have legitimate authority on their behalf to proclaim a constitution in effect, or were they restrained by the act of assembly that scheduled the election of delegates, provided for holding the convention, and required a ratification referendum?[38]

Some Democrats who insisted on disfranchisement of Black men had argued since before the May 1900 party convention that as elected representatives of the people chosen to write a new constitution, convention delegates enjoyed unrestrained legitimate authority to proclaim a constitution in force. Other men, including Braxton, believed otherwise. He argued that if voters elected members of a constitutional convention with no restraints, that might be the case; but in May 1901 when voters elected delegates, the voters' superior sovereign authority required the men whom they elected to submit the constitution to them for ratification or rejection. Thus, the question of ratification or proclamation carried over from the May 1900 Democratic Party convention and came directly before the convention at the very beginning. It resurfaced several times and was not settled until nearly a year later.

The work of the constitutional convention is well documented, although not so thoroughly as it appears to be at first glance. The convention published its official journal in a very large volume together with scores of committee reports and other documents and a second large volume of more than seven hundred pages that contains the nearly three hundred resolutions that members introduced.[39] A special committee of former convention members oversaw the publication four years later of two volumes of debates, some of which had been reported in Richmond newspapers. The 3,300 large pages of small type do not, however, include everything. From time to time throughout the convention, the Democratic members caucused off the floor, usually in the evenings. Important as those discussions undoubtedly were, they did not take place during formal sessions and were not included in the published edition of convention debates. Aside from some newspaper coverage, some notes and memoranda in Allen Caperton Braxton's papers, and several entries that Walter A. Watson made in his diary during the early months of 1902, those Democratic caucuses are not well documented. Watson's incomplete diary, which is in the Virginia Historical Society, Braxton's voluminous personal papers in the library at the University of Virginia, and the newspaper reports contain most of the surviving documentation of the Democrats' informal work.[40]

The convention met in Richmond from 6 June 1901 through 25 July 1902. It held its sessions in the chamber of the House of Delegates in the Capitol until 19 February 1902 and for part of that time, shared the room with the House of Delegates. In February, the convention moved to nearby Mechanic's Hall.[41] The delegates adjourned for the day on 7 September 1901, after President William McKinley was shot, and again on 14 September, after he died. A five-member delegation of convention members attended McKinley's funeral, and a few days later, several members delivered orations, and a Richmond clergymen preached a funeral sermon before the convention.[42] On 1 January 1902, the convention transacted no business because by special invitation, the new governor, lieutenant governor, and attorney general took the oaths of office during a session of the convention, and the governor delivered his inaugural address to the members.[43]

The convention recessed several times. It adjourned from 3 August until 22 August 1901 to allow Democrats to attend the party's state convention[44] (the Republican Party state convention met during that adjournment, too) and again from 25 October to 7 November for the conclusion of the campaign for election of statewide officers and members of the General Assembly. "From the 8th of March to the 29th," according to long note in the published record of the debates, "the Convention did not engage in any deliberations. On each day, immediately after the roll-call, the Convention adjourned, and the Democratic members . . . went into conference upon the Suffrage question. For these twenty-one days there is an intermission of the stenographic report of the proceedings of the Convention, as nothing of interest occurred during that period."[45] The routine adjournments for three weeks allowed members who answered the roll call to receive their per diem allowances while they participated in the Democratic caucuses. From 4 April to 22 May 1902, the convention adjourned while its Committee on Final Revision and Adjustment assembled all the articles in proper, final form;[46] and it adjourned again from 7 to 25 June while the convention staff prepared the enrolled constitution, schedule, and other formal documents necessary to put the constitution into effect.[47]

The published debates and the published journal of the convention both contain incomplete records of the convention's transactions. The journal, but not the debates, records leaves of absence for members and the receipt of scores of petitions on subjects such as the franchise, public education, appropriation of public funds to sectarian institutions, and the sale of alcoholic beverages but with no indication of the substance of any of them. The record of debates scarcely mentions receipt of petitions at all, and only the Committees on Education and Public Instruction, on Public Institutions and Prisons, and on Corporations preserved any of them with the convention's working papers. That is too bad because the committees no doubt took the content of those petitions into account before they reported draft articles to the full convention. We do not know, for example, how industriously Black people organized to petition against their proposed disfranchisement or what arguments they made; nor do we have a good way of ascertaining the range of options that advocates of disfranchisement suggested to the convention.

Or on other subjects. "We have had a great many memorials here to confer suffrage upon women," a delegate commented early in the session. "We do not intend to do it, because they are the power behind the throne; they are the rulers, anyhow."[48] Nothing else in either the record of debates or the journal indicates that any petitions concerned woman suffrage. Some of them could have been ingenious, such as a plan that L. W. W. published in a Richmond newspaper ten days before the convention first met. She or he proposed to authorize women to vote if they or their families owned $1,500 or more in property and paid taxes, not unlike what the Constitution of 1830 had specified for white men. "I do not wish to pose as a special champion of woman suffrage," L. W. W. explained, "But I recognize that it will come sooner than later, and that the Virginia Convention, by taking it up now can settle the suffrage question." Under the plan, many more prosperous white women than Black women would be eligible to vote, and therefore "the negroes would be thrown into a helpless minority in the State and without any violation whatever of either the Fourteenth or Fifteenth amendments. And it should also be borne in mind that the introduction into the voting population of a large body of property-owning women, or those who expect to become owners of property on the death of their husbands, would be apt to have a very conservative influence in our State politics."[49]

Even collating the texts of the published journal and debates leaves some of the convention's proceedings obscured. For instance, early in the day Saturday, 9 November 1901, when the members were discussing whether to limit the number of terms county treasurers could serve, the published debates includes this curious passage: "Various amendments and substitutes were offered and briefly discussed," with nineteen named members "participating in this running and colloquial debate."[50] According to an abbreviated report of that episode in the next day's *Richmond Times*, "the Committee of the Whole got into an inextricable parliamentary tangle . . . and got out of it by referring the subject back to the County Government Committee."[51]

A week later, the same newspaper under the headline "HOT DEBATE IN CONVENTION" summarized a passionate exchange in which some Democrats charged that some Republicans opposed racial segregation in public schools and linked that with the implications of Booker T. Washington's dining at the White House with President Theodore Roosevelt a few weeks earlier. The charge, according to the newspaper, "precipitated an acrimonious political colloquy which fairly sizzled with warmth at intervals,"[52] but none of it was included in the published record of convention debates.

By an agreement reached before the convention first met, its members resolved themselves into a Committee of the Whole on most days.[53] Freed from rules that limited how often members could speak on any one topic and how long they could speak, some of them spoke often on the same subject, and many of them spoke at great length, which is one reason why the convention lasted for an entire year. Several times, members proposed to limit the length of speeches, but none of the limitations stuck. As was always the case in constitutional conventions, some members seldom or never spoke, and others were on their feet speaking nearly every day.

Some of the lawyers were extremely able advocates, most notably Alfred P. Thom of Norfolk, Charles V. Meredith of Richmond, Eppa Hunton of Fauquier County, Alexander Hamilton of Petersburg, and A. Caperton Braxton of Staunton. Several were also particularly long-winded or particularly particular. At the end of the long series of Democratic caucus meetings on suffrage in the spring of 1902, Walter Watson recorded in his diary, "At the close of our session on Saturday I offered the following resolution: 'Resolved: That the turbulent impetuosity of Wm. A. Anderson, the hair-splitting quibbles of Wood Bouldin, the interminable commas of C. V. Meredith and J. C. Wysor are tolerable but the endless prolixity of A. C. Braxton is grievous unto death.'"[54]

Most of the members, like Goode in his opening address, disavowed any dislike of Black people, but they were nearly all extremely critical of Black Virginians, especially of their participation in public life. During a long rant one day on wasting the tax money of decent white people in a futile attempt to educate ineducable Black children, Walter Watson made the most disgusting comment among the many distasteful things any delegate said in the convention. Watson boasted that "we have been a high-minded and an arbitrary people; that we have shot some folks and cut the throats of others, always everywhere, under all circumstances shoving them out in order that we should assert our liberty not only to live ourselves, but to progress in our own way, unfettered and untrammelled by any who dare oppose the way."[55] He wrote in his diary that he was willing to "give up anything and everything to disfranchise all the negroes."[56] The convention delegate, former judge, and future congressman had little or no sympathy for democracy and absolutely none for Black people.

Convention members returned again and again to the subject of Black voting, but when they talked about the political process, they talked exclusively about white Virginia men—"our people," as President John Goode had referred to them. Carter Glass, a member of the Senate of Virginia and a Lynchburg newspaper publisher who eventually took the lead in framing the disfranchisement article of the new constitution, explained that members of the convention won election with the votes of Virginia men who knew that "the term 'people' did not comprehend all the people," only "the *white* people of Virginia."[57] Insofar as members of the convention were concerned, the body politic did not include Black people, precisely in the same way that white men had constituted the whole of the body politic when the Convention of 1776 had amended George Mason's draft language for the Virginia Declaration of Rights to make it clear that enslaved people were not to be regarded as having any of the rights that it protected, specifically including a right to freedom.[58]

Members of the convention discussed other topics at length, too. They talked about saving taxpayers money and made proposals to that purpose to allow smaller juries than twelve members, to allow some trials to take place without juries, to reduce the number and frequency of elections, and to reduce the frequency and length of meetings of the General Assembly. In doing so, some members also disclosed some deep suspicions about the democratic political process. Could they trust the voters? For instance, they discussed whether the constitution should authorize the state board of education to specify which textbooks were to be used in the state's public schools in order to guard against agents of textbook publishers bribing weak members of local school boards; but that could be done only at the expense of local voters' rights to control the schools their own children attended. Those members of the convention feared that corporations might corrupt legislators and that railroad companies might continue to influence elections. If voters could not be trusted to elect qualified men to public office, who could be trusted to select them?

While discussing whether voters, legislators, or the governor should select judges, school trustees, or members of the new State Corporation Commission, convention members complained that voters, even though they should have the choice, were not always wise enough to make good choices. Entrusting that power to corruptible members of the General Assembly might risk the rights of the people, but empowering the governor to appoint too many officers would dangerously enlarge his power. At the same time, the new constitution took away from the General Assembly the authority to appoint the state treasurer, secretary of the commonwealth, superintendent of public instruction, and commissioner of agriculture and made those officials elective for the first time.

Convention members apparently never came to a consensus on any of those questions, with the result that many provisions of the constitution that they adopted could be interpreted in contradictory ways. For example, did the grant to the governor of a new authority to veto specific items in appropriation bills dangerously increase the power of the executive, or was it a prudent check on irresponsible actions of the people's elected representatives?

The Constitution of 1902

On 6 June 1902, the convention adopted the constitution by a vote of 90 to 10. Republicans cast all the negative votes.[59] The Constitution of 1902, even before it was amended several times, and the 1928 revision of it were by far the longest of all Virginia's constitutions. At more than 29,000 words, the Constitution of 1902 was more than twice the length of the Constitution of 1869, which it replaced, and more than eight times the length of the Constitution of 1776. As for all the state's constitutions since that of 1830, the convention divided the Constitution of 1902 into articles and sections, but it numbered the new constitution's 197 sections consecutively throughout the fifteen articles rather than numbered the sections separately within each article. The new constitution also retained a revised, separate, one-sentence article declaring the separation of legislative, executive, and judicial powers, but it moved it from its old position as Article II in the Constitution of 1869 to be Article III in the Constitution of 1902.

The constitution's length was in part the result of several long new sections, including the articles on suffrage, municipal government, and the State Corporation Commission. In many other respects, as with other state constitutions elsewhere in the country early in the twentieth century, it was long because it contained much more precise detail on each of a larger number of topics than nineteenth-century constitutions typically had. Prescriptive and proscriptive details were common in state constitutions then, both to give constitutional status to new institutions and practices and to restrict the capacities of elected officials to be innovative or corrupt. Many of those provisions more nearly resembled ordinary laws than the more general authorizations and limitations of authority that had been in state constitutions from the American Revolution through the early decades of the nineteenth century. The length, form, and style of the Constitution of 1902 as well as the many subjects that it comprehended all reveal how Virginia law and American law had evolved in many important ways since independence a century and a quarter earlier.

PREAMBLE

Members of the convention debated early in the session whether it was a wholesome reminder of the patriotism of the American Revolution to retain Thomas Jefferson's long preamble from the Constitution of 1776 with its itemized list of reasons for declaring independence. Some members argued that the preamble was no longer of any practical use and that it was not necessary 125 years after independence to continue to abuse King George III. The preamble as it stood in 1901 also contained a long cumulative recitation of the authorities under which each of the state's constitutions was prepared and put into force. Some members were reluctant to retain that section and thereby accept the legitimacy of the Constitutions of 1864 and 1869. On 3 June 1902, those members added to the recitation condemnations of the Convention of 1864, "in which the great body of the people of this Commonwealth had no representation" and that had promulgated a state constitution "which was never ratified by the people of this Commonwealth"; and also of the Constitution of 1869 because "the military power and authority of the United States of America" unfairly imposed it on Virginians. The motion to add that language passed 31 to 22; but then, in one of the last important actions of the convention— after the members had decided to proclaim the constitution in effect and not submit it to a ratification referendum—they voted 37 to 18 to delete the whole preamble. They therefore began the Constitution of 1902 with three short paragraphs, similar to those in the preamble to the Constitution of 1776, that only asserted the convention's own authority.[60]

THE BILL OF RIGHTS

Convention members made several important changes to the text of the Bill of Rights in Article I. They amended Section 8, which declared "That no man shall be deprived of his life, or liberty, except by the law of the land, or the judgment of his peers; nor shall any man be compelled in any criminal proceeding to give evidence against himself." They added, "nor be put twice in jeopardy for the same offence, but an appeal may be allowed to the Commonwealth in all prosecutions for the violation of a law relating to the state revenue." The second part of that addition placed into the constitution the essence of a provision that was apparently first inserted into the annual tax law that the General Assembly passed early in 1840.[61] Members of the convention may have thought that addition was wise as a consequence of years of expensive and protracted litigation during the 1870s and 1880s in which the state tried to enforce laws to prevent payment of taxes with interest-bearing coupons from state bonds.[62] The members also revised language in that section to allow a trial without a jury in a criminal case if the accused pleaded guilty. Those changes amplified the provisions of an amendment to the Constitution of 1869 that was ratified on 6 November 1894.

The Committee on the Preamble and Bill of Rights omitted from its report to the full convention several important clauses that the Conventions of 1864 and 1867–68 had added to the Bill of Rights.[63] No delegate objected or sought to reinsert them. So, without any public debate in 1901 and 1902 the delegates quietly left out of the constitution the clauses that abolished and prohibited slavery; repudiated secession by declaring that Virginia would always remain one of the United States; declared that acts of Congress and treaties made under the authority of the Constitution of the United States were the supreme law of the land, which thereby repudiated the antebellum doctrine of states' rights; and "That all citizens of the State are hereby declared to possess equal civil and political rights and public privileges. The declaration of the political rights and privileges of the inhabitants of this State is hereby declared to be a part of the Constitution of this Commonwealth, and shall not be violated on any pretence whatever."

The published record is silent on the subject, but there is little reason to doubt from convention members' comments on the Civil War and its aftermath and their criticisms of the Constitutions of 1864 and 1869 that the committee's omission of those provisions and the convention's acceptance of the committee's report constituted a deliberate repudiation of the 1860s additions to the Bill of Rights. Only the few people who knew exactly what the Conventions of 1864 and 1867–68 had added to the Bill of Rights would have noticed those omissions and understood their significance. Seldom or never have such important changes in the state's fundamental law slipped by with such little public notice.

John Garland Pollard, a Richmond lawyer who had ahead of him a long career in politics and as a Baptist lay leader, moved to delete the word *Christian* from the conclusion of the religious liberty section that George Mason wrote in 1776, "that it is the mutual duty of all to practice Christian forbearance, love and charity, towards each other." Pollard believed in the absolute separation of church and state, which he thought that the 1786 Act for Establishing for Religious Freedom (part of the state constitution since 1830) required. For him, that meant that the state's constitution should contain no wording preferential to any religion, not even to Christianity. "The amendment I offered may be of itself comparatively unimportant," Pollard explained, "but it involves a great principle; and, knowing how even a slight violation of principle often leads to a denial of the principle itself, I thought it not unimportant, inasmuch as we are here to draft anew the fundamental law of the land, to rid it of any suggestion that it is the province of government to judge between the virtues of the religions professed by its citizens." He eventually declined to call for a vote on his proposal for fear that voters might refuse to ratify or obey the constitution if they knew that the reference to Christianity had been removed.[64]

SUFFRAGE

Article II contained twenty-one substantial sections, some of which were several paragraphs long, and was by itself almost as long as the entire Constitution of 1776. Disfranchisement of Black Virginians was the primary objective of a large majority of convention members, but the variety of methods members proposed, such as poll taxes and literacy tests, and the consequences that some of those methods presented, such as denying the vote to poor or illiterate white men, provoked months of contentious debate.

Before members of the convention began work on the suffrage article, they requested information from officers of the state bureaucracy on a number of subjects, including reports on the state's population by age, race, and sex; felony and misdemeanor charges; the number of Black people in the state's prisons; payments of taxes by race; delinquent taxes by race; the amount of tax money cities and counties collected in school taxes; and other subjects that delegates obviously considered important in identifying reasons for and in devising methods of disfranchising people without specifically relying on race, which was a violation of the Fifteenth Amendment.[65] The way was wide open so long as race was not the stated purpose of disfranchisement. The Supreme Court of the United States had, only three years earlier, ruled in *Williams v. Mississippi* that state constitutions that placed restrictions on the suffrage that applied to all potential voters irrespective of race, such as payment of poll taxes or literacy tests, did not violate the equal protection clause of the Fourteenth Amendment or the Fifteenth Amendment.[66]

John Warwick Daniel, chair of the suffrage committee, missed most of the autumn sessions of the convention. During his long absence, no other member took the lead in trying to draw together into one cohesive plan a draft article that met the agreed-on objective of disfranchising Black men without risking a serious reduction in the number of white men who would be able to register. Even after the senator returned prior to the long March recess, during which the closely divided Democratic caucus debated alternatives, he offered little leadership and proposed no plan of his own.[67] "I am sorry he returned to the Convention," Walter Watson grumbled in his diary; "he is willing to do no effective thing on Suffrage."[68] Eventually, Carter Glass, who was not even a member of the suffrage committee, took the lead in the caucus meetings and shaped the final committee report on the subject, which Daniel acknowledged when he introduced it to the convention on 31 March 1902.[69]

Convention members debated and amended the draft suffrage article and on 4 April adopted it with a vote of 59 to 20.[70] The 3 to 1 approval of the article did not reflect a consensus on its provisions after the long and heated debates and arguments. Many delegates were unhappy with the article, some because they believed that it did not go far enough in assuring that all Black voters would be disfranchised; some because the methods of disfranchising Black men jeopardized the ability of some white men to register; some doubted that disfranchisement of any white men was a price worth paying to disfranchise most or all Black men; and some others, that disfranchising poor or poorly educated white men was itself also a wholesome objective.[71]

Section 18, the first in the article, included a new requirement that in order to register and vote, adult men had to have paid a poll tax. A poll tax requirement had been added to the Constitution of 1869 in 1876, but it was repealed in 1882. The new requirement remained in the Constitution until 1971, five years after the Supreme Court of the United States declared in *Harper v. Virginia State Board of Elections* that the poll tax violated the Constitution of the United States.[72]

Almost everything else in the article was a prohibition on voting or an obstacle to registration. Section 23 disqualified men who had been disqualified under the state's previous constitutions: "Idiots, insane persons, and paupers; persons who, prior to the adoption of this Constitution, were disqualified from voting, by conviction of crime, either within or without this State, and whose disabilities shall not have been removed," including having taken part in a duel. And Section 24 disqualified servicemen temporarily stationed in Virginia, inmates of charitable institutions, and students in the state's universities who enrolled as residents of other states.

Section 19 decreed that for the first election to be held after it went into effect, adult men could register to vote if they had served in the armed or naval forces of the United States or the Confederate States, had paid their taxes for the previous year, or could read and satisfactorily explain a section of the new constitution. Section 20 required that thereafter, every person who wished to vote had to pay an annual poll tax of $1.50 and be paid up for three full years prior to an election, except veterans, who were exempted from the tax payment.

Then, each man had to seek out a registrar and, "unless physically unable" in "his own handwriting, without aid, suggestion, or memorandum" provide his name, age, date and place of birth, place of residence and occupation at the time and for the two previous years, whether and where he had previously voted, and "answer on oath any and all questions affecting his qualifications as an elector, submitted, to him by the officers of registration." That was a literacy test, although not so called. A failure to provide full and correct details for any of the requirements was grounds for denial of registration.

Section 30 authorized the General Assembly to impose an optional "property qualification not exceeding two hundred and fifty dollars for voters in any county or subdivision thereof, or city or town, as a prerequisite for voting in any election for officers, other than the members of the General Assembly, to be wholly elected by the voters of such county or subdivision thereof, or city, or town." Little noticed at the time and probably never invoked, that section was in the nature of a last resort, just in case, in spite of the difficulty of registration, Black men in any community appeared able to register in such numbers as to form a majority of voters and be able to elect local officers. In 1915, when John Garland Pollard was attorney general, he explained the purpose of that section in precisely those terms to the president of the Equal Suffrage League of Virginia, who, in her campaign for votes for women, had to respond to charges that enfranchisement of women could endanger the disfranchisement of Black men that the Constitution of 1902 imposed in Virginia and lead to the election of Black men as public officials.[73]

Having corrupted the registration process to achieve their disfranchisement objective, members of the convention then cleaned up the voting process so as to be able to pretend and boast that they had ended the corruption that they had condemned before the convention. The provisions of Article II included some that very specifically and clearly prohibited some of the fraudulent or unfair practices voters had faced during the previous two decades. Section 27 ordered, "The ballotbox shall be kept in public view during all elections, and shall not be opened, nor the ballots canvassed or counted, in secret," and "So far as consistent with the provisions of this Constitution, the absolute secrecy of the ballot shall be maintained." Section 28 required the state to supply "ballots without any distinguishing mark or symbol, for use in all state, county, city, and other elections by the people, and the form thereof shall be the same in all places where any such election is held. All ballots shall contain the names of the candidates, and of the offices to be filled, in clear print and in due and orderly succession."

Section 36 required the General Assembly to "enact such laws as are necessary and proper for the purpose of securing the regularity and purity of general, local and primary elections, and preventing and punishing any corrupt practices in connection therewith." Other sections contained clear and detailed instructions for counting and reporting the votes, all of which could be considered as substantial victories for people—even the ones who were intent on disfranchising Black men—who wished to reform electoral practices and make them less unfair and more nearly democratic.

In defending the final text of the article, Norfolk attorney Alfred P. Thom was chillingly honest in his description of the dishonest purpose of the article. "I expect the examination with which the black man will be confronted" when he attempted to register "to be inspired by the same spirit that inspires every man upon this floor and in this convention. I would not expect an impartial administration of the clause. . . . We do not come here prompted by an impartial purpose in reference to negro suffrage. We come here to sweep the field of expedients for the purpose of finding some constitutional method of ridding ourselves of it forever; and we have the approval of the Supreme Court of the United States in making this effort," meaning the Supreme Court's 1898 ruling in *Williams v. Mississippi*.[74]

"Gentlemen," Republican delegate Albert P. Gillespie complained a little later in the final day of debates, "I have been taught to believe that where a man was guilty of a fraud or of cheating another man, the man who committed the fraud should be punished, that a man who steals a vote should be punished. . . . . The remedy suggested here is to punish the man who has been injured. It is now proposed to right a wrong by punishing those have been defrauded of their votes to the extent of destroying their right of suffrage; in other words, the negro vote of this Commonwealth must be destroyed to prevent Democratic election officers from stealing their votes, for it seems that, as long as there is a negro vote to be stolen, there will be a Democratic election officer ready to steal it."[75]

During the final minutes of the months-long exchanges on the suffrage article, Carter Glass boasted, "This plan of popular suffrage will eliminate the darkey as a political factor in this State in less than five years, so that in no single county of the Commonwealth will there be the least concern felt for the complete supremacy of the white race in the affairs of government. . . . Our politics will be purified and the public service strengthened." Glass tried to reassure skeptical delegates "that the article of suffrage which the Convention will today adopt does not necessarily deprive a single white man of the ballot, but will inevitably cut from the existing electorate four-fifths of the negro voters. (Applause.) That was the purpose of this Convention; that will be the achievement."

Pedigo interrupted Glass at that point and asked, "Will it not be done by fraud and discrimination?"

Glass answered, "By fraud, no; by discrimination, yes. But it will be discrimination within the letter of the law, and not in violation of the law." The published record of the exchange does not indicate that Glass then paused briefly to reflect on the implications of the question; but with an exclamation point the stenographer left the impression that Glass suddenly realized that Pedigo might have implied that discrimination was a bad thing. "Discrimination!" Glass exclaimed, "Why, that is precisely what we propose; that, exactly, is what this Convention was elected for—to discriminate to the very extremity of permissible action under the limitations of the Federal Constitution, with a view to the elimination of every negro voter who can be gotten rid of, legally, without materially impairing the numerical strength of the white electorate. As has been said, we have accomplished our purpose strictly within the limitations of the Federal Constitution by legislating against the characteristics of the black race, and not against the 'race, color or previous condition' of the people themselves. It is a fine discrimination, indeed, that we have practiced in the fabrication of this plan."[76]

By the phrase "the characteristics of the black race," Glass evidently meant the characteristics that members of the convention believed and had repeatedly described, including illiteracy, ignorance, incompetence, untrustworthiness, and dishonesty, not to mention a thirty-five-year history of voting for Readjusters and Republicans. The suffrage article was not only openly racist in purpose, it was also plainly partisan.

THE GENERAL ASSEMBLY

Article IV of the new constitution contained twenty-nine sections. It allowed the General Assembly to set the number of members of the House of Delegates between ninety and one hundred and the number of senators between thirty-three and forty. It left in place the apportionment of seats in both houses that was adopted in 1892 but provided for a new apportionment in 1906. Thereafter, as in all the constitutions since that of 1830, it required the General Assembly to redistrict the state following each federal census. The constitution did not require equality of population in legislative districts, but it continued to require approximate equality in congressional districts that the Constitution of 1830 had included for the first time.

Members of the convention retained most of the provisions concerning the General Assembly from the Constitution of 1869 with some revisions, but the members directed a great deal of criticism at the General Assembly. They made proposals to reduce the frequency and length of legislative sessions that had many supporters on the floor of the convention. They complained that the General Assembly passed too many bills and that too many of the bills that the assembly passed were poorly drafted or inadequately considered. Some of those criticisms revealed distrust of its members, others skepticism about the ability of voters to elect competent legislators. Several members criticized high rates of turnover at election times and logrolling in the selection of judges.

Remedies that some convention members proposed included reduction of the length of assembly sessions to make it more difficult for legislators to pass so many bills and to limit the number of topics on which legislators could act in order to give them time to do better work on the most necessary bills. Some members of the convention therefore supported popular election of more public officials rather than entrust their selection to elected legislators; but if it was voters who elected untrustworthy legislators, perceived problems and proposed solutions became entangled in mutually contradictory ways.

Advocates of extending the terms for members of the House of Delegates from two years to four and of requiring the General Assembly to meet every fourth year rather than every second commanded considerable support on the floor of the convention.[77] Near the very beginning, perhaps after drinks at a bar one evening, one delegate joked, "There are a good many gentlemen here who are disposed to deride the Legislature and its powers. I believe, according to the views of some, they would elect members of the Legislature for life and then provide that they should never meet. (Laughter.)"[78] The final vote to retain two-year terms for delegates and biennial sessions did not come until the spring of 1902.[79]

Section 10 of the schedule that they adopted, along with the new constitution, required for the first time that beginning in 1907, all senators be elected at the same time, not in a rotation that as in the past had provided for election of one-fourth of the senators every year or one-half every second year. Beginning 1907, all the senators were elected at the mid-point of a governor's one four-year term of office. Whether that was a deliberate change to provide voters with something of a checking referendum on a governor midway through his term is not clear from the published debates.

The new limitations and authorizations in Article IV addressed some but by no means all of the concerns. Section 46 reduced the length of the regular biennial session from ninety days to sixty days with an option to add an additional thirty days. Section 50 specified in detail how bills should be printed and read in full on three separate days before the final vote. Section 51 created a permanent joint committee of seven delegates and five senators to review all proposed local legislation and report to the house in which it originated whether the subject matter could better be, or had already been, treated with general laws. That was evidently intended to reduce the number of bills on local matters that the full membership of the General Assembly had to deal with each session. Section 68 created a joint auditing committee, the better to keep a legislative eye on the operations of the state's auditors, treasurer, secretary of the commonwealth, and other government officials. And Section 63 included a list of twenty topics on which it forbade the assembly to pass laws that were applicable only to one locality.

Section 62 granted the General Assembly "full power to enact local option or dispensary laws, or any other laws controlling, regulating, or prohibiting the manufacture or sale of intoxicating liquors." Temperance and prohibition were both very controversial issues in Virginia politics at the time and remained so for several decades. Sale of alcohol was probably the subject of more petitions to the convention than any other one topic except suffrage.

Section 67 prohibited the General Assembly from making any appropriation of public funds "to any church, or sectarian society, association, or institution of any kind whatever, which is entirely or partly, directly or indirectly, controlled by any church or sectarian society; nor shall the General Assembly make any like appropriation to any charitable institution, which is not owned or controlled by the State." Adoption of that section followed a long discussion on retaining the 1851 prohibition on incorporation of religious organizations[80] and another long discussion about the propriety of the assembly or local governments appropriating public money to such charitable institutions as the Little Sisters of the Poor and St. Joseph's Orphanage, two Catholic charities in Richmond that supplied important social services that the city did not. Overt anti-Catholic language did not appear in the recorded discussions, but some anti-Catholicism may have figured in the thinking of some advocates of the restrictive language.[81]

The limitations that the convention placed on the General Assembly in the new constitution arose for the most part from contemporary events, many of them involving political logrolling or outright corruption. The one principal authorization to the assembly, to legislate on alcoholic beverages, was a contemporary political issue, too, but it was the only major clarifying grant of authority to the General Assembly in the new constitution. From the time of the American Revolution, lawyers, judges, and learned commentators had all agreed that state constitutions implicitly invested legislatures with all the authority on every subject that the constitutions did not explicitly deny to them. The Constitution of 1902 was fully within that tradition.[82] The Virginia Supreme Court of Appeals in 1918 affirmed that long-accepted understanding in the state's constitutional law. In *Strawberry Hill Land Co. v. Starbuck*, the court declared that "the State Constitution is not a grant of power, but only the restriction of powers otherwise practically unlimited, that, except so far as restrained by the Constitution, the legislature has plenary power, and that every fair doubt must be resolved in favor of the constitutionality of an act of the General Assembly."[83]

THE EXECUTIVE

Article V on the executive consisted of seventeen sections, some of which affected the authority of the General Assembly, as well. Most of the article on the executive in the Constitution of 1869 remained substantially unchanged, including the prohibition on governors running for reelection.

The most important change was authorization in Section 76 to veto specific items in appropriations bills (a power that the president of the Confederate States had possessed), subject to a two-thirds vote in both houses to override the veto. The carefully worded paragraph specified that a veto of an item in any appropriation bill did not invalidate the whole of the bill. Members of the convention did not discuss this innovation at any length. The section also contained a new provision that allowed the governor to return a bill to the General Assembly with a proposal to amend part or parts of it, which the assembly could accept or reject by the same procedure for considering a veto. The bill in its original or amended form would then return to the governor who "may act upon it as if it were then before him for the first time."

The obvious inference to be drawn from the grant of new authorities to the governor was that it empowered him to place a check on some of the wasteful or frivolous measures that irresponsible legislators might incorporate into appropriations bills. Considering the many criticisms of the General Assembly during the course of the convention, that obvious explanation is almost certainly the correct one. That, together with explicit authorizations for the governor to oversee and remove from office employees or officers of the executive department, substantially augmented the governor's authority to direct and supervise executive agencies.

However carefully drafted the item veto provision appeared to be, the critical word *item* is not therein defined. In 1940, in *Commonwealth v. Dodson*, the Supreme Court of Appeals invalided several vetoes the governor handed down earlier that year. In doing so, the court had to specify more precisely what an item was. The court began with an analogy to preface the definition; "If the Commonwealth were to determine to erect a library building and were to set apart a certain sum for structural steel, another for a heating plant, etc., and were finally to provide for a supervising architect at a stated salary, plainly the Governor could not, by veto, dispense with the services of an architect, although the sum to be paid for his services might, in a limited sense, be regarded as an item. That term," the court concluded, "as used in the Constitution, refers to something which may be taken out of a bill without affecting its other purposes or provisions. It is something which can be lifted bodily from it rather than cut out. No damage can be done to the surrounding legislative tissue, nor should any scar tissue result therefrom."[84]

Sections 80 and 81 directed that the voters, for the first time, elect the secretary of the commonwealth and the state treasurer for four-year terms that coincided with the governor's term. Section 86 authorized the General Assembly to establish a Bureau of Labor Statistics. The new constitution omitted Article III, Section 15, of the old constitution that authorized the General Assembly to establish Bureaus of Agricultural Chemistry, Agriculture and Immigration, and Public Works in the executive department and replaced it with Article X that created a new independent Board of Agriculture and Immigration.

Sections 77 and 78 repeated with no consequential change the former constitution's provisions for the lieutenant governor, including the right to cast a deciding vote, first introduced in 1869, in case of a tie vote in the Senate. Section 78 retained the language that had been in the state's constitutions since 1851 when the modern office of lieutenant governor was created that "In case of the removal of the Governor from office, or of his death, failure to qualify, resignation, removal from the State, or inability to discharge the powers and duties of the office, the said office, with its compensation, shall devolve upon the Lieutenant-Governor."

THE JUDICIARY

The twenty-three sections of Article VI included much new detail on the state's courts and their jurisdictions and made some important changes. Sections 88 through 91 authorized the General Assembly, as had been the case since 1869, to elect five judges of the Supreme Court of Appeals for twelve-year terms. Correcting a perceived defect in the Constitution of 1869,[85] it specified that at the first election of judges, one judge be elected for a term of four years, one for a term of six, one for a term of eight, one for a term of ten, and one for a term of twelve years so that their terms of office should be staggered from the very beginning; and it further specified that appointments to fill vacancies on the bench be for the remainder of the unexpired term and not for a full term of twelve years. The article repeated the requirement in the previous constitution that the court "shall hold its sessions at two or more places in the State, to be fixed by law." Since a law enacted in 1870, the court had held annual sessions in Wytheville, in southwestern Virginia, and in Staunton, in the Shenandoah Valley in addition to its annual sessions in the capital city of Richmond.[86] It continued to do so until the Constitution of 1971 dispensed with that requirement.

Section 89, for the most part carried over from the Constitution of 1869, authorized the General Assembly to "provide for a Special Court of Appeals to try any cases on the docket of the Supreme Court of Appeals in respect to which a majority of the judges are so situated as to make it improper for them to sit; and also to try any cases on said docket which cannot be disposed of with convenient dispatch." By then, nearly a century after the docket of the Supreme Court of Appeals had become clogged with an unmanageable backlog of cases, the court had finally cleared its docket.[87] The General Assembly temporarily revived the Special Court of Appeals by a statute in 1924.[88]

The article created twenty-four judicial circuits and specified which counties and cities were to be included in each, although the constitution granted the General Assembly authority to change the composition of the circuits after 1 January 1906. The judges of the new circuit courts replaced the individual trial judges for each county that the former constitution authorized. The

General Assembly retained its power to elect all judges of courts of record, but Section 103 established maximum and minimum salary ranges for the judges of each court.

Most members of the convention regarded those provisions as the final elimination of the original county court system that had first been established in Virginia in the 1620s, but in fact, the creation of the board of supervisors form of county government in 1869 had effectively abolished the county courts as the sole institutions of local government in Virginia's counties. Advocates of the change in the convention successfully overcame objections, some of which were based in sentimentality, to the final abolition of the office of judge of the old county courts and therefore, they feared, the convivial tradition of court day.[89]

The article authorized the General Assembly to create courts of land registration, in anticipation that the Torrens system of land registration would be adopted in Virginia. It was not as appealing and popular as it initially appeared, and Virginia was one of a large majority of states that did not adopt it.[90] One of the more important innovations in the article was Section 101 that authorized clerks of circuit courts to oversee the probate of estates, which removed the proving of wills and settling of accounts from action in open court.

COUNTY GOVERNMENT

Article VII, Organization and Government of Counties, was shorter (but not by much) in the Constitution of 1902 than its counterpart in the Constitution of 1869. The six sections in effect reauthorized the essential organization and structure of county government as provided for in the amendments ratified in 1874 that had modified and somewhat simplified the original board of supervisors form of county government created in 1869. The new article authorized voters to elect a treasurer, sheriff, commonwealth's attorney, supervisor of the poor, surveyor, and clerk of court in each county and so many commissioners of the revenue as the General Assembly should provide for each. It empowered residents of each magisterial district to elect one member of the county's board of supervisors. Those officers, named in the state constitution, came later to be called "constitutional officers," as distinguished from other county officials whose offices state laws or local ordinances created. By the time the constitutional convention met in 1901, few members proposed to change the basic form of government that had been in place in the counties for more than thirty years or to reduce the number of locally elected officials further.[91] Not only was Article VII comparatively brief, it was one of the few in the new constitution that did not in some way abridge or encroach on the democratic elements of government that the Constitutional Revolution of 1850–70 created in Virginia.

MUNICIPAL GOVERNMENT

The thirteen long sections in the 2,800-word Article VIII, Organization and Government of Cities and Towns, were entirely new. It was the first (and only) article in any Virginia constitution that explicitly and solely treated city and town governments. At the beginning of the twentieth century, cities were becoming more numerous, more populous, and more important to the state than they had ever been.

Section 116 designated incorporated jurisdictions with more than 5,000 inhabitants as cities and with fewer than 5,000 inhabitants as towns. The article left each existing chartered town or city the option to retain its charter, "except so far as it shall be repealed or amended by the General Assembly: provided, that every such charter is hereby amended so as to conform to all the provisions, restrictions, limitations and powers set forth in this article, or otherwise provided in this Constitution."

Section 123 authorized mayors to veto ordinances that city and town councils passed subject to a two-thirds vote of the council or of both branches of a bicameral council to override the veto. Mayors, like the governor, gained an item veto in appropriation of public money, subject to the same override provisions. The article authorized voters in cities and towns to elect their own constitutional officers—a commonwealth's attorney, commissioner of revenue, and treasurer, so many clerks of court as the General Assembly should determine—and a city clerk in cities that had their own deed records. Section 120 designated mayors as the chief executive officers in their cities, specified their duties and responsibilities in detail, including their supervision and inspection of the offices of subordinate executive officers and the suspension of them if required.

The language of existing city and county charters governed the lengths of terms of office, but jurisdictions could elect to conform their governmental structures and election schedules to those specified in the new constitutions. The constitution permitted cities and towns with fewer than 10,000 residents to opt for unicameral councils but required that cities of more than 10,000 inhabitants have bicameral councils with ward boundaries drawn so as "to give as far as practicable, to each ward of such city, equal representation in each branch of said council in proportion to the population of such ward." Until ratification of the Constitution of 1971, that was the only requirement for approximate equality of population in any electoral districts other than those for the election of members of the House of Representatives.[92]

The constitution placed restrictions on private corporations that used or applied to use public streets and ways, which is another evidence that members of the convention and their constituents had experienced problems with modern corporate institutions and were determined to protect the public interest from them. "No street railway," it declared, "gas, water, steam, or electric heating, electric light or power, cold storage, compressed air, viaduct, conduit, telephone, or bridge, company, nor any corporation, association, person or partnership, engaged in these or like enterprises, shall be permitted to use the streets, alleys, or public grounds of a city or town, without the previous consent of the corporate authorities of such city or town." The constitution also secured the rights of every city and town "in and to its water front, wharf property, public landings, wharves, docks, streets, avenues, parks, bridges, and other public places"; and it prohibited any city from selling its "gas, water, and electric works . . . except by an ordinance or resolution passed by a recorded affirmative vote of three-fourths of all the members elected" to its council.

The long and detailed Section 127 concerned new municipal debt. It prohibited cities from issuing bonds to borrow a sum of money that "shall at any time, exceed eighteen per centum of the assessed valuation of the real estate in the city or town subject to taxation, as shown by the last preceding assessment for taxes." Section 128 required, "In cities and towns the assessment of real estate and personal property for the purpose of municipal taxation, shall be the same as the assessment thereof for the purpose of state taxation, whenever there shall be a state assessment of such property."

The provisions of Article VIII incorporated into the constitution institutions of municipal government that had grown up during a century or more of slow, unplanned evolution of Virginia's unique system of city-county separation. By the end of the nineteenth century, each independent city, as they all came to be designated, had all its own legislative, executive, law enforcement, and other officers and was also a separate jurisdiction enumerated in legislative and congressional district statutes. The state's system of district courts followed city and county boundaries. Each city was as legally independent of the adjacent (or surrounding) county or counties as the counties were independent of each other.[93] In September 1901, just as the constitutional convention was getting up to speed, the Supreme Court of Appeals explicitly acknowledged, in *Supervisors of Washington County v. Saltville Land Co.*, that under the terms of the Constitution of 1869 a city, unlike a town, was entitled "to a separate government, and when incorporated is not part of the county for governmental purposes."[94]

EDUCATION

Article IX on Education and Public Instruction had fourteen sections and was considerably longer and more detailed than the corresponding article in the Constitution of 1869 that had created the state's first public school system. The General Assembly had formerly appointed the superintendent of public instruction, but Section 130 provided that voters elect the superintendent for a four-year term at the same time that they elected the governor.

The section designated the governor, attorney general, and superintendent of public instruction as members of the State Board of Education, as before. Appointment of city and county superintendents of schools was the subject of long debate. Some convention members preferred that voters elect county and city school trustees who would in turn appoint local school superintendents. Other delegates thought that the apparent expertise and superior knowledge that presidents or faculty members at the state's colleges and universities possessed made those educators better qualified to choose superintendents. The convention voted to enlarge the State Board of Education from three members to eight and to empower the board to appoint superintendents. Section 130 provided for the appointment to the board of three "experienced educators" from a panel of faculty members at the publicly supported colleges and universities. It authorized the board to appoint to the board "two division superintendents of schools, one from a county and the other from a city, who shall hold office for two years." The article empowered the board to appoint a school superintendent for each county and city, oversee the public school system of the state, and prescribe textbooks to be used in the schools. Advocates of central control and of empowering supposed educational experts at universities to take part in appointing school superintendents and setting policy prevailed over advocates of local, democratic selection of county and city superintendents of schools.

Section 138 stated, "The General Assembly may, in its discretion, provide for the compulsory education of children between the ages of eight and twelve years, except such as are weak in body or mind, or can read and write, or are attending private schools, or are excused for cause by the district school trustees."

Section 140 was the shortest in the entire constitution and almost certainly the least controversial. When the Committee of the Whole was working on final amendments to the article on 23 November 1901, the section, then number 10 in the draft article, was approved without debate as follows:

"The Chairman: The Secretary will read the next section.

"Section 10. White and colored children shall not be taught in the same school.

"The Chairman: Is there any amendment to section 10? If not, the Secretary will read the next section."[95]

None of the sixty-seven members of the convention who answered the roll call at the beginning of the day's session[96] objected to mandatory racial segregation in the public schools. It would have been astonishing at that time if any member of the convention had objected. Section 140 remained in the state constitution until 1971, seventeen years after the Supreme Court of the United States ruled in *Brown v. Board of Education of Topeka* that it violated the equal protection clause of the Fourteenth Amendment.[97]

The article also placed the management of the state's library under the authority of the Board of Education rather than of the secretary of the commonwealth and the General Assembly's Joint Committee on the Library. Section 132 authorized the Board of Education to appoint a library board to oversee the institution and hire the librarian, "but the Supreme Court of Appeals shall have the management of the law library and the appointment of the librarian and other employees thereof."[98]

INDEPENDENT BOARDS AND COMMISSIONS

New Articles X and XI authorized three of the four new independent state commissions that the constitution created. The first created a Department of Agriculture and Immigration under the direction of a Board of Agriculture and Immigration. It replaced the old statutory commissioner of agriculture and consisted of one "practical farmer" from each of the state's congressional districts, whom the governor nominated and the Senate of Virginia confirmed, plus the president of Virginia Polytechnic Institute ex officio. In turn, the president of the board became ex officio a member of the board of visitors of Virginia Polytechnic Institute. The article empowered voters to elect the commissioner for a four-year term.

Section 148 made the state's prison system a constitutionally authorized body. It provided that the governor appoint, subject to confirmation by the Senate, a five-member board of directors and authorized it to hire, supervise, and fire all prison officials and to establish prisons as well as prison farms outside of the capital city.

Sections 149 through 151 authorized the governor to appoint, subject to confirmation by the Senate, a three-member board of visitors for each of the public mental hospitals in the state or any others to be established later, and it created a state board to oversee the system. The state board consisted of all the members of all the boards of individual hospitals under the chairmanship of the Commissioner of State Hospitals for the Insane, whom the governor also appointed for a four-year term subject to confirmation by the Senate. The article also made the commissioner chair of each of the individual hospital boards.

STATE CORPORATION COMMISSION

Article XII contained fifteen long sections, some of them several paragraphs long and some with numerous complex subsections, that established the independent State Corporation Commission. At more than 6,600 words, the article was by far the longest ever to appear in a Virginia constitution, longer than the entire Constitution of 1830 and about twice the length of the Constitution of 1776. Its extraordinarily minute detail was a consequence of its purpose, which was to impose public regulation on private corporations without depriving those corporations of what, during the second half of the nineteenth century, came to be called substantive due process of law. State legislatures and municipalities had attempted to impose regulations on or to set maximum rates of charge for railroads and other corporations through legislative or administrative actions, but the corporations fought back in federal court and usually prevailed by arguing that the regulations and prescribed rates deprived them of their property—profits—arbitrarily and without compensation or due process of law—a judicial process—in violation of the Fourteenth Amendment.

The task of A. Caperton Braxton, who was the foremost advocate for the creation of the commission, chair of the Committee on Corporations, and the principal architect of the article, was to find a constitutional way to immunize the commission from challenges on those grounds. He boldly conceived the original idea of creating a separate department of government for the purpose of regulating corporations, making it a court of record, and requiring it to function like a court at every step in the regulatory process. All procedural and substantive rulings of the commission could be appealed directly and immediately to the Supreme Court of Appeals.[99]

Braxton prepared even more thoroughly for his role in creating the commission than he had done for his support for disfranchisement. He actually cared more about public regulation of railroads than about disfranchisement, but he was clearly the best prepared member of the convention on the many legal questions that both subjects presented. He was extremely diligent in his compilation of data from state regulatory authorities elsewhere in the United States and from the Interstate Commerce Commission in Washington, DC, as well as in his legal research into corporate and constitutional law. Braxton's personal papers are a monument to dedication and industry.

"For many long weary weeks and months" during the autumn of 1901 and early in the winter, Joseph C. Wysor, a member of the Committee on Corporations recalled, Braxton "worked upon this article in the basement of the Capitol. The members frequently referred to him jocosely as being in the catacombs."[100] Braxton sought the advice and assistance of an able collaborator, economist H. Parker Willis, who had a long career as a professor of political economy at Washington and Lee and at George Washington Universities, as an editor of the New York *Journal of Commerce*, and as an advisor to Carter Glass when Glass was a member of the House of Representatives and one of the sponsors of the Federal Reserve Act of 1913.[101] Both the text of the article that created the State Corporation Commission and Braxton's explanation and defense of the committee report on the floor of the convention demonstrated his considerable talent as a legal draftsman and advocate.

When Braxton presented the committee draft to the convention on 4 February 1902, he spoke for more than three hours. He was well-organized, persuasive, and at times eloquent in a speech that comprehensively treated the economics of the railroad industry, which operated as a natural, unregulated monopoly in most places. He also addressed the politics of regulation; the many complex legal technicalities involved in imposing fair public regulations on private corporations; the necessity for observing due process of law scrupulously; the structure of the commission and the operational details that he incorporated into the draft article; immediate access to the Supreme Court of Appeals on procedural and substantive actions of the commission; and the benefits that adoption of the article and creation of the commission would produce. Braxton's answers to questions during his speech were as precise and persuasive as his formal presentation.[102] Braxton believed that he had the support for his proposal of about two-thirds of the members of the convention and of most of the professional and trade organizations in the state.[103]

Members of the convention debated the draft article for three weeks early in February and for another week beginning at the end of the month.[104] Braxton calmly and confidently took charge of the convention. Even the very able arguments of Eppa Hunton, as well as those of other members who preferred to leave regulation to the General Assembly and therefore probably make it ineffective or legally vulnerable, did not deter Braxton. He accepted friendly amendments when he perceived their value or to accommodate skeptics.

The article created a State Corporation Commission of three members whom the governor appointed for staggered six-year terms subject to confirmation by the General Assembly. The article prohibited appointment to the commission of any person in any way employed by or associated with any regulated business and required that at least one of the members had to be qualified to serve on the Supreme Court of Appeals. The State Corporation Commission exercised legislative, administrative, and judicial powers in what may have been the first state agency of its kind in the country. The article authorized the commission to establish bureaus for the regulation of insurance and banking as well as of all transportation and transmission companies, such as telephone and telegraph companies, and to absorb the responsibilities and take charge of the records of the old Board of Public Works and of the statutory and impotent office of railroad commissioner.

The commission's jurisdiction was necessarily limited to businesses that were chartered in the state or that operated entirely within the state. Article I, Section 2, of the Constitution of the United States conferred on Congress the power to regulate interstate and foreign commerce. Whether that power was exclusive or concurrent with the authorities of states in local business activity that was directly connected with or part of interstate or foreign commerce had been, was, and remained a subject of disagreement and litigation. At the time that the convention created the commission, much more commerce was local or regarded as local—intrastate—than later came to be the case.

The commission became the sole agent of the state to grant charters of incorporation, amend charters, or revoke them. It also specified procedures by which corporations operating under charters issued in other states (called "foreign corporations") could be licensed to do business in Virginia. The article contained a kind of grandfather clause to permit Virginia corporations to continue to operate under their original charters.

The article included very precise legal definitions of all the entities to be regulated or licensed. It prohibited discriminatory freight and passenger rates on railroads and other common carriers. It also prohibited the practice of providing legislators and other public officials free passes on railroads—excepting members of the commission, itself, when they were on official business.

Section 162 abolished the fellow servant rule for the railroad industry "so far as it affects the liability of the master for injuries to his servant resulting from the acts or omissions of any other servant or servants of the common master." With a long list of definitions of the kinds of work that men were employed in on the dangerous railroads, the section entitled injured men or the survivors of men who were killed on the job to receive compensation. That largely terminated the abilities of railroad companies to escape liability for injuries or deaths on the job by invoking the old Common Law rule that an owner or employer was not liable through the negligence or incapacity of another employee, or fellow servant. Thereafter, railroads were responsible at their own peril for the safety of all engines, cars, track, and for the proper training and supervision of employees. That the convention abolished one of the mainstay legal doctrines that corporations had used to shield themselves from liability was clear evidence that public dissatisfaction with corporations, railroads in particular, was very strong in Virginia. In a state known then and thereafter as friendly to businesses, abolition of the fellow servant rule on railroads was one of the most remarkable actions of the entire convention.

Because of the broad, new authorities that the constitution granted to members of the new commission, some convention delegates believed that the voters should elect the judges of the commission. Braxton and other members doubted whether voters could make wise choices because of the technical expertise in financial and business matters that judges of the commission should have, and they favored authorizing the General Assembly to elect them or have the governor appoint them, subject to confirmation by the assembly. Suspicion about the capacity of ordinary voters to make wise choices in the election of members of the commission was very evident in that part of the convention's work.[105] In the end, they compromised by authorizing the governor to appoint the judges subject to confirmation by the assembly but empowered the assembly to grant voters the right to elect them at any time after 1 January 1908. In 1918, the General Assembly granted voters the authority to elect members of the commission,[106] then in 1926, the assembly authorized the governor to appoint the judges, subject to approval of the General Assembly.[107]

Braxton was very pleased at the end result. In 1904 he published an article in the *Virginia Law Register* on the creation of the commission, its purposes, methods, and importance. In that article, he defended the many regulatory powers with which the commission was invested as necessary for the public good and for the good of the corporations themselves. When properly regulated, he explained, corporations could not engage in exploitive practices that would give socialists and opponents of corporations reason to advocate more radical measures.[108] Indeed, having deflected all charges of his own radicalism during the convention, Braxton became general counsel of the Richmond, Fredericksburg, and Potomac Railroad in 1904. He was elected president of the Virginia State Bar Association in 1906.[109]

TAXATION AND FINANCE

Article XII on Taxation and Finance was also quite long, more than 3,700 words in twenty-two sections, some of which had several subsections. Sections 168 and 169 required uniformity of taxation at fair market value for both state and local taxes, and Section 171 required reassessments of all taxable property every fifth year. Section 170 retained the General Assembly's power to tax incomes in excess of $600 per annum and authorized it to levy taxes on franchises (businesses that operated under licenses from other corporations). It also placed limitations on the authority of cities to tax certain private properties. Section 173 authorized the General Assembly to levy the poll tax required in the article on suffrage and to devote the revenue from it to the public schools.

Section 175 declared, "The natural oyster beds, rocks, and shoals, in the waters of this State shall not be leased, rented or sold, but shall be held in trust for the benefit of the people of this State, subject to such regulations and restrictions as the General Assembly may prescribe." Delegate Joseph A. Bristow, holder of a patent on a deepwater oyster tong, introduced the original version of that provision.[110] That section could have been added to the Bill of Rights inasmuch as it did not clearly concern taxation or public finance but a personal right of access to a public place for a lawful purpose. The convention may have inserted it into Article XII to replace Section 2 of Article X in the Constitution of 1869 which had declared that oysters harvested from natural oyster beds were to be free from taxation, but which allowed sales of those oysters to be taxed. An amendment ratified in 1901 had deleted that section from the old constitution.

Sections 176 through 182 contained detailed procedures for ascertaining the taxable value of corporations and of shares of stock in corporations, with the State Corporation Commission charged with assessing some species of that property. Section 183 contained a long list of classes of property or of owners of property that the state could not tax, including property of the state and its cities, counties, and schools and earnings on municipal bonds; property of churches or religious societies used exclusively for religious purposes; family burial grounds; property used for schools and academies for educational purposes, specifically including by name the Virginia Historical Society, the Association for the Preservation of Virginia Antiquities, the Confederate Memorial Literary Society, and the Mount Vernon Ladies' Association of the Union. The section also specified that the state could not tax "Real estate belonging to, actually and exclusively occupied, and used by, and personal property, including endowment funds, belonging to Young Men's Christian Associations, and other similar religious associations, orphan or other asylums, reformatories, hospitals and nunneries, which are not conducted for profit, but purely and completely as charities," as well as the property of fraternal associations.

The article also retained, with some modifications in language, the provisions in the Constitutions of 1864 and 1869 that prohibited the state from incurring new public debt except as needed to offset temporary shortfalls in revenue or to pay for emergency expenses in protecting the public safety. It contained revised language that was consistent with the Fourteenth Amendment concerning indebtedness incurred during the Civil War: "no appropriation shall be made for the payment of any debt or obligation created in the name of the State during the war between the Confederate States and the United States. Nor shall any county, city, or town pay any debt or obligation created by such county, city, or town in aid of said war." Section 187 created a new sinking fund for paying the remainder of the state's pre–Civil War public debt that the General Assembly had refinanced in 1892.[111] Section 188 prohibited the state from collecting more revenue than was necessary for meeting the state's obligations and paying off the debt.

MISCELLANEOUS PROVISIONS

Article XIV included a more detailed version of the homestead exemption created under the corresponding article in the Constitution of 1869 and a shorter version of the provision that prohibited so-called stay laws to defer payment of legal debts. It eliminated, presumably as it was no longer necessary, the provision in the Constitution of 1869 concerning ownership of church property "affected by the late civil war"; but it retained, as Section 195, the clause that legalized marriages entered into before the end of slavery and legitimized the acknowledged children of such marriages.

AMENDMENTS AND CONVENTIONS

Article XV, Section 196, provided that the General Assembly could propose amendments to the state constitution by the same procedure adopted in 1869. Both houses had to approve the language in the same form both before and after an election for members of the House of Delegates, then the proposed amendment would be submitted to the voters for ratification or rejection by majority vote. And Section 197, the last in the new constitution, authorized the General Assembly to schedule referenda for calling a convention to revise the constitution whenever it desired.

Proclaiming the Constitution

The report from the Committee on Preamble and Bill of Rights, which the convention received on 20 July 1901, contained a preamble that recited the authority under which members of the convention were elected and concluded with language very like that in the Constitution of 1776, "We, therefore, the delegates of the good people of Virginia so elected and in convention assembled, do ordain and declare the future form of government of Virginia to be as followeth." The active verbs "do ordain and declare" provoked an extended debate about the relative merits and the wisdom, legality, and political expediency of proclaiming the constitution in force without a ratification referendum. On 2 September, the convention postponed further consideration for the time being.[112]

On 23 May 1902, members of the convention began a week of hot debate about whether to proclaim the constitution in effect or to submit it to a ratification referendum, and if they did submit it to a ratification referendum, whether to the existing electorate or to the electorate envisioned under the new constitution.[113] They again debated the question whether they were empowered as the people's direct representatives to ordain the constitution, even though the enabling act under which they were elected required a referendum.

Charles V. Meredith made the disfranchisement case for proclamation more concisely than other delegates when he replied to a western Democrat who said that he would vote to proclaim if it was necessary but remained unconvinced. "Sir," Meredith addressed him and the other delegates, "let the question be decided by those of us who have struggled under it, and who have suffered. We tell you that we know the danger of submitting this instrument to 147,000 negroes ... who may be affected by it. We know that if it is defeated we must remain in the slavery that comes from being prevented to exercise freedom of thought. Is not the emergency sufficient?" No delegate challenged Meredith's misstatement that white citizens lived in slavery to Black Virginians or had been "prevented to exercise freedom of thought."

Meredith concluded, "Sir, for years we have been saying to the people that we were struggling under a Constitution forced upon us by the Underwood Convention. For years we have been justifying everything by the plea of the fear of negro supremacy. The people sent us here to work out our salvation—to relieve this State of all chance of such an evil. What shall we say to them if we now fail? In proclamation lies absolute safety. Any other course will be surrounded by danger. We can bring relief, if we will, to the old State. The people, appreciating the necessity, will justify our course. For these reasons I am for proclamation. (Great applause.)"[114] A. Caperton Braxton changed his mind before the final debate and offered a bargain to unite eastern and western Virginians on the two fundamental questions of disfranchisement and regulation of railroads. He advised western Virginians, who he believed cared less about Black voting than eastern Virginians, to give the easterners the disfranchisement they demanded in order to secure for themselves the protection of their own financial interests that the State Corporation Commission provided. And he advised easterners to vote for the commission to engage westerners' support for disfranchisement.[115]

On 29 May, the convention voted 52 to 33 (plus seven sets of pairs) against submitting the constitution to the existing electorate, voted 58 to 24 (plus six sets of pairs) against submitting it to the new electorate, and then voted 47 to 38 (plus six sets of pairs) to ordain the new constitution without a referendum.[116] Only 5 western members voted to proclaim the constitution, but 42 eastern members voted in favor. Braxton voted in favor of submitting the constitution to the new electorate but not to the old and for proclamation as his only hope to create the State Corporation Commission. The most controversial action by far of the entire convention (and one of the most important) was by a close vote that only 53 of the 100 elected delegates approved.

The convention appended to the constitution a very long schedule so that "no inconvenience may arise from the adoption of this Constitution, and in order to provide for carrying it into complete operation." Section 25 of the schedule declared, "This Constitution shall, except as is otherwise provided in the schedule, go into effect on the tenth day of July, nineteen hundred and two, at noon."[117]

Section 22 required that on 15 July, all members of the General Assembly take the oath specified in Article III Section 34 and swear allegiance to the new constitution; and that by 20 July, all executive officials at the capital and all judges of courts of record take that same oath. It also dropped an axe: "upon the failure of any such officer executive or judicial, to take such oath by the day named, his office shall thereby become vacant."

The coercive requirement in Section 22 of the schedule was part of the implementation of the constitution—it forced public officials to acknowledge its legitimacy or lose their jobs—and worked to secure it against legal challenges. Eleven months after the constitution went into effect, the Supreme Court of Appeals ruled in a criminal case, *Taylor v. Commonwealth*, that was appealed to the court on the grounds, among other things, that the constitution was not properly ratified and therefore prosecution under its authority was not legal. The judges unanimously cited the taking of the oath required in the schedule as acceptance of the legitimacy of the new constitution by all the state's legislative, executive, and judicial officials, including themselves. The constitution "having been thus acknowledged and accepted by the officers administering the government and by the people of the State, and being, as a matter of fact, in force throughout the State," it was therefore "the only rightful, valid, and existing Constitution of this State, and that to it all the citizens of Virginia owe their obedience and loyal allegiance."[118]

In 1904, the Supreme Court of the United States ruled on two pleas that officers of election could not conduct elections under authority of the new constitution, but by then the elections in question had already been held. The court stated in *Jones v. Montague*, and then relied on that case in *Selden v. Montague*, that "the thing sought to be prohibited has been done and cannot be undone by any order of this court."[119] Fait accompli. Those three court opinions settled the legal question about the proclamation and legal legitimacy of the Constitution of 1902. It functioned without another legal challenge and only occasional complaint about its legitimacy much as had the Constitutions of 1776 and 1864 that had also not been ratified.

The convention also adopted An Ordinance to Provide for the Registration of Voters Under this Constitution, and Prior to the Year Nineteen Hundred and Four (1904). It appointed by name several officers of registration at each of the several hundred polling places in the state.[120] Utterly unnoticed in any of the scholarship on the convention and constitution, that ordinance almost certainly named only Democrats and was evidence of the partisan nature of the convention and the constitution it created.

Amendments

In 1910 the General Assembly submitted the first four proposed amendments to the voters for ratification, only one of which they ratified. On 8 November voters ratified an amendment to Article VII, Section 110, to remove a limitation that county treasurers could not serve more than two consecutive terms and to require that all, not merely some, county commissioners of the revenue be elected for four-year terms and that they all be eligible for reelection. Limitations on terms of those officials had been placed in the constitution to reduce the ability of men to enrich themselves at public expense, but with those officials being important local political leaders, too, the limitation weakened the ability of the Democratic Party apparatus to retain its political power. But voters rejected a two-part amendment to Article VIII that would have revised Section 119 to require that all commissioners of revenue in cities be elected for four-year terms and that they be eligible for reelection. The amendment to Section 120 would have permitted city treasurers to be reelected to more than two consecutive terms.[121]

Voters also rejected an amendment to Section 46 to increase the length of regular legislative sessions from sixty to ninety days;[122] and they rejected an amendment to Article IV, Section 50, that would have allowed reading of a bill "by title" only rather than "at length," or in full, on each of the three days it was being considered prior to passage.[123]

In 1912, the General Assembly resubmitted the amendments to Article VIII, Sections 119 and 120, but separately rather than as one amendment with two parts,[124] which created doubts among some lawyers that the resubmission was consistent with the constitution.[125] A citizen of Richmond filed suit in a Richmond court for an injunction to prevent the ratification referendum because the two amendments had been defeated in 1910, and the constitution granted the General Assembly no authority to resubmit them in a second referendum without beginning the amendment process all over again. The judge refused to grant the injunction on the grounds that courts could not interfere with an incomplete legislative process or, by analogy, with an incomplete amendment process, which only a ratification referendum could complete. In *Scott v. James, Secretary of the Commonwealth*, the Supreme Court of Appeals affirmed the judge's ruling without comment,[126] one week after voters ratified both amendments.[127] The merits of the case about resubmission of the amendments in a second referendum remained undecided, but the amendments remained in the constitution.

On election day in 1912, voters also ratified an amendment to Section 117 of Article VIII to authorize the General Assembly to permit cities of more than 15,000 inhabitants to hold referenda on creating forms of municipal government different from the one specific, precisely defined model provided for in the original constitution.

In November 1920, voters, including women for the first time ever, ratified six amendments. One of them added an exception to the requirement that men be resident in the district, city, or county in which they held office to permit appointment of men who did not live in the jurisdiction "to fill positions under a municipal government requiring special technical or professional training and experience," such as civil engineers and managers of public utilities.

Another amendment replaced much of Article VIII, Section 117, with new provisions that granted the General Assembly broader leeway to authorize different forms of municipal government from those stipulated in the original article or the amendment ratified in 1912.

An amendment to Article IX, Section 133, stated, "Men and women may serve as school trustees in said districts, and in cities and in towns forming separate school districts." That was the first authorization in a Virginia constitution for women to serve in any public office.

An amendment to Article IX, Section 136, replaced a limitation on local governments taxing real estate at a higher rate than five mills on the dollar of assessed value for their school funds with an authorization for the General Assembly to establish a maximum rate by law.

Voters ratified a simplified Article IX, Section 138, to authorize the General Assembly to "provide for the compulsory education of children of school age" without any of the exceptions that had originally been in the section.

In 1920, voters also ratified an amendment to Article XIII, Section 184, that created an exception to the prohibition on creation of new state debt to allow the state to issue bonds and borrow money "to construct, or reconstruct, public roads."

Voters ratified three amendments on 8 November 1927, one year before the General Assembly submitted a revised constitution to the voters for consideration. By a large majority, they approved an addition to Article II, Section 22, that had read, "No person, who, during the late war between the States, served in the army or navy of the United States, or the Confederate States, or any state of the United States, or of the Confederate States, shall at any time be required to pay a poll tax as a prerequisite to the right to register or vote." The addition extended the exemption to "the wife or widow of such person." That for the first time recognized in the state constitution that women were eligible to vote, although under authority of the Nineteenth Amendment, they had voted since 1920.

An amendment to Article XIII, Section 170, modified the authority of city and town charters to tax all residents to pay for construction of streets, alleys, sewers, and the like that benefitted owners of property that fronted a street more than owners of property that abutted their property but did not front the street. The amendment added a clarifying clause, "Except in cities and towns and counties having a population greater than five hundred inhabitants per square mile, as shown by the United States census." One contemporary observer speculated that the exception probably then applied to Arlington County, only.[128] If so, that is the first constitutional recognition of suburban areas in Virginia.

Voters also ratified an amendment to Article XIII, Section 186, that brought the constitution into conformity with the state's new fiscal year budget cycle. It increased the effective authority of appropriation laws from two to two and a half years.

The Constitution of the United States

Two amendments to the Constitution of the United States modified the manner in which government under the new Constitution of Virginia functioned. The Seventeenth Amendment, ratified in 1913, empowered voters, not state legislatures, to elect each state's two members of the United States Senate. And the Nineteenth Amendment, ratified in 1920, granted women the right to vote and effectively deleted the restrictive word *male* from Article II, Sections 18 and 22—"Every male citizen of the United States"—that specified who could register to vote.

The Constitution of 1902 in Operation

The two most important innovations in the new constitution, the State Corporation Commission and the disfranchisement article, achieved their intended purposes.

The State Corporation Commission attracted wide attention, earned praise from the beginning, and has remained the fourth branch of state government ever since.[129] During the first twenty-five years of the commission's existence, the General Assembly granted it authority to regulate insurance providers, banks, valuation for tax purposes of public utility companies, rates of pilotage, and regulation or licensing of motor vehicles, commercial trucks, and aeronautics.[130]

In 1904, the Supreme Court of Appeals, in *Norfolk and Portsmouth Belt Line Railroad Co. v. Commonwealth*, ruled that the commission was well within its constitutional right to declare that a common carrier—a railroad—was subject to its regulation of charges for incidental use of a private conveyor to deliver goods between cars on the railroad's track and private property as an essential part of the business of transporting freight.[131] That affirmed the extensive scope of the commission's powers over corporations engaged in intrastate commerce. In 1906, the court, in the case *Winchester and Strasburg Railroad Co. v. Commonwealth*, accepted the blending of legislative and judicial powers in the one commission.[132] And in 1908, in *Prentis v. Atlantic Coast Line Co.*, the Supreme Court of the United States accepted the constitution's definition of the commission as a lawful court.[133]

The restrictions on the franchise also worked as its creators had intended and just as unfairly as Alfred P. Thom had predicted. Indeed, soon after the convention adjourned, Walter Watson met the registrars in Amelia County, one of the two counties he had represented in the convention, and instructed them "to disfranchise the negro under the new Constitution." When Watson registered in Nottoway County in September, he deliberately chose to be examined on his understanding of the constitution rather than take the easier way of qualifying as a taxpayer "or as the son of a soldier" in order to "set an example to the more illiterate whites who might be indisposed to submit to an examination." He wanted the process to intimidate those men into disfranchising themselves.[134]

Watson later recorded in his diary that he "came across an old slave darkey"—that is, a man who had been born into slavery—"who believed great harm of the new Constitution and told me the negroes held me accountable for what they consider a serious attempt upon their liberty."[135] Watson was surprised that any Black person could have had the presumption to believe that he or she was entitled to any civic rights at all in Virginia. Watson would have been even more surprised had he heard how Charles Wilson Butler, a Black resident of Warren County, responded when a registrar asked him to explain the meaning of a section of the constitution. Rather than even make the attempt, Butler indignantly responded, "You men have no right to refuse to register me";[136] but they had the power, and they used it. John Mitchell had clearly warned readers of his *Richmond Planet* of that power at the time.[137]

The detailed provisions for the poll tax and registration deliberately made both processes difficult and expensive.[138] For one thing, the constitution prohibited state and local officials from actively collecting the poll tax. Men who hoped to vote had to find a county or city treasurer and voluntarily pay the tax six months before the election. Republicans and Black Virginians had to hope that the treasurer would be willing to receive the tax payment and not impose obstacles such as allow tax payments only at limited or unpublicized office hours, send them away from the office because the tax rolls were at the treasurer's house, or send them away from the house because the tax rolls were in the office. Convention members knew that the tax, though apparently a small amount, would be difficult for poor people to pay and more difficult for most Black men than for most white men. In addition, both Democrats and Republicans illegally raised money and paid poll taxes of men and women who they hoped would vote for their candidates,[139] even though the Supreme Court of Appeals clearly stated in *Tilton v. Herman* in 1909 that the requirement in the constitution for personal payment of the tax required that it be paid from the personal resources of the person who intended to register to vote.[140]

Registrars could also make themselves difficult to find with the same elusive tactics that treasurers employed, and they could also impose other impediments to registration. After 1904, they could, and did, extralegally stretch the specifications of Article II, Section 20, of the constitution and the enabling laws in Chapter 8, Section 73, of the Code of Virginia that applicants correctly answer questions about their qualifications. Some registrars required satisfactory answers to other questions that had nothing to do with the qualifications listed in the constitution or repeated in the enabling acts, as if questions about politics, the structure of the federal governmental, who discovered the Rocky Mountains, what colony was originally called Albemarle, or other topics that were not specified in the constitution or laws as topics that could be used to disqualify persons who sought to register.[141]

Registration and voting dropped precipitately as a result of the Constitution of 1902 and the laws adopted to implement it. In the 1900 presidential election, 264,240 Virginia men voted; in 1904, a mere 135,867 Virginia men voted,[142] a reduction in the whole number of votes of 48.6 percent. The Republican vote fell from 43.8 percent to 35.2 percent of the total. The number of white voters declined by almost 50 percent, and the small number of remaining Black voters declined by about 90 percent[143] and remained insignificantly small in all but a few communities until the 1960s. In spite of what Carter Glass promised, more white men than Black men probably lost the right to vote as a consequence of the disfranchisement provisions that he prepared and pushed through the convention.

Because most of the white men were Republicans or were poor and could not afford to pay the poll tax or manage to defeat the complex voter registration process, the effect of the Constitution of 1902 was to reduce the Virginia electorate to a smaller proportion of the adult male population than at any time in Virginia's history and significantly increase the chances of Democratic Party victories. Indeed, a smaller proportion of adult Virginians voted during the first half of the twentieth century than in any other state in the country or in any other country in the world that had or pretended to have a representative democracy.[144]

Senator John Warwick Daniel was openly pleased, and Senator Thomas Martin was no doubt privately pleased, that the new constitution reduced the political power of Black and Republican men. Martin was no doubt additionally pleased that, as administered, those provisions significantly strengthened the capacity of his faction of the Democratic Party to maintain its dominance. Constitutional officers in the counties and cities, called the courthouse rings, not only ran local governments but also ran the local Democratic Party apparatus. The state government regulated the fees that some of those officers continued to collect, as they had since early in the seventeenth century, and employed that regulation as a tool with which to keep the members of the courthouse rings in line. They got away with illegally assisting poor or illiterate Democrats pay poll taxes and fill out registration forms, and they sometimes even went so far as to help by casting votes for voters who did not go the poll. In Albemarle County, a judge that the Democratic majority in the General Assembly had elected routinely appointed a Democrat to be the Republican judge of elections in one precinct.[145] The importance of the courthouse rings to the Democratic Party can scarcely be overstated.

Three of the amendments to the Constitution of 1902 had very important and long-lasting consequences to the state's politics and public policy. The amendments of 1912 and 1920 that relaxed the strict definitions of municipal government structure followed a 1908 innovation in Staunton which hired the first professional city manager in the country and effectively removed administrative supervision of all city bureaus and offices from the mayor. The Constitution of 1902 had designated mayors as chief executive officers of cities. The innovation rapidly caught on nationwide and spread throughout Virginia in just a few years.[146]

For the most part, however, the state government during the twentieth century continued, as it had during the previous centuries, to accord localities limited freedom to experiment without previous, clear legislative authorization. The General Assembly and the state's courts functioned as if they were required to adhere to the Dillon Rule, named for a judge and law professor John F. Dillon. In his 1871 book, *The Law of Municipal Corporations*, Dillon stated a truism, that municipal governments had no inherent powers of their own, as state governments did, but only the legal capacity to act on matters and in manners that state constitutions and laws specifically authorized.[147] In 1882, the Supreme Court of Appeals formally adopted the rule in *Kirkham v. Russell*. The judges cited Dillon's book "in respect to municipal corporations. For as upon them is conferred a portion of the authority which properly appertains to the sovereign power of the State, the public interests require that they be confined not only to the powers, but to a reasonable exercise of the powers, which are clearly granted by the terms of their charters."[148]

The General Assembly retained sole authority to grant or amend city charters, which it did by passing a law for each instance. Legislators who represented other, often distant, jurisdictions rather than the residents had the final say on the provisions of city charters.[149] And by law, the assembly permitted cities to annex portions of neighboring counties through a judicial condemnation process that denied the residents of both an opportunity by referendum to take part in deciding whether to approve a proposed annexation.[150]

Under authority of the 1920 amendment that permitted the state to issue bonds to raise money for road construction, the General Assembly submitted a referendum to the voters in November 1923 whether to issue $50 million in bonds to pay for enlarging and improving the new statewide system of public highways.[151] The new chair of the state Democratic Party central committee, Harry Flood Byrd, led the opposition to the bond issue, which for some voters recalled the long debt controversy of the nineteenth century and the resultant short-term success of the biracial Readjuster Party. Byrd advocated construction of highways with revenue raised from licenses on motor vehicles and taxes on gasoline and tires—"pay as you go"—rather than with bonds. Voters defeated the referendum 127,187 to 81,220.[152] Paying for highway construction out of current revenue provided less money immediately than bonds would have made available, which meant slower progress but at a lower long-term cost than with bonds.[153]

Byrd's success in the referendum immediately after his leadership in the successful 1922 campaign to wrest the Ninth Congressional District in southwestern Virginia out of Republican hands[154] propelled him into the governor's office in 1925.[155] By then he was the acknowledged leader of what had been the late Thomas Martin's undemocratic wing of the Democratic Party.[156] Members of the Byrd organization, as it soon came to be known, imposed rigid racial segregation in the state during the decades when American apartheid reached its low point. At that time, the state maintained separate sets of land tax books for "white" and "colored" landowners and segregated "white" and "colored" lists of registered voters. In 1910, the General Assembly changed state law to define as "colored," and therefore subject to all the restrictive laws of Jim Crow, every person with one-sixteenth or more of African ancestry in place of the one-fourth that had been law in Virginia for more than a century.[157] The 1924 Act to Preserve Racial Integrity changed the definition again to any discernible or known trace of African ancestry—what came to be called the "one drop" rule.[158] The General Assembly passed a law in 1904 to empower streetcar conductors to use force if necessary to enforce racially segregated seating[159] and another in 1906 to require racially segregated cars on passenger trains.[160] A 1912 law gave cities and towns an option to require residential racial segregation,[161] and a 1925 law introduced one of the strictest racial segregation regimes in the country for public assemblies of every kind.[162] In 1924, the assembly legalized surgical sterilization of inmates of public institutions whom its officers deemed feeble-minded or likely to have inherited criminal tendencies or had illegitimate children.[163] In short, they continued to "purify" Virginia society much as the disfranchisers in the Convention of 1901–2 believed that they were purifying the electorate.[164]

The Future

The Constitution of 1902, the longest in Virginia's history, remained in force in the state for the longest time of any constitution until the Constitution of 1971 superseded it at noon on 1 July 1971. In June 1928, however, voters ratified a revised version of the constitution that, at the governor's suggestion, the General Assembly submitted to them as an amendment in the form of a substitute. The revised constitution contained numerous changes, some of them technical, some of them substantive, but none that fundamentally altered the structures of state and local government provided for in 1902.

CHAPTER 8

The Constitutional Revision of 1928

Governor Harry Flood Byrd announced in his inaugural address on 1 February 1926, "I construe my election as a mandate to me as a business man to institute the best methods of efficiency and economy in State affairs, so that the people may obtain in the public service a dollar's value for every dollar spent."[1] The next day he submitted to the General Assembly a proposal to reform the state's tax code,[2] and the day after that he addressed both houses of the assembly and outlined his plans for reorganizing and simplifying the state government, which led directly to the revision of the state constitution that voters ratified in November 1928.[3] No new governor of Virginia had ever got off to such a speedy beginning with such a long list of major recommendations for change.

The Program of Progress

Byrd called his administration's collection of governmental reform proposals the Program of Progress,[4] and it gained him a national reputation among public administrators and a somewhat exaggerated reputation as a progressive reformer. Most of his recommendations fit into what historians have described as a post–World War I southern "business progressivism." Its objectives did not comprehend many of the social or economic reforms generally associated with the Progressive movement before the war but with making changes to keep taxes low and regulation of businesses even lower in the interest of stimulating business and industrial development.[5]

Byrd was not yet forty years old, but he was a ten-year veteran of service in the Senate of Virginia and had been described as a young man in a hurry. Of limited formal education, he owned and published the newspapers in Winchester and Harrisonburg and owned some of the largest and most profitable apple orchards in the state. Well connected politically, he was the son of a former Speaker of the House of Delegates and a nephew of a prominent member of Congress. Byrd had become chair of the Democratic Party's State Central Committee in 1922, helped wrest the Ninth Congressional District in southwestern Virginia out of Republican control later that same year, and in 1923, led the campaign to defeat a referendum to authorize a bond issue to speed up the pace of highway construction. In place of bonds, Byrd proposed to finance road construction with a "pay as you go" system that relied on revenue collected on licenses for motor vehicles and taxes on gasoline and tires. He won the 1925 Democratic Party nomination for governor and in November, he easily won election to a four-year term of office.[6]

Byrd took command immediately on being sworn in as governor. The state's two-year budget cycle normally required that a new governor had to work for the first half of his single four-year administration with the budget that his predecessor had proposed and whatever amendments he might be able to persuade the General Assembly to make to that budget during the relatively short regular session that was nearly half done with its work when the new governor took office; but Byrd submitted his own budget to the assembly, introduced his own ideas about reforming the state's tax code, and then plunged into the business of reorganizing the executive branch of government.

Byrd began his 3 February speech to the assembly, not surprisingly for a businessman, with, "Energy and efficiency of administration of the business of a great corporation requires concentration of authority as well as responsibility in the executive head. Virginia is a great business corporation, collecting and disbursing thirty-three million dollars annually. In ten years State expenditures have increased from eight million to thirty-three million dollars, and the cumbersome machinery with which we worried along a decade ago will not operate with modern efficiency."[7]

Byrd's proposals were wide ranging, including proposals for amendments to the Constitution of 1902. "I would urge," he told the legislators,

"1. That the General Assembly submit constitutional amendments to popular vote so that Virginia can adopt the short ballot and elect by direct popular vote only the Governor, Lieutenant Governor, and the Attorney General.

"2. That the administrative heads of departments be appointed by the Governor, who is directly responsible to the people for administrative efficiency.

"3. That the bureaus, boards, and commissions, be grouped in eight or ten departments, that may be abolished, and a business survey be conducted to make clear the way to economies."[8]

Byrd's short ballot proposal was to make the offices of secretary of the commonwealth, treasurer, superintendent of public instruction, and commissioner of agriculture and immigration appointive rather than elective. Byrd also proposed what he called tax segregation, to reserve taxes on land and personal property for the state's cities and counties and to finance state government chiefly from income taxes and other revenue. Because most of the state agencies that Byrd wanted to reorganize into large departments had been created by law, most of his recommendations could be achieved through legislation. The General Assembly passed laws in the special session in 1927 and the regular session of 1928 to make most of the changes; but the short ballot and tax segregation required changes in the state's constitution.

Byrd's was not the first proposal for reform of the state's administrative structure. A study of the state government that a graduate student at the Johns Hopkins University published in 1912 identified the heart of the problem. "The governor of Virginia," he noted, "is not at the head of a system. . . . He works with department heads who may be subordinate or insubordinate, as they like."[9] In 1918, the General Assembly created the state's first executive budget process that improved fiscal management of the state,[10] and in 1924, a legislative committee published a plan to simplify and reorganize the state's many statutory agencies, but it led to no legislative action.[11] Byrd studied those reports and as a member of the General Assembly probably paid closer attention to the details of the state's appropriation and tax laws than any other member. Consequently, he knew in considerable detail what he wanted to do and how he wanted to do it before he took the oath of office as governor. Unlike his predecessors, he devised a cohesive overall plan, provided energetic leadership, and had the political authority to achieve what he wanted.

Byrd recommended an appropriation of $15,000 to hire a professional management consultant to make an efficiency survey of the executive branch prior to the General Assembly taking action, but he also recommended some specific changes for immediate consideration: that all public employees work an eight-hour day (seven hours was then the standard); that all funds expended be by warrant from the auditor and be part of the appropriated budget; and the abolition or consolidation of many separate state agencies. He also recommended ways to end confusions for budget planning that resulted from having an appropriation year that began on 1 March, a fiscal year that began on 1 July, a taxation year that began on 1 January, and a licensing year that began on 1 May.[12]

In 1928, Byrd recommended that the General Assembly act to increase industrial development; attract new residents and investments; promote tourism; create Shenandoah National Park; further the development of port facilities in Hampton Roads; construct airports; protect and preserve the seafood industry; revive markets for and production of the state's principal agricultural products; reduce taxes on agricultural producers and other taxes; and advertise Virginia as a good place to live and do business. "Virginia industrially is neither North or South," Byrd explained in a speech to the General Assembly in 1928 at the time that the assembly submitted a proposed constitution to the voters for ratification and after it had enacted many of the statutory reforms that he had recommended. "She sits midway between the accumulated wealth and enormous consuming power of the East and the new millions and the awakened producing capacity of the South. She is the gateway to the new South now welcoming an industrial invasion."[13]

"This economic development," Byrd went on, "great as it has been, is merely a promise of the development we have good reason to expect in the years just ahead. New wealth, new capital, new income creates new taxable values and the larger these values the less the tax rate has to be. Economic development therefore means more money for schools, for roads, for health preservation, for law enforcement to the point where enlightened economy may suggest further reduction in taxes."[14] It was perhaps easy for some people who listened to Byrd's speech or read the widely distributed printed text to anticipate that he and his administration would spend the money that the administrative reforms saved on improvements to the schools, roads, and public health services he mentioned. But that was not correct. Byrd stated his limited objective plainly, stimulation of business and industrial development and "further reduction in taxes."

The New York Bureau of Municipal Research

In the summer of 1926, Byrd hired the New York of Bureau of Municipal Research to make professional evaluations of the organization and functioning of the state bureaucracy and of the government of Virginia counties. He did not include municipal government in his charge to the consultants, perhaps because the recent transition to the city manager form of government in most of the state's cities had solved organizational or budgeting problems that became evident after the promulgation of the Constitution of 1902.

The New York Bureau was the creation of Luther Gulick, then probably the most prominent expert on public administration in the country. One team of his staff examined agencies of the state bureaucracy, and another studied twelve more or less representative counties in different regions of the state.

Byrd watched closely as two teams under the direction of the bureau's Arthur E. Buck worked and made suggestions and recommendations.[15]

The report on executive agencies, including the State Corporation Commission, was about two hundred pages long and very detailed, both in its analysis of the work of each of several core state agencies and in its recommendations for consolidating them or shifting their responsibilities. The report reflected the bureau agents' belief, which they shared with Byrd, that efficient management of the state could be achieved by employing proven best practices in business. The numerous offices and agencies had come into being as a result of individual legislative acts without adequate consideration for overlapping functions, coordination of related activities, or administrative or fiscal oversight. Almost nothing about the state's bureaucracy was modern. Indeed, the report began, "it should not require any argument to convince even the most skeptical that the present State government of Virginia is greatly in need of complete reorganization. Many parts of the present machinery of administration are completely antiquated. They belong almost to the era of the stage coach and the tallow candle; and here they are trying to function in the age of motor cars and incandescent lights. No wonder it costs more than it should to operate the State government under these conditions."[16]

"As long as the present system is maintained," the report continued, "waste, bungling, and inefficiency are almost inevitable, and the cost of the State government will continue to go up at a rapid rate."[17] The report made specific detailed proposals to reduce administrative expenses; concentrate administrative authority in the governor; remove unnecessary detail from the constitution; reform all aspects of financial administration; reform tax collection; reform the budgeting process; provide for proper auditing and fiscal oversight in each agency; and create a unified, classified public employee system.

The report also contained a long section on the State Corporation Commission.[18] It was less detailed than most of the other sections but warned that because of many changes in the corporate world during the twenty-five years since the commission was created, "The time has now come for constitutional housecleaning on the subject of corporations. . . . Old functions are gone or diminished in importance, and new responsibilities are on the horizon. These are the problems of gasoline price fixing, water power development, giant power, busy lines, and air routes."[19]

The New York Bureau's hundred-page report on county government was in several respects even more damning than its report on the state executive departments. On the second page of the report, Buck made his conclusions crystal clear. "The present county government has no responsible head," it began; "it is without a chief administrative officer and the board of supervisors controls through appointment only a small part of the county administration. Authority for carrying on the administrative work of the county at the present time rests with many individuals. The voters of the county have very little power in the determination of county policies. It is true that they elect a number of administrative officers besides the members of the board of supervisors, but this serves only to dissipate authority and to increase the difficulties of securing effective and economical county government. In fact, there is nothing to commend the present form of county government in Virginia. In many of the counties, it is grossly political, careless, wasteful, and thoroughly inefficient. It has been that way for years, but still it exists and seems to flourish."[20]

The report contained a damning criticism of fractured authority, inadequate oversight and auditing, lack of budgetary planning, lack of coordination of work, and frequent vacancies in some public offices. It proposed centralized accounting, placing all legislative authority in the board of supervisors, and reducing the number of officers and making them less political. It also recommended consolidating adjacent, lightly populated counties to increase efficiency of the administrative apparatus in order better to meet transportation and educational needs.[21] Buck's working group estimated that the recommendations, if adopted, could reduce the total $28 million per annum cost of county government in Virginia by about $1.5 million.[22]

The report recommended abolition of the fee system that had been in place since the early years of the seventeenth century by which county clerks and some other officials collected fees rather than salaries for doing their work.[23] "There is no budgetary or other control over employment in the various county offices, especially those that work under the existing fee system," the condemnation on the fee system began. "The treasurer or the clerk, for example, receives from fees and commissions a certain amount of money and perhaps a small appropriation (many of the clerks do) from the board of supervisors. Out of the total amount he runs his office; that is, pays the salaries of his employees and other office expenses, and retains the balance as his own compensation. . . . The State control, up to the present time, through the fee commission, has not been very satisfactory, and county officials have nearly all retained practically all the fees and commissions they collected. While their salaries have been limited by an act of the General Assembly, they have, in a number of instances, expended the surplus from their fees and commissions on their office force, bringing in members of their families, relatives, or political supporters. This means an overloaded payroll in many of the county offices. While this is evident in a number of cases, it is hard to get at because the official regards employment in their offices as their own private business. Very few of them will tell the amount of salary paid each employee; sometimes they are even unwilling to give the number of employees. Obviously, many of the county offices which are on a fee basis are overmanned. In some of the clerks' offices obsolete methods of recording are still retained; for example, writing everything in long hand, merely to give more employees jobs. If modern methods were used in such cases, one person might do the work of four."[24]

The secretive, proprietary attitude of the fee officers that Buck's investigators encountered in the 1920s resembled practices and attitudes some Virginians complained about two and a half centuries earlier at the time of Bacon's Rebellion of 1676 when county officers refused to let men see public records or told them that how the powerful justices of the peace did their—the public's—business was not the business of anybody else.[25]

The Reed and Prentis Commissions

In addition to hiring the New York Bureau of Municipal Research in 1926, Byrd appointed two advisory committees. The Citizens Committee on Consolidation and Simplification in State and Local Governments was usually referred to at the time as the Reed Commission, after its chair, Richmond tobacco executive William T. Reed. The forty members included Henry C. Stuart, a former governor, and John Garland Pollard, a former attorney general, both of whom had served with commission member George Keezell in the Convention of 1901-2. Several members were respected business executives, and a few were Republicans, but most members were Byrd's loyal political supporters. "I have a big program I am trying to get through," Byrd privately told a Democratic Party official. "As a matter of fact ninety-five per cent of my appointments up to this time have been my own friends."[26] The Reed Commission also had six women members, the first Virginia women ever who had a formal, though limited, role in the process of constitution making.

The Commission to Suggest Amendments to the Constitution to the General Assembly of Virginia was usually referred to at the time as the Prentis Commission, after its chair, Robert R. Prentis, then president of the Virginia Supreme Court of Appeals.[27] The seven members were all judges, law professors, or lawyers, including Byrd's Winchester friend and neighbor R. Gray Williams, a former president of the Virginia State Bar Association.

The Reed Commission provided for a measure of public participation in the final proposals Byrd made to the General Assembly for reorganizing the state bureaucracy, and the New York Bureau of Municipal Research and the Prentis Commission provided professional and apolitical analysis and suggestions for the Reed Commission and the governor to evaluate. That is not to say that the governor waited until the bureau submitted its report before he and the chair of the Reed Commission made important decisions. Byrd and Reed were close friends and political allies. Reed was in fact the closest political advisor Byrd had at the time and one of the few he trusted implicitly. They monitored the work of Buck and his agents as they studied the state bureaucracy and the administration of county governments, and they helped shape the Reed Commission's report, which was published scarcely a month after the bureau's report on state government.[28]

Byrd and Reed effectively killed the bureau's report on county government by delaying its publication for an entire year and allowing it to die an almost unnoticed death. The governor never formally submitted it to the Reed Commission or to the General Assembly. Had any or most of the recommendations of the bureau been adopted, the courthouse rings, as they were called, that ran county governments and also ran the Democratic Party apparatus in the counties would have been seriously undermined or even destroyed. The Reed Commission's short nineteen-page report endorsed the bureau's recommendations on the state bureaucracy and ignored the bureau's analysis of county government.[29] The long and detailed recommendations for constitutional amendments that the Prentis Commission published also made no reference to the then unpublished report on county government.[30] The Reed Commission report worked in large measure as Byrd intended. It helped him control the process, and it won over many skeptics to the generally popular idea of streamlining the state bureaucracy and making it more efficient.

The Constitutional Revision of 1928

The General Assembly amended and approved the constitutional revision in a special session in 1927, and after the election that autumn, approved it again by a vote of 64 to 4 in the House of Delegates and 25 to 8 in the Senate during the 1928 regular session[31] so that it could be submitted to the electorate for ratification or rejection later in 1928. Delegates Sarah Lee Fain, of Norfolk, and Sallie Cook Booker, of Henry County and Martinsville, voted for the revision in 1928. They were the first women legislators who cast votes on a question of constitutional revision in Virginia.

The revision of the state constitution proceeded swiftly. The state's superintendent of public printing published the New York Bureau of Municipal Research report on state government early in 1927 and the Reed and Prentis Commission reports in February of that year. The General Assembly began and completed its review and revisions in a special session that met for one month, from 16 March through 15 April 1927. Governor Byrd's careful preparation, the clear recommendations of the respected independent bureau, the ringing endorsement of the Reed Commission, the detailed recommendations of the apparently nonpolitical Prentis Commission, and Byrd's overpowering influence as Democratic Party leader enabled the assembly to proceed with dispatch and also—and this was singularly important—almost exactly as the governor wished. The process was speedy because Byrd had it under careful control.

That control is best seen in the decision to have the General Assembly, rather than an elected constitutional convention, revise the constitution. It is unclear whose idea that was. Article XV, Section 196, of the Constitution of 1902 empowered the General Assembly to propose amendments and submit them to a ratification referendum. (Section 197 provided for calling state constitutional conventions.) In effect, what the assembly did in 1927 and 1928 was to propose what in parliamentary practice was called an amendment in the form of a substitute. The proposition submitted to the voters began, "Strike out from the Constitution of Virginia, articles one to fifteen thereof, both inclusive, and sections one to one hundred and ninety-seven thereof, both inclusive," except the sections voters separately voted on as part of the short ballot initiative and another to provide for tax segregation, "and insert the following."[32] The Supreme Court of Appeals declared in *Staples v. Gilmer* in 1945 that with the favorable ratification vote, "Virginia had a new Constitution.... No one challenged its validity on the ground that it had been revised and amended in its entirety under the provisions of section 196 instead of by a convention under the provisions of section 197."[33]

For the most part, the Prentis Commission recommended, and the General Assembly proposed, amendments to streamline language and to omit obsolete sections—what might be regarded as technical amendments of the sort skilled lawyers and judges would identify and recommend. As a consequence, the constitution that voters ratified in November 1928 was in essence a revised constitution, not a wholly new constitution as had been each of the constitutions that conventions had rewritten in the eighteenth and nineteenth centuries and in 1901–2. As ratified, the constitutional revision was about 30,260 words long, about 1,000 words longer than the unamended Constitution of 1902.

PREAMBLE AND BILL OF RIGHTS

The General Assembly did not append a preamble to the revised constitution, which begins with Article I, the Bill of Rights, which contained only a few changes. It moved the addition made to Section 8 in 1902 that allowed the commonwealth an appeal in criminal proceedings involving collection of the public revenue to Article VI, Section 88, in the article on the judiciary. Section 8 of the Bill of Rights included a revised and more concise statement of the procedures for allowing trials with fewer than twelve jurors and for trials of accused people who pleaded guilty.

SUFFRAGE

Article II on the suffrage omitted the section that had directed how voter registration be conducted prior to 1904 and omitted the word *male* from the Sections 18 and 20, the first of which began, "Every male citizen of the United States, twenty one years of age," in order to bring the state constitution into conformity with the Constitution of the United States. Just to be sure, it also paraphrased the Nineteenth Amendment, "The right of citizens to vote shall not be denied or abridged on account of sex."

The revised article reduced the required length of residence in Virginia from two years to one year and in the county, city, or town, from twelve months to six. It provided for a general system of registration without all the long, complicated stipulations in the old Section 19. The revision left most of the remainder of long Article II, which had been designed to reduce the number of Black Virginians who could register and vote, substantially unchanged. But Section 31 authorized circuit or corporation court judges to appoint a three-member electoral board for each county and city for three-year terms. A new provision at the end of the section appeared to provide a small new measure of nonpartisanship to the boards: "in appointing judges of election, representation as far as possible shall be given to each of the two political parties which, at the general election next preceding their appointment, cast the highest and next highest number of votes."

SEPARATION OF POWERS

One-sentence Article III repeated, without change, the requirement for separation of legislative, executive, and judicial powers.

GENERAL ASSEMBLY

Article IV on the General Assembly made some minor changes but few major changes. It retained the limitations on the length of legislative sessions and most of the authorizations and limitations imposed on the General Assembly in 1902. Section 50 required reading of bills on each of three separate days in each chamber, but the General Assembly readily accepted the recommendation of the Prentis Commission to change the wording to allow the readings to be "by title" only and not "at length," or in full.³⁴ In 1910, the assembly had proposed that change as an amendment, but voters failed to ratify it.³⁵

The Prentis Commission recommended the addition of a new paragraph in Section 63, which read in full, "The authority of the General Assembly shall extend to all subjects of legislation, not herein forbidden or restricted; and a specific grant of authority in this Constitution upon a subject shall not work a restriction of its authority upon the same or any other subject. The omission in this Constitution of specific grants of authority heretofore conferred shall not be construed to deprive the General Assembly of such authority, or to indicate a change of policy in reference thereto, unless such purpose plainly appear." The addition was meant, the commission's report explained, "to obviate the necessity of conferring powers on the General Assembly in other sections; and to prevent any misunderstandings on account of omission."³⁶

Judge Robert Prentis, himself, probably made the suggestion and drafted the language. He had been author of the opinion of the Supreme Court of Appeals in the 1918 case *Strawberry Hill Land Co. v. Starbuck* that declared, "the State Constitution is not a grant of power, but only the restriction of powers otherwise practically unlimited, that, except so far as restrained by the Constitution, the legislature has plenary power, and that every fair doubt must be resolved in favor of the constitutionality of an act of the General Assembly."³⁷ Prentis's opinion had stated a commonplace understanding concerning state constitutions: that they were essentially limitations on state legislatures, not authorizations to empower legislatures. Since the American Revolution and elimination of the office of king from American governments, state legislatures exercised all legislative powers their constitutions did not specifically deny them.³⁸

EXECUTIVE

Article V on the executive department made both minor and major changes. Section 72 replaced language that had set the governor's annual salary at $5,000 a year with, "He shall receive for his services a compensation to be prescribed by law, which shall neither be increased nor diminished during the period for which he shall have been elected." The section retained the final sentence, "While in office he shall receive no other emolument from this or any other government."

The article, as former constitutions had done, gave the governor authority to command the militia of the state. To Section 73, which granted the governor power to issue reprieves and pardons, it added what amounted to an authorization for the General Assembly to create a "pardoning board, not exceeding three in number, to be appointed by the Governor and to serve during his pleasure. Such board may be vested with exclusive pardoning power over sentences in cases not felonious."

The article contained no changes to the governor's general veto power, the governor's use of item veto on appropriations bills, or the governor's ability to suggest amendments to bills, nor on how a veto could be overridden; nor did it change the brief sections that defined the duties of the lieutenant governor. As part of Byrd's short ballot initiative, the article vested appointment of the secretary of the commonwealth in the governor, subject to General Assembly approval; and voters separately ratified the revised Section 81 which transferred appointment of the state treasurer from the voters to the governor. An addition to the final section in the article prohibited any person that the governor appointed to an office that required confirmation by the General Assembly from serving ad interim or being eligible to reappointment after the assembly failed to confirm the appointment.

JUDICIARY

As with the article on the executive department, Article VI on the judiciary made few important changes but contained some minor adjustments to language. It increased the number of members of the Supreme Court of Appeals from five to seven, to be appointed by the General Assembly for staggered twelve-year terms; designated them justices rather than judges, as from the beginning; and specified that the justice with the longest service on the court henceforth be the chief justice, not president of the court as in the past. Section 88 authorized the court to hold sessions "in bank, or in two divisions, consisting of not less than three judges each, as the court may, from time to time, determine."

The Prentis report recommended the increase in the number of justices. "This, however," it explained, "will afford little relief unless the court sits in two divisions.... The public business requires for its dispatch that the appellate court should be almost continuously in session, and judges cannot write opinions that are worth the writing while hearing arguments, and engaged in conferences with reference to the current business. They should have time to write their opinions. A division into two sections, sitting alternately, affords these opportunities."[39] For a few years after ratification of the revised constitution, the court often sat with a quorum of four or five members (not officially designated as "divisions" of the court) rather than with the full bench of seven, which reduced the workload of each justice to a certain extent. Those cases, when published in *Virginia Reports*, either indicated which justices were not present or which took part in the decision.[40]

Section 89 provided for a Special Court of Appeals in almost the same language as in the Constitution of 1902. Special Courts of Appeals had served through much of the nineteenth century to help the Supreme Court of Appeals clear its overcrowded docket. The General Assembly did not revive the court under authority of the Constitution of 1902 until 1924 and then only for a brief period of about three years as a subordinate court to which the Supreme Court of Appeals delegated certain cases. The assembly did not revive the court again under authority of the revised constitution.[41]

Sections 94 and 95 reauthorized the General Assembly to establish circuit courts and provide for their jurisdiction. An addition to Section 102 allowed the General Assembly to "enact such laws as it may deem necessary for the retirement of the said judges with such compensation and such duties at it may prescribe." Most of the remainder of the article was substantially the same as in the Constitution of 1902.

COUNTY GOVERNMENT

Members of the General Assembly never saw even a draft of the New York Bureau of Municipal Research's report on county government during the initial 1927 special session and made few changes in the old Article VII. The article in the new constitution repeated most of the language on county governments that was in the former constitution. A new sentence added to Section 58 on the General Assembly empowered the assembly to "provide for the consolidation of existing counties on a vote of a majority of the qualified voters of each of such counties voting at an election held for that purpose." It contained new paragraphs appended to Section 110 that invested the General Assembly with authority to create separate superintendents of the poor for individual counties and such officers as might be desirable to act for two or more adjacent counties in managing charitable and penal institutions. It allowed counties, as cities had been able since amendments ratified in 1912 and 1920, to adopt other forms of government than the one specified in 1902. It also allowed counties to hire professional managers comparable to city managers. Several counties adopted modified county manager forms of government during the following decade.

MUNICIPAL GOVERNMENT

With one exception, the revised constitution repeated, with no consequential changes, all the provisions in Article VIII on government of cities and towns as amended in 1920 to allow city manager forms of government. New Section 171 prohibited the state from levying taxes on real estate and personal property and authorized only cities and counties to tax property. Urban and suburban growth in Virginia during the life of the revised 1928 constitution produced more demands for variation even than in counties. Well before ratification of the Constitution of 1971, the General Assembly made numerous changes to municipal government law, some of them of a general nature, more of them of an ad hoc nature, to meet new needs. Those changes, together with changes that also took place in county government, contributed to the major revisions of the provisions on municipal government in the Constitution of 1971.[42]

EDUCATION

A note in the Prentis Commission report to Section 129, the first in Article IX on education, indicated that its recommendations did not enjoy unanimous support. About the composition of the State Board of Education, how its members should be appointed, and precisely what its responsibilities should be, "It is impossible to settle the vexed questions which have been raised with respect to this difficult subject. Those most interested therein do not agree. Their various proposals were studied carefully, and the amendments submitted express the conclusions of this Commission. They are not, of course, ideal, but in the present confusion of thought and conflict of desire it is the best that we can do at this time."[43]

Section 130 changed the composition of the State Board of Education to a seven-member board appointed by the governor and subject to confirmation by the General Assembly. The governor, attorney general, and superintendent of public instruction no longer served as members ex officio, and the revision eliminated representatives from the state's colleges and universities and the two public school superintendents from the board. Separately ratified Section 130 changed the office of superintendent of public instruction from an elective office and provided that the governor appoint the superintendent "for a term coincident with that of each Governor making the appointment," subject to confirmation by the General Assembly.

Sections 132 and 133 gave local school districts a role for the first time in selecting school superintendents, but it limited boards by requiring that they could select only from lists of three qualified educators whom the state board submitted to them for consideration. Revised Section 133 altered the method of selection of local school boards in cities with more than 150,000 inhabitants and gave them more discretion in drawing school district boundaries. The revised constitution made no consequential changes to the method of funding public schools provided for in 1902. And the final provision in Section 132 deprived the state board of education of the authority to appoint the governing board of the state library. By law, the governor thereafter gained the right to appoint the board.

DEPARTMENT OF AGRICULTURE AND IMMIGRATION

The revised constitution made only one consequential change in Article X on agriculture and immigration. Separately ratified Section 145 made the commissioner of agriculture and immigration, which had been an elective office since 1902, an appointive office "for a term coincident with that of each Governor making the appointment," subject to confirmation by the General Assembly.

PUBLIC WELFARE AND PENAL INSTITUTIONS

Section 147 in Article XI replaced the provision, "There shall be a state penitentiary, with such branch prisons and prison farms as may be provided by law" with "Such public welfare, charitable, sanitary, benevolent, reformatory or penal institutions as the claims of humanity and the public good may require shall be established and operated by the Commonwealth under such organization and in such manner as the General Assembly may provide"; and, "Unless otherwise prescribed by law, the existing institutions and laws with respect thereto shall continue."

The revision eliminated Sections 148, which created the state board of prisons, 149, which created a separate three-member board for each of the state's mental hospitals, 150, which created a state board to govern the state's mental hospital system, and 151, which authorized the state board to appoint directors of individual mental hospitals. In place of Section 152, which had provided for the appointment of a commissioner of state mental hospitals, the revision declared, "The office of commissioner of State hospitals for the insane is hereby abolished."

STATE CORPORATION COMMISSION

Robert Prentis was one of the first members of the State Corporation Commission before he went on the Supreme Court of Appeals and no doubt had firm and well-informed opinions about the constitutional provisions for the State Corporation Commission. His commission ignored the New York Bureau of Municipal Research's recommendations for significant revisions to Article XII. The only modifications of consequence to the article on corporations vested selection of the three members of the State Corporation Commission in the General Assembly rather than allowed the assembly to make them elective or permit the governor to appoint them, subject to approval of the assembly. A study published in 1933 demonstrated that in only a small number of instances did people or corporations appeal rulings of the commission to the Supreme Court of Appeals, and that in only a small number of those instances did the court reverse or revise the commission's rulings. That suggests a general satisfaction among interested parties with the manner in which the commission transacted its business.[44]

TAXATION AND FINANCE

Article XIII on Taxation and Finance omitted some old features and included some new ones. Among the most important of the new provisions was one to prohibit the state government from collecting taxes on land and personal property and to reserve those sources of revenue exclusively to cities and counties, what at the time Byrd called "tax segregation." Separately ratified Section 171 contained that provision. The article made a number of technical changes to definitions of taxable property and the method of ascertaining taxable value. It eliminated considerable detail from several of the subsections of Section 183 that listed types of property exempted from taxation. An addition to Section 184 authorized the General Assembly by majority votes of all members elected to each house to submit to public referenda questions of issuing bonds for capital construction projects, with a limitation, "The aggregate amount of the debts authorized by this section shall not at any one time exceed one per centum of the assessed value of all the taxable real estate in the State, as shown by the last preceding assessment."

Section 189, the last in the article, replaced the section of the same number in the Constitution of 1902 that had specified rates of taxation for certain species of property with a new section on a completely different subject. As part of Governor Byrd's plan to attract new business and industrial development to the state, it declared, "The General Assembly may, by general law, authorize the governing bodies of cities, towns and counties to exempt manufacturing establishments and works of internal improvement from local taxation for a period not exceeding five years, as an inducement to their location."

MISCELLANEOUS PROVISIONS

The six sections of Article XIV left unchanged the provisions that treated homestead exemptions, prohibited stay laws that delayed the payment of private debts, and provided for legalizing marriages entered into during slavery times and legitimizing the acknowledged children of such marriages.

AMENDMENTS AND CONVENTIONS

The only change of note to Article XV on proposing amendments was a change to the sentence that required the General Assembly to approve them at two regular sessions with an election of members of the House of Delegates intervening. It added some flexibility as to timing by allowing the second approval at "any subsequent extra session of" that second General Assembly. Whether that change was in the nature of adding a safety valve for allowing resubmission of rejected amendments, as the assembly had done in 1912, is uncertain.[45]

RULES OF CONSTRUCTION

The Prentis commission recommended, and the General Assembly accepted, addition of a brief new Article XVI entitled Rules of Construction. Its Section 198 had four short sentences: "In this Constitution, the singular shall include the plural and the masculine the feminine"; "In conferring a power or imposing a duty, 'may' is permissive and 'shall' is mandatory"; "Omissions, having been often made for brevity, or because a part omitted was superfluous, do not necessarily imply a change of policy"; and "These rules do not apply where a contrary intent plainly appears."

"This is entirely new matter," the Prentis report explained. "It is necessary because it would be tedious and require many changes to draft a Constitution without using the masculine pronoun. To say 'he or she,' or 'him or her' on every occasion would be awkward in the extreme. The meaning and purpose of the other rules of construction is obvious, and the Commission believes their insertion in the Constitution is advisable."[46]

Ratification

Governor Byrd personally and energetically directed the campaign for ratification. He published and circulated three pamphlets, each entitled *A Discussion of the Amendments Proposed to the Constitution of Virginia* on the main body of the constitution, the short ballot, and tax segregation.[47] On 19 June 1928, voters ratified the main body of the revised constitution 74,109 to 60,531. On the same day, they separately ratified, by narrower margins, the sections of the governor's short ballot initiative: new Section 81 by a vote of 68,665 to 65,816 which allowed the governor to appoint the treasurer; new Section 131 by a vote of 68,756 to 65,695 which allowed the governor to appoint the superintendent of public instruction; and new Section 145 by a vote of 69,034 to 65,176 which allowed the governor to appoint the commissioner of agriculture and immigration. And voters separately approved new Section 171 by a vote of 75,160 to 59,600 to impose tax segregation that reserved all taxes on real and personal property to the cities and counties. Byrd's short ballot did not go down so well as the remainder of his Program of Progress, perhaps because opponents feared too much consolidation of power in the governor's office, and it reduced the number of democratically elected state officials. Byrd was already the most politically powerful person in the state, but the short ballot initiative did not immediately increase his personal political or appointive power because none of its features went into effect until the end of his administration.

Amendments

Between 1946 and 1966, voters ratified eleven amendments to the revised constitution, and in 1945 and 1956, the General Assembly authorized limited-purpose conventions to write and add amendments to the constitution without ratification referenda.

Payment of the poll tax as a prerequisite to voting led to the first proposal to amend the revised constitution. At the 1944 regular session of the General Assembly, the legislators passed a law to create a public fund for paying the poll taxes of members of the armed services who were on duty outside Virginia and could not comply with the law that required them to pay the poll tax in person prior to registering.[48] In November of that year, in *Staples v. Gilmer*, the Supreme Court of Appeals declared that law unconstitutional, relying in part on the court's 1909 ruling in *Tilton v. Herman* that the requirement for personal payment of the poll tax meant that the money be paid directly out of the personal resources of the taxpayer.[49] "It is readily seen," the court explained in 1944, "that the Act is a scheme to circumvent the intendment and the terms of the Constitution, and to avoid the State's declared policy. The fact that it was conceived in altruistic motives renders it none the less obnoxious and offensive, to constitutional restrictions and limitation."[50]

At a special session of the General Assembly a few weeks after the court handed down that decision, legislators called for a referendum on a proposal to hold a constitutional convention limited expressly to the purpose of promulgating an amendment to permit members of the armed services to vote without having to pay the poll tax or register in person. The law also empowered the convention to proclaim the amendment to be a part of the constitution without submitting it to a referendum.[51] An amendment to the state constitution to produce the same effect would ordinarily have required many months or as long as two years and deprived service members of the right to vote in the 1945 primary and general elections. Legislators therefore authorized the speediest possible method of clearing the way for them to vote, which was by holding a quick referendum to authorize the convention and grant it authority to place the desired amendment in the constitution without a ratification referendum.

That proposal raised several questions concerning procedures for amending the constitution. Did the General Assembly exceed its authority by attempting to limit the proposed convention to the one subject? Could the assembly in effect limit the voters' delegation of authority to the convention by that limitation or by the authorization to the convention to dispense with a ratification referendum? And did the calling of the convention to amend the constitution under Article XV, Section 196, violate the letter and intent of both sections of Article XV, Section 196, that governed how the General Assembly could propose constitutional amendments, and Section 197 that governed how it could call constitutional conventions, presumably for the purpose of wholesale revision of the constitution?[52]

Early in 1945 in a second case also styled *Staples v. Gilmer*, the Supreme Court of Appeals with only one dissent ruled that the actions of the General Assembly complied with the terms of the state constitution inasmuch as nothing in the constitution explicitly prohibited the assembly from making the proposal in the form that it did.[53] Interestingly, the sole dissenter was Chief Justice Preston W. Campbell, who had been a member of the Convention of 1901–2. He quoted at length an exchange between convention members A. Caperton Braxton and John Strode Barbour to support his own recollection and belief in 1945 that Section 197 did not authorize the assembly to proceed as it had done and limit the scope of subjects that the convention could consider.[54]

Voters approved the convention in a referendum on 6 March by a vote of 54,515 to 30,341;[55] voters elected forty white men from the state's senatorial districts on 24 April; and the convention met in the Capitol in Richmond from 30 April to 3 May.[56] On the latter date, the convention "proclaimed, established, ordained and declared" a new Article XVII "to be on and after the third day of May, 1945, a permanent part of the said Constitution of Virginia." The amendment provided that "No member of the armed forces of the United States, while in active service in time of war, shall be required to pay a poll tax or to register as a prerequisite to the right to vote in any and all elections, including legalized primary elections." It "canceled and annulled" poll taxes those service members owed for 1942, 1943, and 1944 and prohibited assessment of poll taxes on members of the armed services then and thereafter during wartime.

University of Virginia political scientist Robert K. Gooch, in a critical analysis of the majority's opinion in the second *Staples v. Gilmer* decision, explained that the legislators had proceeded as they did in authorizing the convention and empowering it to add the new provisions to the constitution without a ratification referendum so as to prevent opponents of the poll tax from going farther and using the occasion to attempt to abolish the poll tax.[57]

In 1948, the General Assembly proposed an amendment to do just that and also to create a new state board of elections and new local boards of elections. For reasons that are not clear, but perhaps to detach the question of the poll tax from the presidential campaign of 1948, the act that submitted the proposed amendment to the voters delayed the referendum until 8 November 1949.[58] Voters on that date refused to ratify it by a vote of 206,542 to 56,687.[59]

An amendment that voters ratified on 5 November 1946 removed from Section 183 a reference to property owned by the United States government from the list of property exempt from taxation.

On 2 November 1948, voters ratified an amendment that deleted Section 51 that in 1902 had created a permanent Joint Committee of the General Assembly to review all bills on local subjects to ascertain whether the subject matter had already been, or could better be, treated by general laws.

Voters on 2 November 1954 narrowly defeated a proposed amendment to Section 115 that would permit cities and counties to borrow money from the state Retirement System for constructing schools without a prior referendum to approve issuing bonds to repay the loan.[60]

Early in 1956, the General Assembly provided for another limited-purpose convention to amend the constitution without a ratification referendum.[61] The purpose was to allow public money to be paid to private schools that people created after the Supreme Court of the United States ruled in 1954 in *Brown v. Board of Education of Topeka* that compulsory racial segregation in public schools violated the equal protection clause of the Fourteenth Amendment.[62] In order to evade the Supreme Court's directive to desegregate the public schools, Virginia adopted what quickly became known as a policy of "massive resistance," part of which was to allow public subvention to private schools for white children. Article IX, Section 141, of the Constitution of 1902 prohibited appropriation of public money to schools and colleges not wholly owned by the state or by any city or county. The 1955 decision of the Supreme Court of Appeals in *Almond v. Day* had invalidated state educational grants to orphans of service members killed in the two world wars on the grounds that even though the state paid the money directly to the students' families, the money in reality went to the private schools in violation of Section 141.[63] That meant that the state could not make similar grants to members of white families who desired to send their children to private racially segregated schools rather than to public schools that might come under federal court orders to desegregate.

Voters authorized the convention by a vote of 304,154 to 146,164 on 9 January 1956;[64] voters elected forty white men from senatorial districts on 21 February; and the convention met in the Capitol on 5, 6, and 7 March 1956.[65] The convention approved new language for Article IX, Section 141, that omitted obsolete references to bonds issued in the nineteenth century that had since been paid off and inserted a 175-word provision that permitted state and local governments to appropriate money for private nonsectarian schools and institutions of higher education. The convention ordained the amendment in effect as of 7 March 1956.[66]

Voters ratified three amendments on 6 November 1956. They approved an amendment to Article IV, Section 69, to change the date for inauguration of the governor from the third Wednesday in January after the election to the second Wednesday in January. Amendments to Sections 155 and 161 deleted language in the article on the State Corporation Commission that required railroads to provide free transportation for commission members who were on official business. And an amendment to Section 169 added to the requirement that cities and counties tax all personal property based on its fair market value: "The General Assembly may define as a separate subject of taxation household goods and personal effects and may allow the governing bodies of counties, cities, and towns to exempt or partially exempt such property from taxation."

An amendment ratified on 4 November 1958 to Section 151, which governed how counties could contract public debts, allowed the General Assembly to authorize "by general law, the school board of any county to contract to borrow money from the Virginia Supplemental Retirement System, or any successor thereto, for the purpose of school construction, with the approval of the governing body of the county."

An amendment to Article XVII ratified on 8 November 1960 removed the words "in time of war" from the first sentence, "No member of the armed forces of the United States, while in active service in time of war, shall be required to pay a poll tax or to register, as a prerequisite to the right to vote in any and all elections, including legalized primary elections." On that same date, voters rejected proposed amendments to Sections 110, 118, 119, and 120 to permit constitutional officers in certain cities and counties to serve in adjacent cities and counties at the same time and to enable the General Assembly to consolidate charitable and penal institutions in adjacent counties and cities if the voters of each approved.[67]

On 6 November 1962, voters ratified an amendment to Article II, Section 20, concerning registration of voters that the registrar "may"—not "must," "shall," or "will"—provide applicants a printed "form" on which to supply all the required information without aid or assistance. The amendment permitted the General Assembly to outlaw the practice of registrars handing applicants blank pieces of paper that they had to fill out unaided.[68] On that same day, voters rejected an amendment to Article II, Section 30, that the General Assembly could require that only freeholders—owners of real estate—be permitted to vote in referenda on issuance of state bonds or bonds of any of its political subdivisions.[69]

And also on 6 November 1962, a mere two weeks after the Cuban Missile Crisis began, voters ratified a new provision to Section 51 in Article III: "In any case of enemy attack upon the soil of Virginia by nuclear fusion or fission bombs or devices, if the Governor by proclamation declares that due to the emergency created thereby a quorum of the General Assembly cannot be assembled, a lesser number, but not less than two-fifths of the members elected to each house, may meet, and may enact legislation" by the vote of four-fifths of the members of each house present, but such laws would not be in force for longer than one year.

Voters ratified the final amendment to the constitution on 8 November 1966. It changed the name of the Board of Agriculture and Immigration to the Board of Agriculture and Commerce and the title of the administrator from Commissioner of the Board of Agriculture and Immigration to the Commissioner of the Board of Agriculture and Commerce in order that the responsibilities of the board and commissioner could be revised accordingly.

Constitution of the United States

The only change to the Constitution of the United States that directly changed any part of the Constitution of Virginia as it was revised in 1928 was the Twenty-Fourth Amendment, which was ratified in 1964 without the consent of the General Assembly of Virginia. It prohibited imposition of a poll tax as a prerequisite to vote in elections for presidential elector and for senators and representatives in Congress. Two years later, the Supreme Court of the United States, in *Harper v. Virginia State Board of Elections*, which combined two challenges to the poll tax in Virginia, ruled that the poll tax was an unconstitutional infringement on the right to vote in all elections.[70]

A large number of federal laws and federal court cases that arose as a consequence of the Civil Rights movement in the 1950s and 1960s directly affected numerous state laws and in one instance invalidated a section of the state constitution. In 1954, the Supreme Court of the United States ruled in *Brown v. Board of Education of Topeka*, that mandatory racial segregation in public schools violated the equal protection clause of the Fourteenth Amendment.[71] That invalidated Section 140 of the state constitution that since 1902 had mandated that "White and colored children shall not be taught in the same school."

Revised Constitution in Operation

The primary purpose of Governor Byrd's Program of Progress was to concentrate administrative and appointive powers in the office of the governor in the interest of efficiency and saving money. As a measure to improve public administration, it achieved its primary objective. It also magnified the political influence of the governor's office. Indeed, a study late in the life of the revised constitution declared the governor of Virginia to be one of the most powerful governors in the country.[72] But the constitutional revision also had a powerful political result. It allowed increased concentration of political power in the upper echelons of the dominant wing of the state's Democratic Party, which Byrd personally directed. Only once between ratification of the revised Constitution in 1928 and Byrd's death in 1966 did his own personal first or second choice for governor fail to win the nomination and general election. The exception was New Deal sympathizer James H. Price in 1937. Because Byrd remained the most influential political leader in the state and nearly always had a sympathetic or hand-chosen political ally in the governor's office, Byrd had the longest successful leadership of a dominant political organization in the history of the country.

The governor's constitutional responsibilities and authorities were only part of the source of the governor's power. With the backing (almost always) of the party's leaders, the governor of the one-party state usually spoke for and to the party's members, including overwhelmingly large majorities in both houses of the General Assembly. The governor therefore set the agenda for each biennial legislative session, both by proposing a budget and by making other recommendations in his message to the opening session of each new assembly. In that circumstance, the political authority of the governor amplified the actual legal authority.[73]

The Constitution granted the General Assembly power to elect judges of all the state's courts and judges of the State Corporation Commission, but because the assembly met for only sixty days every second year (about 8 percent of the time), the governor's authority to fill vacancies on all courts and the

State Corporation Commission actually meant that the governor's effective appointive power was much greater than it appeared at first glance. Governors appointed almost all the new judges, and their political allies in the General Assembly nearly always elected them to full terms.[74]

In 1927, while Byrd was still governor, he appointed Everett Randolph Combs state comptroller to keep his eye on the state's money. Combs had been chair of the Ninth District Democratic Party in 1922 when he and Byrd led the redemption of the congressional district from the Republicans. Promoted to the State Compensation Board in 1934, Combs was in charge of policing the salaries and expenditures of members of the courthouse rings who received fees for performing their jobs. As Byrd's personal watchdog and enforcer in state government until 1949, he became the second most influential man in the state.[75] During the 1930s, L. McCarthy Downs, the auditor of public accounts and a Byrd organization member in good standing, instituted new auditing procedures for fee officers to reduce the likelihood of financial scandals in the courthouse rings of the sort that Byrd always feared and that the New York Bureau of Municipal Research's report on county government had identified.[76]

Byrd and Combs supervised the unreformed courthouse rings closely and resisted changes, such as modification or elimination of the fee system, that could weaken their control. The Democratic Party leaders controlled the courthouse rings and through legislative and judicial enforcement of the Dillon Rule also controlled local government, which in many places was the same thing, the same people, as the courthouse rings. Local needs could fall victim to political orthodoxy or political considerations. In 1940, the Virginia Commission on County Government issued a stern condemnation of the existing political and legal constraints on counties. "If local government perishes," the commission warned, "democratic self-government is in danger. The Commission is convinced that unless rapid progress is made in the reorganization and rehabilitation of Virginia county government the last vestiges of 'home rule' in Virginia counties will shortly be lost. . . . If the present rapid trends toward 'state consolidation' continue," the commissioners predicted, "within ten years, and assuredly within this generation, the Virginia county as we know it will remain only a name and its officers will perform 'state functions' in the 'provinces' which were once self-governing counties."[77]

Along with controlling the courthouse rings, the Byrd organization's ability to keep the electorate small was another key to its long-running success. The poll tax as a prerequisite for voter registration, first introduced in 1902, was the object of much scorn for decades because of its undemocratic character.

Late in the administration of Governor James Price—the only administration during the course of forty years that was unfriendly toward Byrd and his organization—the governor requested a report and recommendations on the poll tax from the Virginia Advisory Legislative Council. Completed in 1941 for the council of legislators that included a few opponents of the Byrd organization and one or more Republicans, the report was largely the work of University of Virginia political science professor Robert K. Gooch. The report damned the poll tax as a source of political corruption and an embarrassment to the state. It declared bluntly that the tax was "founded on disbelief in political democracy as the basis of government. Advocacy of retention of the poll-tax and genuine belief in political democracy are basically irreconcilable."[78] The council declined to release or publish the report, and as late as the 1960s, legislative officials refused to let a graduate student even see a copy; so, in 1969, Gooch published his own carbon copy, instead.[79]

Under Byrd's dominating leadership, Virginia's congressional delegation was more consistently hostile to the New Deal, the Fair Deal, the New Frontier, and the Great Society than the delegation of any other southern state. The party's leaders were probably more resistant to change than the party's loyal members. Presidential election returns demonstrated during the 1930s and 1940s that Virginia voters—even the limited number who could then vote—gave President Franklin D. Roosevelt very large majorities four times. Other than that, no voting constituency was powerful enough to challenge the Byrd organization's ability to get its way.[80] In fact, a smaller proportion of adult Virginians voted during the life of the revised constitution than in any other state in the country. "By contrast," political scientist V. O. Key concluded in his important 1949 study of southern politics, "Mississippi is a hotbed of democracy."[81] Until the mid-1960s, Byrd dominated the party and the state without serious challenges.

The Future

Sixteen months into the forty-three-year life of the revised constitution, the stock market crash of 1929 ushered in a decade-long depression. The depression destroyed any likelihood that Harry Byrd's Program of Progress would stimulate business and industrial growth in Virginia. That was the first of many unforeseen events of transformative importance during the revised constitution's existence. The Great Depression, the revolutionary changes in the relationship between the federal government and the economy that the New Deal of the 1930s created, the ramifications of those changes for state government in Virginia, World War II, the Civil Rights movement, rapid urbanization and suburbanization after the war, and the collapse of the Byrd organization after the death of Byrd in 1966 together meant that by the end of the 1960s, Virginia scarcely resembled the state as it had been in 1928.[82] Those changes during the second and third quarters of the twentieth century, much as the radical changes that had taken place in Virginia during the first and second quarters of the nineteenth century, provided the occasion for the state's political leaders to rewrite the state's constitution again.

CHAPTER 9

The Constitution of 1971

A demographic revolution in Virginia that began well before World War II and two revolutions in American law after the war had profound effects on the state. Together, they undermined the foundations for the state's regime of racial segregation that had hardened into place at the beginning of the twentieth century, and they undermined the foundations for the undemocratic political organization that Democrats had created late in the nineteenth century. That organization, under the leadership of Harry Flood Byrd since 1922, had dominated Virginia politics and government for more than four decades before the constitutional revision of 1928. The demise of that organization and the demographic and legal revolutions helped bring about the Constitution of 1971.

The Demographic Revolution

Two world wars and the Great Depression of the 1930s redistributed both the population of the state and the center of political gravity within the state. Between 1900 and 1970, the population of Virginia increased about 250 percent, from approximately 1,850,000 people to 4,650,000. Just as importantly, the increase was not uniform across the state. By the 1950s, more Virginians resided in urban and suburban areas than in rural and small-town regions. A rapid growth in the number of densely concentrated people who resided in three clusters that formed a large arc from the northern suburbs of the District of Columbia, through the capital region with Richmond at its center, and to the naval and shipbuilding centers in Hampton Roads created a new asymmetry in the state's population.[1]

Changes in people's relationships to, and requirements of, their governments accompanied the important demographic changes. Twentieth-century Virginians, like other twentieth-century Americans, expected state and local governments to provide good public schools, fire and police protection, public health facilities and hospitals, water and sewer services, expensive public roads, airports, and in some places public meeting halls or large-scale venues for sporting and other entertainment events. People's expectations pulled even the slow-moving government of Virginia away from the "pay as you go," limited-government philosophy that had always informed the Byrd organization's leadership. Federal aid to schools, public libraries, roadways, and other state and local government projects complicated relations between the state and federal governments, required creation of new corresponding state administrative agencies to oversee the grants, and in effect made people rely more than ever before on government at all levels.

The early twentieth-century governmental institutions that agents of the New York Bureau of Municipal Research had analyzed and found inadequate in its study of local government in 1926[2] became more and more inadequate as time passed, especially institutions of local government. To meet some of the expectations of Virginia's people, the General Assembly individually empowered cities and counties to enlarge their responsibilities or to act cooperatively. Some cities annexed densely populated portions of neighboring counties. During the 1960s, cities and towns annexed territory sixty-five times, affecting more than 160,000 people, and some cities merged with neighboring counties or towns. The city of Hampton merged with, or absorbed, Elizabeth City County and the town of Phoebus in 1952; the city of Newport News merged with Warwick County in 1958; in 1963, the city of Virginia Beach absorbed Princess Anne County; and, also in 1963, the city of South Norfolk and Norfolk County merged to form the new city of Chesapeake. The rural county of Nansemond received a charter in 1972 and merged with the small city of Suffolk in 1974. Each of the named counties became extinct with the merger.[3] In some instances, as in Nansemond County, the assembly granted charters to counties to enable county governments to function more like city governments, with the result that by the 1960s, Virginia had cities as well as rural, urban, and suburban counties, and in one instance, a largely rural city.[4]

Between 1942 and 1970, the General Assembly also authorized creation of more than three hundred independent or semi-independent public authorities to provide specific public services. In many instances, those authorities had jurisdiction in more than one county or in a county and adjacent city. A commentator concluded in 1970 that the many districts "made it possible for a vast array of urban services to be provided outside of Virginia's cities, but the price has been a hodge-podge of overlapping statutes causing confusion, administrative difficulty, and troublesome planning problems." Those institutional complications and enlarged responsibilities appeared to be incompatible in many instances with the provisions for city and county governments in the state constitution—in particular, the restrictions on how local units of government could borrow money for long-term projects and how much money they could borrow.[5]

That undoubtedly made adaptations or systematic overhaul of local government institutions very difficult or perhaps even impossible, given the General Assembly's predilection to provide for individual changes piecemeal rather than to devise comprehensive, long-term adaptations to new circumstances. Members of the state's Metropolitan Areas Study Commission emphasized in 1967 that "what were once thought to be local problems are no longer local in their effects on the region of the State. Where local leadership lacks an area-wide perspective and where problems are accumulating, the State has provided neither leadership nor incentives to positive action." The commission's members concluded, "When great movements of people, fundamental alterations of economics, and radically new transportation and communications systems come into being with all the resulting interdependence of people, areas, and states, it is vitally necessary that the State adjust itself to meet the new circumstances. The units of government were originally designed to meet the governmental requirements of the 17th, 18th, and 19th Centuries. Obviously, the State must now adjust itself to meet the problems of the 20th Century." The commission recommended a significantly increased role for the state government in devising plans for future growth and supporting and coordinating the necessary work of cities and urbanized portions of counties.[6]

Whether demographic changes and their consequences by themselves would have eventually eroded the bases for the state's regime of white supremacy and the dominance of the Byrd organization sufficiently to destroy them remains unclear. During the first two-thirds of the twentieth century, the organization relied on a combination of a severely restricted electorate and malapportionment of seats in the General Assembly to retain its political control of the state.[7] The demographic revolution clearly made maintenance of the Byrd organization's dominance and the preservation of political control through the old courthouse rings much more difficult before the two revolutions in law that made it impossible. But even as late as the 1960s, the cumulative changes had not yet pulled the Byrd organization apart.

The Civil Rights and Representation Revolutions

The Civil Rights movement, which began before World War II and continued into the 1970s, terminated or undermined numerous laws and social practices in Virginia and overturned two provisions of the state's constitution.[8] The 1954 ruling of the Supreme Court of the United States in *Brown v. Board of Education of Topeka* declared that mandatory racial segregation of public schools violated the equal protection clause of the Fourteenth Amendment.[9] That invalidated Section 140 of the Constitution of 1902 that provided, "White and colored children shall not be taught in the same school." In 1964, the Twenty-Fourth Amendment (which the General Assembly of Virginia did not ratify) prohibited imposition of a poll tax as a prerequisite to vote in elections for presidential elector and members of the two houses of Congress. The Supreme Court's decision two years later in *Harper v. Virginia State Board of Elections*, which combined two challenges to the Virginia poll, declared the poll tax to be an unconstitutional burden on citizens in any election in the country.[10] That invalidated the requirements in Article II of the Constitution of 1902 that made payment of the poll tax a prerequisite for the franchise.

Starting in the 1940s, through a practice known as "incorporation," the Supreme Court of the United States began individually declaring that the fundamental rights enumerated in the Bill of Rights constituted the main body of liberties that the Fourteenth Amendment prohibited the states from denying to any person. Relying on that new interpretation of the Fourteenth Amendment and on the commerce clause in the Constitution of the United States, the federal government renewed the campaign that it had abandoned in the 1880s to construct new societies and polities in the states of the former Confederacy—indeed, throughout the country—on the basis of equal civil and political rights for all people. State laws on many subjects fell victim to litigation in federal courts.

The increased power of the federal government at the expense of state authority generated stiff opposition in Virginia and elsewhere in the country, both because it abridged traditional states' rights in many areas of law and public policy and also because of how many state and local racial segregation laws were overturned by the Civil Rights movement and the application of the Bill of Rights to the states. Federal laws, including the Civil Rights Act of 1964 and the Voting Rights Acts of 1965, together with a cascade of federal court rulings invalidated most of Virginia's racial segregation statutes, laws dating from the seventeenth century that prohibited interracial marriage, as well as laws and social practices that had permitted different treatment of white and

Black Virginians under the "separate but equal" doctrine that the Supreme Court of the United States had endorsed in *Plessy v. Ferguson* in 1896.[11]

The Voting Rights Act was of the utmost importance because it placed under federal supervision all voting laws and practices in states and parts of states with histories of discrimination against racial minorities. No new laws and no changes to old laws, including electoral district boundaries, in those regions could take effect without the approval of the Department of Justice or the United States District Court for the District of Columbia. The enumerated jurisdictions to which the law applied specifically included all of Virginia.[12] Thereafter, the government of Virginia was without the legal ability to enforce or revise old laws or enact new ones that could bolster the authority of the Byrd organization or extend the life of Jim Crow segregation.

The Byrd organization's initial reaction to the school desegregation decision of 1954—the first of the sweeping Civil Rights cases—was to adopt a policy of "massive resistance" to prohibit enforcement of the federal court orders in Virginia. Later in the decade when that policy brought about closings of public schools in Norfolk, Front Royal, and Charlottesville and threatened closings in other cities, a significant number of Virginia Democrats abandoned massive resistance in order to preserve the public school system. As a consequence, by the 1960s, the Byrd organization was in danger of crumbling.

And during that very same decade of the 1960s, what can be termed the Representation Revolution,[13] of which the Voting Rights Act was a part, further transformed Virginia politics. In a series of landmark rulings, the Supreme Court of the United States required that all elections and electoral districts in the United States had to provide for equality of representation based on the principle of "one person, one vote."[14] Inasmuch as the General Assembly of Virginia had repeatedly devised legislative districts that awarded seats on a discriminatory basis, that seriously undermined the ability of the Byrd organization to retain the malapportionment that gave small numbers of white voters in rural and southeastern areas the ability to elect more members of the assembly than larger numbers of white and Black voters in urban and suburban areas were able to elect.[15] The Representation Revolution of the 1960s eventually terminated the districting tactics that had helped the Byrd organization's base in the rural and southeastern parts of the state retain its dominance. At the same time, the demographic revolution and the demands of people in urban and suburban areas for more public services increased pressures for other kinds of changes.

The apparently firm control that the Byrd organization exercised over Virginia government and politics eventually gave way under the weight of the simultaneous strains of the demographic and legal revolutions. Harry Byrd, a member of the United States Senate, became increasingly preoccupied during the 1950s and early 1960s with his battles against the enlarged role that the federal government assumed in American society, especially in Civil Rights, and his attempts to prevent or limit the growth of the federal budget. Byrd's retirement from the Senate in 1965 because of ill health and his death the following year left the organization without an identifiable successor as its leader.[16] His retirement and death occurred during, and were parts of, what in hindsight we can clearly see was a critical turning point in the state's political history.

The Commission on Constitutional Revision

In 1964, two years before Byrd died, Lieutenant Governor Mills E. Godwin Jr., who as a state senator had been one of the leaders of massive resistance in the 1950s even though he was not an organization insider, broke with Byrd to endorse and campaign for Lyndon B. Johnson in that year's presidential election. Johnson carried Virginia, the first Democrat to do so since 1948 and the last until 2008; then in 1965, Godwin won election as governor.[17] He had shrewdly realized before almost any other major political leader in Virginia that in the changed circumstances of the 1960s, neither racial segregation nor the existence of the Byrd organization would be a good foundation on which to win elections or fashion a new politics that could move farther away from the old Byrd orthodoxy to meet the needs of the people during and after the continuing demographic revolution. During Godwin's four years in office, he persuaded the General Assembly to abandon that orthodoxy in several major ways. At his recommendation, the assembly passed a sales tax to increase revenue; increased appropriations for public schools; created the state's first community college system; and borrowed money for needed infrastructure projects. Godwin recognized that those important breaks with the past could not be fully effective during the remaining decades of the twentieth century because of the constraints that the state's antiquated constitution placed on the state government and on local governments.[18]

In Godwin's 10 January 1968 address to the General Assembly midway through his term as governor, he enumerated the accomplishments legislators had approved during the previous session in 1966 but lamented that city and county governments, as well as the state government, lacked constitutional authority to raise the necessary money or to do more. "In these last few turbulent years of growth and change," Godwin began his proposal for constitutional revision, "Virginia's new dimensions have many times extended to the

Constitution itself.... Now, the time has come, in my judgment, for a studied and impartial analysis of its provisions in the light of today."[19]

Godwin proposed that the General Assembly undertake the revision rather than summon a constitutional convention for that purpose.[20] He requested that the General Assembly authorize him to appoint a select Commission on Constitutional Revision to be composed of "impartial and eminently qualified citizens, whose stature is commensurate with the task to be performed, and whose recommendations would command the respect and thoughtful consideration of the General Assembly and the people of Virginia." Such nonpartisan or bipartisan commissions of experts and representatives of the public had precedent. Several other states during the twentieth century had employed constitutional revision commissions to prepare drafts or suggestions for a convention or legislature,[21] including the Commission to Suggest Amendments to the Constitution to the General Assembly of Virginia that Governor Harry F. Byrd appointed in 1926 to reduce proposals for revising the state constitution into a draft revisal of the constitution for the General Assembly to consider.[22]

Proceeding by these "thorough and deliberate means" rather than by summoning a potentially expensive and uncontrollable convention, Godwin planned for the General Assembly to act on the commission's recommendations at a special session in 1969 and then, at the regular session in 1970, formally submit a new constitution to a ratification referendum that autumn.[23] Godwin's proposal appealed to the Democratic Party majority in both houses of the assembly who would thereby be in full control of what the proposed new constitution would contain and what it would not.[24]

Later in January, Godwin appointed a bipartisan eleven-member commission, which included men from all regions of the state except the southwesternmost counties. Its chair was former Democratic governor Albertis Harrison, who had recently become a justice of the Supreme Court of Appeals. The other members included Lewis F. Powell, a future justice of the Supreme Court of the United States, as well as a sitting and a future federal judge, the dean of the law school at the University of Virginia who later served on the World Court, and Richmond Civil Rights attorney Oliver W. Hill, the only member of the commission who was the first Black man to have a formal role in preparing a state constitution since the two dozen men who served in the Convention of 1867–68.[25] To be the commission's executive director, the members appointed University of Virginia law professor A. E. Dick Howard, author of the 1968 book, *The Road from Runnymede: Magna Carta and Constitutionalism in America*.[26] The governor appointed no women to the commission.

The commission conducted five public hearings at different places in the state to gather public opinion. The commission's executive director and five committees coordinated a massive research project in the summer of 1968 in which attorneys and law students prepared almost 150 memoranda on different aspects of the state's constitution and laws and on constitutional innovations in other states during the middle decades of the twentieth century.[27] Those reports and most of the records of the commission are preserved in the state's archives in the Library of Virginia and in the library of the law school at the University of Virginia.[28] Moreover, the June 1968 issue of the *Virginia Law Review*, published at the University of Virginia law school, contained a symposium on state constitutions, including Howard's own "'For the Common Benefit': Constitutional History in Virginia as a Casebook for the Modern Constitution-Maker," and Wythe W. Holt Jr.'s "Constitutional Revision in Virginia, 1902 and 1928: Some Lessons on Roadblocks to Institutional Reform."[29]

The commission and its staff made several recommendations of major importance in addition to the specific changes that they submitted to the General Assembly. The bipartisan commission was able to make its proposals without generating suspicions of excessive partisanship that had derailed or almost derailed proposed constitutional revisions in several other states during the 1960s; and the commission recommended that some of the proposed provisions be voted on separately, at the time of the ratification referendum, in order to reduce the likelihood that opposition to some one or another of the most controversial sections threaten ratification of the whole constitution. The provisions to be voted on separately were to allow the General Assembly to alter the boundaries of the capital city; to permit appropriation of public funds for the benefit of handicapped children who attended private schools; to retain the authority that an amendment of 1956 granted to the General Assembly to appropriate money to private schools; to delete the old constitution's prohibition on lotteries that had been in state constitutions since 1851;[30] to allow the General Assembly to issue general obligation bonds subject to approval in a referendum; and to allow the General Assembly to issue revenue bonds by a two-thirds vote of each house, the bonds to be paid off from revenue-generating projects such as toll roads.[31]

In January 1969, the commission delivered its 542-page report to the governor and General Assembly. The clear introduction explained the philosophy of the proposed constitutional revision, in particular that the constitution should consist for the most part in general provisions and not include, as the Constitution of 1902 and its 1928 revision, detail of the kind that ought to be left to the General Assembly to determine by law as circumstances changed. The excellent report also included the texts of the state constitution as it existed as of 1969 and the proposed revision in parallel columns that allowed legislators, journalists, and others to see easily what the commission members proposed to change and what they planned to leave unchanged.[32]

The General Assembly Sessions of 1969 and 1970

The 1969 special session of the General Assembly met for two months, from 26 February through 25 April, about twice the length of the 1927 assembly session that prepared the proposed revision that voters ratified in 1928. Transcriptions of voice recordings of the proceedings in both houses have been published in two large volumes. Each volume includes texts in parallel columns of the proposal of the Constitutional Revision Commission, the text as reported from the relevant legislative committees, the text as approved before being sent to the other house, and the final text that was submitted to the voters for ratification.[33]

William Ferguson Reid, a Henrico County dentist, was a member of the House of Delegates in the sessions of 1969 and 1970, the only elected Black public official since the two dozen who had served in the Convention of 1867–68 ever to participate in writing a new Virginia constitution. The first three women who ever took part in writing an entirely new Virginia constitution were Eleanor P. Sheppard, of the city of Richmond, who served in the House of Delegates both sessions; Mary A. Marshall, of Arlington County; and Dorothy S. McDiarmid, of Fairfax County. These three women were members of the House of Delegates in the 1969.

The House of Delegates approved the main body of the constitution by a vote of 89 to 3 on 25 April 1969, and the Senate approved it by a vote of 34 to 0 on the same day.[34] Both houses also approved the propositions to be voted on separately at the time of the ratification referendum. During the 1970 regular session, the House of Delegates voted 96 to 0 and the Senate voted 38 to 0 submit the constitution to the voters that autumn.[35] At that time, the legislators approved four of the separate amendments but declined to give a second approval to the proposal to allow public subvention of handicapped children in private schools and to allow the General Assembly to alter the boundaries for the capital city. They also decided to allow the 1956 amendment that permitted public money to be appropriated for private, racially segregated schools to remain in the constitution without giving voters a chance to approve or reject it.

The Constitution of 1971

As with the constitutional revision of 1928, the General Assembly proposed the new constitution to the voters in November 1970 in the form known in parliamentary practice as an amendment in the form of a substitute. The Supreme Court of Appeals had ruled in *Staples v. Gilmer* in 1945 that the General Assembly had the authority to submit a new or revised constitution to the voters in that form.[36] The question on the ballot asked voters whether to delete the entire old constitution (except the sections to be voted on separately and the one to be silently incorporated into the new constitution) and in its place, insert the new.[37] At about 18,430 words, the proposed constitution, even with substantial additions made to several sections, was less than two-thirds the length of the more than 29,000 words in the Constitution of 1902 and the 30,000 in the 1928 revision. Like the old constitution, the new constitution had no preamble. Unlike the old, with its sixteen articles (and a seventeenth added in 1945) and 197 consecutively numbered sections (200 as of 1945), the new was divided into twelve articles with the sections in each separately numbered. The new constitution omitted many provisions that were legislative in character and left them to the discretion of the General Assembly, such as the whole Article IX on the State Board of Agriculture and Immigration, which by an amendment to the old constitution ratified in 1966 had become the office of the Commissioner of Agriculture and Commerce; Article X on prisons and other institutions; and the homestead exemption provision in Article XI. It also omitted obsolete provisions, such as the requirement in Article III for payment of a poll tax as a prerequisite for registration to vote, and the whole of the 1945 Article XVII on that subject; Article XVI's "Rules of Construction" of the 1928 revision of the constitution that were not needed for the new constitution; and the outdated former Section 195 on the legal ability of acknowledged children of people who married during slavery times to inherit property from their parents. By a separate vote at the time of the ratification referendum, voters agreed 491,124 to 290,168 to omit the prohibition on lotteries that had been in the state's constitutions since 1851.[38]

Each article in the new constitution is the subject of a separate chapter in A. E. Dick Howard's two-volume 1974 *Commentaries on the Constitution of Virginia* and in the 2014 second edition of John Dinan's *The Virginia State Constitution*.[39] In each book, each section (and sometimes each subsection) is the subject of one or more paragraphs or pages of descriptive analysis. Howard's analyses include carefully documented historical background, references to state and federal case law that contributed to the text as ratified in 1971, relevant legal scholarship on some topics, and discussions of instances in which the General Assembly modified or rejected recommendations of the Commission on Constitutional Revision. Dinan's volume includes concise accounts of the court rulings, official opinions of the attorney general, and legal scholarship that elucidated the application of the evolving text of the Constitution of 1971 as it was amended to 2014. For our purpose of understanding how the Constitution of 1971 is part of the long historical evolution of Virginia's constitutions, this account focuses on what the Constitution of 1971 preserved, modified, or omitted from the state's previous constitutions, as well as the amendments that modified the text that voters ratified in 1970.

BILL OF RIGHTS

Article I of the Constitution of 1971 included almost all the provisions of the Bill of Rights that were in the Constitution of 1902 with a few modifications, some of which transferred modified language from other portions of the old constitution into the Bill of Rights in the new.

The first important change to an old section was to Section 9, that since 1776 had read, "That excessive bail ought not to be required, nor excessive fines imposed, nor cruel and unusual punishments inflicted." The revision brought up into the Bill of Rights some related subjects that since 1830 had been in the article on the General Assembly and had prohibited the assembly from enacting certain classes of laws. The change added to the original section, "that the privilege of the writ of habeas corpus shall not be suspended unless when, in cases of invasion or rebellion, the public safety may require; and that the General Assembly shall not pass any bill of attainder, or any ex post facto law."

Section 11 included similar modifications. As revised, the section read, "That no person shall be deprived of his life, liberty, or property without due process of law; that the General Assembly shall not pass any law impairing the obligation of contracts, nor any law whereby private property shall be taken or damaged for public uses, without just compensation, the term 'public uses' to be defined by the General Assembly; and that the right to be free from any governmental discrimination upon the basis of religious conviction, race, color, sex, or national origin shall not be abridged, except that the mere separation of the sexes shall not be considered discrimination." Early in the assembly's consideration of the commission's report, Delegate Dorothy McDiarmid persuaded the relevant committees of both houses to add the prohibition of sexual discrimination to the Bill of Rights.[40]

To Section 12 that protected the rights of free speech and the press, the General Assembly added language from the First Amendment to the Constitution of the United States to protect the rights of assembly and petition. Members of the General Assembly included in Section 13 a new constitutional right to bear arms, which they borrowed from the Second Amendment to the Constitution of the United States.

The General Assembly accepted recommendations of the Commission on Constitutional Revision to make two important additions to Section 15, which, since Patrick Henry proposed the language in 1776, had read, "That no free government, nor the blessings of liberty, can be preserved to any people, but by a firm adherence to justice, moderation, temperance, frugality, and virtue; and by frequent recurrence to fundamental principles." To that, the new constitution added, "and by the recognition by all citizens that they have duties as well as rights, and that such rights cannot be enjoyed save in a society where law is respected and due process is observed." The revised section also contained a new sentence, "That free government rests, as does all progress, upon the broadest possible diffusion of knowledge, and that the Commonwealth should avail itself of those talents which nature has sown so liberally among its people by assuring the opportunity for their fullest development by an effective system of education throughout the Commonwealth."

That language should be read together with the new language of Article VIII, Section 1, "The General Assembly shall provide for a system of free public elementary and secondary schools for all children of school age throughout the Commonwealth, and shall seek to ensure that an educational program of high quality is established and continually maintained." With an authorization to the General Assembly to require compulsory education for school-age children, the government's constitutional obligation to provide good quality public education for all Virginia children guaranteed them the right to receive an education at public expense. The Supreme Court of Virginia stated as much—"education is a fundamental right under the Constitution"—in 1994 in *Scott v. Commonwealth*, when it ruled that the state's constitution nevertheless did not require perfect equality of funding for all the state's school districts. No longer would it be constitutionally permissible for a locality to abolish its public schools as Prince Edward County had done in the 1950s as part of the massive resistance to prevent desegregation of the schools.[41]

SUFFRAGE AND QUALIFICATIONS FOR OFFICE

Article II omitted several large portions of the 1902 text, including the poll tax, that had been designed to prevent Black men from voting or to suppress the number who could qualify. The article revised other sections, in some instances substantially, and added new language that was clearer than the old or that brought the state's constitution into line with federal Civil Rights laws and the several important Supreme Court cases of the Representation Revolution.

Section 2 required voter registrars to provide "a standard form"—thus making it impossible in the future for registrars to hand applicants blank sheets of paper to fill in without aid[42]—on which they had to record their "full name, including the maiden name of a woman, if married; date of birth; marital status; occupation; social security number, if any; whether the applicant is presently a United States citizen; address and place of abode and length of residence in the Commonwealth and in the precinct; place and time of any previous registrations to vote."

Section 2 omitted language from Section 24 of the former constitution that had prohibited voting by active members of the armed forces temporarily stationed in the state in keeping with recent Supreme Court decisions, particularly *Carrington v. Rash* that in 1965 invalidated a similar but even more restrictive provision in the Texas constitution.[43] The new constitution also omitted the provision in the old Section 24 that prohibited registration and voting by people who temporarily resided in Virginia while attending school. Legislators agreed to that deletion in light of the Supreme Court of Appeals' 1966 ruling in *Kegley v. Johnson* that under the state and federal constitutions students could not be treated differently than other applicants.[44] The revised Section 2 included a new sentence, "Nothing in this Article shall preclude the General Assembly from requiring as a prerequisite to registration to vote the ability of the applicant to read and complete in his own handwriting the application to register."

Comparatively brief Section 3 on voting replaced several long, restrictive sections and began, "No ballot or list of candidates upon any voting machine shall bear any distinguishing mark or symbol, other than words identifying political party affiliation; and their form, including the offices to be filled" and the names of candidates. This inclusion was a direct repudiation of some of the unfair tactics some members of the Byrd organization had employed at polling places earlier in the century to influence or control the outcomes of elections.[45]

Section 6 required, "Members of the House of Representatives of the United States and members of the Senate and of the House of Delegates of the General Assembly shall be elected from electoral districts established by the General Assembly. Every electoral district shall be composed of contiguous and compact territory and shall be so constituted as to give, as nearly as is practicable, representation in proportion to the population of the district. The General Assembly shall reapportion the Commonwealth into electoral districts in accordance with this section in the year 1971 and every ten years thereafter." The section for the first time extended to legislative districts the requirement for compact and contiguous districts that contained as nearly as practicable equal populations that had applied only to congressional districts since ratification of the Constitution of 1830 and to the few bicameral city councils since promulgation of the Constitution of 1902. These changes brought the redistricting provisions of the state constitution into line with the federal Supreme Court case law of the Representation Revolution.[46]

SEPARATION OF POWERS

Article III of the new constitution retained the requirement for separation of legislative, executive, and judicial powers and the prohibition on any public official exercising more than one authority at a time that had, though slightly modified several times, been in every Virginia constitution since that of 1776.

THE GENERAL ASSEMBLY

Article IV retained most of the cardinal features respecting the General Assembly from the old constitution, including authority for the assembly to set the size of the House of Delegates at from ninety to one hundred members and the Senate from thirty-three to forty. The assembly did not change the number of members of either house (one hundred delegates, forty senators) before or after ratification of the new constitution.

The new article was shorter than the old. Voters separately voted to eliminate the prohibition on the assembly authorizing lotteries, and the article also omitted the disqualification for service in the assembly based on taking part in a duel. It also eliminated sections that prohibited the assembly from creating new counties with fewer than six hundred square miles of territory or eight thousand inhabitants; that specifically authorized the assembly to pass laws concerning alcohol; and the long Section 68 that the Convention of 1901–2 had added to the constitution that created the joint auditing committee. Moreover, some of the prohibitions on legislative action appeared for the first time in the Bill of Rights and were no longer embedded in Article IV as restrictions on the powers of the General Assembly.

The most important legislative matter in which the 1969 session of the General Assembly rejected the recommendations of the Commission on Constitutional Revision concerned the frequency of legislative sessions. The Virginia Constitution of 1851 had authorized the assembly to meet every other year rather than annually as had been the case since 1776. The Constitutions of 1864 and 1869 restored annual sessions, but an amendment ratified in 1876 reintroduced biennial sessions, and the Constitution of 1902 and the 1928 revision retained that requirement. The Commission on Constitutional Revision researched changing patterns in twentieth-century state constitutions and discovered that as of 1947, only six of the forty-eight states had annual sessions, but by the time of the constitutional revision, almost all had annual sessions. The Commission recommended retaining biennial sessions but extending them to ninety days rather than sixty every other year. However, members of the General Assembly restored annual legislative sessions and retained the sixty-day limit on sessions in even-numbered years, when new legislators took office and adopted the state's two-year budget. The new constitution limited sessions in odd-numbered years to thirty days but, as with the previous constitutions, authorized members of the assembly to extend, by a two-thirds vote of both houses, each session by thirty days.

Section 14 retained the list of twenty specific subjects on which the previous constitution had prohibited the General Assembly from passing laws of special or local application only. The constitution did not define the words *special* and *local*, which could make drafting constitutional bills difficult. Legislators had sometimes evaded the specific prohibition on special or local bills by passing bills that contained language couched in general terms but limited in application in some manner, such as making them applicable only in jurisdictions with populations that fell within a narrow range so as to make them operative only in one or a few cities or counties.[47]

THE EXECUTIVE

The Commission on Constitutional Revision and the members of the 1969 session of the General Assembly made few important changes to the substance of Article V on the executive department, but they streamlined the language and revised the sequence of some sections in the interest of clarity and brevity. As with public officials mentioned elsewhere in the new constitution, the revision omitted the provision that set the annual salary for the governor and left it to the discretion of the assembly to set the salary.

The constitution retained the four-year term for the governor with no eligibility for reelection and the four-year terms for lieutenant governor and attorney general. Because Section 2 of the schedule ratified along with the constitution directed that all elected officials then in office serve out their terms, the first election after ratification of the new constitution, scheduled for November 1971, allowed the four-year rotation of elections for Virginia governors and members of the Senate of Virginia and the two-year rotation for members of the House of Delegates to continue without alteration. Some twentieth- and twenty-first-century commentators and observers indicated that they understood the election of governors in the odd-numbered years immediately following presidential elections and the election of members of the General Assembly in odd-numbered years, too, as a deliberate and wise requirement that tended to separate federal from state politics; but in fact, the timing was the result of a fortuitous accident.

The Constitutional Convention of 1867–68 provided for a ratification referendum and election of statewide officers and members of the General Assembly in 1868, which for the first time would have synchronized state and federal elections, although that was undoubtedly not the purpose of the provision, which was to put the new constitution into operation immediately. The contentious politics of the decade prevented ratification of the constitution and with it the first elections to be held under its authority until July 1869. Thereafter, every other odd-numbered year, voters elected the governor, lieutenant governor, and attorney general, every odd-numbered year, all members of the House of Delegates, and until 1907, half the state senators; and after that year, voters elected all state senators in odd-numbered years midway through the four-year terms of governors. The Constitution of 1971 and the schedule simply continued that rotation schedule.

Section 6 preserved the governor's authority to veto bills and particular items in appropriations bills, as well as the governor's ability to suggest amendments to bills that the assembly had passed. The two houses could accept or reject the proposed amendments, after which the governor could sign or reject the bill as if it were new. As of 1971, the governor of Virginia was one of only three in the country who had constitutional authority to introduce amendments to bills that legislators had already passed.[48]

The new article omitted the sections from the old article that provided for the appointment of the secretary of the commonwealth, state treasurer, auditor of public accounts, and commissioner of the bureau of labor statistics. That left the General Assembly fully empowered to create, abolish, or modify those and other executive departments as needed and to specify their responsibilities.

Sections 13 and 14 basically repeated the brief provisions for the lieutenant governor that had been in the previous constitution, but Section 13 specifically declared, "there shall be no limit on the terms of the Lieutenant Governor." (Five lieutenant governors had won election to more than one consecutive term since 1902.) Section 17 authorized the lieutenant governor to "discharge the powers and duties" of the governor in the event a governor-elect failed to qualify or died before taking office, and in the event of a vacancy in the office of governor, it specified a line of succession: lieutenant governor, attorney general, and Speaker of the House of Delegates; and if none of them qualified, "the House of Delegates shall convene and fill the vacancy." The section also contained detailed provisions, perhaps inspired by and very similar to the recent Twenty-Fifth Amendment to the Constitution of the United States, for authorizing the lieutenant governor to become acting governor in case of a temporary incapacity of a governor and for restoring the governor to full authority.

The Constitution of 1971 specified that "No person shall be eligible for election or appointment to the office of Attorney General unless he is a citizen of the United States, has attained the age of thirty years, and has the qualifications required for a judge of a court of record." The section left it to the General Assembly, as in the past, to define the responsibilities of the office, and added that, as with judges, the attorney general's "compensation shall neither be increased nor diminished during the period for which he shall have been elected." Unlike for the governor but as was the case with the lieutenant governor, "There shall be no limit on the terms of the Attorney General." (Five attorneys general had won election to consecutive terms since 1902, including John R. Saunders who won election in 1917 and won reelection repeatedly until he died in office in 1934.)

The constitution authorized the governor to request official opinions on the duties of the office from the attorney general, but the attorney general, being a separately elected state official, did not, in 1971, properly become a member of the executive department of government and therefore subordinate to the governor. In several instances, political and legal conflicts arose when the two officials' responsibilities or desires appeared to conflict.[49]

By law and under the constitutional provisions for the State Corporation Commission, the attorney general represented the interests of the state in both state and federal courts and before the commission. Since the very beginning in 1776, attorneys general also rendered advisory opinions when public officials requested legal advice. Beginning in the 1880s, attorneys general published an annual report to the governor that contained, among other information, copies of the important advisory rulings they had made at the request of public officials. Those opinions did not have the force of law and did not serve as binding precedent in court, but the Supreme Court of Appeals acknowledged in *Barber v. City of Danville* in 1928 and in *Beck v. Shelton* in 2004, that they were "of the most persuasive character" and therefore "entitled to due consideration."⁵⁰ Public officials who requested the opinions relied on the authority of the attorneys general and probably almost always followed their recommendations in administering the laws.

THE JUDICIARY

Section 1 of Article VI began, "The judicial power of the Commonwealth shall be vested in a Supreme Court and in such other courts of original or appellate jurisdiction subordinate to the Supreme Court as the General Assembly may from time to time establish." That clearer and more ample authority than had been granted in the previous constitution allowed the assembly to create or abolish any court in the state or change its jurisdiction except, of course, it could not abolish the Supreme Court.

The General Assembly accepted most of the recommendations that the Commission on Constitutional Revision suggested to Article VI in order to streamline the article and strip out of it many specific provisions that both agreed should be left to the discretion of the General Assembly, such as several long sections that listed the counties and cities in which individual circuit court judges served. The article renamed the Supreme Court of Appeals as the Supreme Court of Virginia and rather than designate the senior justice in terms of service as chief justice, as the constitutional revision of 1928 had done, left it to the General Assembly to direct how the chief justice be selected. The General Assembly initially left in place the former constitution's rule, but in 2002, it authorized the members of the court to elect the chief justice from among their number.⁵¹

Section 2 retained the number of justices at seven but authorized the General Assembly to enlarge the number to eleven, which the assembly has never done. The article also authorized the court to "sit and render final judgment en banc or in divisions as may be prescribed by law" except in cases in which a matter was alleged to violate the Constitution of Virginia or of the United States. As before, it required a majority of the whole number of justices to agree to declare a law or action unconstitutional.

The new article omitted the section in the old constitution that authorized the creation from time to time of a Special Court of Appeals,⁵² and it also omitted the requirement that the Supreme Court meet in two or more cities in the state, which left it to the discretion of the General Assembly to require or discontinue the practice that dated to 1831.⁵³ The assembly discontinued the annual court sessions in Wytheville and Staunton in 1971.⁵⁴ In 1983, the General Assembly created a new Court of Appeals subordinate to the Supreme Court[55] and able to take much of the business of the Supreme Court on itself.[56]

The new article provided that "The justices of the Supreme Court shall be chosen by the vote of a majority of the members elected to each house of the General Assembly for terms of twelve years" and all other judges "for terms of eight years." It empowered the governor, as in previous constitutions, to fill judicial vacancies that occurred when the General Assembly was not in session, but those judges could not serve longer than "thirty days after the commencement of the next session of the General Assembly" unless the assembly elected them to a full term. Moreover, "Upon election by the General Assembly, a new justice or judge shall begin service of a full term."

Section 4 increased the authority of the chief justice and declared, "The Chief Justice of the Supreme Court shall be the administrative head of the judicial system. He may temporarily assign any judge of a court of record to any other court of record except the Supreme Court and may assign a retired judge of a court of record, with his consent, to any court of record except the Supreme Court. The General Assembly may adopt such additional measures as it deems desirable for the improvement of the administration of justice by the courts and for the expedition of judicial business."

The new language of Section 5 increased the constitutional authority of the court: "The Supreme Court shall have the authority to make rules governing the course of appeals and the practice and procedures to be used in the courts of the Commonwealth, but such rules shall not be in conflict with the general law as the same shall, from time to time, be established by the General Assembly."

Section 9 authorized the General Assembly to create a retirement system for judges older than "a prescribed age" to be defined by law, and Section 10 provided for creation of a "Judicial Inquiry and Review Commission consisting of members of the judiciary, the bar, and the public and vested with the power to investigate charges which would be the basis for retirement, censure, or removal of a judge," including judges of the State Corporation Commission. The section authorized the Supreme Court to remove from office any judge who had "engaged in conduct prejudicial to the proper administration of justice." Section 12 prohibited judges from making any appointments to local offices. Some early twentieth-century laws had given circuit court judges authority to appoint local school boards and electoral boards, a power that some of them evidently used for partisan purposes.[57] In 1969, the Commission on Constitutional Revision and the General Assembly regarded such roles as entirely improper for any judge.

LOCAL GOVERNMENT

Article VII replaced the two separate articles in the 1928 revision of the Constitution of 1902 that had prescribed distinct forms of government for counties and cities.[58] It included some revised portions of each of the old articles, such as the provisions for constitutional officers, but stripped out a considerable amount of detail that, in some instances, had become obsolete by virtue of the General Assembly granting individual waivers to localities to adopt city manager or county manager forms of government or otherwise deviate from the forms that the Constitution of 1902 originally required. It also omitted several long and detailed sections that had minutely described and defined procedures in city councils and the roles and authorities of mayors.

Section 2 required the General Assembly to "provide by general law for the organization, government, powers, change of boundaries, consolidation, and dissolution of counties, cities, towns, and regional governments." The section in effect left in place the existing laws that allowed cities to annex portions or all of adjacent counties through a judicial process without a referendum in which residents could have an option to determine for themselves in which to live.[59] It also prohibited the General Assembly from individually changing county and city boundary lines. The assembly session of 1969 proposed to authorize a separate ratification referendum on a new section to allow the General Assembly to change the boundaries of the capital city of Richmond at any time, but in 1970, the assembly members elected not to submit that proposal to the voters, so it was never included in the constitution.[60]

For the most part, Article VI treated counties and cities in much the same manner and to some extent blurred the distinctions between the two. The new article preserved the state's unique system of independent incorporated cities, but towns remained parts of the counties in which they were located. The new article required a minimum population of 5,000 for a town to become an incorporated city. The article also specifically legitimized the numerous special districts or regional government bodies that the General Assembly had created to meet needs for new or expanded public services that accompanied the demographic revolution.[61]

The 1969 session of the General Assembly elected to preserve the essence of the Dillon Rule and declined to accept the recommendation of the Commission on Constitutional Revision to abandon or reduce reliance on it in governing the relationship between local governments and the state government. The unwritten rule was named for a judge and law professor, John F. Dillon. In his 1871 book, *The Law of Municipal Corporations*, Dillon stated a truism: that municipal governments had no inherent powers of their own, as state governments did, but only the legal capacity to act on matters and in manners that state constitutions and laws specifically authorized.[62] Some states provided in their constitutions or by general laws that local governments could operate freely within specified parameters, as the Commission on Constitutional Revision recommended, called Home Rule.[63] The commission believed that strict application of the Dillon Rule thwarted democratic government at the local level and proposed to add a new sentence to Article VII, Section 3, that "A charter county or a city many exercise any power or perform any function which is not denied to it by this Constitution, by its charter, or by laws enacted by the General Assembly";[64] but the legislators did not include a Home Rule provision in the article and refused to relinquish reliance on the Dillon Rule. They thereby preserved to themselves and their successors the ability to continue to have final say-so on changes to all consequential and many minor local government functions.[65]

Officials of the Virginia Municipal League and the Virginia Association of Counties both opposed relaxation of the rule. That opposition may have been because of the increasing number of Virginia cities and towns with African American majorities or increasingly large African American minorities. Preservation of the Dillon Rule could allow the General Assembly to prevent alterations in municipal government boundaries and policies that new African American majorities might seek to adopt.[66]

Section 2 of new Article VII allowed some localities to modify their forms of government by popular referendum and to create additional regional government units. Section 5 also directed, "If the members are elected by district, the district shall be composed of contiguous and compact territory and shall be so constituted as to give, as nearly as is practicable, representation in proportion to the population of the district." It also required revision of electoral districts in the year following each federal census. That brought the article on local government into line with the Representation Revolution of the 1960s and extended to all elected local governing bodies in the state the requirement for approximate equality of population in electoral districts that, until that time, the state's constitutions had required only for members of the House of Representatives since 1830 and for bicameral city councils since 1902. Together with the requirements of the Voting Rights Act of 1965, these changes eventually terminated at-large election of members of city councils and introduced single-member municipal government in most of the state's cities by the 1980s.[67]

Section 10 contained significantly revised procedures for how local units of government could borrow money, which was one of the several important recommendations Governor Godwin had itemized in his 1968 speech that set constitutional revision in motion. The section authorized cities, counties, and towns to issue bonds but only after approval by majority vote in a referendum called for that specific purpose. The new provisions retained the old prohibition on any city, town, or county issuing bonds in aggregate value totaling more than 18 percent of its taxable property, but it authorized voters in counties to elect to borrow money under the more lenient provisions of the constitution that applied to cities.

EDUCATION

Article VIII,[68] Section 1, began, "The General Assembly shall provide for a system of free public elementary and secondary schools for all children of school age throughout the Commonwealth, and shall seek to ensure that an educational program of high quality is established and continually maintained." It empowered the State Board of Education to establish standards of quality but reserved to the General Assembly authority to revise the standards. Section 3 allowed the General Assembly to impose compulsory education on all children of school age. And seventeen years after the Supreme Court of the United States ruled in *Brown v. Board of Education of Topeka* that mandatory racial segregation in public schools violated the equal protection clause of the Fourteenth Amendment,[69] the new constitution omitted Section 140 of the Constitution of 1902 that ordered, "White and colored children shall not be taught in the same school."

The article, like most others in the new constitution, was shorter than the article on education that was in the 1902 constitution as it had been revised in 1928. It created a nine-member State Board of Education whose members the governor appointed for staggered four-year terms subject to confirmation or rejection by the General Assembly. Section 6 continued the authorization in a section of the 1928 revision of the constitution for the governor to appoint the superintendent of public instruction for a four-year term to coincide with the term of the governor, with the General Assembly also authorized to confirm or reject the governor's appointment. Section 7 created local school boards but left it to the General Assembly to determine how to select members.

Section 8, as in the former constitution, devoted the earnings from the state's old Literary Fund to the support of the public schools but for the first time placed administration of the fund in the hands of the board. Section 141 of the old constitution, as amended in 1956, permitted the state to provide tax money to private, nonsectarian schools. The amendment had allowed the government to support private schools for white children whose parents wished to keep them out of public schools that were desegregated or might become desegregated. During the 1969 session of the General Assembly, legislators hotly debated what to do with that provision, and in 1970, decided that if voters ratified the body of the constitution, old Section 141 would quietly become Section 10 of Article VIII. In that way, supporters of the new constitution reduced the risk that strongly held opinions on either side about that section might jeopardize ratification of the new constitution.[70]

Section 11 contained a new provision that allowed the General Assembly to authorize loans to students who attended nonprofit institutions of higher education "whose primary purpose is to provide collegiate or graduate education and not to provide religious training or theological education." The assembly also gained authority to create a state agency to assist such institutions in borrowing money for construction of educational facilities, "provided that the Commonwealth shall not be liable for any debt created by such borrowing."

STATE CORPORATION COMMISSION

Article IX drastically reduced the length and detail in the article that originally created the State Corporation Commission from fifteen long sections totaling more than 6,600 words in 1902 to seven more-conventional sections totaling about 1,110 words. Most of the deletions consisted of provisions that the Commission on Constitutional Revision believed were legislative in nature, such as specifying that the commission's offices be open six days a week, rather than of fundamental, constitutional importance. The new article omitted several whole sections, some of which were vitally important in 1902, that were legislative in nature or had become obsolete through changes in commercial law and business operations. The original article had been very long because A. Caperton Braxton, its chief author, had included definitions, detailed rules of procedure, and other requirements to guarantee that the commission and its actions could not be successfully challenged in court for depriving any person or corporation of full due process of law.[71]

Section 1 of the revised article provided for the State Corporation Commission to consist of three judges, which the General Assembly elected for staggered six-year terms. It authorized the assembly to increase the number of judges to five, which the assembly never did. The section retained the requirement that at least one judge be qualified to serve as a judge in a court of law, even though the Commission on Constitutional Revision had recommended that all the members be so qualified, and empowered the governor to fill vacancies when the assembly was not in session. The section contained a new authorization for the assembly to prescribe a mandatory retirement age for members of the commission.

Section 2 repeated the concisely defined authority of the commission: "the Commission shall be the department of government through which shall be issued all charters, and amendments or extensions thereof, of domestic corporations and all licenses of foreign corporations to do business in this Commonwealth," which it defined in Section 5 as corporations that were chartered in or had headquarters in another state or country. Brief Section 3 required that in the commission's proceedings and the rules and regulations that it adopted, all parties receive due notice and have the protection of due process of law, but "The General Assembly shall have the power to adopt such rules, to amend, modify, or set aside the Commission's rules, or to substitute rules of its own." As in the original 1902 article, Section 4 provided that appeals from decisions or about the proceedings of the commission be directly to the Supreme Court of Virginia and no other.

In specifically reserving to the General Assembly the authority to make all necessary laws for the governance of corporations, the revised Section 6 authorized elected representatives, rather than appointed commissioners, to fashion the general and specific public policies relating to corporate bodies. The issue of who should be so empowered—elected representatives or appointed experts—had generated much debate in the Convention of 1901-2. As Braxton had then explained the original article, "we say in so many words, that in all such matters the power of the General Assembly to legislate shall remain supreme and paramount, and in all matters, except the fixing of rates, the General Assembly can tie the hands of this commission just as tight as it is possible to tie them. There is no rule or regulation they can make which the General Assembly cannot rescind. There is no restriction that can be put upon them which the General Assembly is not capable of putting upon them, except the fixing of rates." Section 6 explicitly embodied that constitutional principle.[72]

In 2017, the Supreme Court of Virginia affirmed Braxton's interpretation in a politically controversial case, *Old Dominion Committee for Fair Utility Rates et al. v. State Corporation Commission*. The court unanimously determined that a 2015 law that postponed the commission's scheduled biennial rate reviews for Appalachian Power Company and for Dominion Power (the most politically powerful corporation in the state as a result of its campaign contributions and large staff of lobbyists[73]) was a legitimate constitutional exercise of legislative power and not an infringement on the constitutional authority of the commission on the grounds that the Constitution of 1971 explicitly granted the General Assembly authority to supplant commission rates and rules.[74]

TAXATION AND FINANCE

Article X is one of the longest in the Constitution of 1971 and contains some of the most complex and technical provisions as well as one of the longest new provisions. Section 6 included a revised and expanded list that had its beginning in the Constitution of 1851 of persons and entities granted exemption from taxation, including charitable, benevolent, and religious organizations.[75] Unlike most other provisions that the Commission on Constitutional Revision recommended or endorsed, the section consisted for the most part of detailed exemptions of the sort that commission members usually regarded as legislative in character rather than of constitutional consequence. Dick Howard summarized the discussions of commission members on this subject: "After repeated efforts to rewrite section 183" of the previous constitution that included the list, "the Commissioners threw up their hands and left the basic structure as it was."[76] The General Assembly created a dense maze of statutes on the subject of tax exemptions for religious and charitable organizations.[77] The assemby submitted to the voters, and they ratified, the largest number of amendments to any part of the constitution.

Section 9 that treated public debt, Howard explained in his *Commentaries on the Constitution of Virginia*, "begins with a prohibition: state debt shall not be contracted save on the terms allowed in the section. The prohibition is simple; it takes but one sentence. The rest of the section, perhaps the most technical and involved provision in the Constitution, takes several pages and carefully spells out the manner in which money may be borrowed and within what limitations."[78] The long section replaced several sections in the old constitution.

The 578 words of separately ratified Section 9-B authorized the General Assembly to issue general obligation bonds for capital projects and pledge the full faith and credit of the commonwealth to pay the principal and interest if approved in a popular referendum. The 429 words of separately ratified Section 9-C authorized the General Assembly to issue revenue bonds for the construction of projects (such as toll roads or dormitories) that produced revenue with which to pay the principal and interest.

Section 10 prohibited the state and its subdivisions from purchasing stock in private corporations, but it contained an exception: "This section shall not be construed to prohibit the General Assembly from establishing an authority with power to insure and guarantee loans to finance industrial development and industrial expansion and from making appropriations to such authority." And Section 11 included a new constitutional requirement that "The General Assembly shall maintain a State employees retirement system to be administered in the best interest of the beneficiaries thereof."

CONSERVATION

As Howard summarized the new article XI on Conservation, the article did not create or recognize a citizen's legally defensible right to a healthy environment, nor did it "purport to direct the General Assembly to enact environmental legislation." Instead, relatively early in the national evolution of the environmental preservation movement, "in addition to authorizing certain action by the Assembly, the article turns its attention to a much broader concern: a constitutional statement of public policy which serves to bind state agencies and officials, as well as courts, and which gives meaning and substance to Virginia's public trust in its land, water, and other natural resources."[79]

The article declared, "To the end that the people have clean air, pure water, and the use and enjoyment for recreation of adequate public lands, waters, and other natural resources, it shall be the policy of the Commonwealth to conserve, develop, and utilize its natural resources, its public lands, and its historical sites and buildings. Further, it shall be the Commonwealth's policy to protect its atmosphere, lands, and waters from pollution, impairment, or destruction, for the benefit, enjoyment, and general welfare of the people of the Commonwealth." The new article concluded with the repetition of a section that was added to the article on taxation in the Constitution of 1902, "The natural oyster beds, rocks, and shoals in the waters of the Commonwealth shall not be leased, rented, or sold but shall be held in trust for the benefit of the people of the Commonwealth."

AMENDMENTS AND CONVENTIONS

Article XII, entitled "Future Changes," repeated with minor changes of language the provisions in the Constitutions of 1869 and 1902 and the 1928 revision that the General Assembly could propose amendments to the constitution if both houses agreed to the text, with an election of members of the House of Delegates intervening, and that voters by a majority vote could ratify them. Section 2 empowered the General Assembly to call conventions to revise the constitution but did not require referenda beforehand, as the previous constitution had required. A new paragraph in Section 2 directed the General

Assembly to "provide for the submission, in such manner as it shall prescribe and not sooner than ninety days after final adjournment of the convention, of the proposals of the convention to the voters qualified to vote in elections by the people" for ratification or rejection.

Ratification

Governor A. Linwood Holton, a Republican who succeeded Mills Godwin in office in January 1970, asked Dick Howard to form a Virginians for the Constitution committee to direct the campaign for ratification. Holton chaired the bipartisan committee, and Godwin served as its honorary chair. The committee secured endorsements from such influential state organizations as the Virginia Education Association, the Virginia Congress of Parents and Teachers, the Virginia Municipal League, the Virginia Association of Counties, the Retail Merchants Association, the Virginia State AFL-CIO, the League of Women Voters, the Virginia Federation of Women's Clubs, and the Black political action group, the Crusade for Voters. Howard and other commission members personally visited numerous editors of the state's newspapers and directed a wide-ranging and effective campaign on behalf of ratification. Opposition existed in all parts of the state, but the general approval of the new constitution and the opportunity for voters to vote separately on the potentially most controversial matters reduced the likelihood that opposition to those matters would jeopardize ratification of the main body of the constitution.[80]

On 3 November 1970, voters ratified the new constitution by a vote of 576,776 to 226,219, or a 71.8 percent margin. By a 62.9 percent margin (491,124 to 290,168) they deleted the prohibition on lotteries. By a 65.9 percent margin (504,315 to 261,220) they separately ratified Article X Section 9-B to permit the General Assembly to issue general obligation bonds, if approved in a popular referendum, and by a 64.6 percent margin (484,274 to 265,784) they separately ratified Article X Section 9-C to permit the General Assembly to issue revenue bonds for capital projects.[81]

Amendments

The Constitution of 1971 was a major improvement over its predecessor in almost every respect, including conciseness, clarity, flexibility, and elimination of legislative detail. Nevertheless, during its first half century of existence, the General Assembly submitted sixty-one amendments to the voters, who ratified fifty-two of them. Some amendments arose from political debates on contentious issues, but others appeared to the legislators who proposed them to be necessary to refine further the provisions of the constitution at the time it was ratified or to solve new problems.[82]

Amendments made three changes to Article I, the Bill of Rights. In 1996, voters added a new Section 8-A entitled "Rights of victims of crime." It required "That in criminal prosecutions, the victim shall be accorded fairness, dignity and respect by the officers, employees and agents of the Commonwealth and its political subdivisions and officers of the courts and, as the General Assembly may define and provide by law, may be accorded rights to reasonable and appropriate notice, information, restitution, protection, and access to a meaningful role in the criminal justice process." The rights specifically included but were not limited to, "The right to protection from further harm or reprisal through the imposition of appropriate bail and conditions of release"; "The right to be treated with respect, dignity and fairness at all stages of the criminal justice system"; "The right to address the circuit court at the time sentence is imposed"; "The right to receive timely notification of judicial proceedings"; "The right to restitution"; "The right to be advised of release from custody or escape of the offender, whether before or after disposition"; and "The right to confer with the prosecution."

In 2012, voters ratified a major change to the portion of Section 11 that dealt with eminent domain, the right of the state to take private property for public use and that required "just compensation" for the property so taken. The General Assembly submitted the amendment to the voters after widespread public outrage that the Supreme Court of the United States generated in 2005 with its 5 to 4 ruling in *Kelo v. City of New London*, which affirmed the right of the Connecticut city to condemn private land and, through an economic development project, convert it to a different private purpose that the city hoped would produce more revenue.[83]

The amendment replaced the old language with new language that was much more restrictive than the old: "That the General Assembly shall pass no law whereby private property, the right to which is fundamental, shall be damaged or taken except for public use. No private property shall be damaged or taken for public use without just compensation to the owner thereof. No more private property may be taken than necessary to achieve the stated public use. Just compensation shall be no less than the value of the property taken, lost profits and lost access, and damages to the residue caused by the taking." A provision included in the amendment specified that "A public service company, public service corporation, or railroad exercises the power of eminent domain for public use when such exercise is for the authorized provision of utility, common carrier, or railroad services." The final sentence for the first time endowed some private Virginia corporations with a constitutional right rather than an optional legislative permission to exercise the governmental right of eminent domain that had its origins far back in the king of England's royal prerogative.

In 2006, voters added a new Section 15-A on marriage to the Bill of Rights in order to prohibit efforts to make same-sex marriages legal in Virginia. It stated, "That only a union between one man and one woman may be a marriage valid in or recognized by this Commonwealth and its political subdivisions." It also prohibited civil alliances between people that could confer on the parties benefits akin to the rights married people possessed. A federal judge ruled in 2014 in the case *Bostic v. Rainey* that the prohibition on same-sex marriage and civil unions violated the human right of Americans to marry whomever they chose,[84] based in large part on the Supreme Court's decision in *Loving v. Virginia* that, in 1967, invalidated all laws that had prohibited interracial marriage.[85] Because of that precedent, the attorney general of Virginia did not appear in court to defend the amendment. The Fourth Circuit Court of Appeals affirmed the district court's ruling later that year in *Bostic v. Shaefer*.[86] The Supreme Court of the United States refused to review the circuit court's ruling. That made Article I, Section 15-A, of the Constitution of Virginia void and of no effect, but the General Assembly never submitted to the voters an amendment to remove it from the state constitution.

An amendment that voters ratified in 2000 added a Section 4 to the new Article X on conservation. It could have been added to the Bill of Rights in Article I because it preserved personal rights of Virginians: "The people have a right to hunt, fish, and harvest game, subject to such regulations and restrictions as the General Assembly may prescribe by general law."[87]

In 2016, voters failed to ratify a proposed addition of a new Section 11-A in Article I that would have placed the essence of the state's right to work law into the constitution to make any labor contract that required union membership for employment "an illegal combination or conspiracy."[88]

Between 1972 and 2020, voters ratified several amendments to Article II on Franchise and Officers, some of which changed two or more sections of the article. The very first amendment to the new constitution, which was ratified in 1971, changed the minimum voting age to eighteen in all elections. The constitution had originally required the same minimum age of twenty-one that had been in Virginia voting laws and constitutions since the seventeenth century. During debate on the section in the Senate of Virginia during the 1969 session, senators had failed by one vote to change the minimum age to eighteen in the new constitution.[89] The amendment brought the new constitution into line with the Twenty-Sixth Amendment to the Constitution of the United States which was also ratified in 1971.

Four amendments changed portions of Article II on registration. The first, ratified in 1976, removed the requirement for long residency in a precinct before an election and allowed people who moved shortly before an election to vote in their previous voting place. A 1982 amendment deleted the requirement that married women list their maiden names and occupations in order to register. An amendment ratified in 1996 empowered the General Assembly to determine how and when people who moved from one precinct to another could register as well as vote.

A 1994 amendment to Section 3 specifically provided for absentee voting. Amendments ratified in 1976, 1986, and 1994 simplified Section 4 that imposed requirements on the General Assembly in relation to voter registration, purging registration lists of names of people who had not voted in four years, and voting by absentee ballot.

A 2004 amendment to Section 6 on apportionment added clarifications to require that the mandatory decennial reapportionments of seats in the House of Representatives and both houses of the General Assembly that was scheduled for 2011 be implemented for the next regular elections in November 2011 and members of Congress in November 2012; that elected officials in office at the time of ratification serve out the remainder of their terms; and that people elected to fill a vacancy in the meantime be elected from the old electoral district.

A 1986 amendment added one sentence to Section 8, "No person, nor the deputy or the employee of any person, who holds any elective office of profit or trust under the government of the United States, the Commonwealth, or any county, city, or town of the Commonwealth, shall be appointed an assistant registrar or officer of election."

In 2020, voters ratified an amendment to Section 6 to create a bipartisan Virginia Redistricting Commission to consist of two members of each political party in each house of the assembly and eight citizen members that legislative leaders named from a panel that retired judges proposed. The amendment empowered the commission to prepare electoral districts for members of the House of Representatives and both houses of the General Assembly in the year 2021 and every ten years thereafter. The amendment required that the assembly pass or reject the commission's plan but not have authority to amend it. If the commission failed to draw new district lines or the General Assembly refused to enact the commission's redistricting, the Supreme Court of Virginia would do the work.

Four amendments altered Article IV on the General Assembly, but in 1982, voters rejected a proposed amendment to permit the assembly by two-thirds vote of both houses to place limits on the subjects on which members could introduce bills in the short sessions in odd-numbered years.[90]

A 1980 amendment rewrote Sections 6, 11, and 13 of Article IV and Section 6 of Article V to require the General Assembly to reconvene after the adjournment of every session for a three-day session to enable legislators to consider and have the ability to override vetoes and item vetoes in appropriations bills as well as to consider and accept or reject amendments that the governor suggested. It arose from a large increase in the number of bills that the General Assembly passed in the 1970s and the number of bills the governor vetoed because they were defective or duplicated existing law or other bills.[91] It quickly came to be called the veto session. In 2012, voters ratified a revised version of the 1980 amendment that allowed the General Assembly to change the date on which the veto session would begin.

A 1994 amendment to Article IV, Section 14, that enumerated limitations on the powers of the General Assembly was the direct result of a 1992 decision of the Supreme Court of Virginia. In *Starnes v. Cauoyette*, the court ruled that a 1991 state law to extend the statute of limitations to permit victims of child abuse to sue to recover civil damages longer after the event than formerly allowed had violated the due process clause of the Virginia Bill of Rights. The amendment specifically authorized the assembly to enact such laws.[92]

In 1996, voters, by a very narrow margin, rejected an amendment to the sentence in Section 14 that had been in all the state's constitutions since it was added as Article IV, Section 32, in the Constitution of 1851. The original sentence read, "The General Assembly shall not grant a charter of incorporation to any church or religious denomination, but may secure the title to church property to an extent to be limited by law." The amendment would have deleted part of the sentence and left it as, "The General Assembly may secure the title to church property to an extent to be limited by law."[93] Ten years later, in 2006, voters repealed the entire sentence. A federal judge ruled in *Falwell v. Miller* in 2002 that the prohibition violated the free exercise of religion clause in the First Amendment to the Constitution of the United States. Neither the chair of the State Corporation Commission, listed as defendant in the case, nor the attorney general appeared in court to defend the provision.[94]

Three amendments altered Article V on the executive. The 1980 amendment that created the reconvened, or veto, session of the General Assembly included corresponding changes to Section 6 that specified the governor's responsibilities to meet the deadlines for the session; and a second amendment ratified in 1994 revised the deadlines for the governor's action before and during the reconvened session.

An amendment ratified in 2004 added to Section 16 on succession to the office of governor. "In the event of an emergency or enemy attack upon the soil of Virginia," it began, "and a resulting inability of the House of Delegates to convene to fill the vacancy, the Speaker of the House, the person designated to act in his stead as prescribed in the Rules of the House of Delegates, the President pro tempore of the Senate, or the majority leader of the Senate, in that designated order, shall serve as Acting Governor until such time as the House of Delegates convenes to elect a Governor."

Six amendments modified Article VI on the judiciary. The portion of Section 1 that read, "No appeal shall be allowed to the Commonwealth in a case involving the life or liberty of a person, except that an appeal by the Commonwealth may be allowed in any cases involving the violation of a law relating to State revenue" had raised serious questions about exposing people to double jeopardy.[95] A 1996 amendment replaced the paragraph with more flexible language, "The General Assembly may allow the Commonwealth the right to appeal in all cases, including those involving the life or liberty of a person, provided such appeal would not otherwise violate this Constitution or the Constitution of the United States."

A 1984 amendment granted the Supreme Court sole and original authority "to answer questions of state law certified by a court of the United States or the highest appellate court of any other state."

A 2002 amendment empowered the Supreme Court of Virginia "to consider claims of actual innocence presented by convicted felons in such cases and in such manner as may be provided by the General Assembly" because of a number of well-documented instances in which evidence produced after conviction and expiration of a deadline for filing an appeal clearly demonstrated the convicted person's innocence.

An amendment ratified in 1998 allowed the General Assembly to remove the requirement for secrecy that the constitution imposed in 1971 on proceedings before the Judicial Inquiry and Review Commission. The requirement for confidentiality, though intended to protect judges against whom no findings had yet been entered, came under several legal challenges to the First Amendment right of free speech. In 1990 the Fourth Circuit Court of Appeals, in *Baugh v. Judicial Inquiry and Review Commission*, determined that the statute then in force enacted under the authority of the constitutional provision was unconstitutional on that ground because it had prohibited journalists from mentioning the very existence of an inquiry even if the journalist did not name the judge who was being investigated.[96]

A 1976 amendment to Section 12 that limited judges' capacity to appoint people to fill vacancies in elective governmental positions permitted them to do so should the next scheduled election occur within sixty days of the end of the term to be filled.

Voters ratified three amendments to Article VII on local government. An amendment to Section 1 that they ratified in 1972 permitted incorporated cities and towns to retain their status as cities or towns even if their populations fell below the required minimum of 5,000 for cities and 1,000 for towns.

An amendment ratified in 1984 added a new exception to Section 6 that prohibited elected or appointed officials from holding more than one office, "except that a member of a governing body may be elected or appointed to fill a vacancy in the office of mayor or board chairman if permitted by general law or special act."

A 1980 amendment reduced the total amount of debt any city or town could incur from 18 percent to 10 percent "of the assessed valuation of the real estate in the city or town subject to taxation, as shown by the last preceding assessment for taxes."

Voters ratified two amendments to Article VIII on education, both of which concerned finances. Section 11, which allowed grants to students who attended private colleges and universities, produced two lawsuits in 1972 and 1973, both styled *Miller v. Ayers*. In them, the Supreme Court of Virginia invalidated portions of enabling laws on the grounds that the grants violated the freedom of religion and establishment of religion clauses in the First Amendment to the Constitution of the United States.[97] The General Assembly submitted, and in 1974 voters ratified, a change to Section 11 that allowed the General Assembly to permit the state or any political subdivision "to contract with such institutions for the provision of educational or other related services."

In 1990, voters ratified an amendment to Section 8 that enabled the General Assembly to exempt from deposit in the Literary Fund money derived from the seizure or sale of property confiscated "for a violation of the criminal laws of this Commonwealth proscribing the manufacture, sale or distribution of a controlled substance or marijuana. Such proceeds shall be paid into the state treasury" rather than into the Literary Fund "and shall be distributed by law for the purpose of promoting law enforcement."

Voters have ratified nineteen amendments to Article X on taxation and finance, the largest number for any article and almost 40 percent of the whole number of amendments. A 1976 amendment allowed the General Assembly to reduce the rate of taxation or declare exempt from taxation "Land subject to a perpetual easement permitting inundation by water." It allowed localities that could already exempt or reduce the real estate tax rate on people aged sixty-five or older "who are deemed by the General Assembly to be bearing an extraordinary tax burden on said real estate in relation to their income and financial worth" to grant additional relief to persons who were also "permanently and totally disabled as established by general law." The amendment also allowed the General Assembly to define "as a separate subject of taxation any property" used for "the purpose of transferring or storing solar energy" because at that time, people were experimenting with technology to capture solar energy in water tanks in order that the warmed water could be used for heating purposes in the winter and the water thus thereby cooled for cooling purposes in summer.

In 1978, voters ratified an amendment to permit the General Assembly to authorize "the governing body of any county, city, town, or regional government" to reduce or exempt from taxation property that "by virtue of age and use, have undergone substantial renovation, rehabilitation or replacement."

An amendment ratified in 1980 allowed localities to provide tax relief for real and personal property "owned by, and occupied as the sole dwelling" of poor old people. And on the same date voters ratified an amendment to allow cities and towns to exempt from taxation equipment installed after 1974 "for the purposes of converting from oil or natural gas to coal or to wood, wood bark, wood residue, or to any other alternate energy source for manufacturing, and any co-generation equipment installed since such date for use in manufacturing."

A 1990 amendment allowed local governments to provide tax relief to people older than sixty-five or were "permanently and totally disabled."

An amendment ratified in 1984 authorized the governor to reduce expenditure of appropriated revenue if necessary to keep the budget balanced. A long amendment ratified in 1992 created a Revenue Stabilization Fund, which quickly became popularly known as the rainy day fund, designed to provide a source of money during temporary short-falls in revenue. It authorized the General Assembly to deposit in the fund a limited amount of revenue in good years that it could draw on in lean years. The amendment limited the size of the fund to 10 percent "of the Commonwealth's average annual tax revenues derived from taxes on incomes and retail sales as certified by the Auditor of Public Accounts for the three fiscal years immediately preceding"; but the General Assembly submitted to the voters, and in 2010 they ratified, an amendment to raise the limit to 15 percent.

An amendment of 1996 revised Section 11 to permit employees of local governments and public school systems to participate in the retirement system for state employees.

An amendment of 1998 empowered the General Assembly to allow cities, counties, and towns "the option to exempt or partially exempt from taxation any business, occupational or professional license or any merchants' capital, or both."

An amendment ratified in 2000 created a new Lottery Proceeds Fund into which net profits from the state's lotteries be deposited, the money to be provided solely to the "counties, cities, and towns, and the school divisions thereof, to be expended for the purposes of public education." The amendment allowed for exceptions, however: "The General Assembly may appropriate amounts from the Fund for other purposes only by a vote of four-fifths of the members voting in each house, the name of each member voting and how he votes to be recorded in the journal of the house."

In 2002, voters ratified an amendment to remove from the General Assembly and grant to local governing bodies the authority to classify for tax exemption "Property used by its owner for religious, charitable, patriotic, historical, benevolent, cultural, or public park and playground purposes."

The other seven amendments to Article X, Section 6, extended tax exemptions to certain members of the population. A 2006 amendment permitted localities to provide tax relief for owners of "real estate with new structures and improvements in conservation, redevelopment, or rehabilitation areas." An amendment ratified in 2010 allowed local government bodies "to establish either income or financial worth limitations, or both, in order to qualify for such relief." Another amendment ratified the same day added a new Section 6-A that allowed the General Assembly to grant tax relief on the residential property of any member or veteran of the armed services deemed 100 percent disabled in the line of duty and to the surviving spouse "so long as the surviving spouse does not remarry and continues to occupy the real property as his or her principal place of residence." A 2014 amendment allowed the General Assembly to "exempt from taxation the real property of the surviving spouse of any member of the armed forces of the United States who was killed in action" and "who occupies the real property as his or her principal place of residence," so long as the survivor did not remarry. An amendment ratified in 2016 authorized local governments to extend similar tax exemptions to "the surviving spouse of any law-enforcement officer, firefighter, search and rescue personnel, or emergency medical services personnel who was killed in the line of duty, who occupies the real property as his or her principal place of residence." Two amendments ratified in 2018 removed from the provisions that the survivors continue to reside in the same house and not move to another in Virginia.

Another amendment ratified in 2018 permitted the General Assembly to provide for relief from local taxation on real estate "subject to recurrent flooding upon which flooding abatement, mitigation, or resiliency efforts have been undertaken." And an amendment ratified in 2020 specifically excluded from taxation one passenger vehicle belonging to disabled members of the armed services, disabled veterans, and their spouses.

The Constitution of 1971 in Operation

Section 1 of the Schedule that was ratified along with the Constitution of 1971 specified that the new constitution become effective at noon on 1 July 1971. Section 5 ordered the General Assembly to convene in January 1971 to "enact such laws as may be deemed proper, including those necessary to implement this revised Constitution." That thoughtful innovation meant that for the very first time, a new state constitution and a revised legal code went into effect in Virginia at the same time.

How a state constitution functions and what that means for the people who live in the state depend on the words in the constitution and on how legislators, executive officials, and judges interpret and apply the words. And words, even some words and phrases that appear to have stable, specific meanings in law, are often subject to differing interpretations. Many words do not have stable and specific meanings in law. In some instances, the Constitution of Virginia and the Constitution of the United States contain the same language, such as the section that has been in the state Bill of Rights since 1776 and in the federal Bill of Rights since 1791: "That excessive bail ought not to be required, nor excessive fines imposed, nor cruel and unusual punishments inflicted." The words *excessive*, *cruel*, and *unusual* did not and do not have precisely defined legal meanings and are therefore subject to varying interpretations that legislators or courts may give them; and the phrase *ought not* does not clearly impose a prohibition on what legislators or judges might determine to be excessive, cruel, or unusual.

Must state courts and federal courts interpret such language identically? Should state courts interpret similar but not identical language in a state constitution in exactly the same way as federal courts interpret the federal constitution?[98] Do, or should, changes in interpretation in federal courts automatically propagate in state law? For example, the "right to keep and bear arms" language of the Second Amendment in the United States Constitution, which was ratified along with the remainder of the Bill of Rights in 1791, became part of the Constitution of Virginia in 1971. (Before 1971, no Virginia court had occasion to rule on what the original language respecting the militia had meant.) Did incorporation into the state constitution of that language, which federal courts had interpreted before that date, include those interpretations as of 1971? And if so, did that preclude state judges from interpreting it differently or require that they reinterpret it after 2008 when the Supreme Court of the United States, in *District of Columbia v. Heller*, changed federal interpretation and application of that language to declare that it was not a collective right of community self-defense (as the original reference to the "well organized militia" suggested) but an individual, personal right to self-defense?[99]

Virginia's Supreme Court has tended to rule that language in the state constitution be understood as "coextensive" with federal court interpretations of corresponding provisions—whether identical or merely similar—in the Constitution of the United States. That is, that the state language means the same thing as the federal language and protects people in the enjoyment of all of, but not necessarily of more, rights than federal judges have declared protected under the federal constitution and laws. Among the rights in the Virginia Bill of Rights that the state's courts have explicitly declared to be coextensive are the right to a speedy trial, against self-incrimination, double jeopardy, search and seizure, due process, antidiscrimination, free speech, freedom of the press, freedom of assembly and petition, the right to bear arms, religious freedom, and against religious establishment.[100]

In one instance, the Supreme Court of Virginia deferred to federal courts and federal law when the federal constitution contained no comparable language. In 1973, in *Archer and Johnson v. Mayes et al.*, the seven white, male justices ruled that the protection against governmental discrimination based on sex that was added to Virginia's Bill of Rights in 1971 ("that the right to be free from any governmental discrimination upon the basis of religious conviction, race, color, sex, or national origin shall not be abridged") could not be interpreted to allow women more rights in Virginia than women were entitled to under federal law and the Constitution of the United States, even though the federal constitution included no explicit prohibition on discrimination based on sex or gender; and the Fourteenth Amendment's requirement for equal protection of the laws that could be understood as prohibiting states from treating women and men differently did not bind the federal government.[101]

During the half century and more in which the Constitution of 1971 has been in force, the political character of Virginia has changed dramatically in ways that the authors of the constitution probably could not have anticipated. For eighty-five years before ratification of the constitution, Virginia was in effect a one-party state, and that one party was under the domination of one undemocratic, politically conservative faction. During the 1970s and 1980s, the state's Democratic Party, in part because of the Civil Rights and Representation Revolutions, became more progressive and inclusive, and the state's Republican Party became more conservative, both in keeping with trends in their national counterparts. And during that time and the remainder of the twentieth century, the state became politically competitive, often with an observable advantage for Republicans, in spite of gerrymandering that allowed Democrats to maintain majorities in both houses of the General Assembly well into the 1990s. Then, in the first decades of the twenty-first century, in spite of gerrymandering that allowed Republicans to maintain majorities in both houses of the General Assembly, Democrats gained political ground to such an extent that they elected four of six governors, carried the state for their presidential candidates four times in succession, and in 2019, won majorities in both houses of the General Assembly for the first time in more than two decades.[102]

Those changes in the political landscape modified some of the ways in which public officials functioned under the constitution. For example, governors retained the power to fill vacancies on all the state's courts and on the State Corporation Commission when the General Assembly was not in session. Even with the creation of the short, thirty-day sessions of assembly in odd-numbered years, the assembly was in session only about 12 percent of the time (as opposed to 8 percent since 1902), which meant that governors still had the initial opportunity to fill a majority of the vacancies that occurred. But a governor could no longer reasonably anticipate that the General Assembly would appoint that judge to a full term if the other party held a majority in either or both houses of the assembly. In the event that one party had a majority in the House of Delegates and the other in the Senate of Virginia, vacancies could, and in some instances did, remain unfilled for many months. That changed political circumstance suggested to some people the propriety of amending the constitution to provide for some other method of selecting judges—by popular election as in some states; by gubernatorial appointment with senatorial or General Assembly confirmation; or by some other method subject to fewer partisan political considerations.[103]

The slow conversion of Virginia from a one-party Democratic state to a competitive two-party state occurred independently of the workings of the state constitution. The Representation Revolution of the 1960s had a large part in that transformation. The one person, one vote requirement imposed on the states in the 1960s gradually led the General Assembly to abandon the use of multimember districts, dating from the very beginning in 1619. Since 1982, all redistricting laws made all districts in both houses of the General Assembly into single-member districts. Something comparable took place in the cities that had previously had provisions for at-large election of city council members. Single-member districts allowed for the election of more Republicans and of more African American Democrats to the General Assembly, which helped break the back of one-party politics in the state and contributed in important ways to Virginia becoming a politically competitive state.[104]

Republican governor A. Linwood Holton, who was in office when voters ratified the Constitution of 1971, probably never thought of himself as continuing or completing anything that his distant predecessor, Harry Flood Byrd, had done or begun. Holton had devoted his career in public life to overturning the Byrd organization and undermining one-party politics. Nevertheless, Holton in effect completed the work that Byrd began in the 1920s of making the governor the state's genuine rather than nominal chief executive. The state bureaucracy had continued to grow in size and complexity by the 1960s. In 1972, at Holton's recommendation, the assembly created the first full-fledged cabinet system for the state. It organized about ninety-five state agencies into six cabinet departments, each under the administration of a cabinet officer whom the governor appointed, subject to legislative confirmation.[105]

The governor's increased administrative authority as a powerful chief executive together with the governor's preparation of the biennial state budget and the annual address to the General Assembly at the opening of each session gave the governor an ever-larger influence in setting the agenda for legislative action. As always in the past, the governor's ability to succeed in reaching those objectives rested on personal popularity, persuasive ability, and political support in the General Assembly. Even without the powerful old Byrd organization that had played a large role in augmenting the effective political power of Virginia governors during the first decades of the twentieth century, by the first decades of the twenty-first, the governor of Virginia was very well positioned under the provisions of the Constitution of 1971 to remain one of the more powerful governors in the country.

That does not mean that legislators did not make some extremely consequential changes in law and practice in Virginia at the same time. During the 1970s and 1980s, for reasons that arose largely from local considerations and, in some instances, the heritage of mandatory racial residential segregation, the General Assembly granted several counties immunity from annexation, in part to protect white residents from being shifted into cities with Black majorities or increasing Black minorities. To some extent, that prohibited cities and neighboring counties from improvising to meet new challenges as some of them had done in the 1950s and 1960s or to take advantage of new opportunities. Within a matter of less than two decades, annexations and consolidations virtually ceased.[106]

That was one of many instances in which the General Assembly employed its constitutional authority to require units of local government to function according to the desires of state legislators, not necessarily according to the desires of residents of cities. Annexation was one of many issues that sparked occasional renewals of the debates about the Dillon Rule. Some scholarly studies suggest that even a fairly strict (but sometimes inconsistent) application and interpretation of the rule did not prevent local initiative because the assembly often granted local requests for alterations in city or county charters or governmental practices;[107] and beginning early in the twenty-first century the General Assembly authorized an increasingly large number of local referenda on proposals to change city, county, or regional policies.[108] Still, strict application of the Dillon Rule perpetuates state control over local governments in Virginia to an extent that is unusual in the United States.

The Future

Several major changes to the functioning of state government that amendments have implemented, such as the veto session and the rainy day fund, have not changed the basic structure of the government as initially prescribed in 1971. The other amendments have allowed adaptations to the constitution to keep it functioning properly. Absent any unforeseeable demands for major changes, the constitution will probably continue in effect without major structural changes with little or no visible prospect of another comprehensive constitutional revision. To that extent, the constitution has met the purposes of its creators.[109]

CHAPTER 10

The Age of Constitutional Amendments

Each state's constitution is unique, just as its laws and political culture are unique. In one very important respect, though, they all share a long evolutionary history that began with the Revolutionary-era constitutional conventions. During the century and a quarter that began in 1776, elected delegates assembled in Virginia conventions and wrote state constitutions eight times (including one for Kentucky in 1792 and one for West Virginia in 1861–1862); a ninth convention, which met in 1861 to deal with the secession crisis, acted like a constitutional convention after the issue of secession was decided and submitted a revised constitution to voters, who refused to ratify it. After the election of delegates to the constitutional convention in Virginia in 1901, for almost another century and a quarter (as of this present writing), no Virginians met in convention to write a state constitution. In fact, no state held a constitutional convention after the 1980s and only two did so after the 1960s. Perhaps the age of state constitutional conventions is a thing of the past and that extraordinarily important and revolutionary invention of the Revolutionary generation has quietly expired without many people noticing the death of that creature and creator of representative democracy.[1]

In Virginia, as elsewhere in the United States, an age of state constitutional amendments succeeded the age of state constitutional conventions.[2] In Virginia, as in a majority of states, legislators, not elected members of constituent conventions, determined what, if any, changes to a state's constitution qualified voters had an opportunity to ratify or reject. That magnified the real authority of the General Assembly of Virginia, which, since 1910 when it first proposed amendments to the Constitution of 1902, exercised sole control over the process of constitutional change, subject only to voters' actions at ratification referenda. Amendments that the General Assembly proposed to the Constitution of 1971 have not been widely discussed, and, with the exceptions of the ban on same-sex marriages and the creation of the bipartisan redistricting commission, usually had no networks of well-organized advocates. Voters probably heard little about and therefore seldom debated the amendments on which they, in their sovereign capacity, made the final decisions. In that respect, for more than a century, state constitutional change in Virginia took place absent the important public discussions about the states' fundamental laws and peoples' rights and responsibilities that had normally engaged the body politic before, during, and after the constitutional conventions of 1776, 1829–30, 1850–51, 1864, 1867–68, and 1901–2.

I moved to Virginia eight weeks after the Constitution of 1971 became effective and have lived in the state ever since, but when I began to research Virginia's constitutions, I realized that I did not even recall many of the constitutional amendment referenda in which I had voted. That raised a profoundly important question in my mind: If voters pay little attention to amendments that legislators propose, to what extent has the age of constitutional amendments that succeeded the age of constitutional conventions undermined the American understanding that state constitutions embody the will of the people in their sovereign capacity? Has state constitutional evolution become a new and largely unrecognized engine of legislative authority that has in effect taken the place of that venerable expression of the sovereign will, the constituent convention, that our Revolutionary ancestors invented when they invented state constitutions? What does that suggest about the future?

Virginia's constitutions and their cumulative history across more than four centuries chart change and continuity to explain in part how Virginians lived at any one time during their long history. I have no doubt that a comprehensive account of each of the other forty-nine states' constitutional histories would be just as interesting as that of Virginia, though doubtless for different reasons and in different ways in each, and just as important to the people of each state in how they live. If, as Louis Brandeis famously remarked in *New State Ice Company v. Liebmann* in 1932, states can serve as experimental laboratories for the development of American democratic government,[3] then each state's constitution is of the utmost importance because it defines, enables, or constrains the ability of the people to make the public law of the state in which they live.

NOTES

Abbreviations and Short Titles

Acts	*Acts of the General Assembly of Virginia* (variant titles) with session date
DVB	John T. Kneebone et al., eds., *Dictionary of Virginia Biography* (Richmond, 1998–)
DVB online	Online *Dictionary of Virginia* biographies accessible via the site index on the Library of Virginia's website at http://www.lva.virginia.gov
Election Records	MS Election Records, Office of the Secretary of the Commonwealth, Record Group 13, Library of Virginia
Enrolled Bills	Records of the General Assembly, Enrolled Bills, Record Group 87, Library of Virginia
EV	Virginia Humanities online *Encyclopedia Virginia*
Hening, *Statutes*	William Waller Hening ed., *The Statutes at Large: Being a Collection of All the Laws of Virginia, from the First Session of the Legislature, in the Year 1619* . . . (Richmond, 1809–23)
JHB	John Pendleton Kennedy and H. R. McIlwaine eds., *Journals of the House of Burgesses of Virginia*, 13 unnumbered volumes (Richmond, 1905–15) with dates from title pages
JHD	*Journal of the House of Delegates* (variant titles) with session date
JS	*Journal of the Senate of Virginia* (variant titles) with session date
LVA	Library of Virginia, Richmond
Official Election Results	Virginia State Board of Elections, *Official Election Results* . . . (variant titles), pamphlets reporting official results of ratification referenda, with date; most results since 1958 posted on the Department of Elections website at https://www.elections.virginia.gov
RG	Record Group
Statement of Vote	Secretary of the Commonwealth, *Statement of the Vote* . . . (variant titles), pamphlets reporting official results of ratification referenda, with date, posted on the Department of Elections website at https://www.elections.virginia.gov
Tarter, *Grandees*	Brent Tarter, *The Grandees of Government: The Origins and Persistence of Undemocratic Politics in Virginia* (Charlottesville, 2013)

VMHB   *Virginia Magazine of History and Biography*
VNL   *University of Virginia News Letter* (1925–97), *Virginia News Letter* (1997–2018)
WMQ   *William and Mary Quarterly*

Introduction

1. George Washington to John Augustine Washington, 31 May–4 June 1776, in *The Papers of George Washington: Revolutionary War Series*, ed. Philander D. Chase et al. (Charlottesville 1985–), 4:412.

2. Thomas M. Cooley, *A Treatise on the Constitutional Limitations which Rest upon the Legislative Power of the States of the American Union* (Boston, 1868); William J. Brennan Jr., "State Constitutions and the Protection of Individual Rights," *Harvard Law Review* 90 (1977): 489–504.

3. A. E. Dick Howard, "'For the Common Benefit': Constitutional History in Virginia as a Casebook for the Modern Constitution-Maker," *Virginia Law Review* 54 (1968): 818–902; and the chapter-length introductions to A. E. Dick Howard, *Commentaries on the Constitution of Virginia*, 2 vols. (Charlottesville, 1974), 1:1–24; and to John Dinan, *The Virginia State Constitution: A Reference Guide*, rev. 2nd ed. (Oxford, 2014), 1–32.

4. George Brown Oliver, "A Constitutional History of Virginia, 1776–1860" (PhD, Duke University, 1959); Robert P. Sutton, *Revolution to Secession: Constitution Making in the Old Dominion* (Charlottesville, 1989).

5. William A. Anderson, "Virginia Constitutions," *Proceedings of the Virginia State Bar Association* 13 (Richmond, 1900), 145–78; David L. Pulliam, *The Constitutional Conventions of Virginia from the Foundation of the Commonwealth to the Present Time* (Richmond, 1901); Jacob N. Brenaman, *A History of Virginia Conventions* (Richmond, 1902); William J. Van Schreeven, *The Conventions and Constitutions of Virginia, 1776–1966* (Richmond, 1967).

Chapter 1. The Constitution of the Colony

1. [Richard Bland], *An Inquiry into the Rights of the British Colonies, Intended as an Answer to the Regulations Lately Made Concerning the Colonies, and the Taxes Imposed upon Them Considered. In a Letter Addressed to the Author of that Pamphlet* (Williamsburg, 1766), 13.

2. William Blackstone, *Commentaries on the Laws of England*, 4 vols. (Oxford, 1765–69), 1:68–73, 76–77, quotation on 76; *Black's Law Dictionary*, s.v. "Memory; Legal Memory."

3. Susan M. Kingsbury, "A Comparison of the Virginia Company with the Other English Trading Companies of the Sixteenth and Seventeenth Centuries," *Annual Report of the American Historical Association for the Year 1906*, 2 vols. (Washington, DC, 1908), 1:159–76; Wesley Frank Craven, *The Virginia Company of London, 1606–1624* (Jamestown, 1957); Ken MacMillan, *Sovereignty and Possession in the English New*

World: The Legal Foundations of Empire, 1576-1640 (Cambridge, 2006), 79-89; Anthony Pagden, "Law, Colonization, Legitimation, and the European Background," in *The Cambridge History of Law in America*, ed. Michael Grossberg and Christopher Tomlins, 3 vols. (Cambridge, 2008), 1:1-31; Mary Sarah Bilder, "Charter Constitutionalism: The Myth of Edward Coke and the Virginia Charter," *North Carolina Law Review* 94 (2016): 1545-97; Alexander B. Haskell, *For God, King, and People: Forging Commonwealth Bonds in Renaissance Virginia* (Chapel Hill, 2017), 151-64.

4. Samuel M. Bemiss, ed., *The Three Charters of the Virginia Company of London, with Seven Related Documents, 1606-1621* (Williamsburg, 1957), 1-12, quotation on 9.

5. Bemiss, *Three Charters*, 13-22.

6. James Horn, *A Land as God Made It: Jamestown and the Birth of America* (New York, 2005); Karen Ordahl Kupperman, *The Jamestown Project* (Cambridge, MA, 2007).

7. Bemiss, *Three Charters*, 13-22, 42-43.

8. William Strachey, comp., *For the Colony in Virginea Britannia: Lawes Divine, Morall and Martiall, & c.*, (London, 1611); Walter F. Prince, "The First Criminal Code of Virginia," *Annual Report of the American Historical Association for the Year 1899* (Washington, 1900) 1:311-63; David H. Flaherty, *For The Colony in Virginea Britannia: Lawes Divine, Morall and Martiall, Etc.*, comp. William Strachey (Charlottesville, 1969); Introduction to David Thomas Konig, "'Dale's Laws' and the Non-common Law Origins of Criminal Justice in Virginia," *American Journal of Legal History* 26 (1982): 354-75; Brent Tarter, "Lawes Divine Morall and Martiall," *EV* (2011).

9. Bemiss, *Three Charters*, 76-94.

10. Susan Myra Kingsbury, ed., *Records of the Virginia Company of London*, 4 vols. (Washington, DC, 1906-35), 3:98-109.

11. *Oxford English Dictionary*, s.v. "burgess."

12. William J. Van Schreeven and George H. Reese, eds., *Proceedings of the General Assembly of Virginia, July 3-August 4, 1619* (Jamestown, 1969).

13. *Oxford English Dictionary*, s.v. "assembly."

14. Kingsbury, *Records of the Virginia Company*, 3:483-84. The 1619 instructions are evidently lost, but company officials copied them for Sir Francis Wyatt's use later.

15. Warrant dated 26 January 1623/4; Kingsbury, *Records of the Virignia Company*, 3:483-84.

16. Bemiss, *Three Charters*, 51.

17. Schreeven and Reese, *Proceedings of the General Assembly of Virginia*, 58.

18. Wesley Frank Craven, *Dissolution of the Virginia Company: The Failure of a Colonial Experiment* (New York, 1932).

19. Charles I, *By the King. A Proclamation for Setling the Colony of Virginia* (London, 1625); also printed in Clarence S. Brigham, ed., *British Royal Proclamations Relating to America, 1603-1783* (Worcester, MA, 1911); and in *Transactions and Collections of the American Antiquarian Society* 12 (1911): 52-55.

20. Jon Kukla, *Political Institutions in Virginia, 1619-1660* (New York, 1989), 76-79, 96-97; Warren M. Billings, *A Little Parliament: The Virginia General Assembly in the Seventeenth Century* (Richmond, 2004), 5-10; Warren M. Billings, with the assistance

of Maria Kimberly, ed., *The Papers of Sir William Berkeley, 1605–1677* (Richmond, 2007), 29–35; Haskell, *For God, King, and People*, 210–34.

21. Hening, *Statutes*, 2:311–14.

22. Public Record Office (hereafter PRO) Colonial Office (hereafter CO) 5/1355, 94–95, National Archives of the United Kingdom; text also copied as last document in a manuscript volume of the 1705 revision of the laws, LVA.

23. PRO CO 1/34, fol. 202.

24. Mary Sarah Bilder, "English Settlement and Local Governance," in *Cambridge History of Law in America*, 1:63–103.

25. Billings, *Papers of Sir William Berkeley*, 393–97; Philip Alexander Bruce, *Institutional History of Virginia in the Seventeenth Century; An Inquiry into the Religious, Moral, Educational, Legal, Military, and Political Condition of the People, Based on Original and Contemporaneous Records*, 2 vols. (New York, 1910).

26. Most of the surviving original colonial archive is in Colonial Papers, RG 1, LVA; a portion of the executive records of the last royal governor is in the George Chalmers Papers, New York Public Library.

27. Brent Tarter, "A Rich Storehouse of Knowledge: A History of the Library of Virginia," in *The Common Wealth: Treasures from the Collections of the Library of Virginia*, ed. Sandra Gioia Treadway and Edward D. C. Campbell, Jr. (Richmond, 1997), 14.

28. Jon Kukla, "Preface to the Second Edition," in *Legislative Journals of the Council of Colonial Virginia*, rev. 2nd ed., 3 vols., ed. H. R. McIlwaine (Richmond, 1979), viii–x.

29. *JHB, 1619–1658/59*, 114.

30. General Court Records, Virginia Historical Society, printed in H. R. McIlwaine, ed., *Minutes of the Council and General Court of Colonial Virginia* (Richmond, 1924), 206–461.

31. PRO CO 5/1405, printed in H. R. McIlwaine, ed., *Legislative Journals of the Council*, 1:3–10.

32. PRO CO 5/1405, printed as the first document in volume 1 of H. R. McIlwaine, Wilmer L. Hall, and Benjamin L. Hillman, eds., *Executive Journals of the Council of Colonial Virginia*, 6 vols. (Richmond, 1925–66).

33. William Noel Sainsbury and J. W. Fortescue, eds., *Calendar of State Papers, Colonial Series, America and West Indies, 1677–1680* (London, 1896), 468–69; PRO CO 5/1355, 400, 410; McIlwaine, Hall, and Hillman, *Executive Journals of the Council*, 1:485.

34. Kukla, *Political Institutions*, 11A–14.

35. Henry Hartwell, Edward Chilton, and James Blair, *The Present State of Virginia, and the College*, ed. Hunter Dickinson Farish (London, 1727; Williamsburg, 1940), 21–37. Originally written in the 1690s.

36. Robert Beverley, *History and Present State of Virginia*, ed. Susan Scott Parrish (London, 1705; Chapel Hill, 2013), 190–92.

37. *Oxford English Dictionary*, s.v. "lieutenant."

38. Beverley, *History*, 191.

39. Leonard Woods Labaree, *Royal Instructions to British Colonial Governors, 1670–1776*, 2 vols. (New York, 1935), 1:74, 77, 78–79.

40. William Byrd to Francis Otway, 10 February 1741, in *The Correspondence of*

the *Three William Byrds of Westover, Virginia, 1684–1776*, ed. Marion Tinling, 3 vols. (Charlottesville, 1977), 1:355.

41. Hartwell, Chilton, and Blair, *Present State of Virginia, and the College*, 62–64; Beverley, *History*, 214–15; James Titus, *The Old Dominion at War: Society, Politics, and Warfare in Late Colonial Virginia* (Columbia, SC, 1991).

42. Hartwell, Chilton, and Blair, *Present State of Virginia, and the College*, 49–51; Beverley, *History*, 196; Junius Rodes Fishburn, "The Office of Secretary of State in Colonial Virginia" (PhD, Tulane University, 1971); John M. Hemphill II and Gail S. Terry, "The Wheels of Government and the Machinery of Justice: The Workings of Virginia's Colonial Capital," *Virginia Cavalcade* 38 (1988): 52–65.

43. Billings, *Papers of Sir William Berkeley*, 60.

44. Hartwell, Chilton, and Blair, *Present State of Virginia, and the College*, 59–60; Beverley, *History*, 197; George Webb, *Office and Authority of a Justice of Peace* (Williamsburg, 1736), 115–19; Percy Scott Flippin, *The Financial Administration of the Colony of Virginia* (Baltimore, 1915), 21–37.

45. Hartwell, Chilton, and Blair, *Present State of Virginia, and the College*, 16–20; Beverley, *History*, 197.

46. Sarah Shaver Hughes, *Surveyors and Statesmen: Land Measuring in Colonial Virginia* (Richmond, 1979).

47. Kingsbury, *Records of the Virginia Company*, 3:478.

48. McIlwaine, *Minutes of the Council and General Court*, 3–202.

49. Bruce, *Institutional History*, 1:653–89; William E. Nelson, *The Common Law in Colonial America*, vol. 1, *The Chesapeake and New England* (Oxford, 2008), 13–22.

50. Kingsbury, *Records of the Virginia Company*, 3:447.

51. Brent Tarter, "The Library of the Council of Colonial Virginia," in *"Esteemed Bookes of Lawe" and the Legal Culture of Early Virginia*, ed. Warren M. Billings and Brent Tarter (Charlottesville, 2017), 37–56.

52. Hening, *Statutes*, 1:174, 187.

53. E.g., Hening, *Statutes*, 1:270–72, 345–46.

54. Hening, *Statutes*, 3:9–10.

55. Labaree, *Royal Instructions*, 1:318; Jon Kukla, "Robert Beverley Assailed: Appellate Jurisdiction and the Problem of Bicameralism in Seventeenth-Century Virginia," *VMHB* 88 (1980): 415–29; Billings, *Little Parliament*, 149–71.

56. Joseph Henry Smith, *Appeals to the Privy Council from the American Plantations* (New York, 1950). See also Sharon Hamby O'Connor and Mary Sarah Bilder, "Appeals to the Privy Council from the American Colonies: An Annotated Digital Catalogue," accessed 29 September 2015, http://amesfoundation.law.harvard.edu/ColonialAppeals/.

57. Labaree, *Royal Instructions*, 2:752–60.

58. Labaree, *Royal Instructions*, 1:336.

59. Hening, *Statutes*, 3:489–40; Hartwell, Chilton, and Blair, *Present State of Virginia, and the College*, 46–48; Webb, *Office and Authority of a Justice of Peace*, 106–7; Hugh F. Rankin, *Criminal Trial Proceedings in the General Court of Colonial Virginia* (Charlottesville, 1965).

60. Hening, *Statutes*, 3:176–79.

61. George H. Reese, ed., *Proceedings in the Court of Vice-Admiralty of Virginia, 1698–1775* (Richmond, 1983); Webb, *Office and Authority of a Justice of Peace*, 107.

62. McIlwaine, *Legislative Journals of the Council*, 443; this is the last record of the governor attending the council during a legislative session.

63. Kukla, *Political Institutions*, 110–22; and Billings, *Little Parliament*, 27–28, correcting Thomas Francis Moran, *The Rise and Development of the Bicameral System in America* (Baltimore, 1895).

64. Hening, *Statutes*, 1:372, 428, 431.

65. Tarter, *Grandees*, 43.

66. Kukla, *Political Institutions*, 148–204; Warren M. Billings, *Sir William Berkeley and the Forging of Colonial Virginia* (Baton Rouge, 2004), 123–29.

67. Labaree, *Royal Instructions*, 1:318; Kukla, "Robert Beverley Assailed," 415–29; Billings, *Little Parliament*, 149–71.

68. E.g., Hening, *Statutes*, 1:422–27.

69. Hening, *Statutes*, 1:268–69.

70. Hening, *Statutes*, 1:549.

71. Billings, *Little Parliament*, 36–40.

72. *JHB, 1619–1658/59*, 114.

73. Hening, *Statutes*, 1:172, 177.

74. Warren M. Billings, *Statute Law in Colonial Virginia: Governors, Assemblymen, and the Revisals that Forged the Old Dominion* (Charlottesville, 2021).

75. Hening, *Statutes*, 1:299–300.

76. Hening, *Statutes*, 2:20, 272–73.

77. Hening, *Statutes*, 3:236–46; *JHB, 1713–1727/26*, 138, 178.

78. Hening, *Statutes*, 1:378; E. G. Swem, "The Disqualification of Ministers in State Constitutions," *WMQ*, 1st ser., 26 (1917): 73–78; Wilbur Samuel Howell, ed., *Jefferson's Parliamentary Writings* in *The Papers of Thomas Jefferson*, 2nd ser. (Princeton, 1988), 60, 178.

79. Hening, *Statutes*, 1:333–34.

80. Hening, *Statutes*, 2:280.

81. Hening, *Statutes*, 3:26.

82. Hening, *Statutes*, 3:172–75, quotation on 172.

83. Hening, *Statutes*, 4:475–76; Albert Edward McKinley, *The Suffrage Franchise in the Thirteen American Colonies* (Philadelphia, 1903), 40.

84. Hening, *Statutes*, 3:92–94.

85. Flippin, *Financial Administration*, 47–50; Jack P. Greene, "The Attempt to Separate the Offices of Speaker and Treasurer in Virginia, 1758–1766," *VMHB* 71 (1963): 11–18; Tarter, *Grandees*, 90–91.

86. Webb, *Office and Authority of a Justice of Peace*, 17–22; Lucille Blanche Griffith, *The Virginia House of Burgesses, 1750–1774*, rev. ed. (University, 1970); Billings, *Little Parliament*.

87. Labaree, *Royal Instructions*, 1:92.

88. Billings, *Little Parliament*, 59–60, 119–20.

89. Labaree, *Royal Instructions*, 1:125.

90. Labaree, *Royal Instructions*, 1:141–43, 218–19.

91. Labaree, *Royal Instructions*, 1:140–41.

92. Gwenda Morgan, "'The Privilege of Making Laws': The Board of Trade, the Virginia Assembly and Legislative Review, 1748–1754," *Journal of American Studies* 10 (1976): 1–15; Justin W. Aimonetti, "Colonial Virginia: The Incubator of Judicial Review," *Virginia Law Review* 105 (2020): 765–810, on 781–94.

93. Kingsbury, *Records of the Virginia Company*, 4:483–84; Billings, *Papers of Sir William Berkeley*, 29.

94. McIlwaine, *Legislative Journals of the Council*, 1:420–21, 428, 487, 591, 623–24, 634, 1349; unpublished journal of the convention session of the House of Burgesses, 1685, Monson Family Papers, Library of Congress; Warren M. Billings, ed., *The Papers of Francis Howard Baron Howard of Effingham, 1643–1695* (Richmond, 1989), 234–35, 237–40, 263–64, 420–22; Billings, *Little Parliament*, 185; Labaree, *Royal Instructions*, 1:212–13; R. A. Brock, ed., *Official Letters of Alexander Spotswood*, 2 vols. (Richmond, 1882–85), 1:53–54; George H. Reese, ed., *The Official Papers of Francis Fauquier, Lieutenant Governor of Virginia, 1758-1768*, 3 vols. (Charlottesville, 1980–83), 3:1202, 1250.

95. Kingsbury, *Records of the Virginia Company*, 3:98–109, 468–82.

96. Hening, *Statutes*, 1:125.

97. Hening, *Statutes*, 1:131–33.

98. Hening, *Statutes*, 1:140.

99. Hening, *Statutes*, 1:168–70, renewed and amplified September 1632, 1:185–87.

100. Susie M. Ames, ed., *County Court Records of Accomack-Northampton, Virginia, 1632-1640* (Washington, DC, 1954); Nelson, *Common Law in Colonial America*, 1:23–47.

101. Hening, *Statutes*, 1:224; Jon Kukla, "The Founding of Virginia Counties—1634?" *Magazine of Virginia Genealogy* 22 (August 1984): 3–6.

102. Hening, *Statutes*, 2:69–71.

103. Hening, *Statutes*, 1:302–3; Warren M. Billings, "Some Acts Not in Hening's *Statutes*: The Acts of Assembly, April 1652, November 1652, and July 1653," *VMHB* 83 (1975): 51.

104. Turk McCleskey and James C. Squire, "Knowing When to Fold: Litigation on a Writ of Debt in Mid-Eighteenth-Century Virginia," *WMQ*, 3rd ser., 76 (2019): 509–44.

105. Beverley, *History*, 197–98.

106. Warren M. Billings, "Pleading, Procedure, and Practice: The Meaning of Due Process of Law in Seventeenth-Century Virginia," *Journal of Southern History* 47 (1981): 569–84; Jessica K. Lowe, *Murder in the Shenandoah: Making Law Sovereign in Revolutionary Virginia* (New York, 2018).

107. Webb, *Office and Authority of a Justice of Peace*, 89–104, 200–7, 292–306; Warren M. Billings, "A Virginia Original: George Webb's *Office and Authority of a Justice of Peace*," in *"Esteemed Bookes of Lawe,"* 157–77.

108. John Ruston Pagan, "English Statutes in Virginia, 1660–1714," in *"Esteemed Bookes of Lawe,"* 57–94, on 61–62, 65–68.

109. Billings and Tarter, *"'Esteemed Bookes of Lawe,'"* frontispiece.

110. Hening, *Statutes*, 3:102–3; Webb, *Office and Authority of a Justice of Peace*, 107; Oliver Perry Chitwood, *Justice in Colonial Virginia* (Baltimore, 1905), 97–101.

111. Edward L. Bond, *Damned Souls in a Tobacco Colony: Religion in Seventeenth-Century Virginia* (Macon, Ga., 2000); Edward L. Bond, ed., *Spreading the Gospel in Colonial Virginia: Sermons and Devotional Writings* (Lanham, Md., 2004); John K. Nelson, *Blessed Company: Parishes, Parsons, and Parishioners in Anglican Virginia, 1690–1776* (Chapel Hill, 2001); Brent Tarter, "Reflections on the Church of England in Colonial Virginia," *VMHB* 112 (2004): 339–71.

112. Hening, *Statutes*, 3:171.

113. Hugh Jones, *The Present State of Virginia* . . . (London, 1724), 48.

114. Bemiss, *Three Charters*, 100.

115. Hening, *Statutes*, 1:240–43, 399–400; Billings, "Some Acts not in Hening's *Statutes*," 31.

116. Hening, *Statutes*, 1:240–43; Warren M. Billings, ed., "Some Acts Not in Hening's *Statutes*," 31.

117. George Chalmers, ed., *Opinions of Eminent Lawyers on Various Points of English Jurisprudence, Chiefly Concerning the Colonies, Fisheries and Commerce of Great Britain*, rev. ed. (Burlington, 1858), 53–60; Hartwell, Chilton, and Blair, *Present State of Virginia, and the College*, 65–67; George MacLaren Brydon,' *Virginia's Mother Church and the Political Conditions under Which It Grew*, 2 vols. (Richmond, 1947–52) 1:344–53, 517–34.

118. John Ruston Pagan, *Anne Orthwood's Bastard: Sex and Law in Early Virginia* (Oxford, 2003), 120–22.

119. Hening, *Statutes*, 1:421, 520–21.

120. Hening, *Statutes*, 2:201–2, 3:82, 325–28, 530–34, 5:245–46, 426–30; William H. Seiler, "Land Processioning in Colonial Virginia," *WMQ*, 3rd ser., 6 (1949): 416–36; Tarter, *Grandees*, 44–45.

121. Waverly K. Winfree, comp., *The Laws of Virginia: Being a Supplement to Hening's "The Statutes at Large," 1700–1750* (Richmond, 1971), 295–305.

122. Nelson, *Blessed Company*, 43–47, 326.

123. Hartwell, Chilton, and Blair, *Present State of Virginia, and the College*, 67–68; Thad W. Tate, "Blair, James," *DVB*, 1:539–43; Edward L. Bond, "Clayton, John," *DVB*, 3:285–86.

124. Beverley, *History*, 209–11; Tarter, *Grandees*, 35–52.

125. Bland quoted in *Godwin et al. v. Lunan*, Thomas Jefferson, *Reports of Cases Determined in the General Court of Virginia. From 1730, to 1740; and from 1768, to 1772*, ed. Thomas Jefferson Randolph (Charlottesville, 1829), 108.

126. Jon Kukla, "Order and Chaos in Early Virginia: Political and Social Stability in Pre-Restoration Virginia," *American Historical Review* 90 (1985): 275–98; Tarter, *Grandees*, 35–82.

127. These paragraphs are based on Tarter, *Grandees*, 85–110, and the sources cited therein.

128. Warren M. Billings, "'Virginia's Deploured Condition,' 1660–1676: The Coming of Bacon's Rebellion" (PhD diss., Northern Illinois University, 1968), 103–6.

129. John Gilman Kolp, *Gentlemen and Freeholders: Electoral Politics in Colonial Virginia* (Baltimore, 1998), 36–58, which significantly and convincingly revises downward

the estimates in Robert E. Brown and B. Katherine Brown, *Virginia, 1705–1786: Democracy or Aristocracy?* (Lansing, Mich., 1964), 125–50.

130. Hening, *Statutes*, 2:170.

131. Hening, *Statutes*, 2:260.

132. Hening, *Statutes*, 3:447–62.

133. Pagan, *Anne Orthwood's Bastard*, 71–78, 99–101; Barton, *Virginia Colonial Decisions*, 2:45–50.

134. This and the following paragraph follow Tarter, *Grandees*, 59–82; Brent Tarter, "Bacon's Rebellion, the Grievances of the People, and the Political Culture of Seventeenth-Century Virginia," *VMHB* 119 (2011): 3–41; Haskell, *For God, King, and People*, 340–52.

135. This account follows Jack P. Greene, ed., "The Case of the Pistole Fee: The Report of a Hearing on the Pistole Fee Dispute before the Privy Council, June 18, 1754," *VMHB* 66 (1958): 399–422; and Tarter, *Grandees*, 95–97.

136. Hening, *Statutes*, 6:568–69, 7:240–41; this and the following two paragraphs follow Smith, *Appeals to the Privy Council*, 607–26; and Tarter, *Grandees*, 97–100.

137. Arthur P. Scott, "The Constitutional Aspects of the 'Parson's Cause,'" *Political Science Quarterly* 31 (1916): 558–77; Jon Kukla, *Patrick Henry, Champion of Liberty* (New York, 2017), 39–46.

138. This account follows Tarter, *Grandees*, 100–4.

139. *JHB, 1761–1765*, 302 (quotation), 303–4, the whole set in decorative italic type.

140. William J. Van Schreeven, Robert L. Scribner, and Brent Tarter, eds., *Revolutionary Virginia, The Road to Independence: A Documentary Record*, 7 vols. (Charlottesville, 1973–83), 1:19–21 (quotation on 20), 7:722–27.

141. Kukla, *Patrick Henry*, 80–97.

142. [Bland], *Inquiry into the Rights of the British Colonies*, 13.

143. Haskell, *For God, King, and People*, 353–55, 360–68.

144. John Phillip Reid, *Constitutional History of the American Revolution*, 4 vols. (Madison, 1986–93).

145. [Thomas Jefferson], *A Summary View of the Rights of British America: Set Forth in Some Resolutions Intended for the Inspection of the Present Delegates of the People of Virginia, Now in Convention, by a Native, and Member of the House of Burgesses* (Williamsburg, 1774).

146. John Phillip Reid, *The Concept of Liberty in the Age of the American Revolution* (Chicago, 1988), esp. 100–1, 104–5; Jack P. Greene, *The Constitutional Origins of the American Revolution* (Cambridge, 2010), esp. 19–66; and (with some reservations) Eric Nelson, *The Royalist Revolution: Monarchy and the American Founding* (Cambridge, MA, 2014), 29–107.

147. 6 George III, ch. 12.

148. Carl Bridenbaugh, "Violence and Virtue in Virginia, 1766: or, The Importance of the Trivial," *Proceedings of the Massachusetts Historical Society*, 3rd ser., 76 (1964): 3–29; J. A. Leo LeMay, "Robert Bolling and the Bailment of Colonel Chiswell," *Early American Literature* 6 (1971): 99–142; George Wythe in Alexander Purdie and John Dixon's *Virginia Gazette*, 1 August 1766 (quotation).

149. John Phillip Reid, *The Concept of Representation in the Age of the American Revolution* (Chicago, 1989); Peverill Squire, *The Rise of the Representative: Lawmakers and Constituents in Colonial America* (Ann Arbor, 2017).
150. Labaree, *Royal Instructions*, 1:362–65.
151. *JHB, 1766–1769*, 218.
152. *JHB, 1773–1776*, 132.
153. Brent Tarter, *Virginians and Their Histories* (Charlottesville, 2021), 130–31.

Chapter 2. The Constitution of 1776

1. Richard Henry Lee to Charles Lee, 29 June 1776, in *The Letters of Richard Henry Lee*, ed. James Curtis Ballagh, 2 vols. (New York, 1911–14), 1:203.
2. J. Franklin Jameson, "The Early Political Uses of the Word Convention," *American Historical Review* 3 (1898): 477–87.
3. *Oxford English Dictionary*, s.v. "delegate."
4. Texts of extant resolutions printed in William J. Van Schreeven, Robert L. Scribner, and Brent Tarter eds., *Revolutionary Virginia, The Road to Independence, A Documentary Record*, 7 vols. (Charlottesville, 1973–83), 1:105–68.
5. Van Schreeven, Scribner, and Tarter, *Revolutionary Virginia*, 1:219–39.
6. Worthington C. Ford et al., eds., *Journals of the Continental Congress, 1774–1789*, 34 vols. (Washington, DC, 1904–37), 1:75–80.
7. Elections of committees and their surviving records are all printed in vols. 3–7 of Van Schreeven, Scribner, and Tarter, *Revolutionary Virginia*; Larry Bowman, "The Virginia County Committees of Safety, 1774–1776," *VMHB* 79 (1971): 322–37, even though at the time they were never called committees of safety.
8. Van Schreeven, Scribner, and Tarter, *Revolutionary Virginia*, 2:334–89.
9. Van Schreeven, Scribner, and Tarter, *Revolutionary Virginia*, 3:303–510; convention's ordinances published in *Ordinances Passed at a Convention held at the Town of Richmond, in the Colony of Virginia, on Monday, the 17th of July, 1775* (Williamsburg, 1775); and in Hening, *Statutes*, 9:9–74.
10. Committee of Safety's records published in volumes 3–7 of Van Schreeven, Scribner, and Tarter, *Revolutionary Virginia*.
11. Hening, *Statutes*, 9:54–55.
12. Clarence S. Brigham, ed., *British Royal Proclamations Relating to America, 1603–1783* (Worcester, MA, 1911), in *Transactions and Collections of the American Antiquarian Society* 12 (1911): 228–29.
13. Van Schreeven, Scribner, and Tarter, *Revolutionary Virginia*, 5:334–35.
14. 16 George III, chap. 5.
15. Van Schreeven, Scribner, and Tarter, *Revolutionary Virginia*, 5:3–439; the convention's ordinances are printed in *Ordinances Passed at a Convention held at the Town of Williamsburg, in the Colony of Virginia, on Friday, the 1st of December, 1775* (Williamsburg, 1776); and in Hening, *Statutes*, 9:75–107.
16. Ford et al., *Journals of the Continental Congress*, 3:403–4.
17. Ford et al., *Journals of the Continental Congress*, 4:342, 357–58.

18. Election records in Van Schreeven, Scribner, and Tarter, *Revolutionary Virginia*, 6:292–494 passim, 7:28–29, 212, 225–26.

19. [Brent Tarter], "Introductory Note," Van Schreeven, Scribner, and Tarter, *Revolutionary Virginia*, 6:286–90.

20. Roger Atkinson to Sammy [Samuel Pleasants Jr.?], 20 November 1776, Letter Book of Roger Atkinson, University of Virginia.

21. Richard Henry Lee to Patrick Henry, 20 April 1776, in Ballagh, *Letters of Richard Henry Lee*, 2:177.

22. John Page to Thomas Jefferson, 26 April 1776, in *Papers of Thomas Jefferson*, ed. Julian P. Boyd et al. (Princeton, 1950–), 1:288.

23. Thomas Jefferson to Thomas Nelson Jr., 16 May 1776, in Boyd et al., *Papers of Thomas Jefferson*, 1:292.

24. John E. Selby, "Richard Henry Lee, John Adams, and the Virginia Constitution of 1776," *VMHB* 84 (1976): 387–400.

25. Undated, unsigned handbill, Williams College, printed in Van Schreeven, Scribner, and Tarter, *Revolutionary Virginia*, 6:367–68.

26. [John Adams], *Thoughts on Government: Applicable to the Present State of the American Colonies. In a Letter from a Gentleman to His Friend* (Philadelphia, 1776).

27. [Carter Braxton], *An Address to the Convention of the Colony and Ancient Dominion of Virginia; on the Subject of Government in General, and Recommending a Particular Form to Their Consideration. By a Native of That Colony* (Philadelphia, 1776).

28. Patrick Henry to John Adams, 20 May 1776, in *Papers of John Adams*, ed. Robert J. Taylor et al. (Cambridge, MA, 1977–), 4:200–2.

29. J. A. Washington to Richard Henry Lee, 18 May 1776, Lee Family Papers, University of Virginia.

30. Thomas Ludwell Lee to Richard Henry Lee, 1 June 1776, Lee Family Papers, University of Virginia.

31. The sixth and seventh volumes of Van Schreeven, Scribner, and Tarter, *Revolutionary Virginia* contain texts of all the essential extant documents and the official manuscript journal of the Convention of 1776, most of which are preserved in Revolutionary Convention Papers, Convention of 1776, RG 89, LVA. The convention's ordinances are printed in *Ordinances Passed at a General Convention of Delegates and Representatives, from the Several Counties and Corporations of Virginia, Held at the Capitol, in the City of Williamsburg, on Monday the 6th of May, Anno Dom: 1776* (Williamsburg, 1776); and in Hening, *Statutes*, 9:119–51.

32. Van Schreeven, Scribner, and Tarter, *Revolutionary Virginia*, 7:145–46.

33. Van Schreeven, Scribner, and Tarter, *Revolutionary Virginia*, 7:142–43, 145–47.

34. Van Schreeven, Scribner, and Tarter, *Revolutionary Virginia*, 7:143.

35. Van Schreeven, Scribner, and Tarter, *Revolutionary Virginia*, 7:22, 182–83.

36. Thomas Jefferson, *Notes on the State of Virginia*, ed. William Peden (Chapel Hill, 1955), 121–25.

37. Edmund Randolph, *History of Virginia*, ed. Arthur H. Shaffer (Charlottesville, 1970), 252–53, 262.

38. Thad W. Tate, "The Social Contract in America, 1774–1787," *WMQ*, 3rd ser., 22 (1965): 375–91; Gordon S. Wood, *The Creation of the American Republic, 1776–1787* (Chapel Hill, 1969), 273–91, 306–43; Marc W. Kruman, *Between Authority and Liberty: State Constitution Making in Revolutionary America* (Chapel Hill, 1997), 15–33; Christian G. Fritz, "Fallacies of American Constitutionalism," *Rutgers Law Journal* 35 (2004): 1327–69; Christian G. Fritz, *American Sovereigns: The People and America's Constitutional Tradition before the Civil War* (Cambridge, 2008), 31–35.

39. St. George Tucker, ed., *Blackstone's Commentaries: With Notes of Reference to the Constitution and Laws, of the Federal Government of the United States; and of the Commonwealth of Virginia*, 5 vols. (Philadelphia, 1803), 1:Appendix C, 83–88.

40. Randolph, *History of Virginia*, 255.

41. Committee report printed as a handbill by Alexander Purdie (Williamsburg, n.d. [May 1776]); Van Schreeven, Scribner, and Tarter, *Revolutionary Virginia*, 7:9–10, 269–272 271–72, 276–277, 300, 302, 341, 351, 364, 417, 430, 449–50, 458; A. E. Dick Howard, *Commentaries on the Constitution of Virginia*, 2 vols. (Charlottesville, 1974), 1:33–39, 56–313.

42. Randolph, *History of Virginia*, 253.

43. Randolph, *History of Virginia*, 254.

44. 1 William and Mary chap. 18.

45. Hening, *Statutes*, 3:171, 361.

46. Lewis Peyton Little, *Imprisoned Preachers and Religious Liberty in Virginia* (Lynchburg, 1938); Rhys Isaac, *The Transformation of Virginia, 1740–1790* (Chapel Hill, 1982); Jewel L. Spangler, *Virginians Reborn: Anglican Monopoly, Evangelical Dissent, and the Rise of Baptists in the Late Eighteenth Century* (Charlottesville, 2008); Tarter, *Grandees*, 117–21.

47. Van Schreeven, Scribner, and Tarter, *Revolutionary Virginia*, 7:456–58; William T. Hutchinson et al., eds., *Papers of James Madison, Congressional Series*, 17 vols. (Chicago and Charlottesville, 1962–91), 1:170–75 (first quotation); Randolph, *History of Virginia*, 254 (second quotation).

48. Kruman, *Between Authority and Liberty*, 35–40; G. Alan Tarr, *Understanding State Constitutions* (Princeton, 1998), 77–78; Dan Friedman, "Tracing the Lineage: Textual and Conceptual Similarities in the Revolutionary-Era State Declarations of Rights of Virginia, Maryland, and Delaware," *Rutgers Law Journal* 33 (2002): 929–1029.

49. Brent Tarter, "Virginia Declaration of Rights," in *To Secure the Blessings of Liberty: Rights in American History*, ed. Josephine F. Pacheco (Fairfax, VA, 1993), 48–51.

50. Brent Tarter, "Virginians and the Bill of Rights," in *The Bill of Rights: A Lively Heritage*, ed. Jon Kukla (Richmond, 1987), 3–18.

51. Robert A. Rutland, ed., *The Papers of George Mason, 1725–1792*, 3 vols. (Chapel Hill, 1970), 1:299–302.

52. Alexander B. Haskell, *For God, King, and People: Forging Commonwealth Bonds in Renaissance Virginia* (Chapel Hill, 2017), 67–81.

53. Jackson Turner Main, *The Sovereign States, 1775–1783* (New York, 1975), 143–221; Willi Paul Adams, *The First American Constitutions: Republican Ideology and the Making of the State Constitutions in the Revolutionary Era* (Chapel Hill, 1980), 59–93.

54. Edmund Pendleton to Thomas Jefferson, 24 May 1776, in *The Letters and Papers of Edmund Pendleton, 1734–1803*, ed., David J. Mays, 2 vols. (Charlottesville, 1967), 1:180.

55. George Mason to Richard Henry Lee, 18 May 1776, in Rutland, *Papers of George Mason*, 1:271; Brent Tarter, "George Mason and the Conservation of Liberty," *VMHB* 99 (1991): 279–304.

56. Randolph, *History of Virginia*, 252.

57. Van Schreeven, Scribner, and Tarter, *Revolutionary Virginia*, 7:12–13, 594–98, 603–6, 621, 628, 636–39, 641–44, 649–54, 657–58.

58. Wood, *Creation of the American Republic*, 150–61; Kruman, *Between Authority and Liberty*, 109–23.

59. Hening, *Statutes*, 4:475–78; Tucker, *Blackstone's Commentaries*, 1:Appendix, 96–99.

60. Hening, *Statutes*, 12:120–21.

61. Hening, *Statutes*, 9:126–28.

62. Randolph, *History of Virginia*, 256–57.

63. Boyd et al., *Papers of Thomas Jefferson*, 1:362; David N. Mayer, *The Constitutional Thought of Thomas Jefferson* (Charlottesville, 1994), 54–83; Matthew Crow, *Thomas Jefferson, Legal History, and the Art of Recollection* (Cambridge, 2017), esp. 82–131.

64. Kruman, *Between Authority and Liberty*, 131–48.

65. Kruman, *Between Authority and Liberty*, 123–26.

66. Randolph, *History of Virginia*, 255–56.

67. Hening, *Statutes*, 12:722–33; *Acts*, 1815–16 Sess., chap. 82.

68. Hening, *Statutes*, 1:378.

69. E. G. Swem, "The Disqualification of Ministers in State Constitutions," *WMQ*, 1st ser., 26 (1917): 73–78.

70. Van Schreeven, Scribner, and Tarter, *Revolutionary Virginia*, 7:651, 657.

71. Jackson Turner Main, *The Upper House in Revolutionary America, 1763–1788* (Madison, 1967), 128–30; George Brown Oliver, "A Constitutional History of Virginia, 1776–1860" (PhD diss., Duke University, 1959) 243–48.

72. Pagan, "English Statutes in Virginia," in Warren M. Billings and Brent Tarter, eds., *"Esteemed Bookes of Lawe" and the Legal Culture of Early Virginia* (Charlottesville, 2017), 72, 75; McIlwaine, *Legislative Journals of the Council*, 493; Hening, *Statutes*, 3:516–17.

73. Edmund Pendleton to Thomas Jefferson, 10 August 1776; and Jefferson to Pendleton, 26 August 1776, in Boyd et al., *Papers of Thomas Jefferson*, 1:489, 503–4.

74. Main, *Upper House in Revolutionary America*; Wood, *Creation of the American Republic*, 162–96, 206–26, 237–55.

75. Thomas M. Cooley, *A Treatise on the Constitutional Limitations which Rest upon the Legislative Power of the States of the American Union* (Boston, 1868), esp. 9–10, 88, 90; Tarr, *Understanding State Constitutions*, 6–9, 15–17; Robert F. Williams, *The Law of American State Constitutions* (Oxford, 2009), 247–53.

76. *Strawberry Hill Land Co. v. Starbuck*, 124 Va 71 (1918) quotation on 77.

77. Schreeven, Scribner, and Tarter, *Revolutionary Virginia*, 7:655, 659n24.

78. Oliver, "Constitutional History of Virginia," 166–71, 176–86; James Laverne Anderson, "The Virginia Councillors and the American Revolution: The Demise of an Aristocratic Clique," *VMHB* 82 (1974): 56–74; Main, *Upper House in Revolutionary America*; Wood, *Creation of the American Republic*, 132–50; Kruman, *Between Authority and Liberty*, 126–30.

79. James Madison to Thomas Jefferson, 16 March 1784, in Hutchinson et al., *Papers of James Madison, Congressional Series*, 8:9.

80. Emory G. Evans, "Executive Leadership in Virginia, 1776–1781: Henry, Jefferson, and Nelson," in *Sovereign States in an Age of Uncertainty*, ed. Ronald Hoffman and Peter J. Albert (Charlottesville, 1981), 185–225; Stuart Lee Butler, *Defending the Old Dominion: Virginia and Its Militia in the War of 1812* (Lanham, MD, 2013).

81. Brent Tarter, "'If the ritual doesn't change, the times do': Swearing in Virginia's Governors," *Virginia Cavalcade* 50 (2001), 168–77.

82. John Tyler to Thomas Jefferson, 12 May 1810, in *The Papers of Thomas Jefferson: Retirement Series*, ed. J. Jefferson Looney et al. (Princeton, 2004–), 2:386 (quotation), Thomas Mann Randolph to Jefferson, 27 July 1821 and Jefferson to Randolph, 30 July 1821, ibid., *Papers of Thomas Jefferson: Retirement Series* 17:320, 382.

83. George Webb, *Office and Authority of a Justice of Peace* (Williamsburg, 1736), 202–3.

84. Hening, *Statutes*, 769–70; the archives of Virginia preserve only one small folder of documents in RG 103, LVA.

85. Francis H. McGuire, "The General Court of Virginia," *Report of the Seventh Annual Meeting of the Virginia State Bar Association* (Richmond, 1895), 197–229, on 202–22.

86. James E. Herget, "The Missing Power of Local Government: A Discrepancy between Text and Practice in Our Early State Constitutions," *Virginia Law Review* 62 (1976): 999–1015.

87. *Case of the County Levy*, 5 Call (9 Va) (n.d., ca. 1789) 139.

88. Hening, *Statutes*, 3:102–3.

89. Tucker, *Blackstone's Commentaries*, 1:Appendix, 115–16.

90. Van Schreeven, Scribner, and Tarter, *Revolutionary Virginia*, 7:708.

91. *Papers of Jefferson: Retirement Series*, 17:320; Hening, *Statutes*, 9:164–67.

92. Gordon S. Wood, "Introduction: State Constitution-Making in the American Revolution," *Rutgers Law Journal* 24 (1992): 911–26.

93. Van Schreeven, Scribner, and Tarter, *Revolutionary Virginia*, 7:654–55.

94. Hening, *Statutes*, 9:128–30.

95. Hening, *Statutes*, 9:126–28.

96. Hening, *Statutes*, 9:119–22.

97. Hening, *Statutes*, 9:130–32.

98. Hening, *Statutes*, 9:149–51.

99. Van Schreeven, Scribner, and Tarter, *Revolutionary Virginia*, 7:708–9.

100. Hening, *Statutes*, 9:127.

101. *Case of the County Levy*, 5 Call (9 Va) (n.d., ca. 1789) 139.

102. John Page to Thomas Jefferson, 6 July 1776, in Boyd et al., *Papers of Thomas Jefferson*, 1:454–455.

103. Thad W. Tate, "The Coming of the Revolution in Virginia: Britain's Challenge to Virginia's Ruling Class, 1763–1776," *WMQ*, 3rd ser., 19 (1962): 323–43; John E. Selby, *The Revolution in Virginia, 1775–1783* (Williamsburg, 1988); Woody Holton, *Forced Founders: Indians, Debtors, Slaves, and the Making of the American Revolution in Virginia* (Chapel Hill, 1999); Tarter, *Grandees*, 107–10, 113–18.

104. Raymond C. Bailey, *Popular Influence upon Public Policy: Petitioning in Eighteenth-Century Virginia* (Westport, CT, 1979); Tarter, *Grandees*, 126–33.

105. The many footnotes and appendices in St. George Tucker's edition of *Blackstone's Commentaries* clearly indicate how numerous and significant the changes that the General Assembly made to the laws during the first twenty-five years after independence were.

106. Hening, *Statutes*, 9:226–27.

107. Hening, *Statutes*, 12:138–40.

108. Holly Brewer, "Entailing Aristocracy in Colonial Virginia: 'Ancient Feudal Restraints' and Revolutionary Reform," *WMQ*, 3rd ser., 54 (1997): 307–46, correcting C. Ray Keim, "Primogeniture and Entail in Colonial Virginia," *WMQ*, 3rd ser., 25 (1968): 545–86.

109. Thomas E. Buckley, SJ *Church and State in Revolutionary Virginia, 1776–1787* (Charlottesville, 1977); Thomas E. Buckley, SJ, *Establishing Religious Freedom: Jefferson's Statute in Virginia* (Charlottesville, 2013), 55–81; Spangler, *Virginians Reborn*; John Ragosta, *Wellspring of Liberty: How Virginia's Dissenters Helped Win the American Revolution and Secured Religious Liberty* (New York, 2010); Tarter, *Grandees*, 118–23.

110. Hening, *Statutes*, 12:84–86, quotation on 86.

111. Thomas E. Buckley, SJ, "Evangelicals Triumphant: The Baptists' Assault on the Virginia Glebes, 1786–1801," *WMQ*, 3rd ser., 45 (1988): 33–69.

112. Hening, *Statutes*, 11:164–66, 272–75.

113. *Peter Kamper v. Mary Hawkins*, 3 Va (1 Va Cases) 20 (1793), quotation on 37; Charles F. Hobson, ed., *St. George Tucker's Law Reports and Selected Papers, 1782–1825*, 3 vols. (Chapel Hill, 2013), 1:264–66, 274–90.

114. *Commonwealth v. Caton*, 4 Va (2 Va Cases) 5 (1782), quotation on 8.

115. *Commonwealth v. Caton*, 4 Va (2 Va Cases) 5 (1782), quotation on 20.

116. Margaret Virginia Nelson, *A Study of Judicial Review in Virginia, 1789–1928* (New York, 1947), 31–53.

117. *Case of the County Levy*, 139–42.

118. *Kamper v. Hawkins*, 3 Va (1 Va Cases) 20 (1793); *Asbury Crenshaw and Thomas B. Crenshaw v. The Slate River Company*, 27 Va (6 Randolph) 245 (1828).

119. Constitution of 1851, Article VI, Section 11.

120. John P. Kaminski, "Restoring the Declaration of Independence: Natural Rights and the Ninth Amendment," and Charles F. Hobson, "The Tenth Amendment and the New Federalism of 1789," in Kukla ed., *Bill of Rights, A Lively Heritage*, 50, 153–63.

121. Tarter, "Virginians and the Bill of Rights," 15; *Barron v. Baltimore*, 32 US 243 (1833), quotation on 250.

122. *Journal of the First Constitutional Convention of Kentucky, Held in Danville, Kentucky, April 2 to 19, 1792* (Lexington, 1942); John D. Barnhart, "Frontiersmen and Planters in the Formation of Kentucky," *Journal of Southern History* 7 (1941): 19–36; Joan Wells Coward, *Kentucky in the New Republic: The Process of Constitution Making* (Lexington, 1979); Harry S. Laver, "'Chimney Corner Constitutions': Democratization and its Limits in Frontier Kentucky," *Register of the Kentucky Historical Society* 95 (1997): 337–67; Robert M. Ireland, *The Kentucky State Constitution* (New York, 2011), 3–7.

123. Barnhart, "Frontiersmen and Planters," 34–35, evidently relying in part on Clara Campbell Holmes, "The First Kentucky Constitution" (MS thesis, Louisiana State University, 1940); Lowell H. Harrison, *Kentucky's Road to Statehood* (Lexington, 1992), 57–61, 104, 116. See also E. Merton Coulter, "Early Frontier Democracy in the First Kentucky Constitution," *Political Science Quarterly* 39 (1924): 665–77.

124. Printed in Harrison, *Kentucky's Road to Statehood*, 152–68.

125. Ireland, *Kentucky State Constitution*, 7–10.

126. Tarter, "Virginia Declaration of Rights," 47–51.

127. Silvana R. Siddali, *Frontier Democracy: Constitutional Conventions in the Old Northwest* (Cambridge, 2016), 43.

Chapter 3. The Constitution of 1830

1. *Alexandria Herald*, 3 June 1816.

2. This and the following paragraphs follow William G. Shade, *Democratizing the Old Dominion: Virginia and the Second Party System, 1824–1861* (Charlottesville, 1996), esp. 18–24; and Tarter, *Grandees*, 173–76.

3. *A Tabular Statement, Shewing the Free White, Free Coloured, Slave and Total Population in Each Count of the Commonwealth of Virginia, According to the Census of 1790, 1800, 1810, and 1820, Respectively; Prepared in Compliance with a Resolution of the Convention of Virginia, Passed on the 10th October, 1829*, printed as Document No. 9 with *Journal, Acts and Proceedings of a General Convention of the Commonwealth of Virginia, Assembled in Richmond* (Richmond, 1829 [i.e., 1830]).

4. *Acts*, 1815–16 Sess., chap. 17; Richard L. Morton, "The Virginia State Debt and Internal Improvements, 1820–38," *Journal of Political Economy* 25 (1917): 339–73; Carter Goodrich, "The Virginia System of Mixed Enterprise: A Study of State Planning of Internal Improvements," *Political Science Quarterly* 44 (1940): 355–86.

5. Julian P. Boyd et al., eds., *Papers of Thomas Jefferson* (Princeton, 1950–), 6:284–94.

6. Boyd et al., *Papers of Thomas Jefferson*, 6:294–308.

7. Thomas Jefferson, *Notes on the State of Virginia*, ed. William Peden (Chapel Hill, 1955), 117–20, quotations on 118, 119.

8. *Alexandria Herald*, 3 June 1816.

9. Proceedings and public declaration printed in Richmond *Enquirer*, 31 August 1816; and *Niles' Weekly Register* 3 (14 September 1816): 37–40, quotation on 38.

10. *JHD*, 1815–16 Sess., 167–68.

11. Hening, *Statutes*, 10:140–45; Tarter, *Grandees*, 130–31.

12. *Acts*, 1816–17 Sess., chap. 5.

13. J. Jefferson Looney et al., eds., *The Papers of Thomas Jefferson: Retirement Series* (Princeton, 2004–), 10:162–63, 220–21, 322–23, 367–68, 435–36.

14. Thomas Jefferson to Henry Tompkinson, i.e., Samuel Kercheval, 12 July 1816; Looney, *Papers of Thomas Jefferson: Retirement Series*, 10:222–28, quotations on 222, 223.

15. Looney et al., *Papers of Thomas Jefferson: Retirement Series*, 10:226; Merrill D. Peterson, "Mr. Jefferson's 'Sovereignty of the Living Generation,'" *Virginia Quarterly Review* 52 (1976): 437–47.

16. Tarter, *Grandees*, 165–76.

17. William J. Van Schreeven, *The Conventions and Constitutions of Virginia, 1776–1966* (Richmond, 1967), 31; Legislative Petitions, Records of the General Assembly, RG 78, LVA.

18. Earl G. Swem, "A Bibliography of the Conventions and Constitutions of Virginia, Including References to Essays, Letters and Speeches in the Virginia Newspapers" printed in *Bulletin of the Virginia State Library* 3 (1910): 380–96.

19. Shade, *Democratizing the Old Dominion*, esp. 61–63; see also Robin L. Einhorn, *American Taxation, American Slavery* (Chicago, 2006).

20. Tarter, *Grandees*, 93, 132–33.

21. *Daily Richmond Whig*, 15 October 1829; *Proceedings and Debates of the Virginia State Convention of 1829–30* (Richmond, 1830), 25–31.

22. *Fifth Census, or, Enumeration of the Inhabitants of the United States, 1830* (Washington, DC), 86, 88.

23. Michael J. Dubin, *United States Presidential Elections, 1788–1860: The Official Results by County and State* (Jefferson, NC, 2002), 50; *Vote on the Convention Question* printed with Governor's Message, and Accompanying Documents, 50, printed with *JHD*, 1828–29 Sess.

24. *Fifth Census*, 86, 88.

25. *Richmond Enquirer*, 20 October 1829.

26. *JHD*, 1824–25 Sess., 148–50; *JS*, 1824–25 Sess., 93–95.

27. *Richmond Enquirer*, 5, 9 (including address), 11 August 1825.

28. *JHD*, 1826–27 Sess., 112–13.

29. *JHD*, 1827–28 Sess., 33–34; *JS*, 1827–28 Sess., 76–77.

30. *Acts*, 1827–28 Sess., chap. 24.

31. *Vote on the Convention Question* printed with Governor's Message, and Accompanying Documents, 50, printed with *JHD*, 1828–29 Sess.

32. *Acts*, 1828–29 Sess., chap. 15.

33. Robert P. Sutton, "The Virginia Constitutional Convention of 1829–30: A Profile Analysis of Late Jeffersonian Virginia" (PhD, University of Virginia, 1967); Trenton E. Hizer, "'Virginia Is Now Divided': Politics in the Old Dominion, 1820–1833" (PhD, University of South Carolina, 1997), 211–13; Tarter, *Grandees*, 179–80.

34. Sutton, "The Virginia Constitutional Convention of 1829–30"; Sutton, *Revolution to Secession*, 75–77, 92; Shade, *Democratizing the Old Dominion*, 72.

35. Merrill D. Peterson, ed., *Democracy, Liberty, and Property: The State Constitutional Conventions of the 1820's* (Indianapolis, 1966), 271; Dickson D. Bruce Jr., *The Rhetoric of Conservatism: The Virginia Convention of 1829-30 and the Conservative Tradition in the South* (San Marino, CA, 1982); Alison Goodyear Freehling, *Drift Toward Dissolution: The Virginia Slavery Debate of 1831-1832* (Baton Rouge, 1982), 36-81; Sutton, *Revolution to Secession*, 72-102; Hizer, "'Virginia Is Now Divided,'" 221-68; Kevin R. C. Gutzman, *Virginia's American Revolution: From Dominion to Republic, 1776-1840* (Lanham, MD, 2007), 135-205.

36. Laura J. Scalia, *America's Jeffersonian Experiment: Remaking State Constitutions, 1820-1850* (DeKalb, IL, 1999), 33-38.

37. *Journal, Acts and Proceedings of a General Convention of the Commonwealth of Virginia, Assembled in Richmond* (Richmond, 1829 [i.e., 1830]).

38. Records of the Virginia Constitutional Convention of 1829-30, RG 91, LVA.

39. *Proceedings and Debates*; Trenton E. Hizer, "Rough Index to the Proceedings and Debates of the Virginia State Convention of 1829-1830" (n.p., n.d., [1993]).

40. Joanne L. Gatewood, ed., "Richmond during the Virginia Constitutional Convention of 1829-30: An Extract from the Diary of Thomas Green, October 1, 1829, to January 31, 1830," *VMHB* 84 (1976): 287-332; Hugh B. Pleasants, "Sketches of the Virginia Convention of 1829-30," *Southern Literary Messenger* 17 (1851): 147-54; Hugh Blair Grigsby, Diary, Virginia Historical Society; Grigsby, *The Virginia Convention of 1829-30* (Richmond, 1854); and Grigsby, "Sketches of Members of the Constitutional Convention of 1829-30," *VMHB* 61 (1953): 219-332.

41. *Journal, Acts and Proceedings*, 3-5.

42. *Journal, Acts and Proceedings*, 21-23.

43. James Madison to Lafayette 1 February 1830, draft, James Madison Papers, Library of Congress; printed with stylistic modifications in William Cabell Rives, ed., *Letters and Other Writings of James Madison*, 4 vols. (Philadelphia, 1865), 4:58-61.

44. William T. Hutchinson et al., eds., *Papers of James Madison, Congressional Series*, 17 vols. (Chicago and Charlottesville, 1962-91), 14:163-64; Tarter, *Grandees*, 165-67.

45. Scalia, *America's Jeffersonian Experiment*, 134-46.

46. This and the following paragraphs follow Tarter, *Grandees*, 180-88; Bruce, *Rhetoric of Conservatism*, 90, 175-95; Sutton, *Revolution to Secession*, 72-92.

47. *Proceedings and Debates*, 65-79.

48. *Proceedings and Debates*, 160.

49. George Brown Oliver, "A Constitutional History of Virginia, 1776-1860" (PhD diss., Duke University, 1959), 178-86.

50. Bruce, *Rhetoric of Conservatism*, 90; Sutton, *Revolution to Secession*, 79-92; Shade, *Democratizing the Old Dominion*, 72-73.

51. *Proceedings and Debates*, 750, 786-87.

52. Hening, *Statutes*, 3:172-75.

53. Hening, *Statutes*, 12:120.

54. Christopher M. Curtis, "Reconsidering Suffrage Reform in the 1829-1830 Virginia Constitutional Convention," *Journal of Southern History* 74 (2008): 89-124; Cur-

tis, *Jefferson's Freeholders and the Politics of Ownership in the Old Dominion* (New York, 2011).

55. Hening, *Statutes*, 1:333–34.

56. Hening, *Statutes*, 2:272–73.

57. Brent Tarter, *Gerrymanders: How Redistricting Has Protected Slavery, White Supremacy, and Partisan Minorities in Virginia* (Charlottesville, 2019), 24–28.

58. Hening, *Statutes*, 12:84–86.

59. St. George Tucker, Enquiry into the causes of the Accumulation of Business in the Courts of Chancery & Court of Appeals; & of the means of remedying the same, January 1807, with draft bill, in Charles F. Hobson, ed., *St. George Tucker's Law Reports and Selected Papers, 1782–1825*, 3 vols. (Chapel Hill, 2013), 3:1576–1601.

60. Thomas R. Morris, *The Virginia Supreme Court, An Institutional and Political Analysis* (Charlottesville, 1975), 65–68.

61. *Asbury Crenshaw and Thomas B. Crenshaw v. The Slate River Company*, 27 Va (6 Randolph) 245 (1828), quotation on 277.

62. Margaret Virginia Nelson, *A Study of Judicial Review in Virginia, 1789–1928* (New York, 1947), 31–53.

63. *Proceedings and Debates*, 505.

64. Jefferson to Tompkinson, 12 July 1816, *Papers of Thomas Jefferson: Retirement Series*, 10:223; St. George Tucker, ed., *Blackstone's Commentaries: With Notes of Reference to the Constitution and Laws, of the Federal Government of the United States; and of the Commonwealth of Virginia*, 5 vols. (Philadelphia, 1803), 1:Appendix C, 83–88.

65. *Frederick Justices v. Bruce et al.*, 45 Va (4 Grattan) 281 (1848).

66. Oliver, "Constitutional History," 199–200.

67. Albert O. Porter, *County Government in Virginia, A Legislative History, 1607–1904* (New York, 1947), 155–226.

68. *Proceedings and Debates*, 789–91.

69. *Journal, Acts and Proceedings*, 296–97.

70. Madison to Lafayette, 1 February 1830, draft, Madison Papers, Library of Congress, printed with stylistic modifications in Rives, *Letters and Other Writings of James Madison*, 4:58–61; Drew R. McCoy, *The Last of the Fathers: James Madison and the Republican Legacy* (Cambridge, 1989), 217–52.

71. *Proceedings and Debates*, 790.

72. *Wheeling Gazette*, 3 April 1830.

73. Ratification referendum totals printed in *Proceedings and Debates*, 903, compared with 1828 *Vote on the Convention Question; Entire Official Poll on the New Constitution of Virginia*.

74. Ambler, *Sectionalism in Virginia*, 172–74.

75. *Fifth Census*, 86, 88.

76. *A Statement of the Number of Persons in Each County of This Commonwealth*, printed as Document No. 7 with *Journal and Proceedings*.

77. *Vote on the Convention Question*.

78. Shade, *Democratizing the Old Dominion*, 63–64.

79. Dubin, *United States Presidential Elections, 1788–1860*, 50, 58–60.

80. James Madison to Thomas Jefferson, 16 March 1784, in Hutchinson et al., *Papers of James Madison, Congressional Series*, 8:9; Thomas Jefferson to Henry Tompkinson, i.e., Samuel Kercheval, 12 July 1816, *Papers of Thomas Jefferson, Retirement Series*, 10:223.

81. Oliver, "Constitutional History," 187–89.

82. Journal of the Council of State, RG 3, LVA.

83. Patrick H. Breen, *The Land Shall Be Deluged in Blood: A New History of the Nat Turner Revolt* (Oxford, 2015), 125–26, 243n49.

84. Joseph C. Robert, *The Road from Monticello: A Study of the Virginia Slavery Debate of 1832* (Durham, NC, 1941); Freehling, *Drift toward Dissolution*, 122–228; Hizer, "Virginia Is Now Divided," 322–79; Eric S. Root, *All Honor to Jefferson? The Virginia Slavery Debates and the Positive Good Thesis* (Lanham, MD, 2008); and Eric S. Root, ed., *Sons of the Fathers: The Virginia Slavery Debates of 1831–1832* (Lanham, MD, 2010).

85. Thomas Nelson Page, *The Negro: The Southerner's Problem* (New York, 1904), 235.

86. Hening, *Statutes*, 3:102–3; *Acts*, 1831–32 Sess., chap. 22.

87. *Acts*, 1832–33 Sess., chap. 12.

88. *Acts*, 1848 Sess., chap. 10.

89. Recorded in Charles H. Ambler, ed., "Diary of John Floyd," *John P. Branch Historical Papers of Randolph-Macon College* 5 (1918): 173.

Chapter 4. The Constitution of 1851

1. Merrill D. Peterson, "Mr. Jefferson's 'Sovereignty of the Living Generation,'" *Virginia Quarterly Review* 52 (1976): 437–47.

2. Hugh Blair Grigsby, *The Virginia Convention of 1829–30* (Richmond, 1854), 94–99.

3. *Richmond Enquirer*, 26 October 1832.

4. *Norfolk and Portsmouth Herald and General Advertiser*, 13 May 1835.

5. Charles Henry Ambler, *Sectionalism in Virginia from 1776 to 1861* (Chicago, 1910), 172–74.

6. Francis Pendleton Gaines, "The Virginia Constitutional Convention of 1850–51: A Study in Sectionalism" (PhD diss., University of Virginia, 1950), esp. 17–22, 73–74; William G. Shade, *Democratizing the Old Dominion: Virginia and the Second Party System, 1824–1861* (Charlottesville, 1996), esp. 262–83; Trenton E. Hizer, "'Virginia Is Now Divided': Politics in the Old Dominion, 1820–1833" (PhD, University of South Carolina, 1997).

7. Ambler, *Sectionalism in Virginia*, 252; *Documents, Containing Statistics of Virginia; Ordered to be Printed by the State Convention Sitting in the City of Richmond, 1850–51*, and *Tables to Accompany Statement A. in the Report of the Committee on the Basis of Representation*, both bound with *Journal, Acts and Proceedings of a General Convention of the State of Virginia, Assembled at Richmond, on Monday, the Fourteenth Day of October, Eighteen Hundred and Fifty* (Richmond, 1850 [i.e., 1851]).

8. Frederic Bancroft, *Slave-Trading in the Old South* (Baltimore, 1931), 384–87.

9. Ambler, *Sectionalism in Virginia*, 224–28, 240–44; Gaines, "Virginia Constitutional Convention," 70–73; Shade, *Democratizing the Old Dominion*, 191–224; Robin Einhorn, *American Taxation, American Slavery* (Chicago, 2006); Tarter, *Grandees*, 191–92, 213–16; Paul E. Herron, *Framing the Solid South: The State Constitutional Conventions of Secession, Reconstruction, and Redemption, 1860–1902* (Lawrence, KS, 2017), 44–64.

10. Tarter, *Grandees*, 137–61, and sources cited 412–15.

11. John Letcher to the editor, 25 June 1858, in *Daily Richmond Enquirer*, 30 June 1858.

12. John J. Zaborney, *Slaves for Hire: Renting Enslaved Laborers in Antebellum Virginia* (Baton Rouge, 2012).

13. Lacy K. Ford, *Deliver us from Evil: The Slavery Question in the Old South* (Oxford, 2009).

14. Gaines, "Virginia Constitutional Convention," 1–18, 42–49, 74–79; Shade, *Democratizing the Old Dominion*, 1–49.

15. Ambler, *Sectionalism in Virginia*, 1–3.

16. Brent Tarter, *Gerrymanders: How Redistricting Has Protected Slavery, White Supremacy, and Partisan Minorities in Virginia* (Charlottesville, 2019), 17–28; *Acts*, 1816–17 Sess., chap. 5; 1827–28 Sess., chap. 4; Constitution of 1830, Article III, Sections 2, 3, and 4.

17. Tarter, *Grandees*, 203–6.

18. Shade, *Democratizing the Old Dominion*, esp. 15–16, 282.

19. *Acts*, 1815–16 Sess., chap. 17; Carter Goodrich, "The Virginia System of Mixed Enterprise: A Study of State Planning of Internal Improvements," *Political Science Quarterly* 44 (1940): 355–86; Tarter, *Grandees*, 175.

20. Ambler, *Sectionalism in Virginia*, 175–85, 237–44; George Brown Oliver, "A Constitutional History of Virginia, 1776–1860" (PhD diss., Duke University, 1959), 122–23.

21. Robert P. Sutton, *Revolution to Secession: Constitution Making in the Old Dominion* (Charlottesville, 1989), 113–14; Peter C. Stewart, "Railroads and Urban Rivalries in Antebellum Eastern Virginia," *VMHB* 81 (1973): 3–22; Ambler, *Sectionalism in Virginia*, 243.

22. Ambler, *Sectionalism in Virginia*, 253–54; Oliver, "Constitutional History," 118–19, 389–91; Earl G. Swem, *A Bibliography of the Conventions and Constitutions of Virginia, Including References to Essays, Letters and Speeches in the Virginia Newspapers*, in *Bulletin of the Virginia State Library* 3 (1910): 396–406.

23. *Proceedings of the Convention* printed with *JHD*, 1842–43 Sess., as Doc. 29.

24. Gaines, "Virginia Constitutional Convention," 84; Oliver, "Constitutional History," 125–33.

25. Gaines, "Virginia Constitutional Convention," 80–82, 85–88; Sutton, *Revolution to Secession*, 111–12.

26. *Acts*, 1849–50 Sess., chap. 8; *Statement Shewing the Data Upon Which Apportionment of Representation, in the Bill Concerning a Convention, Are Based*, House Doc. 40, printed with *JHD*, 1849–50 Sess.; Gaines, "Virginia Constitutional Convention," 89–90; Tarter, *Grandees*, 190.

27. *JHD*, 1849–50 Sess., 261, 340 (quotation); *JS*, 1849–50 Sess., 126.

28. Gaines, "Virginia Constitutional Convention," 296–99, tabulated from incomplete original manuscript returns in Records of the Convention of 1850–51, RG 92, LVA; Sutton, *Revolution to Secession*, 117; Secretary of the Commonwealth, Executive Journal, 1849–1850, RG 13, LVA, 197, without recording vote total.

29. Oliver, "Constitutional History," 142–44; Sutton, *Revolution to Secession*, 120–21.

30. Sutton, *Revolution to Secession*, 207–30; Shade, *Democratizing the Old Dominion*, 269–72.

31. *Journal, Acts and Proceedings*, 75–76.

32. *Journal, Acts and Proceedings, and also Documents, Containing Statistics of Virginia: Ordered to be Printed by the State Convention Sitting in the City of Richmond, 1850–51* (Richmond, 1851).

33. Records of the Convention of 1850–51, RG 92, LVA.

34. Esp., John Janney Papers, University of North Carolina; Ellis-Munford Papers and Smith-Carrington Papers, Duke University; William Cabell Rives Papers, Library of Congress.

35. Gaines, "Virginia Constitutional Convention," 115–20.

36. *Register of the Debates and Proceedings of the Va. Reform Convention* (Richmond, 1851).

37. An index to the supplements is in *DVB* files, LVA.

38. *Journal, Acts and Proceedings*, 5.

39. Frances Leigh Williams, "The Heritage and Preparation of a Statesman, John Young Mason, 1799–1859," *VMHB* 75 (1967): 305–30.

40. *Journal, Acts and Proceedings*, 420–21, quotation on 420.

41. Laura J. Scalia, *America's Jeffersonian Experiment: Remaking State Constitutions, 1820–1850* (DeKalb, IL, 1999), esp. 50–51, 66–69, 73–75, 134–55.

42. Craig M. Simpson, *A Good Southerner: The Life of Henry A. Wise of Virginia* (Chapel Hill, 1985), 80–83; William A. Link, *Roots of Secession: Slavery and Politics in Antebellum Virginia* (Chapel Hill, 2003), 20–21.

43. Gaines, "Virginia Constitutional Convention," 121–226; Oliver, "Constitutional History," 389–408; Sutton, *Revolution to Secession*, 129–34; Link, *Roots of Secession*, 13–24.

44. Gaines, Virginia Constitutional Convention," 227–51; Oliver, "Constitutional History of Virginia," 439–41; Sutton, *Revolution to Secession*, 134–36.

45. Constitution of 1830, Article III, Section 15.

46. Ambler, *Sectionalism in Virginia*, 261–66; Gaines, "Virginia Constitutional Convention," 121–226; Oliver, "Constitutional History of Virginia," 149–50, 389–408; Sutton, *Revolution to Secession*, 111–12, 129–34.

47. Tarter, *Gerrymanders*, 29–39; cf. the different tabulation in Gaines, "Virginia Constitutional Convention," 211.

48. Constitution of 1830, Article III, Section 6; Constitution of 1851, Article IV, Sections 13 and 14.

49. Gaines, "Virginia Constitutional Convention," 252–57; Sutton, *Revolution to Secession*, 127–28; James E. Pate, "Constitutional Revision in Virginia Affecting the Gen-

eral Assembly," *WMQ*, 2nd ser., 10 (1930): 105–22, contains almost no useful analysis of the Constitution of 1851.

50. Constitution of 1830, Article III, Section 7.

51. Silvana R. Siddali, *Frontier Democracy: Constitutional Conventions in the Old Northwest* (New York, 2016), 347–77.

52. *McCulloch v. The State of Maryland*, 17 US 316 (1819), quotation on 431.

53. Richard L. Morton, "The Virginia State Debt and Internal Improvements, 1820–38," *Journal of Political Economy* 25 (1917): 339–73.

54. Benjamin Ulysses Ratchford, *American State Debts* (Durham, NC, 1941), 124, 133.

55. Thomas E. Buckley, SJ, *Establishing Religious Freedom: Jefferson's Statute in Virginia* (Charlottesville, 2013), 68, 70–72, 78–81, 215–20; Mathew D. Staver and Anita L. Staver, "Disestablishmentarianism Collides with the First Amendment: The Ghost of Thomas Jefferson Still Haunts Churches," *Cumberland Law Review* 33 (2002): 43–105.

56. Thomas E. Buckley, SJ, "'A Great Religious Octopus': Church and State at Virginia's Constitutional Convention, 1901–1902," *Church History* 72 (2003): 333–60.

57. Oliver, "Constitutional History," 190; Sutton, *Revolution to Secession*, 124–25.

58. *JHD*, 1852 Sess., 44, 54.

59. *JHD*, 1850–51 Sess., 404–5.

60. Gaines, "Virginia Constitutional Convention," 267–69; Oliver, "Constitutional History," 318–22; Kermit L. Hall, "The Judiciary on Trial: State Constitutional Reform and the Rise of an Elected Judiciary, 1846–1860," *Historian* 45 (1983): 337–54; Scalia, *America's Jeffersonian Experiment*, 69–110, esp. 71–72; Siddali, *Frontier Democracy*, 170–99.

61. *Acts*, 1830–31 Sess., chap. 4.

62. Margaret Virginia Nelson, *A Study of Judicial Review in Virginia, 1789–1928* (New York, 1947), 40–45.

63. David A. Sutelan and Wayne R. Spencer, "The Virginia Special Court of Appeals: Constitutional Relief for an Overburdened Court," *William and Mary Law Review* 8 (1967): 244–76, esp. 247–54; Thomas R. Morris, *The Virginia Supreme Court, An Institutional and Political Analysis* (Charlottesville, 1975), 36, 64–64n. 13, 68.

64. *Acts*, 1847–48 Sess., chap. 68.

65. *Sharpe v. Robertson*, 46 Va (5 Grattan) 518 (1849), quotation on 518.

66. *Sharpe v. Robertson*, 46 Va (5 Grattan) 518 (1849).

67. West Virginia Constitution of 1863, Article VI, Section 9.

68. Gaines, "Virginia Constitutional Convention," 269–76; Oliver, "Constitutional History," 364–68.

69. Albert O. Porter, *County Government in Virginia, A Legislative History, 1607–1904* (New York, 1947), 227–41.

70. *Journal, Acts and Proceedings*, 419.

71. Gaines, "Virginia Constitutional Convention," 281–85.

72. Gaines, "Virginia Constitutional Convention," 279–85.

73. Gaines, "Virginia Constitutional Convention," 286–87, 306–9, tabulated from official returns in Records of the Convention of 1850–51.

74. Gaines, "Virginia Constitutional Convention," 296–309.

75. *JHD*, 1852 Sess., 44, 54.

76. Michael J. Dubin, *United States Presidential Elections, 1788–1860: The Official Results by County and State* (Jefferson, NC, 2002), 114, 133; Shade, *Democratizing the Old Dominion*, 108.

77. Ambler, *Sectionalism in Virginia*, 300–38; Shade, *Democratizing the Old Dominion*, 283–91, with 1860 statistics on 285; Link, *Roots of Secession*.

78. John E. Stealey III, *West Virginia's Civil War–Era Constitution: Loyal Revolution, Confederate Counter-Revolution, and the Convention of 1872* (Kent, OH, 2013), 34–35; Tarter, *Grandees*, 213–16; Adam J. Zucconi, "'Preserve Us From Such Democracy': Politics, Slavery, and Political Culture in Antebellum Northwest Virginia, 1850–1861," *VMHB* 123 (2015): 324–54.

79. Stealey, *West Virginia's Civil War–Era Constitution*, 40–67; Tarter, *Grandees*, 214–16; for one instance, see Brent Tarter, *Daydreams and Nightmares, A Virginia Family Faces Secession and War* (Charlottesville, 2015), 46–50, 78.

80. George H. Reese, ed., *Proceedings of the Virginia State Convention of 1861*, 4 vols. (Richmond, 1965), 4:545; Roman J. Hoyos, "Peaceful Revolution and Popular Sovereignty: Reassessing the Constitutionality of Southern Secession," in *Signposts: New Directions in Southern Legal History*, ed. Sally E. Hadden and Patricia Hagler Minter (Athens, GA, 2013), 241–64; Herron, *Framing the Solid South*, 83–94.

81. Attested enrolled copy, Ordinances of the Convention of 1861, No. 39, RG 93, LVA.

82. Certificate of the secretary of the commonwealth, 14 June 1861, Secretary of the Commonwealth Executive Journal (1861), 234, also printed in *Daily Richmond Enquirer*, 18 June 1861 and several other state newspapers; Tarter, *Grandees*, 216.

83. Henry Thomas Shanks, "Conservative Constitutional Tendencies of the Virginia Secession Convention," in *Essays in Southern History*, ed. Fletcher Melvin Green (Chapel Hill, 1949), 28–48; constitution printed as last document in vol. 3 of *Journals and Papers of the Virginia State Convention of 1861*, 3 vols. (Richmond, 1866, 1966).

84. *Journal and Papers of the Virginia State Convention of 1861*, 1:441–2.

85. Secretary of the Commonwealth Executive Journal, RG 3, LVA (1862), 120.

86. Tarter, *Grandees*, 223–28.

87. James G. Randall, *Constitutional Problems under Lincoln* rev. ed., (1926; repr., Urbana, IL, 1951), 433–61; Victor Langford, "Constitutional Issues Raised by West Virginia's Admission into the Union," *West Virginia History* 2 (1940): 12–35; Sheldon Winston, "Statehood for West Virginia an Illegal Act?" *West Virginia History* 30 (1969): 530–34; Vasan Kesavan and Michael Stokes Paulsen, "Is West Virginia Unconstitutional?" *California Law Review* 90 (2002): 291–400, esp. 301–25.

88. Virgil A. Lewis, ed., *How West Virginia Was Made: Proceedings of the First Convention of the People of Northwestern Virginia at Wheeling May 13, 14, and 15 1861, and the Journal of the Second Convention of the People of Northwestern Virginia at Wheeling, Which Assembled, June 11th, 1861, and Continued in Session until June 25th, Adjourned until August 6th, 1861, Reassembled on that Date, and Continued in Session Until August 21st, When it Adjourned sine die, With Appendices and an Introduction, Annotations and Addenda* (Charleston, WV, 1909).

89. Charles H. Ambler, Frances Haney Atwood, and William B. Mathews, eds., *Debates and Proceedings of the First Constitutional Convention of West Virginia (1861–1863)*, 3 vols. (Huntington, WV, 1939), with text of Constitution and schedule at 3:859–888, and ratification votes on 1:44, 57; Robert M. Bastress, *The West Virginia State Constitution* (Oxford, 2011), 12–17; Stealey, *West Virginia's Civil War-Era Constitution*, 72–106.

90. John E. Stealey III, "West Virginia's Constitutional Critique of Virginia: The Revolution of 1861–1863," *Civil War History* 57 (2011): 9–47; Stealey, *West Virginia's Civil War-Era Constitution*, 72–106.

Chapter 5. The Constitution of 1864

1. Virginius Dabney, *Virginia, The New Dominion* (Garden City, NY, 1971); Ronald L. Heinemann et al., *Old Dominion, New Commonwealth: A History of Virginia, 1607–2007* (Charlottesville, 2007); Peter Wallenstein, *Cradle of America: Four Centuries of Virginia History* (Lawrence, KS, 2007), although the constitution is very briefly mentioned in the second edition (Lawrence, KS, 2014), 198. See, however, Brent Tarter, *Virginians and Their Histories* (Charlottesville, 2020), 260–62.

2. Richard G. Lowe, *Republicans and Reconstruction in Virginia, 1856–70* (Charlottesville, 1991), 21–23; Sara B. Bearss, "'Restored and Vindicated': The Virginia Constitutional Convention of 1864," *VMHB* 122 (2014): 156–81.

3. *Acts*, 1863 Richmond Sess., chap. 57.

4. Bearss, "'Restored and Vindicated,'" 157–58.

5. Virgil A. Lewis, ed., *How West Virginia Was Made: Proceedings of the First Convention of the People of Northwestern Virginia at Wheeling May 13, 14, and 15 1861, and the Journal of the Second Convention of the People of Northwestern Virginia at Wheeling, Which Assembled, June 11th, 1861, and Continued in Session until June 25th, Adjourned until August 6th, 1861, Reassembled on that Date, and Continued in Session Until August 21st, When it Adjourned sine die, With Appendices and an Introduction, Annotations and Addenda* (Charleston, WV, 1909), 37–38.

6. Wheeling *Daily Intelligencer*, 21 June 1861; Brent Tarter, "'If the ritual doesn't change, the times do': Swearing in Virginia's Governors," *Virginia Cavalcade* 50 (2001): 168–77.

7. Tarter, *Grandees*, 219–20.

8. Abraham Lincoln to the Senate and House of Representatives, 4 July 1861, *Congressional Globe*, 37th Cong., 1st Sess., Appendix 2.

9. Lowe, *Republicans and Reconstruction*, 12–16.

10. Edward S. Evans, *The Seals of Virginia* (Richmond, 1911), 39–40, and illustration, 17; also published as a part of the official *Report of the Virginia State Library for the Year 1909–1910* (Richmond, 1911).

11. Charles Henry Ambler, *Francis H. Pierpont, Union War Governor and Father of West Virginia* (Chapel Hill, 1937), 213–46; Robert Nelson Anderson, "The City of Alexandria—One Time Capital of Virginia," *Arlington Historical Magazine* 3 (October 1968): 35–52.

12. Bearss, "'Restored and Vindicated,'" 159–60.

13. Constitution of 1851, Article IV, Section 21.
14. Ambler, *Pierpont*, 30, 34–42, 160, 201, 219.
15. *JHD*, 1863–64 Alexandria Sess., 15–16.
16. *Acts*, 1863–64 Alexandria Sess., chap. 2
17. Bearss, "'Restored and Vindicated,'" 165–66.
18. *Daily Richmond Enquirer*, 24 December 1860.
19. *Journal of the Constitutional Convention Which Convened at Alexandria on the 13th Day of February, 1864* (Alexandria, 1864), 3–4.
20. Bearss, "Restored and Vindicated," 166–69.
21. *Journal of the Constitutional Convention*, 4; Bearss, "Restored and Vindicated," 169.
22. *Journal of the Constitutional Convention; Constitution of the State of Virginia, and the Ordinances Adopted by the Convention which Assembled at Alexandria, on the 13th Day of February, 1864* (Alexandria, 1864).
23. Records of the Virginia Convention of 1864, RG 95, LVA.
24. Virginia Historical Society old catalog record Mss13:1864 Apr 7:1.
25. *New York Times*, 11 March 1864.
26. Constitution of 1869, Article XI, Section 4, para. 4.
27. Catherine M. Jones, "More than a Contract, Less than a Right: Regulating Marriage in Postwar Virginia, 1865–1885" (unpublished paper, 2018).
28. Constitution of 1830, Article II, Section 14.
29. Constitution of 1851, Article III, Section 1.
30. Constitution of 1851, Article IV, Section 5; Brent Tarter, *Gerrymanders: How Redistricting Has Protected Slavery, White Supremacy, and Partisan Minorities in Virginia* (Charlottesville, 2019), 29–39.
31. Constitution of 1830, Article III, Section 6; Constitution of 1851, Article III, Section 14.
32. Constitution of 1851, Article IV, Section 8.
33. Brent Tarter, *A Saga of the New South: Race, Law, and Public Debt in Virginia* (Charlottesville, 2016), 13–14, 18, 153–73.
34. Richard L. Morton, "The Virginia State Debt and Internal Improvements, 1820–38," *Journal of Political Economy* 25 (1917): 339–73; Carter Goodrich, "The Virginia System of Mixed Enterprise: A Study of State Planning of Internal Improvements," *Political Science Quarterly* 44 (1940): 355–86; Tarter, *Saga of the New South*, 11–14.
35. *Journal of the Convention*, 46–47; Bearss, "Restored and Vindicated," 170–71.
36. *Journal of the Convention*, 46; Bearss, "Restored and Vindicated," 171.
37. *Journal of the Convention*, 49.
38. *Journal of the Convention*, 50; Bearss, "Restored and Vindicated," 171.
39. *Journal of the Convention*, 51–52.
40. *Journal of the House of Representatives*, 37th Cong., 2d Sess., 47, 379, 490.
41. *JHD*, 1864–65 Alexandria Sess., 21.
42. *Journal of the Senate*, 38th Cong., 2d Sess., 15, 148–50.

43. *JS*, 1864–65 Alexandria Sess., 127–29; *JHD*, 1864–65 Alexandria Sess., 54–56; Brent Tarter, "Thirteenth Amendment to the U.S. Constitution," *EV* (2014).

44. *Alexandria Gazette*, 15 June 1865.

45. Janet L. Coryell, "Botts, John Minor," *DVB*, 1:114–17.

46. *Alexandria Gazette*, 15 June 1865.

47. Hamilton J. Eckenrode, *The Political History of Virginia during Reconstruction* (Baltimore, 1904), 22.

48. William A. Anderson, "Virginia Constitutions," *Virginia State Bar Association Proceedings* 13 (1900), 160.

49. Ralph C. McDanel, *The Virginia Constitutional Convention of 1901–1902* (Baltimore, 1928), 122.

50. E.g., William F. Swindler, *Government by the People: Theory and Reality in Virginia* (Charlottesville, 1969), 46; A. E. Dick Howard, *Commentaries on the Constitution of Virginia*, 2 vols. (Charlottesville, 1974), 1:14; John Dinan, *The Virginia State Constitution*, rev. 2nd ed. (Westport, CT, Oxford, 2014), 19; and Paul E. Herron, *Framing the Solid South: The State Constitutional Conventions of Secession, Reconstruction, and Redemption, 1860–1902* (Lawrence, KS, 2017), 136–37.

51. E. Lee Shepard, "Brockenbrough, John White," *DVB*, 2:253–55.

52. Undated legal brief of John White Brockenbrough filed with suit papers in *Elijah R. Walker v. William H. Loving*, Nelson Co. Chancery Causes, 1871-079, LVA.

53. George W. Munford, comp., *Third Edition of the Code of Virginia Including Legislation to January 1, 1874* (Richmond, 1873), esp. 18–21, 23–24, quotation on 18.

54. John B. Minor, *Institutes of Common and Statute Law*, rev. 3rd ed., 4 vols. (Richmond, 1882), 1:191–92.

55. Ambler, *Pierpont*, 261–83; Lowe, *Republicans and Reconstruction*, 23–35; Virginia Case Files for United States Pardons (1865–1867), United States Office of the Adjutant General, RG 94, National Archives and Records Administration.

56. *Acts*, 1865 extra Sess., chap. 6.

57. *Acts*, 1865 extra Sess., chap. 7.

58. *Acts*, 1865 extra Sess., chap. 1.

59. Lowe, *Republicans and Reconstruction*, 24–49; Alan B. Bromberg, "The Virginia Congressional Elections of 1865, A Test of Southern Loyalty," *VMHB* 84 (1976): 75–98.

60. *JHD*, 1865–66 Sess., 30.

61. *Acts*, 1865–66 Sess., chap. 86.

62. Enrolled Bills, 1865–66 Sess., chap. 131, Records of the General Assembly, RG 78, LVA.

63. *Acts*, 1865–66 Sess., chap. 69.

64. John O. Peters, "New Law for a Shocking New Reality" (unpublished paper 2017).

65. *Acts*, 1865–66 Sess., chaps. 84, 85.

66. *Virginia v. West Virginia*, 78 US (11 Wallace) 39 (1871).

67. *JHD*, 1865–66 Sess., 388–90.

68. *JHD*, 1866–67 Sess., 69, 79.

69. Tarter, *Saga of the New South*, 17–18.

70. Constitution of 1851, Article IV, Section 36; *Acts*, 1865–66 Sess., chap. 18.

71. *JHD*, 1864–65 Alexandria Sess., 11–12.

72. Brent Tarter, "The Cohabitation Act of 1866," *EV* (2015); Jones, "More Than a Contract, Less Than a Right."

73. Constitution of 1869, Article XI, Section 7, para. 3.

74. *The Code of Virginia* (Richmond, 1860), 724.

75. *JHD*, 1864–65 Alexandria Sess., 8–9.

76. Brent Tarter, "African Americans and Politics in Virginia, 1865–1902," and "Conference with President Andrew Johnson (June 16, 1865)," both *EV* (2015).

77. *Acts*, 1865–66 Sess., chap. 28; Brent Tarter, "The Vagrancy Act of 1866," *EV* (2015).

78. *Daily Richmond Whig*, 26 January 1866; Tarter, "Vagrancy Act."

79. *JS*, 1866–67 Sess., 101–3; *JHD*, 1866–67 Sess., 101–2.

80. Dan T. Carter, *When the War Was Over: The Failure of Self-Reconstruction in the South, 1865–1867* (Baton Rouge, 1985).

81. 39th Cong., 2d Sess., chap. 63.

82. Brent Tarter, "The First Military District," *EV* (2015).

83. William Thomas Alderson, "The Influence of Military Rule and the Freedmen's Bureau on Reconstruction in Virginia, 1865–1870" (PhD diss., Vanderbilt University, 1952).

84. *Luther v. Borden*, 48 US (7 Howard) 1 (1849).

85. *Texas v. White*, 74 US (7 Wallace) 700 (1868), quotation on 725.

86. Constitution of 1851, Article VI, Section 11; Constitution of 1864, Article VI, Section 11.

87. *Ex Parte Lawhorne* 59 VA (18 Grattan) 90 (1868).

88. 60 Va (19 Grattan) 543–668.

89. *Acts* 1870 Sess., chap. 18.

90. *Acts* 1870 Sess., chap. 11.

91. *Acts* 1870 Sess., chap. 18.

92. *Griffin's Executor v. Cunningham and Washington*, and *Alexandria & Georgetown R. R. Co. v. Alexandria & Washington R.R. Co., et al.*, decided together 14 November 1870 and motion for rehearing denied 13 March 1871 on the same grounds, 61 Va (20 Grattan) 31 (1870, 1871).

93. Computed from *Eighth Census*, 4 vols. (Washington, DC, 1864–66), 1:518, and *Ninth Census*, 4 vols. (Washington, DC, 1872), 1:4–5.

Chapter 6. The Constitution of 1869

1. Records of the Convention of 1867–68, RG 96, LVA.

2. Armistead R. Long, *The Constitution of Virginia: An Annotated Edition* (Lynchburg, 1901), 3.

3. 41st Cong., 1st Sess., chap. 10.

4. *Acts*, 1870 Sess., chap. 18.

5. Described in *Equal Suffrage. Address from the Colored Citizens of Norfolk Va., to the People of the United States* . . . (New Bedford, MA, 1865), 9; Michael Hucles, "Many Voices, Similar Concerns: Traditional Methods of African-American Political Activity in Norfolk, Virginia, 1865–1875," *VMHB* 100 (1992): 543–66.

6. *Equal Suffrage*, 10.

7. *Equal Suffrage*, 10–15.

8. *Equal Suffrage*, 1, 4.

9. Brent Tarter, "African Americans and Politics in Virginia, 1865–1902," *EV* (2015).

10. *Richmond Times*, 7 June 1865; *New-York Tribune*, 17 June 1865; LeRoy P. Graf, et al., eds., *The Papers of Andrew Johnson* (Knoxville, 1967–2000) 8:210–13; John Thomas O'Brien Jr., "Reconstruction in Richmond: White Restoration and Black Protest, April–June 1865," *VMHB* 89 (1981): 259–81; Brent Tarter, "Conference with President Andrew Johnson (June 16, 1865)," *EV* (2015).

11. Philip S. Foner and George E. Walker, eds., *Proceedings of the Black State Conventions, 1840–1865* (1979–80), 2:258–76, quotation on 262.

12. *Proceedings and Debates of the Virginia State Convention, of 1829-30* (Richmond, 1830), 25–31.

13. Richard G. Lowe, *Republicans and Reconstruction in Virginia, 1856–70* (Charlottesville, 1991), 22–24; Brent Tarter, "The Republican Party of Virginia in the Nineteenth Century," *EV* (2014).

14. Charles Henry Ambler, *Francis H. Pierpont, Union War Governor and Father of West Virginia* (Chapel Hill, 1937), 261–83; Lowe, *Republicans and Reconstruction*, 23–35; Virginia Case Files for United States Pardons (1865–67), United States Office of the Adjutant General, RG 94, National Archives and Records Administration.

15. Ambler, *Pierpont*, 261–83.

16. Lowe, *Republicans and Reconstruction*, 35–41; Tarter, "African Americans and Politics."

17. *Daily Richmond Whig*, 6 July 1865.

18. Ambler, *Pierpont*, 287–88.

19. 39th Cong., 2d Sess., chap. 63.

20. Jack P. Maddex Jr., *The Virginia Conservatives, 1867–1879: A Study in Reconstruction Politics* (Chapel Hill, 1970); Brent Tarter, "The Conservative Party of Virginia," *EV* (2014).

21. Acts of 2 and 23 March and a joint resolution of 19 July 1867, 39th Cong., 2d Sess., chap. 63, 40th Cong., 1st Sess., chap. 6, and Joint Res. 40.

22. *Consolidated List of Persons Registered as Voters in the State of Virginia*, printed as Doc. 5 in *Documents of the Constitutional Convention of the State of Virginia* (Richmond, 1867), 51–52.

23. *Acts*, 1827–28 Sess. chap. 24; *Acts*, 1849–50 Sess., chap. 8; *Acts*, 1865 extra Sess., chap. 1.

24. *Consolidated Vote of the State of Virginia at the Election Held October 22, 1867,*

printed as Doc. 5 in *Documents of the Constitutional Convention of the State of Virginia*, 53–56.

25. Secretary of the Commonwealth MS Election Records, Acc. 50706, RG 13, LVA; for an analysis of the voting in one county see Daniel W. Crofts, *Old Southampton: Politics and Society in a Virginia County, 1834–1869* (Charlottesville, 1992), 243–57, 355–56.

26. Brent Tarter, "John C. Underwood (1809–1873)," *EV* (2015).

27. Matthew S. Gottlieb, "James W. Hunnicutt (1814–1880)," *EV* (2015); Steven E. Nash "'The Devil Let Loose Generally': James W. Hunnicutt's Conceptualization of the Union in Fredericksburg," *VMHB* 126 (2018): 334–65.

28. Richard G. Lowe, "Virginia's Reconstruction Convention: General Schofield Rates the Delegates," *VMHB* 80 (1972): 341–60; Richard L. Hume, "The Membership of the Virginia Constitutional Convention of 1867–1868: A Study of the Beginnings of Congressional Reconstruction in the Upper South," *VMHB* 86 (1978): 461–84.

29. *Journal of the Constitutional Convention of the State of Virginia* (Richmond, 1868), 4.

30. Richmond *Daily Whig*, 6 December 1867; *Frank Leslie's Illustrated Newspaper* 25 (15 February 1868): 345–46.

31. *Richmond Times-Dispatch*, 27 January 1968.

32. Cynthia Miller Leonard, *The General Assembly of Virginia, July 30, 1619–January 11, 1978* (Richmond, 1978), 749, 755.

33. Lowe, "Virginia's Reconstruction Convention."

34. Biographies of all of them in *EV* and *DVB* online.

35. E.g., Richmond *Southern Opinion*, 7, 21 December 1867, 15 February, 28 March 1868.

36. Richmond *Southern Opinion*, 21 December 1867.

37. Raleigh Travers Daniel, "Conservative Party State Committee Circular No. 4," 12 February 1868, broadside, LVA.

38. Richmond *Daily Examiner and Inquirer*, 11, 12 December 1867.

39. E.g., Richmond *Daily Dispatch*, 11 December 1867.

40. *Journal of the Constitutional Convention*; *Documents of the Constitutional Convention of the State of Virginia* (Richmond, 1868).

41. *Debates and Proceedings of the Constitutional Convention of the State of Virginia* (Richmond, 1868).

42. Paul E. Herron, *Framing the Solid South: The State Constitutional Conventions of Secession, Reconstruction, and Redemption, 1860–1902* (Lawrence, KS, 2017), 69–184, with some reservations inasmuch as the author did not yet have access to, or did not consult, some then new scholarship that significantly changed the Virginia and West Virginia narratives.

43. 39th Cong., 1st Sess., chap. 31.

44. Laura A. Free, *Suffrage Reconstructed: Gender, Race, and Voting Rights in the Civil War Era* (Ithaca, NY, 2015).

45. Sandra Gioia Treadway, "A Most Brilliant Woman: Anna Whitehead Bodeker and the First Woman Suffrage Association in Virginia," *Virginia Cavalcade* 43 (1994): 166–77.

46. *Debates and Proceedings*, 467.

47. Elsa Barkley Brown, "To Catch the Vision of Freedom: Reconstructing Southern Black Women's Political History, 1865–1880," in *African American Women and the Vote, 1837–1965*, ed. Ann D. Gordon et al. (Amherst, 1997), 66–99, on 73–80.

48. Catherine M. Jones, "More than a Contract, Less than a Right: Regulating Marriage in Postwar Virginia, 1865–1885" (unpublished paper, 2018).

49. Brent Tarter, "When 'Kind and Thrifty Husbands' Are Not Enough: Some Thoughts on the Legal Status of Women in Virginia," *Magazine of Virginia Genealogy* 33 (1995): 79–101.

50. *Proceedings of the Constitutional Convention of South Carolina* (Charleston, SC, 1868), quotation on 785–86; Suzanne D. Lebsock, "Radical Reconstruction and the Property Rights of Southern Women," *Journal of Southern History* 43 (1977): 195–216.

51. *Acts* 1877 Sess., chap. 329; Tarter, "When 'Kind and Thrifty Husbands' Are Not Enough"; Laura F. Edwards, "The Material Conditions of Dependency: The Hidden History of Free Women's Control of Property in the Early Nineteenth-Century South," in *Signposts: New Directions in Southern Legal History*, ed. Sally E. Hadden and Patricia Hagler Minter (Athens, GA, 2013), 171–92; Jones, "More Than a Contract, Less Than a Right."

52. William G. Shade, *Democratizing the Old Dominion: Virginia and the Second Party System, 1824–1861* (Charlottesville, 1996); Tarter, *Grandees*, 172–75, 190–93.

53. Attested enrolled Constitution in Records of the Convention of 1867–68; *The Constitution of Virginia Framed by the Convention Which Met in Richmond, Virginia, on Tuesday, December 3, 1867* (Richmond, 1868).

54. Tarter, *Grandees*, 206–14.

55. Constitution of 1830, Article III, Section 14; Constitution of 1851, Article III, Section 1; Constitution of 1864, Article III, Section 1.

56. Constitution of 1851, Article IV, Section 8.

57. Constitution of 1864, Article IV, Section 8.

58. Constitution of 1864, Article IV, Section 6.

59. Hening, *Statutes*, 1:378; E. G. Swem, "The Disqualification of Ministers in State Constitutions," *WMQ*, 1st ser., 26 (1917): 73–78.

60. *Debates and Proceedings*, 458–61.

61. Thomas M. Cooley, *A Treatise on the Constitutional Limitations Which Rest upon the Legislative Power of the States of the American Union* (Boston, 1868), esp. 9–10, 88, 90.

62. B. A. Glasrud, "African American Militia Units in Virginia (1870–1899)," *EV* (2015).

63. Constitution of 1864, Article VI, Section 1.

64. Constitution of 1851, Article VI, Section 11; Constitution of 1864, Article VI, Section 11.

65. David K. Suelan and Wayne R. Spencer, "The Virginia Special Court of Appeals: Constitutional Relief for an Overburdened Court," *William and Mary Law Review* 8 (1967): 244–76, on 263–67.

66. "A Special Court of Appeals," *Virginia Law Journal* 10 (1886): 62.

67. *Report of the Ninth Annual Meeting of the Virginia State Bar Association* 10 (Richmond, 1897), 27.

68. *Report of the Proceedings and Debates of the Constitutional Convention State of Virginia Held in the City of Richmond June 12, 1901, to June 26, 1902*, 2 vols. (Richmond, 1906), 1:1361–62.

69. Constitution of 1851, Article IV, Section 38; Constitution of 1864, Article IV, Section 35.

70. *Burks v. Hinton*, 77 Va 1 (1883).

71. Margaret Virginia Nelson, *A Study of Judicial Review in Virginia, 1789–1928* (New York, 1947), 117–20; cf. W. Hamilton Bryson, "Judicial Independence in Virginia," *University of Richmond Law Review* 38 (2004): 705–20.

72. John O. Peters, "Virginia's Readjuster Judges, Guilt by Association (unpublished paper, 2016).

73. Constitution of 1902, Section VI, Article 96.

74. Albert O. Porter, *County Government in Virginia, A Legislative History, 1607–1904* (New York, 1947), 241–303.

75. Thomas Jefferson to Henry Tompkinson, i.e., Samuel Kercheval, 12 July 1816, in J. Jefferson Looney et al., eds., *The Papers of Thomas Jefferson: Retirement Series* (Princeton, 2004–), 10:225.

76. Constitution of 1851, Article VI, Section 19.

77. Richard Lee Morton, *The Negro in Virginia Politics, 1865–1902* (Charlottesville, 1919); Luther Porter Jackson, *Negro Office-Holders in Virginia, 1865–1895* (Norfolk, 1945); Charles Wynes, *Race Relations in Virginia, 1870–1902* (Charlottesville, 1961); Joseph P. Harahan, "Politics, Political Parties, and Voter Participation in Tidewater Virginia during Reconstruction, 1865–1900" (PhD diss., University of Michigan, 1973); Tarter, "African Americans and Politics."

78. Porter, *County Government in Virginia*, 242–303, with statistics on 301–3.

79. Marianne E. Julienne and Brent Tarter, "Establishment of the Public School System in Virginia," *EV* (2016).

80. *Journal of the Convention*, 333–34.

81. *JS*, 1869–70 Sess., 485, 489, 507; *JHD*, 1869–70 Sess., 606–7, 615; Julienne and Tarter, "Establishment of the Public School System in Virginia."

82. *Acts*, 1869–70 Sess., chap. 259.

83. J. L. Blair Buck, *The Development of Public Schools in Virginia, 1607–1952* (Richmond, 1952), 65–93; Walter J. Fraser Jr., "William Henry Ruffner and the Establishment of Virginia's Public School System, 1870–1874," *VMHB* 79 (1971): 259–79; Marianne E. Julienne, "William Henry Ruffner (1824–1908)," *EV* (2014).

84. Tarter, *Saga of the New South*, 12–14, 17, 145–74.

85. Paul Goodman, "The Emergence of Homestead Exemption in the United States: Accommodation and Resistance to the Market Revolution, 1840–1880," *Journal of American History* 80 (1993): 470–98; James W. Ely Jr., "Homestead Exemption and Southern Legal Culture," in *Signposts: New Directions in Southern Legal History*, 289–316; Silvana R. Siddali, *Frontier Democracy: Constitutional Conventions in the Old Northwest* (New York, 2016), 236–38.

86. *Acts*, 1866 Sess., chap. 68.
87. *Acts*, 1866–67 Sess., chap. 139.
88. *Acts*, 1870 Sess., chap. 157.
89. *The Homestead Cases* 63 Va (22 Grattan) 266 (1872), quotation on 301.
90. George W. Munford, comp., *Third Edition of the Code of Virginia: Including Legislation to January 1, 1874*, rev. ed. (Richmond, 1873), 1168–78; M. P. Burks, "Homestead Exemptions," *Virginia Law Register* 2 (1896): 167–82.
91. *Acts*, 1866–67 Sess., chap. 210.
92. Nancy A. Hillman, "Drawn Together, Drawn Apart: Black and White Baptists in Tidewater Virginia, 1800–1875" (PhD diss., College of William and Mary, 2013), 295–396.
93. *Acts*, 1865–66 Sess., chap. 18; Brent Tarter, "Cohabitation Act of 1866" *EV* (2015).
94. *Journal*, 389.
95. John C. Underwood to editor, *Washington Chronicle*, 7 January 1868 [sic], reprinted in *New York Times*, 10 January 1869.
96. Tarter, "John C. Underwood"; *Annual Report of the Joint Committee on the State Library* printed as Doc. No. 13 with *JS*, 1872–73; *New York Times*, 22 February 1873; see also, Marianne E. Julienne and Brent Tarter, "The Virginia Ordinance of Secession: A Research Note on Contemporary Copies," *VMHB* 119 (2011): 154–81, on 155–59.
97. Ordinance printed with *Constitution of Virginia*, 40–41.
98. Ordinance printed with *Constitution of Virginia*, 39–40.
99. James L. McDonough, "John Schofield as Military Director of Reconstruction in Virginia," *Civil War History* 15 (1969): 237–56; Brent Tarter, "First Military District," *EV* (2015).
100. Richmond *Daily Dispatch*, 18 April 1868.
101. Maddex, *Virginia Conservatives*, 60–66; Lowe, *Republicans and Reconstruction*, 148–55.
102. Alexander F. Robertson, *Alexander Hugh Holmes Stuart* (Richmond, 1925), 272–77, 278–85, and including the important documents, on 430–45, 448–56; Maddex, *Virginia Conservatives* 67–73; Lowe, *Republicans and Reconstruction*, 159–63.
103. 41st Cong., 1st Sess., chap. 17; *The Statutes at Large and Proclamations of the United States of America, from December 1869 to March 1871* (Boston, 1871), Appendix, 1125–26.
104. *General Orders and Circulars, Headquarters First Military District, 1869* (Richmond, 1870), 3–7.
105. *Richmond Daily Whig* and *Richmond Dispatch*, both 22 September 1869.
106. *JS*, 1869 special Sess., 27–28; *JHD*, 1869 special Sess., 36.
107. 41st Cong., 1st Sess., chap. 10.
108. *Texas v. White*, 74 US (7 Wallace) 700 (1868).
109. 41st Cong., 1st Sess., chap. 10.
110. Richmond *Daily Dispatch*, 28 January 1870.
111. Richmond *Daily Dispatch*, 28 January 1870.
112. *Acts*, 1870 Sess., chap. 18.
113. *Acts*, 1870–71 Sess., chap. 282.

114. Tarter, *Saga of the New South*, 22–28.

115. Allen W. Moger, "Railroad Practices and Policies in Virginia after the Civil War," *VMHB* 59 (1951): 423–57, esp. 425–26, 437–38; Robert K. Burton, "History of Taxation in Virginia, 1870–1901" (Phd diss., University of Virginia, 1962), 128–30; George Harrison Gilliam, "Building a Modern South: Political Economy in Nineteenth-Century Virginia" (PhD diss., University of Virginia, 2013), 200–15, 276–85.

116. This and the following four paragraphs follow Tarter, *Saga of the New South*, 22–81.

117. *Antoni v. Wright* and *Smith v. Wright*, 62 Va (21 Grattan) 833 (1872); Tarter, *Saga of the New South*, 29–32.

118. Tarter, *Grandees*, 256–65; Tarter, *Saga of the New South*, 79–81.

119. Jacob N. Brenaman, *A History of Virginia Conventions* (Richmond, 1902), 122.

120. *Acts*, 1872–73 Sess., chap. 336.

121. Tarter, "African Americans and Politics."

122. Pippa Holloway, "'A Chicken-Stealer Shall Lose His Vote': Disfranchisement for Larceny in the South, 1874–1890," *Journal of Southern History* 75 (2009): 931–62; Pippa Holloway, *Living in Infamy: Felon Disfranchisement and the History of American Citizenship* (New York, 2014).

123. Tarter, *Saga of the New South*, 40–41; Tarter, "African Americans in Politics in Virginia."

124. Constitution of 1851, Article IV, Section 8; Constitution of 1864, Article IV, Section 8; Constitution of 1869, Article V, Section 6.

125. This and the following four paragraphs are based on Charles E. Wynes, *Race Relations in Virginia, 1870–1902* (Charlottesville, 1961); Ronald E. Shibley, "Election Laws and Electoral Practices in Virginia, 1867–1902: An Administrative and Political History" (PhD diss., University of Virginia, 1972), esp. 60–214; Wythe Holt, *Virginia's Constitutional Convention of 1901–1902* (New York, 1990); Tarter, *Grandees*, 262–65; Tarter, "African Americans and Politics"; Tarter, "The Republican Party in the Nineteenth Century," *EV* (2014).

126. *Acts*, 1884 Sess., chap. 158.

127. *Acts*, 1893–94 Sess., chap. 746.

128. Shibley, "Election Laws and Electoral Practices in Virginia," esp. 60–215; Holt, *Virginia's Constitutional Convention of 1901–1902*, 59–74; Tarter, *Grandees*, 264–68.

129. *Dred Scott v. Sandford*, 60 US 393 (1857).

130. Garrett Epps, *Democracy Reborn: The Fourteenth Amendment and the Fight for Equal Rights in Post–Civil War America* (New York, 2006); Laura F. Edwards, *A Legal History of the Civil War and Reconstruction: A Nation of Rights* (New York, 2015); Timothy S. Huebner, *Liberty and Union: The Civil War Ear and American Constitutionalism* (Lawrence, KA, 2016); Eric Foner, *The Seconding Founding: How the Civil War and Reconstruction Remade the Constitution* (New York, 2019).

131. Merrill D. Peterson, "Mr. Jefferson's 'Sovereignty of the Living Generation,'" *Virginia Quarterly Review* 52 (1976): 437–47.

132. Maddex, *Virginia Conservatives*, 120.

133. "The Proposed Constitutional Amendments," *Virginia Law Journal* 10 (1886): 60–61, quotation on 61.

134. Election Records No. 104.

135. Election Records No. 444.

136. Election Records No. 104.

137. C. Vann Woodward, *Origins of the New South, 1877–1913* (Baton Rouge, 1951), 92–100; Carl N. Degler, *The Other South: Southern Dissenters in the Nineteenth Century* (New York, 1974), 264–315; Edward L. Ayers, *The Promise of the New South: Life after Reconstruction* (New York, 1992), 46–47; Steven Hahn, *A Nation under Our Feet: Black Political Struggles in the Rural South, From Slavery to the Great Migration* (Cambridge, MA, 2003), 367–84, 400–11; Tarter, *Grandees*, 242–50; Tarter, *Saga of the New South*, 63–80.

138. Tarter, *Saga of the New South*, 174–84.

Chapter 7. The Constitution of 1902

1. *Report of the Proceedings and Debates of the Constitutional Convention State of Virginia Held in the City of Richmond June 12, 1901, to June 26, 1902*, 2 vols. (Richmond, 1906), 1:19–22, quotation on 19.

2. John Goode, *Recollections of a Lifetime* (New York, 1906).

3. *Proceedings and Debates*, 1:20.

4. James F. Holcombe, "Is Slavery Consistent with Natural Law?" *Southern Literary Messenger* 27 (1858): 401–21, on 408.

5. *Proceedings and Debates*, 1:21.

6. J. Morgan Kousser, *The Shaping of Southern Politics: Suffrage Restriction and the Establishment of the One-Party South, 1880–1910* (New Haven, 1974); Michael E. Perman, *Struggle for Mastery: Disfranchisement in the South, 1888–1908* (Chapel Hill, 2001); Paul E. Herron, *Framing the Solid South: The State Constitutional Conventions of Secession, Reconstruction, and Redemption, 1860–1902* (Lawrence, KS, 2017), 185–225.

7. Esp. *Richmond Planet*, 9 November 1901, 7; *Richmond Planet* 28 June 1902; *Richmond Planet* 5 July 1902.

8. 41st Cong., 1st Sess., chap. 10.

9. Beth Barton Schweiger, "Putting Politics Aside: Virginia Democrats and Voter Apathy in the Era of Disfranchisement," in *The Edge of the South: Life in Nineteenth-Century Virginia*, ed. Edward L. Ayers and John C. Willis (Charlottesville, 1991), 194–218.

10. *Acts*, 1884 extra Sess., chap. 158; *Acts*, 1893–94 Sess., chap. 746.

11. Ronald Edward Shibley, "Election Laws and Electoral Politics in Virginia, 1867–1902: An Administrative and Political History" (PhD diss., University of Virginia, 1972), 60–214; Wythe Holt, *Virginia's Constitutional Convention of 1901–1902* (New York, 1990); Ralph C. McDanel, *The Virginia Constitutional Convention of 1901–1902* (Baltimore, 1928), 30, 33; and Tarter, *Grandees*, 262–64.

12. Charles E. Wynes, *Race Relations in Virginia, 1870–1902* (Charlottesville, 1961);

Allen W. Moger, *Virginia: Bourbonism to Byrd, 1870–1925* (Charlottesville, 1968); Raymond H. Pulley, *Old Virginia Restored: An Interpretation of the Progressive Impulse, 1870–1930* (Charlottesville, 1968); Tarter, *Grandees*, 231–77; Brent Tarter, *A Saga of the New South: Race, Law, and Public Debt in Virginia* (Charlottesville, 2016).

13. Allen W. Moger, "The Rift in Virginia Democracy in 1896," *Journal of Southern History* 4 (1938): 295–317; Tarter, *Grandees*, 256–57.

14. Martin quoted in Walter Edward Harris to Harry F. Byrd, 2 February 1933, Harry Flood Byrd Papers, University of Virginia.

15. Address of 23 October 1883 reported in Richmond *Daily Dispatch*, 26 October 1883.

16. Raymond H. Pulley, "The May Movement of 1899: Irresolute Progressivism in the Old Dominion," *VMHB* 75 (1967): 186–201.

17. Shibley, "Election Laws and Electoral Practices," 215–26; Holt, *Virginia's Constitutional Convention*, 90–109; Perman, *Struggle for Mastery*, 322–24; Herron, *Framing the Solid South*, 185–225.

18. *Acts*, 1899–1900 Sess., chap. 780.

19. Norfolk *Virginian-Pilot*, 3 May 1900.

20. Herron, *Framing the Solid South*, 232.

21. *Acts*, 1899–1900 Sess., chap. 780.

22. Election Records No. 104.

23. Computed from *Twelfth Census*, 10 vols. (Washington, DC, 1902), 1:100–1.

24. Edgar Eugene Robinson, *The Presidential Vote, 1896–1932* (Stanford, CA, 1934), 354.

25. *Proceedings and Debates*, 2:3181.

26. *Acts*, 1901 extra Sess., chap. 243.

27. *Proceedings and Debates*, 1:139–40.

28. *Proceedings and Debates*, 2194–95.

29. George Harrison Gilliam, "Locomotives and Lawyers: The Impact of the Railroads on Virginia Law in the Nineteenth Century" (unpublished paper, 2018).

30. Election Record No. 47.

31. Brent Tarter, "Fighting Ninth District," in *Encyclopedia of Appalachia*, ed. Ruby Abramson and Jean Haskell (Knoxville, 2006), 1593–94.

32. Brent Tarter, "Bristow, Joseph Allen," *DVB* 2:235–36.

33. John Garland Pollard, Data for Biographical Sketches of the Members of the Virginia Constitutional Convention of 1901–2, Mss5:9 P7624:1, Virginia Historical Society; *Richmond Times*, 12 June 1901; Jacob N. Brenaman, *A History of Virginia Conventions* (Richmond, 1902), 96–104.

34. Holt, *Virginia's Constitutional Convention*, 111–12.

35. *Journal*, 49.

36. *Proceedings and Debates*, 1:4–17, 29–88; Braxton's initial remarks in *Proceedings and Debates*, 1:4–5, 7–9, 12–13, and in a second discussion of the topic on 56–71.

37. Allen Caperton Braxton, "Powers of Conventions," *Virginia Law Register* 7 (1901): 79–99, with a supplemental note, "The Powers of the Approaching Constitutional Convention in Virginia," 100–6.

38. *Acts*, 1901 special Sess., chap. 243, sec. 12, 17.

39. *Journal of the Constitutional Convention of Virginia. Held in the City of Richmond, Beginning June 12th, 1901* (Richmond 1901 [i.e., 1902]); *Resolutions of the Constitutional Convention of 1901–1902* (Richmond, 1902).

40. Allen Caperton Braxton Papers, University of Virginia; Mrs. Walter A. Watson [Constance Tinsley Watson], ed., *Notes on Southside Virginia* (Richmond, 1925).

41. *Proceedings and Debates*, 1:1384, 2:2544.

42. *Proceedings and Debates*, 1:319, 415, 435, 471–87.

43. *Proceedings and Debates*, 1:1384, 2:1707–11.

44. Brenaman, *History of Virginia Conventions*, 94.

45. *Proceedings and Debates*, 2:2931; *Journal*, 452–63.

46. *Proceedings and Debates*, 2:3090, 3096.

47. *Proceedings and Debates*, 2:3263, 3266.

48. *Proceedings and Debates*, 1:277.

49. L. W. W. to Editor, *Richmond Times*, 2 June 1901.

50. *Proceedings and Debates*, 1:981.

51. *Richmond Times*, 10 November 1901.

52. *Richmond Times*, 17 November 1901.

53. *Richmond Times*, 12 June 1901.

54. *Notes on Southside Virginia*, 215.

55. *Proceedings and Debates*, 1:1227.

56. *Notes on Southside Virginia*, 211.

57. *Proceedings and Debates*, 1:295.

58. Edmund Randolph, *History of Virginia*, ed. Arthur H. Shaffer (Charlottesville, 1970), 253.

59. *Journal*, 535.

60. *Journal*, 522–24, quotations on 522–23.

61. *Acts*, 1839–40 Sess., Chap. 2, Section 37; Roger D. Scott, "Double Jeopardy and the Commonwealth's Right to Writs of Error in Criminal Cases," *University of Richmond Law Review* 20 (1986): 629–69, on 652–56.

62. Tarter, *Saga of the New South*, 29–32, 45–46, 55–56, 61–63, 82–129.

63. Unnumbered committee report printed with *Journal*.

64. *Record of Debates*, 1:328–30, quotation on 330; Thomas E. Buckley, SJ, *Establishing Religious Freedom: Jefferson's Statute in Virginia* (Charlottesville, 2013), 210–15.

65. Docs. 1, 2, 3, 5, 6, 7, 8, 9, 11, 12, 14, 17, and 18 printed and bound with *Journal* as separately paginated documents.

66. *Williams v. Mississippi*, 170 US 213 (1898).

67. Holt, *Virginia's Constitutional Convention*, 158–59; Perman, *Struggle for Mastery*, 207–8, 218.

68. *Notes on Southside Virginia*, 213.

69. *Proceedings and Debates*, 2:2943–57, on 2943; John W. Daniel, "The Work of the Constitutional Convention," *Reports of the Virginia State Bar Association* 15 (1902): 266–67, 272.

70. *Proceedings and Debates*, 2:2943–3080, with vote on 3079–80.

71. *Proceedings and Debates*, 2:2943–3080; *Notes on Southside Virginia*, 210–14; Tarter, *Grandees*, 267, 269.

72. *Harper v. Virginia State Board of Elections*, 383 US 663 (1966).

73. Lila Meade Valentine to Jessie Townsend, 10 April 1915, and to Mary Elizabeth Pidgeon, 11 October 1919, both Equal Suffrage League of Virginia Records, Library of Virginia; Brent Tarter, Marianne E. Julienne, and Barbara C. Batson, *The Campaign for Woman Suffrage in Virginia* (Charleston, SC, 2020), 47–54, 121, 133, 134.

74. *Proceedings and Debates*, 2:2972–73.

75. *Proceedings and Debates*, 2:3014.

76. *Proceedings and Debates*, 2:3076–77.

77. *Proceedings and Debates*, 1:459–598, 1:1033–36, 2:1844–70.

78. *Proceedings and Debates*, 1:156.

79. *Proceedings and Debates*, 2:3039–96.

80. *Proceedings and Debates*, 1:733–82.

81. *Proceedings and Debates*, 1:783–818; Buckley, *Establishing Religious Freedom*, 223–28.

82. Thomas M. Cooley, *A Treatise on the Constitutional Limitations which Rest upon the Legislative Power of the States of the American Union* (Boston, 1868), esp. 9–10, 88, 90; G. Alan Tarr, *Understanding State Constitutions* (Princeton, 1998), 6–9, 15–17; Robert F. Williams, *The Law of American State Constitutions* (Oxford, 2009), 247–53.

83. *Strawberry Hill Land Co. v. Starbuck*, 124 Va 71 (1918) quotation on 77.

84. *Commonwealth v. Dodson*, 176 Va 281 (1940), quotation on 290.

85. John O. Peters, "Virginia's Readjuster Court: Guilt by Association" (unpublished paper, 2016).

86. *Acts*, 1869–70 Sess., chap. 160.

87. *Proceedings and Debates*, 1:1361–62.

88. David K. Sutelan and Wayne R. Spencer, "The Virginia Special Court of Appeals: Constitutional Relief for an Overburdened Court," *William and Mary Law Review* 8 (1967): 244–76, on 267–70; *Acts*, 1924 Sess., chap. 264.

89. *Proceedings and Debates*, esp., 1:1306, 1314–15, 1430, 1432, 1441–42; *Report of the Ninth Annual Meeting of the Virginia State Bar Association* 10 (Richmond, 1897), 38–39; Holmes Conrad, "The Old County Court System of Virginia: Its Place in History," *Report of the Twentieth Annual Meeting of the Virginia State Bar Association* 21 (Richmond, 1908), 323–50 on 347.

90. Eugene C. Withers, "The Torrens System of Land Registration," *Report of the Twelfth Annual Meeting of the Virginia State Bar Association* 13 (Richmond, 1900), 299–336; John O. Peters, "The Bar Association Movement in Virginia" (unpublished paper, 2018).

91. Albert O. Porter, *County Government in Virginia, A Legislative History, 1607–1904* (New York, 1947), 307–18, 322–41; Patrick M. McSweeney, "Local Government Law in Virginia, 1870–1970," *University of Richmond Law Review* 4 (1970): 174–222, on 194–96.

92. Brent Tarter, *Gerrymanders: How Redistricting Has Protected Slavery, White Supremacy, and Partisan Minorities in Virginia* (Charlottesville, 2019), 26, 50, 63.

93. Chester Ward Bain, *"A Body Incorporate": The Evolution of City-County Separation in Virginia* (Charlottesville, 1967); and Weldon Cooper, "Virginia Local Government, 1776–1976," *VNL* 52 (1976): 41–44, which do not find the origins so far back in time as E. Lee Shepard, "Courts in Conflict: Town-County Relations in Post-Revolutionary Virginia," *VMHB* 85 (1977): 184–99, and Brent Tarter, ed., *The Order Book and Related Papers of the Common Hall of the Borough of Norfolk, Virginia, 1736–1798* (Richmond, 1979), 20–24.

94. *Supervisors of Washington County v. Saltville Land Co.*, 99 Va. 640 (1901).

95. *Proceedings and Debates*, 1:1237.

96. *Journal*, 249.

97. *Brown v. Board of Education of Topeka*, 347 US 483 (1954).

98. Brent Tarter, "A Rich Storehouse of Knowledge, A History of the Library of Virginia," in *The Common Wealth: Treasures from the Collections of the Library of Virginia*, ed. Sandra Gioia Treadway and Edward D. C. Campbell, Jr. (Richmond, 1997), 20–21.

99. A. Caperton Braxton, "The Virginia State Corporation Commission," *Virginia Law Register* 10 (1904): 1–18; Thomas Edward Gay Jr., "Creating the Virginia State Corporation Commission," *VMHB* 78 (1970): 464–80; Holt, *Virginia's Constitutional Convention*, 169–98; George Harrison Gilliam, "Making Virginia Progressive: Courts and Parties, Railroads and Regulators, 1890–1910," *VMHB* 107 (1999): 189–222; Gilliam, "Locomotives and Lawyers."

100. *Proceedings and Debates*, 2:2321.

101. Gay, "Creating the Corporation Commission," 468.

102. *Proceedings and Debates*, 2:2140–71.

103. Gay, "Creating the Corporation Commission," 476; *Proceedings and Debates*, 2:2421.

104. *Proceedings and Debates*, 2:2140–2578, 2:2775–2856; Braxton's extended comments are *Proceedings and Debates*, 2:2140–71, 2: 2228–34, 2:2420–53, 2:2455–78, 2:2787–2856.

105. *Proceedings and Debates*, 2:2178, 2199, 2204, 2319–20, 2327, 2338–41, 2374, 2538–69, 2780–93.

106. *Acts*, 1918 Sess., chap. 55.

107. *Acts*, 1926 Sess., chap. 37.

108. Braxton, "Virginia State Corporation Commission."

109. Wythe W. Holt Jr., "Braxton, Allen Caperton," *DVB* 2:198–200.

110. *Resolutions of 1901–1902 Convention*, No. 203.

111. Tarter, *Saga of the New South*, 130–42.

112. *Proceedings and Debates*, 1:91–92, 119–27, 133–43, 147–50, 152–55, 156–64, 170–73, 176–88, 227–33, 237–42, 256–59, 268–307.

113. *Proceedings and Debates*, 2:3100–3258.

114. *Proceedings and Debates*, 2:3245.

115. Gilliam, "Locomotives and Lawyers"; *Proceedings and Debates*, 2:3258–60.

116. *Journal*, 503–5; *Proceedings and Debates*, 2:3258–60.

117. Schedule appended to text of enrolled Constitution in RG 97, LVA, and printed with the Constitution as a separately paginated document bound in the *Journal*, quotations on 66, 73.

118. *Taylor v. Commonwealth*, 101 Va 829 (1903) on 831.

119. *Jones v. Montague*, 194 US 147 (1904) on 153; *Selden v. Montague*, 194 US 153 (1904).

120. Unnumbered, separately paginated document bound with *Journal*.

121. *Acts*, 1910 Sess., chap. 41.

122. *Acts*, 1910 Sess., chap. 29.

123. *Acts*, 1910 Sess., chap. 40.

124. *Acts*, 1912 Sess., chap. 40.

125. Fred Harper, "Constitutional Amendment in Virginia," *Virginia Law Register* 18 (1912): 321–35.

126. *Scott v. James, Secretary of the Commonwealth*, 114 Va 297 (1912).

127. *Annual Report of the Secretary of the Commonwealth* (Richmond, 1913), 297–98.

128. C. H. Morrissett, "Proposed Amendments to the Constitution of Virginia," *Proceedings of the Thirty-Eighth Annual Meeting of the Virginia State Bar Association* (Richmond, 1927), 372–410 on 374–75; A. E. Dick Howard, *Commentaries on the Constitution of Virginia*, 2 vols. (Charlottesville, 1974), 2:1060–61.

129. L. McCarthy Downs, "The State Corporation Commission," *Virginia Law Review* 35 (1949): 516–30; Ralph T. Catterall, "The State Corporation Commission of Virginia," *Virginia Law Review* 48 (1962): 139–51; Preston C. Shannon, "The Evolution of Virginia's State Corporation Commission," *William and Mary Law Review* 14 (1973): 523–46 on 533–36; Laurence J. O'Toole Jr. and Robert S. Montjoy, *Regulatory Decision Making: The Virginia State Corporation Commission* (Charlottesville, 1984), esp. 30–55.

130. Shannon, "Evolution of State Corporation Commission," 534.

131. *Norfolk and Portsmouth Belt Line Railroad Co. v. Commonwealth*, 103 Va 289 (1904).

132. *Winchester and Strasburg Railroad Co. v. Commonwealth*, 106 264 Va (1906) on 268.

133. *Prentis v. Atlantic Coast Line Co.*, 211 US 210 (1908).

134. *Notes on Southside Virginia*, 218, 210.

135. *Notes on Southside Virginia*, 220.

136. Warren Co. List of Colored Applicants Refused Registration, 1901–3, LVA.

137. *Richmond Planet*, 7, 28 June; *Richmond Planet* 5 July 1902.

138. This and the following paragraph follow Herman L. Horn, "The Growth and Development of the Democratic Party in Virginia since 1890" (PhD diss., Duke University, 1949).

139. Joseph A. Fry and Brent Tarter, "The Redemption of the Fighting Ninth: The 1922 Congressional Election in the Ninth District of Virginia and the Origins of the Byrd Organization," *South Atlantic Quarterly* 77 (1978): 352–70, on 358–63; Tarter, *Grandees*, 288–90.

140. *Tilton v. Herman*, 109 Va (1909) 503.

141. Tarter, *Grandees*, 273–74; and Brent Tarter, Marianne E. Julienne, and Barbara C. Batson, *The Campaign for Woman Suffrage in Virginia* (Charleston, SC, 2020), 149–51, citing A. W. Hunton to Miss Ovington, 25 October 1920, enclosing investigative

report, and [Mary White Ovington?] to Harriet Stanton Blatch, 3 December 1920, both in National Woman's Party Subject File, Voting Hampton Va., 1920, National Association for the Advancement of Colored People Papers, Library of Congress, and Norfolk *Journal and Guide*, 6 November 1920, Tuskegee Institute News Clipping File; Henry W. Anderson, "Popular Government in Virginia," *University of Virginia Record, Extension Series* 11 (June 1927): 66–68.

142. Robinson, *Presidential Vote*, 354.

143. Calculations from Horn, "Growth and Development of the Democratic Party," 102–13.

144. Tarter, *Grandees*, 296–304; V. O. Key, *Southern Politics in State and Nation* (New York, 1949), 17–33.

145. Horn, "Growth and Development of the Democratic Party"; Tarter, *Grandees*, 288–92.

146. LeRoy Hodges, "Reorganization of Municipal Government in Virginia," Bulletin No. 9 of the *Southern Commercial Congress* (1915); William A. Grubert, *The Origin of the City Manager Plan in Staunton, Virginia* (Staunton, VA, 1954).

147. John F. Dillon, *The Law of Municipal Corporations*, 2nd ed., 2 vols. (New York, 1873), 1:92–93.

148. *Kirkham v. Russell*, 76 Va. 956 (1882), quotation on 961–62.

149. Bain, "A Body Incorporate."

150. Chester W. Bain, "Annexation: The Virginia Procedure," *VNL* 37 (1961): 41–44; Bain, *Annexation in Virginia; The Use of the Judicial Process for Readjusting City-County Boundaries* (Charlottesville, 1966).

151. *Acts*, 1923 extra Sess., chap. 146.

152. Election Record No. 64, also in *Annual Report of the Secretary of the Commonwealth* (1923), 489.

153. Ronald L. Heinemann, *Harry Byrd of Virginia*, (Charlottesville, 1996), 40–42.

154. Fry and Tarter, "Redemption of the Fighting Ninth."

155. Heinemann, *Harry Byrd*, 42–46.

156. Henry C. Ferrell Jr., "The Role of Democratic Party Factionalism in the Rise of Harry Flood Byrd," *Essays in Southern Biography* (Greenville, NC, 1965), 146–66; Heinemann, *Harry Byrd*, 42–46.

157. *Acts*, 1912 Sess., chap. 581.

158. *Acts*, 1924 Sess., chap. 371.

159. *Acts*, 1904 session, chap. 85.

160. *Acts*, 1906 Sess., chap. 91, sec. 47.

161. *Acts*, 1912 Sess., chap. 157.

162. *Acts*, 1925 Sess., chap. 569; Richard B. Sherman, "The 'Teachings at Hampton Institute': Social Equality, Racial Integrity, and the Virginia Public Assemblage Act of 1926," *VMHB* 95 (1987): 275–300.

163. *Acts*, 1924 Sess., chap 394; Richard B. Sherman, "The 'Teachings at Hampton Institute.'"

164. Tarter, *Grandees*, 307–32.

Chapter 8. The Constitutional Revision of 1928

1. *Inaugural Address of Harry Flood Byrd, Governor of Virginia, Delivered Before the General Assembly and the People of Virginia, February 1, 1926*, Senate Doc. 6, bound with *JS*, 1926 Sess., 3.

2. *Communication from the Governor of Virginia Transmitting a Message to the General Assembly of Virginia on the Subject of Taxation, Tuesday, February 2, 1926*, Senate Doc. 7, bound with *JS*, 1926 Sess.

3. *Address of Harry F. Byrd Governor on the Subject of Simplification of Government in Virginia, Delivered Before the General Assembly of Virginia, Wednesday, February 3, 1926*, Senate Doc. 8, bound with *JS*, 1926 Sess.

4. Robert T. Hawkes Jr., "Harry F. Byrd, Leadership and Reform," in *The Governors of Virginia, 1860–1978*, ed. Edward E. Younger and James Tice Moore (Charlottesville, 1982), 233–46; Ronald L. Heinemann, *Harry Byrd of Virginia*, (Charlottesville, 1996), 58–84.

5. George B. Tindall, "Business Progressivism: Southern Politics in the Twenties," *South Atlantic Quarterly* 62 (1963): 92–106.

6. Henry C. Ferrell Jr., "The Role of Democratic Party Factionalism in the Rise of Harry Flood Byrd," *Essays in Southern Biography* (Greenville, NC, 1965), 146–66; Joseph A. Fry and Brent Tarter, "The Redemption of the Fighting Ninth: The 1922 Congressional Election in the Ninth District of Virginia and the Origins of the Byrd Organization," *South Atlantic Quarterly* 77 (1978): 352–70; Heinemann, *Harry Byrd*, 40–46.

7. *Address . . . Simplification of Government*, 1–2.

8. *Address . . . Simplification of Government*, 2.

9. Frank A. Magruder, *Recent Administration in Virginia* (Baltimore, 1912), 197.

10. *Acts*, 1918 Sess., chap. 64.

11. *Report of the Commission on Simplification and Economy of State and Local Government to the General Assembly of Virginia, January 1924* (Richmond, 1924).

12. *Address . . . Simplification of Government*, 4–10.

13. *Program of Progress. An Address by Harry Flood Byrd, Governor, Delivered Before the General Assembly of Virginia, January 16, 1928*, printed as Senate Doc. 5, bound with *JS*, 1928 Sess., 3.

14. *Program of Progress*, 13–14.

15. A. E. Buck, "A Survey of Virginia State and County Government," *Social Forces* 6 (1928): 448–52; Byrd's correspondence with Luther Gulick, A. E. Buck, and William T. Reed in Executive Papers of Governor Harry Flood Byrd (1926–30), RG 3, LVA, and with Reed in William T. Reed Papers, Virginia Historical Society.

16. New York Bureau of Municipal Research, *Organization and Management of the State Government of Virginia; Report on a Survey Made for the Governor and His Committee on Consolidation and Simplification* (Richmond, 1927), 6.

17. *Organization and Management of State Government*, 8.

18. *Organization and Management of State Government*, 82–86.

19. *Organization and Management of State Government*, 85.

20. New York Bureau of Municipal Research, *County Government in Virginia: Report on a Survey Made to the Governor and His Committee on Consolidation and Simplification, January 1927* (Richmond, 1928), 6.

21. New York Bureau of Municipal Research, *County Government in Virginia*, esp. 18–19.

22. New York Bureau of Municipal Research, *County Government in Virginia*, 5, 19.

23. Albert O. Porter, *County Government in Virginia, A Legislative History, 1607–1904* (New York, 1947), 28–30, 32–33, 72–79.

24. New York Bureau of Municipal Research, *County Government in Virginia*, 23.

25. Tarter, *Grandees*, 65–69.

26. Harry F. Byrd to Rorer A. James Jr., 21 July 1926, Byrd Executive Papers.

27. Minutes of the meetings of the Prentis Commission are in a bound volume in the state archives in the Library of Virginia.

28. Joseph A. Fry, "Senior Advisor to the Democratic 'Organization': William T. Reed and Virginia Politics," *VMHB* (1977): 445–69.

29. *Report of Citizens Committee on Consolidation and Simplification in State and Local Governments Submitted to the Governor of Virginia in Accordance with Act of General Assembly of 1926* (Richmond, 1927).

30. *The Constitution of Virginia: Report of the Commission to Suggest Amendments to the Constitution to the General Assembly of Virginia* (Richmond, 1927).

31. *JS*, 1928 Sess., 585; *JHD*, 1928 Sess., 763–64.

32. Enrolled Bills, 1928 Sess., chap. 46, LVA.

33. *Staples v. Gilmer*, 183 Va 613 (1945), quotation on 630.

34. *Report of the Commission to Suggest Amendments*, 15.

35. *Acts*, 1910 Sess., chap. 30; official vote published in *Annual Report of the Secretary of the Commonwealth* (1921), 309–11.

36. *Report of the Commission to Suggest Amendments*, 19.

37. *Strawberry Hill Land Co. v. Starbuck*, 124 Va 71 (1918) quotation on 77.

38. Thomas M. Cooley, *A Treatise on the Constitutional Limitations which Rest upon the Legislative Power of the States of the American Union* (Boston, 1868), esp. 9–10, 88, 90; G. Alan Tarr, *Understanding State Constitutions* (Princeton, 1998), 6–9, 15–17; Robert F. Williams, *The Law of American State Constitutions* (Oxford, 2009), 247–53.

39. *Report of the Commission to Suggest Amendments*, ix.

40. Graham C. Lilly and Antonin Scalia, "Appellate Justice: A Crisis in Virginia?" *Virginia Law Review* 57 (1971): 3–64, on 37–41; Thomas R. Morris, *The Virginia Supreme Court: An Institutional and Political Analysis* (Charlottesville, 1975), 63–65.

41. David K. Sutelan and Wayne R. Spencer, "the Virginia Special Court of Appeals: Constitutional Relief for an Overburdened Court," *William and Mary Law Review* 8 (1967): 244–76 on 270–75.

42. Patrick M. McSweeney, "Local Government Law in Virginia, 1870–1970," *University of Richmond Law Review* 4 (1970): 176–222, on 202–22.

43. *Report of the Commission to Suggest Amendments*, x.

44. Lewis F. Powell Jr., "The Relation between the Virginia Court of Appeals and

the State Corporation Commission," *Virginia Law Review* 19 (1933): 433–58, 571–93; Laurence J. O'Toole Jr. and Robert S. Montjoy, *Regulatory Decision Making: The Virginia State Corporation Commission* (Charlottesville, 1984), esp. 56–88.

45. Fred Harper, "Constitutional Amendment in Virginia," *Virginia Law Register* 18 (1912): 321–35.

46. *Report of Commission to Suggest Amendments*, 82.

47. Harry Flood Byrd, *A Discussion of the Amendments Proposed to the Constitution of Virginia*, 3 vols. (Richmond, 1928).

48. *Acts*, 1944 Sess., chap. 287.

49. *Tilton v. Herman*, 109 Va 503 (1909).

50. *Staples v. Gilmer*, 183 Va 338 (1944), quotation on 349.

51. *Acts*, 1944 special Sess., chap. 1.

52. Robert K. Gooch, "The Recent Limited Constitutional Convention in Virginia," *Virginia Law Review* 31 (1945): 708–26, esp. 709–12.

53. *Staples v. Gilmer*, 183 Va 613 (1945).

54. *Staples v. Gilmer*, at 632–42.

55. *Statement of the Vote*, 6 March 1945.

56. Records of the Virginia Constitutional Convention of 1945, RG 98, LVA; *Journal of the Constitutional Convention of the Commonwealth of Virginia to Amend the Constitution of Virginia for Voting by Certain Members of the Armed Forces* (Richmond 1945).

57. Gooch, "Recent Limited Constitutional Convention," 711; John Dinan, *The Virginia State Constitution*, 2nd ed. (Oxford, 2014), 30–32.

58. *Acts*, 1948, chap. 525.

59. *Acts*, 1948 Sess., chap. 526; *Statement of the Vote*, 8 November 1949.

60. *Acts*, 1954 Sess., chap. 711; *Statement of the Vote*, 2 November 1954.

61. *Acts*, 1956 Sess., chap. 1.

62. *Brown v. Board of Education of Topeka*, 347 US 483 (1954).

63. *Almond v. Day*, 197 Va 419 (1955).

64. *Statement of the Vote*, 9 January 1956.

65. Records of the Convention of 1956, Acc. 37566, LVA, including enrolled amendment; *Journal of the Constitutional Convention of the Commonwealth of Virginia to Revise and Amend Sec. 141 of the Constitution of Virginia* (Richmond, 1956).

66. Dinan, *Virginia State Constitution*, 32–34.

67. *Acts*, 1960 Sess., chap. 613; *Statement of the Vote*, 8 November 1960.

68. Emmet M. Frazer, "How Does It Feel to Be Colored?" *Commonwealth* 12 (June 1945): 10–13.

69. *Acts*, 1962 Sess., chap. 643; *Statement of the Vote*, 6 November 1962.

70. *Harper v. Virginia State Board of Elections*, 383 US 663 (1966).

71. *Brown v. Board of Education of Topeka*, 347 US 483 (1954).

72. George W. Spicer, "From Political Chief to Administrative Chief," in *Essays on the Law and Practice of Governmental Administration: A Volume in Honor of Frank Johnson Goodnow*, ed. Charles G. Haines and Marshall E. Dimock (Baltimore, 1935), 94–124; Joseph A. Schlesinger, "The Politics of the Executive," in *Politics in the American States*, ed. Herbert Jacob and Kenneth N. Vines (Boston, 1965), 229.

73. Carter O. Lowance (long-time chief of staff of several Virginia governors), "The Governor of Virginia," *VNL* 36 (1960): 21–24; Rowland Egger (who served in the administration of James H. Price in the 1930s and was an internationally renowned student of public administration), "The Governorship of Virginia, 1776 and 1976," *VNL* 52 (1976), 45–48.

74. Robert J. Austin, "The Virginia Supreme Court of Appeals: Career Patterns and the Selection Process," *VNL* 45 (1968): 13–16; Thomas R. Morris, "The Virginia Judiciary, 1776–1976," *VNL* 53 (1976): 1–4.

75. Minor T. Weisiger, "Combs, Everett Randolph," *DVB* 3:395–97; Tarter, *Grandees*, 287–96.

76. Brent Tarter, "Downs, Lewis McCarthy," *DVB* online.

77. *Report of the Virginia Commission on County Government to the Governor and General Assembly, January 1940* (Richmond, 1940), quotations on 13, 16.

78. Robert K. Gooch, *The Poll Tax in Virginia Suffrage History: A Premature Proposal for Reform* (Charlottesville, 1969), quotations in 21, 22.

79. Ronald Edward Shibley, "Election Laws and Electoral Practices in Virginia, 1867–1902: An Administrative and Political History" (PhD diss., University of Virginia, 1972), 247; Tarter, *Grandees*, 300.

80. Tarter, *Grandees*, 293–96.

81. V. O. Key, *Southern Politics in State and Nation* (New York, 1949), 20.

82. Brent Tarter, *Virginians and Their Histories* (Charlottesville, 2020), 357–420.

Chapter 9. The Constitution of 1971

1. Jean Gottman, *Virginia at Mid-Century* (New York, 1955); Brent Tarter, *Virginians and Their Histories* (Charlottesville, 2020), 357–420.

2. New York Bureau of Municipal Research, *County Government in Virginia: Report on a Survey Made to the Governor and His Committee on Consolidation and Simplification, January 1927* (Richmond, 1928).

3. Chester W. Bain, "Annexation: The Virginia Procedure," *VNL* 37 (1961): 41–44; Bain, *Annexation in Virginia; The Use of the Judicial Process for Readjusting City-County Boundaries* (Charlottesville, 1966); S. J. Makielski Jr. *City-County Consolidation: A Guide for Virginians* (Charlottesville, 1971); David Graham Temple, *Merger Politics; Local Government Consolidation in Tidewater Virginia* (Charlottesville, 1972).

4. William L. Martin and J. E. Buchholtz, "Annexation—Virginia's Dilemma," *Washington and Lee Law Review* 24 (1967): 241–67; Weldon Cooper, "The Charter and Virginia Local Government," *VNL* 45 (1969): 29–32; Edward L. Morton, "Municipal Annexation in Virginia, 1960–1970," *VNL* 48 (1970): 33–36.

5. S. J. Makielski Jr., "State Authorities: Virginia's Governmental Paradox," *VNL* 41 (1965): 41–44; S. J. Makielski Jr., "The Special District Problem in Virginia," *Virginia Law Review* 55 (1969): 1182–99; Patrick M. McSweeney, "Local Government Law in Virginia, 1870–1970," *University of Richmond Law Review* 4 (1970): 174–222 quotation on 202.

6. Metropolitan Areas Study Commission (usually known as the Hahn Commis-

sion report, after its chair, T. Marshall Hahn), *Governing the Virginia Metropolitan Areas: An Assessment* (Richmond, 1967), *and Metropolitan Virginia: A Program for Action* (Richmond, 1967), quotations on 51–52.

7. Brent Tarter, *Gerrymanders: How Redistricting Has Protected Slavery, White Supremacy, and Partisan Minorities in Virginia* (Charlottesville, 2019), 50–57.

8. Tarter, *Virginians and Their Histories*, 381–99 and sources cited on 471.

9. *Brown v. Board of Education of Topeka*, 347 US 483 (1954).

10. *Harper v. Virginia State Board of Elections*, 383 US 663 (1966).

11. *Plessy v. Ferguson*, 163 US 537 (1896); Tarter, *Virginians and Their Histories*, 381–99.

12. 89th Cong., 1st Sess., chap. 110.

13. Tarter, *Gerrymanders*, 58–64.

14. J. Douglas Smith, *On Democracy's Doorstep: The Inside Story of How the Supreme Court Brought "One Person, One Vote" to the United States* (New York, 2014).

15. Tarter, *Gerrymanders*, 58–78.

16. Ronald L. Heinemann, *Harry Byrd of Virginia*, (Charlottesville, 1996), 407–20.

17. James R. Sweeney, "A New Day in the Old Dominion: The 1964 Presidential Election," *VMHB* 102 (1994): 307–48; Sweeney, "Bridge to the New Dominion: Virginia's 1965 Gubernatorial Election," *VMHB* 125 (2016): 246–88; and Sweeney, "Mills Edwin Godwin Jr. (1914–1999)" *EV* (2016).

18. James L. Bugg Jr., "Mills Edwin Godwin Jr.," in *The Governors of Virginia, 1860–1978*, ed. Edward E. Younger and James Tice Moore (Charlottesville, 1982), 373–91; Tarter, *Grandees*, 360–61.

19. *Address of Mills E. Godwin, Jr., to the General Assembly, Wednesday, January 10, 1968*, printed as Doc. 1 with *JS*, 1968 Sess., 10.

20. Tarter, *Grandees*, 335–54.

21. Robert F. William, "Are State Constitutional Conventions Things of the Past? The Increasing Role of the Constitutional Commission in State Constitutional Change," *Hofstra Law and Policy Symposium* 1 (1996): 1–26.

22. *The Constitution of Virginia: Report of the Commission to Suggest Amendments to the Constitution to the General Assembly of Virginia* (Richmond, 1927).

23. *Address of Mills E. Godwin, Jr.*, 11.

24. Tarter, *Grandees*, 387–88.

25. *Richmond Times-Dispatch*, 27 January 1968.

26. A. E. Dick Howard, "Constitutional Revision: Virginia and the Nation," *University of Richmond Law Review* 9 (1974): 1–48, reprinted as Howard, "Adopting a New Constitution: Lessons from Virginia" in *State Constitutions for the Twenty-First Century*, ed. G. Alan Tarr and Robert F. Williams, 3 vols. (New York, 2006), 1:73–110; Jean Hardiman, "Toward Greater Equality: In 1968–1970, Virginia's Leading Legal Minds Came Together to Revise the Constitution," *Virginia Bar Association Journal* 47 (Fall 2020): 19–21; A. E. Dick Howard and William Antholis, "The Virginia Constitution of 1971, An Interview with A. E. Dick Howard," *VMHB* 129 (2021): 346–89, on 349–50.

27. Commission on Constitutional Revision, *The Constitution of Virginia: Report*, (Richmond, 1969), with lists of more than 200 speakers at public hearings on 485–523, and of research memoranda on 527–32.

28. Records of the Commission on Constitutional Revision, RG 87, LVA; Papers of A. E. Dick Howard for the Virginia Commission for Constitutional Revision, 1969–71, Arthur J. Morris Law Library, University of Virginia.

29. A. E. Dick Howard, "'For the Common Benefit': Constitutional History in Virginia as a Casebook for the Modern Constitution-Maker"; Wythe W. Holt Jr., "Constitutional Revision in Virginia, 1902 and 1928: Some Lessons on Roadblocks to Institutional Reform"; Frank P. Grad, "The State Constitution: Its Function and Form for Our Time"; C[arroll] L. W[agner Jr.], "State Constitutional Change: The Constitutional Convention"; David J. Mays, "Some Thoughts on Revision of the Virginia Constitution"; Armistead L. Boothe, "The Adequacy of the Virginia Constitution of 1902," *Virginia Law Review* 54 (1968).

30. Constitution of 1851, Article IV, Section 33.

31. Howard, "Constitutional Revision: Virginia and the Nation," 2–3, 8–10, 17–18.

32. Commission on Constitutional Revision, *Constitution of Virginia*, 8–15.

33. Howard and Antholis, "Virginia Constitution of 1971," 372–75; Charles K. Woltz, ed., *Proceedings and Debates of the Virginia Senate Pertaining to Amendment of the Constitution, Extra Session 1969, Regular Session 1970* (Richmond, 1971); and *Proceedings and Debates of the Virginia House of Delegates Pertaining to Amendment of the Constitution, Extra Session 1969, Regular Session 1970* (Richmond, 1973).

34. *JHD*, 1969 special Sess., 387; *JS*, 1969 special Sess., 307.

35. *JHD*, 1970 Sess., 498–99; *JS*, 1970 Sess., 481.

36. *Staples v. Gilmer*, 183 Va 613 (1945).

37. Enrolled Bills, 1970 Sess., chap. 786; *Acts*, 1970 Sess., chap. 763.

38. *Official Election Returns*, 3 November 1970.

39. A. E. Dick Howard, *Commentaries on the Constitution of Virginia*, 2 vols. (Charlottesville, 1974); John Dinan, *The Virginia State Constitution*, rev. 2nd ed. (Oxford, 2014).

40. *Proceedings and Debates in the House of Delegates*, 482.

41. *Scott v. Commonwealth*, 247 Va 379 (1994), quotation on 386; Commission on Constitutional Revision, *Constitution of Virginia*, 15, 20, 99, 254–56; Howard and Anthlois, "Virginia Constitution of 1971," 356–58; Robert E. Shepherd Jr., "The most Basic Non-Fundamental Right: Education in American Constitutional Law," *VNL* 61 (1985): 69–74; John C. Eastman, "When Did Education become a Civil Right? An Assessment of State Constitutional Provisions for Education, 1776–1900," *American Journal of Legal History* 42 (1998): 1–34; John Dinan, "The Meaning of State Constitutional Education Clauses: Evidence from the Constitutional Convention Debates," *Albany Law Review* 70 (2007): 927–81.

42. Emmet M. Frazer, "How Does It Feel to Be Colored?" *Commonwealth* 12 (June 1945): 10–13.

43. *Carrington v. Rash*, 380 US 89 (1965).

44. *Kegley v. Johnson*, 207 Va 54 (1966).

45. Tarter, *Grandees*, 281–304.

46. Tarter, *Gerrymanders*, 25–26, 65–68.

47. Marshall T. Bohannon, "Local Bills—Some Observations," *Virginia Law Review*

42 (1956): 845–59; Richard S. Harrell, "Special Legislation in Virginia," *Virginia Law Review* 42 (1956): 860–74.

48. Alexander J. Walker, "The Governor's Veto Power," *VNL* 54 (December 1977): 13–16.

49. Michael Singer, "Constitutional Crisis in the Commonwealth: Resolving the Conflict between Governors and Attorneys General," *University of Richmond Law Review* 41 (2006): 43–76; Dinan, *Virginia State Constitution*, 158–60.

50. *Barber v. City of Danville*, 149 Va 418 (1928), quotation on 424; *Beck v. Shelton*, 267 Va 482 (2004).

51. *Acts*, 2002 Sess., chap. 43.

52. David K. Sutelan and Wayne R. Spencer, "The Virginia Special Court of Appeals: Constitutional Relief for an Overburdened Court," *William and Mary Law Review* 8 (1967): 244–76.

53. *Acts*, 1830–31 Sess., chap. 4; *Acts*, 1869–70 Sess., chap. 160.

54. *Acts*, 1971 Sess., chap. 51.

55. *Acts*, 1983 Sess., chap. 413.

56. Graham C. Lilly and Antonin Scalia, "Appellate Justice: A Crisis in Virginia?" *Virginia Law Review* 57 (1971): 3–64.

57. Tarter, *Grandees*, 273–76, 288–93.

58. Donald D. Dixon, "Local Government and the 1971 Virginia Constitution," *VNL* 49 (1973): 37–40; Jack Spain Jr., "The General Assembly and Local Government: Legislating a Constitution 1969–70," *University of Richmond Law Review* 8 (1974): 387–429.

59. Bain, "Annexation: The Virginia Procedure," 41–44; Bain, *Annexation in Virginia*.

60. Howard, *Commentaries*, 2:814.

61. McSweeney, "Local Government Law in Virginia," 205–22; Makielski, "The Special District Problem in Virginia."

62. John F. Dillon, *The Law of Municipal Corporations*, 2nd ed., 2 vols. (New York, 1873), 1:92–93; Tarter, *Grandees*, esp. 385–88.

63. Kenneth E. Vanlandingham, "Municipal Home Rule in the United States," *William and Mary Law Review* 10 (1968): 269–314, which on 273–74 construed provisions of the Constitution of 1902 and then-current statutes as conferring a greater degree of legislative discretion in the application of the Dillon Rule than members of the Constitutional Revision Commission perceived.

64. Commission on Constitutional Revision, *Constitution of Virginia*, 228–30, 385 (quotation).

65. Spain, "The General Assembly and Local Government," 403–4; Howard and Antholis, "Virginia Constitution of 1971," 363–66.

66. Richard C. Schragger and C. Alex Retzloff, "The Failure of Home Rule Reform in Virginia: Race, Localism, and the Constitution of 1971," *Journal of Law and Politics* (forthcoming).

67. Murel M. Jones Jr., "The Impact of Annexation-related City-Council Reapportionment on Black Political Influence: The Cities of Richmond and Petersburg, Vir-

ginia" (PhD diss., Howard University, 1977); Thomas R. Morris and Neil Bradley, "Virginia," in *Quiet Revolution in the South: The Impact of the Voting Rights Act, 1965–1990*, ed. Chandler Davidson and Bernard Grofman (Princeton, 1994), 271–98; Tarter, *Gerrymanders*, 50, 75.

68. Hullihen W. Moore, "In Aid of Public Education: An Analysis of the Education Article of the Virginia Constitution of 1971," *University of Richmond Law Review* 5 (1971): 263–310.

69. *Brown v. Board of Education of Topeka*, 347 US 483 (1954).

70. Howard, *Commentaries*, 2:952–57.

71. A. Caperton Braxton, "The Virginia State Corporation Commission," *Virginia Law Register* 10 (1904): 1–18; Thomas Edward Gay Jr., "Creating the Virginia State Corporation Commission," *VMHB* 78 (1970): 464–80; George Harrison Gilliam, "Making Virginia Progressive: Courts and Parties, Railroads and Regulators, 1890–1910," *VMHB* 107 (1999): 189–222.

72. *Report of the Proceedings and Debates of the Constitutional Convention State of Virginia Held in the City of Richmond June 12, 1901, to June 26, 1902*, 2 vols. (Richmond, 1906), 2:2166 (quotation); Laurence J. O'Toole and Robert S. Montjoy, "Virginia's State Corporation Commission, I: Historical Perspective," *VNL* 56 (1980 no. 8): 13–16; and "Virginia's State Corporation Commission, II: Decision Making Today," *VNL* 57 (1980): without page numbers; and commission member Elizabeth B. Lacy, "Virginia State Corporation Commission: Responsible Regulation for the Commonwealth," *University of Richmond Law Review* 21 (1987): 303–16.

73. Jeff Thomas, *Virginia Politics and Government in a New Century, The Price of Power* (Charleston, SC, 2016), 55–78; and Thomas *The Virginia Way: Democracy and Power after 2016* (Charleston, SC, 2019), 37–60.

74. *Old Dominion Committee for Fair Utility Rates et al. v. State Corporation Commission*, 294 Va 168 (2017).

75. D. W. B., "Property Tax Exemptions for Charitable, Benevolent, and Religious Organizations in Virginia," *Virginia Law Review* 71 (1985): 601–23.

76. Howard, *Commentaries*, 2:1073.

77. Michael Long, "Navigating the Maze—Considering Recent Changes in Virginia Law Concerning the Granting of Property Tax Exemptions for Religious, Charitable, and Certain Other Organizations," *Journal of Local Government Law* 2 (2004): 2–8.

78. Howard, *Commentaries*, 2:1100.

79. Howard, *Commentaries*, 2:1143 (quotation); J. Y. P. Jr., "Toward a Constitutionally Protected Environment," *Virginia Law Review* 56 (1970): 458–86.

80. Howard, "Constitutional Revision: Virginia and the Nation," 10–37; Hardiman, "Toward Greater Equality," 20–21; Howard and Antholis, "Virginia Constitution of 1971," 361, 377–84.

81. *Official Election Returns*, 3 November 1970.

82. John Dinan, "Amendments to Virginia's 1971 Constitution," *VMHB* 129 (2021): 322–45.

83. *Kelo v. City of New London*, 545 US 469 (2005).

84. *Bostic v. Rainey*, 970 F. Supp. 2d 456 (E.D. Va. 2014).

85. *Loving v. Virginia*, 388 US 1 (1967).

86. *Bostic v. Schaefer*, No. 14-1167, U.S. Court of Appeals for the Fourth Circuit.

87. Stephen P. Halbrook, "The Constitutional Right to Hunt: New Recognition for an Old Liberty in Virginia," *William and Mary Bill of Rights Law Journal* 19 (2010): 197–233.

88. *Acts*, 2016 Sess., chap. 735; vote not reported on Virginia State Board of Elections website.

89. *Proceedings and Debates in the Senate of Virginia*, 425.

90. *Acts*, 1982 Sess., chap. 687.

91. Walker, "The Governor's Veto Power," 13–16.

92. *Starnes v. Cauoyette*, 244 Va 202 (1992).

93. *Acts*, 1996 Sess., chap. 908.

94. *Falwell v. Miller*, 203 F. Sup 2d (2002): 624–633; Mathew D. Staver and Anita L. Staver, "Disestablishmentarianism Collides with the First Amendment: The Ghost of Thomas Jefferson Still Haunts Churches," *Cumberland Law Review* 33 (2002): 43–105; Thomas E. Buckley, SJ, "'A Great Religious Octopus': Church and State at Virginia's Constitutional Convention, 1901–1902," *Church History* 72 (2003): 333–60; Thomas E. Buckley, SJ, *Establishing Religious Freedom: Jefferson's Statute in Virginia* (Charlottesville, 2013), 68, 70–72, 78–81, 215–20.

95. Deborah Lee Titus, "Commonwealth Right of Appeal in Criminal Proceedings," *Washington and Lee Law Review* 43 (1986): 295–316; Roger D. Scott, "Double Jeopardy and the Commonwealth's Right to Writs of Error in Criminal Cases," *University of Richmond Law Review* 20 (1986): 629–69, on 661–65; Jeffrey D. McMahan Jr., "Guarding the Guardians: Judges' Rights and Virginia's Judicial Inquiry and Review Commission," *University of Richmond Law Review* 43 (2008): 473–522.

96. *Baugh v. Judicial Inquiry and Review Commission*, 907 F 2d 440 (1990); Brian R. Pitney, "Unlocking the Chamber Doors: Limiting Confidentiality in Proceedings before the Virginia Judicial Inquiry and Review Commission," *University of Richmond Law Review* 26 (1992): 367–90; Dinan, *Virginia State Constitution*, 175–76.

97. *Miller v. Ayers*, 213 Va. 217 (1972); *Miller v. Ayers*, 214 Va. 171 (1973).

98. Robert A. Schapiro, "Identity and Interpretation in State Constitutional law," *Virginia Law Review* 84 (1998): 389–457.

99. Stephen R. McCullough, "Article I Section 13 of the Virginia Constitution: Of Militias and an Individual Right to Bear Arms," *University of Richmond Law Review* 48 (2013): 215–33; *District of Columbia v. Heller*, 554 US 570 (2008).

100. Stephen R. McCullough, "A Vanishing Virginia Constitution," *University of Richmond Law Review* 46 (2011): 347–57; Robert S. Claiborne Jr., "Commonwealth and Constitution," *University of Richmond Law Review* 48 (2013): 415–77.

101. *Archer and Johnson v. Mayes et al.*, 213 Va 633 (1973).

102. Tarter, *Grandees*, 357–75; Tarter, *Gerrymanders*, 79–98.

103. Carl W. Tobias, "Reconsidering Virginia Judicial Selection," *University of Richmond Law Review* 43 (2008): 37–49.

104. Tarter, *Gerrymanders*, 65–78.

105. *Acts*, 1972 Sess., chap. 61; A. Linwood Holton, *Opportunity Time* (Charlottes-

ville, 2018), 112–14; Weldon Cooper, "State Reorganization: The Virginia Experience," *VNL* 46 (1970): 25–28; T. Edward Temple, "The Virginia Cabinet: A Preliminary Assessment," *VNL* 50 (1973): 9–12.

106. Thomas J. Michie and Marcia S. Mashaw, "Annexation and State Aid to Localities: A Compromise is Reached," *VNL* 55 (1979): 41–44; Mary Jo. Fields, "An Update on Local Government Consolidation in Virginia," *VNL* 60 (1983): 19–23; Robert E. Spicer Jr., "Annexation in Virginia: The 1979 Amendments Usher in a New Era in City-County Relations," *University of Richmond Law Review* 17 (1983): 819–43; Jack D. Edwards, "Annexation Resumes in Virginia," *VNL* 60 (1984): 37–41; Jack D. Edwards, *Neighbors and Sometimes Friends: Municipal Annexation in Modern Virginia* (Charlottesville, 1992); Andrew V. Sorrell and Bruce A. Vlk, "Virginia's Never-Ending Moratorium on City-County Annexations," *VNL* 88 (January 2012): 1–9.

107. E.g., A. E. S., "Dillon's Rule: The Case for Reform," *Virginia Law Review* 68 (1982): 693–712; Dick Hall-Sizemore and M. H. Wilkinson, "Home Rule in Virginia: Perception and Reality," *VNL* 66 (March/April 1990): 1–5; Robert M. DeVoursney, "The Dillon Rule in Virginia: What's Broken? What Needs to Be Fixed?" *VNL* (July/August 1992): 1–10; League of Women Voters of the Fairfax Area Education Fund, "Dillon's Rule: Good or Bad for Local Governments?" (October 2004); *Roanoke Times*, 3 March 2007.

108. Most easily seen by the Virginia Board of Elections official online *Official Election Results*.

109. Brent Tarter, "The Virginia Constitution of 1971, The First Half Century," *VMHB* 129 (2021): 291–321.

Chapter 10. The Age of Constitutional Amendments

1. Robert F. Williams, "Are State Constitutional Conventions Things of the Past? The Increasing Role of the Constitutional Commission in State Constitutional Change," *Hofstra Law and Policy Symposium* 1 (1996): 1–26.

2. John Dinan, *State Constitutional Politics: Governing by Amendment in the American States* (Chicago, 2018).

3. *New State Ice Company v. Liebmann*, 285 US 262 (1932), on 311.

SELECT BIBLIOGRAPHIES

General Works

Anderson, William A. "Virginia Constitutions," *Proceedings of the Virginia State Bar Association* 13 (1900): 145–78.
Brenaman, Jacob N. *A History of Virginia Conventions*. Richmond: J. L. Hill Printing Company, 1902.
Dinan, John. *The Virginia State Constitution: A Reference Guide*. 2nd ed. Oxford: Oxford University Press, 2014.
Howard, A. E. Dick. *Commentaries on the Constitution of Virginia*. 2 vols. Charlottesville: University of Virginia Press, 1974.
Howard, A. E. Dick. "'For the Common Benefit': Constitutional History in Virginia as a Casebook for the Modern Constitution-Maker." *Virginia Law Review* 54, no. 5 (1968): 818–902.
Nelson, Margaret Virginia. *A Study of Judicial Review in Virginia, 1789–1928*. New York: Columbia University Press, 1947.
Pate, James E. "Constitutional Revision in Virginia Affecting the General Assembly." *William and Mary Quarterly*, 2nd ser. 10 (1930): 105–22.
Pulliam, David L. *The Constitutional Conventions of Virginia from the Foundation of the Commonwealth to the Present*. Richmond: John T. West, 1901.
Swem, Earl G. "A Bibliography of Conventions and Constitutions of Virginia Including References to Essays, Letters and Speeches in the Virginia Newspapers." *Bulletin of the Virginia State Library* 3, no. 4 (1910): 355–401.
Van Schreeven, William J. *The Conventions and Constitutions of Virginia, 1776–1966*. Richmond, Virginia State Library, 1967.

The Constitution of 1776

PRIMARY

Revolutionary Convention Papers, Convention of 1776, Record Group 89, Library of Virginia.
Ordinances Passed at a General Convention of Delegates and Representatives, from the Several Counties and Corporations of Virginia, Held at the Capitol, in the City of Williamsburg, on Monday the 6th of May, Anno Dom: 1776. Williamsburg, Alexander Purdie, 1776.
Proceedings of the Convention of Delegates Held at the Capitol, in the City of Williamsburg, in the Colony of Virginia, on Monday the 6th of May, 1776. Williamsburg, Alexander Purdie, 1776.
Van Schreeven, William J., Robert L. Scribner, and Brent Tarter, eds. *Revolutionary Vir-*

ginia, *The Road to Independence: A Documentary Record*, 7 vols. Charlottesville: University of Virginia Press, for the Virginia Independence Bicentennial Commission, 1973–83. Volumes 6 and 7 contain all the records of the Convention of 1776.

SECONDARY

Buckley, Thomas E., SJ. *Church and State in Revolutionary Virginia, 1776–1787*. Charlottesville: University of Virginia Press, 1977.

Buckley, Thomas E., SJ. *Establishing Religious Freedom: Jefferson's Statute in Virginia*. Charlottesville: University of Virginia Press, 2013.

Grigsby, Hugh Blair. *The Virginia Convention of 1776: A Discourse Delivered Before the Virginia Alpha of the Phi Beta Kappa Society, in the Chapel of William and Mary College, in the City of Williamsburg, on the Afternoon of July the 3rd, 1855*. Richmond: J. W. Randolph, 1855.

Hilldrup, Robert L. "The Virginia Convention of 1776." PhD diss., University of Virginia, 1935.

Oliver, George B. "A Constitutional History of Virginia, 1776–1860." PhD diss., Duke University, 1959.

Pole, J. R. "Representation in Virginia from the Revolution to Reform." *Journal of Southern History* 24 (1958): 16–50.

Randolph, Edmund. *History of Virginia*. Edited by Arthur H. Shaffer. Charlottesville: University Press of Virginia for the Virginia Historical Society, 1970.

Selby, John E. "Richard Henry Lee, John Adams, and the Virginia Constitution of 1776." *Virginia Magazine of History and Biography* 84, no. 4 (1976): 387–400.

Sutton, Robert P. *Revolution to Secession: Constitution Making in the Old Dominion*. Charlottesville: University Press of Virginia, 1989.

Tarter, Brent. "An Introductory Note." In vol. 7 of *Revolutionary Virginia, The Road to Independence: A Documentary Record*, edited by William J. Van Schreeven, Robert L. Scribner, and Brent Tarter. 7 vols. Charlottesville: University Press of Virginia, for the Virginia Independence Bicentennial Commission, 1973–83.

Tarter, Brent. "The Virginia Declaration of Rights." In *To Secure the Blessings of Liberty: Rights in American History*, ed. Josephine F. Pacheco. Fairfax, VA: George Mason University Press, 1993.

The Constitution of 1830

PRIMARY

Records of the Virginia Constitutional Convention of 1829–30, Record Group 91, Library of Virginia, includes the enrolled constitution.

Journal, Acts and Proceedings of a General Convention of the Commonwealth of Virginia, Assembled in Richmond (Richmond, T. Ritchie, 1829 [i.e., 1830]).

Proceedings and Debates of the Virginia State Convention of 1829–30 (Richmond, S. Shepherd and Co., for Ritchie and Cook, 1830).

SECONDARY

Ambler, Charles H. *Sectionalism in Virginia, 1776 to 1861*. Chicago, University of Chicago Press, 1910.
Bruce, Dickson D., Jr. *The Rhetoric of Conservatism: The Virginia Convention of 1829-30 and the Conservative Tradition in the South*. San Marino, CA, Huntington Library, 1982.
Chandler, Julian A. C. *History of Suffrage in Virginia*. Baltimore, Johns Hopkins Press, 1901.
Chandler, Julian A. C. *Representation in Virginia*. Baltimore, Johns Hopkins Press, 1896.
Curtis, Christopher M. "Reconsidering Suffrage Reform in the 1829-1830 Virginia Constitutional Convention." *Journal of Southern History* 74, no 1. (February 2008): 89-124.
Freehling, Alison Goodyear. *Drift toward Dissolution: The Virginia Slavery Debate of 1831-1832*. Baton Rouge, Louisiana State University Press, 1982.
Gatewood, Joanne L., ed. "Richmond during the Virginia Constitutional Convention of 1829-30: An Extract from the Diary of Thomas Green, October 1, 1829, to January 31, 1830." *Virginia Magazine of History and Biography* 84, no. 3 (1976): 287-332.
Grigsby, Hugh Blair. "Sketches of Members of the Constitutional Convention of 1829-30." *Virginia Magazine of History and Biography* 61, no. 3 (1953): 219-332.
Grigsby, Hugh Blair. *The Virginia Convention of 1829-30*. Richmond, Virginia Historical Society, 1854.
Hizer, Trenton E. "'Virginia Is Now Divided': Politics in the Old Dominion, 1820-1833." PhD diss., University of South Carolina, 1997.
Oliver, George B. "A Constitutional History of Virginia, 1776-1860." PhD diss., Duke University, 1959.
Peterson, Merrill D., ed. *Democracy, Liberty, and Property: The State Constitutional Conventions of the 1820s*. Indianapolis, Bobbs-Merrill Co., 1966.
Pleasants, Hugh B. "Sketches of the Virginia Convention of 1829-30." *Southern Literary Messenger* 17 (1851): 147-54.
Pole, J. R. "Representation in Virginia from the Revolution to Reform." *Journal of Southern History* 24 (1958): 16-50.
Shade, William D. *Democratizing the Old Dominion: Virginia and the Second Party System, 1824-1861*. Charlottesville, University Press of Virginia, 1996.
Sutton, Robert P. *Revolution to Secession: Constitution Making in the Old Dominion*. Charlottesville, University Press of Virginia, 1989.
Sutton, Robert P. "The Virginia Constitutional Convention of 1829-30: A Profile Analysis of Late Jeffersonian Virginia." PhD diss., University of Virginia, 1967.

The Constitution of 1851

PRIMARY

Records of the Convention of 1850-51, RG 92, LVA.
Documents, Containing Statistics of Virginia: Ordered to be Printed by the State Convention Sitting in the City of Richmond, 1850-51. Richmond, W. Culley, 1851.

Journal, Acts and Proceedings, and also Documents, Containing Statistics of Virginia: Ordered to be Printed by the State Convention Sitting in the City of Richmond, 1850–51. Richmond, W. Culley, 1851.

Register of the Debates and Proceedings of the Va. Reform Convention. Richmond, R. H. Gallaher, 1851.

Supplements to Richmond newspapers, incomplete, reporting debates, Library of Virginia, and College of William and Mary.

SECONDARY

Ambler, Charles Henry. *Sectionalism in Virginia, 1776 to 1861.* Chicago, University of Chicago Press, 1910.

Chandler, Julian A. C. *History of Suffrage in Virginia.* Baltimore, Johns Hopkins Press, 1901.

Chandler, Julian A. C. *Representation in Virginia.* Baltimore, Johns Hopkins Press, 1896.

Gaines, Francis Pendleton, Jr. "The Virginia Constitutional Convention of 1850–51: A Study in Sectionalism." PhD diss., University of Virginia, 1950.

Link, William A. *Roots of Secession: Slavery and Politics in Antebellum Virginia.* Chapel Hill, University of North Carolina Press, 2003.

Oliver, George B. "A Constitutional History of Virginia, 1776–1860." PhD diss., Duke University, 1959.

Pole, J. R. "Representation in Virginia from the Revolution to Reform." *Journal of Southern History* 24 (1958): 16–50.

Poteet, H. H. "The Virginia Convention of 1850–51." PhD diss., Johns Hopkins University, 1929.

Shade, William D. *Democratizing the Old Dominion: Virginia and the Second Party System, 1824–1861.* Charlottesville, University Press of Virginia, 1996.

Simpson, Craig. "Political Compromise and the Protection of Slavery: Henry A. Wise and the Virginia Constitutional Convention of 1850–1851." *Virginia Magazine of History and Biography* 83 (1975): 387–405.

Sutelan, David A., and Wayne R. Spencer. "The Virginia Special Court of Appeals: Constitutional Relief for an Overburdened Court." *William and Mary Law Review* 8 (1967): 244–76.

Sutton, Robert P. *Revolution to Secession: Constitution Making in the Old Dominion.* Charlottesville, University Press of Virginia, 1989.

The Constitution of 1864

PRIMARY

Records of the Virginia Convention of 1864, Record Group, 95, Library of Virginia.

Constitution of Virginia, Virginia Historical Society, old catalog record Mss13:1864 Apr 7:1.

Constitution of the State of Virginia, and the Ordinances Adopted by the Convention which Assembled at Alexandria, on the 13th Day of February, 1864. Alexandria, D. Turner, 1864.

Journal of the Constitutional Convention Which Convened at Alexandria on the 13th Day of February, 1864. Alexandria, D. Turner, 1864.

SECONDARY

Bearss, Sara B. "'Restored and Vindicated': The Virginia Constitutional Convention of 1864." *Virginia Magazine of History and Biography* 122 (2014): 156–81.

Belz, Herman. *Reconstructing the Union: Theory and Policy during the Civil War.* Ithaca, NY, Cornell University Press for the American Historical Association, 1969.

Lowe, Richard G. *Republicans and Reconstruction in Virginia, 1856–1870.* Charlottesville, University Press of Virginia, 1991.

The Constitution of 1869

PRIMARY

Records of the Virginia Constitutional Convention of 1867–68, Record Group 96, Library of Virginia, includes the enrolled constitution.

The Constitution of Virginia Framed by the Convention Which Met in Richmond, Virginia, on Tuesday, December 3, 1867 (Richmond, Office of the New Nation, 1868).

The Debates and Proceedings of the Constitutional Convention of the States of Virginia, Assembled at the City of Richmond, Tuesday, December 3, 1867: Being a Full and Complete Report of the Debates and Proceedings of the Convention, Together with the Reconstruction Acts of Congress and Those Supplementary Thereto, the Order of the Commander of the First Military District Assembling the Convention, and the New Constitution. Richmond, William H. Samuel, 1868.

Documents of the Constitutional Convention of the State of Virginia. Richmond, Office of the New Nation, 1868.

Journal of the Constitutional Convention of the State of Virginia, Convened in the City of Richmond, December 3, 1867, by an Order of General Schofield, Dated 2 November, 1867, in Pursuance of the Act of Congress of March 23, 1867. Richmond, Office of the New Nation, 1868.

Summary of the Number of Registered Voters, the Number of Votes Polled, and the Result of the Election on the Question of Acceptance or Rejection of a Proposed Constitution for the State of Virginia, Held on the Sixth (6th) Day of July, 1869 published in *General Orders and Circulars, Headquarters First Military District, 1869.* Richmond, Assistant Advocate General's Office, 1870.

Secretary of the Commonwealth Election Records, No. 427, Record Group 13, Library of Virginia.

SECONDARY

Belz, Herman. "The Problem of Constitutionalism and Constitutional Liberty in the Reconstruction South." In *An Uncertain Tradition: Constitutionalism and the History of the South,* edited by Kermit L. Hall and James W. Ely Jr. Athens, GA, University of Georgia Press, 1989.

Chandler, Julian A. C. *History of Suffrage in Virginia*. Baltimore, Johns Hopkins Press, 1901.
Chandler, Julian A. C. *Representation in Virginia*. Baltimore, Johns Hopkins Press, 1896.
Online edition of the Library of Virginia's *Dictionary of Virginia Biography*, online *Encyclopedia Virginia*, and website of the General Assembly's Martin Luther King Jr. Commission contain biographies of all African American delegates to the convention.
Fairlie, John A. "The Veto Power of the State Governor." *American Political Science Review* 11 (1917): 473–93.
Hume, Richard L. "The Membership of the Virginia Constitutional Convention of 1867–1868: A Study in the Beginnings of Congressional Reconstruction." *Virginia Magazine of History and Biography* 86 (1978): 461–84.
Long, Armistead R. *The Constitution of Virginia: An Annotated Edition*. Lynchburg, J. T. Bell and Co., 1901.
Lowe, Richard G. "Virginia's Reconstruction Convention: General Schofield Rates the Delegates." *Virginia Magazine of History and Biography* 80 (1972): 341–60.
Lowe, Richard G. *Republicans and Reconstruction in Virginia, 1856–1870*. Charlottesville, University Press of Virginia, 1991.

The Constitution of 1902

PRIMARY

Records of the Virginia Constitutional Convention (1901–1902), Record Group 97, Library of Virginia, including enrolled constitution.
Journal of the Constitutional Convention of Virginia. Held in the City of Richmond, Beginning June 12th, 1901. Richmond, J. H. O'Bannon, 1901 [i.e., 1902], includes schedule and ordinances.
Report of the Proceedings and Debates of the Constitutional Convention State of Virginia Held in the City of Richmond June 12, 1901, to June 26, 1902, 2 vols. Richmond, Hermitage Press, 1906.
Resolutions of the Constitutional Convention of 1901–1902. Richmond, no publisher, 1902.
Braxton, Allen Caperton. Papers. University of Virginia.
Braxton, A. Caperton. "The Powers of the Approaching Limited Constitutional Convention in Virginia." *Virginia Law Register* 7 (1901): 100–106, with a supplemental note, "The Powers of the Approaching Constitutional Convention in Virginia." *Virginia Law Register* 7 (1901): 79–99.
Daniel, John W. "The Work of the Constitutional Convention." *Reports of the Virginia State Bar Association* 15 (1902): 257–94.
John Garland Pollard, Data for Biographical Sketches of the Members of the Virginia Constitutional Convention of 1901–1902, Virginia Historical Society, Mss 5:9 P7624:1.
Richmond Times. 12 June 1901, contains brief sketches of convention delegates.

Thomas, A. F. *The Virginia Constitutional Convention and its Possibilities.* Lynchburg, J. P. Bell Co., 1901.
Watson, Walter A. Diary. Virginia Historical Society, entries for 1902 published in Mrs. Walter A. Watson [Constance Tinsley Watson], ed., *Notes on Southside Virginia.* Richmond, Virginia State Library, 1925.

SECONDARY

Chandler, Julian A. C. "Constitutional Revision in Virginia." *Proceedings of the American Political Science Association, Fifth Annual Meeting* 5 (1909): 192–202.
Gay, Thomas Edward, Jr. "Creating the Virginia State Corporation Commission." *Virginia Magazine of History and Biography* 78 (1970): 464–80.
Fairlie, John A. "The Veto Power of the State Governor." *American Political Science Review* 11 (1917): 473–93.
Gilliam, George Harrison. "Making Virginia Progressive: Courts and Parties, Railroads and Regulators, 1890–1910." *Virginia Magazine of History and Biography* 107 (1999): 189–222.
Herron, Paul E. *Framing the Solid South: The State Constitutional Conventions of Secession, Reconstruction, and Redemption, 1861–1902.* Lawrence, KS, University Press of Kansas, 2017.
Holt, Wythe. "The Virginia Constitutional Convention of 1901–1902: A Reform Movement Which Lacked Substance." *Virginia Magazine of History and Biography* 76 (1968): 67–102.
Holt, Wythe. *Virginia's Constitutional Convention of 1901–1902.* New York, Garland Publishing, 1990.
Kousser, J. Morgan. *The Shaping of Southern Politics: Suffrage Restriction and the Establishment of the One-Party South, 1880–1910.* New Haven, Yale University Press, 1974.
McDanel, Ralph C. *The Virginia Constitutional Convention of 1901–1902.* Baltimore, 1928.
McKinley, Albert E. "Two New Southern Constitutions." *Political Science Quarterly* 18 (1903): 480–511.
Matzen, John Mathiason. *State Constitutional Provisions for Education: Fundamental Attitude of the American People Regarding Education as Revealed by State Constitutional Provisions, 1776–1929.* New York, Teachers' College, Columbia University, 1931.
Moger, Allen W. *Virginia: Bourbonism to Byrd, 1870–1925.* Charlottesville, University Press of Virginia, 1968.
Pate, James E. "Constitutional Revision in Virginia Affecting the General Assembly," *William and Mary Quarterly,* 2nd ser., 10 (1930): 105122.
Perman, Michael. *Struggle for Mastery: Disfranchisement in the South, 1888–1908.* Chapel Hill, University of North Carolina Press, 2001.
Porter, Albert O. *County Government in Virginia, A Legislative History, 1607–1904.* New York, Columbia University Press, 1947.

Pulley, Raymond H. *Old Virginia Restored: An Interpretation of the Progressive Impulse, 1870–1930.* Charlottesville, University of Virginia Press, 1968.

Wells, Roger H. "The Item Veto and State Budget Reform." *American Political Science Review* 18 (1924).

The Constitutional Revision of 1928

PRIMARY

Byrd, Harry Flood. *A Discussion of the Amendments Proposed to the Constitution of Virginia.* Richmond, no publisher, 1928. Three pamphlets treating the revised constitution, the short ballot amendments, and the tax segregation amendment.

Enrolled constitution in Enrolled Bills, 1928 Sess., chap. 46, Library of Virginia.

Executive Papers of Governor Harry Flood Byrd (1926–30). Record Group 3, Library of Virginia. Boxes 18, 30, 31, 77, and 7, 8 and correspondence with William T. Reed, Luther Gulick, and A. E. Buck.

Address of Harry F. Byrd Governor on the Subject of Simplification of Government in Virginia, Delivered Before the General Assembly of Virginia, Wednesday, February 3, 1926, Senate Doc. 8, bound with *JS*, 1926 Sess.

Journal of the House of Delegates, extra Sess., 1927.

Journal of the Senate of Virginia, extra Sess., 1927. Ditto

New York Bureau of Municipal Research. *Organization and Management of the State Government of Virginia; Report on a Survey Made for the Governor and His Committee on Consolidation and Simplification.* Richmond, D. Bottom, 1927.

New York Bureau of Municipal Research. *County Government in Virginia: Report on a Survey Made to the Governor and His Committee on Consolidation and Simplification, January 1927.* Richmond, D. Bottom, 1928.

Program of Progress. An Address by Harry Flood Byrd, Governor, Delivered Before the General Assembly of Virginia, January 16, 1928, printed as Senate Doc. 5, bound with *JS*, 1928 Sess., 3.

Reed, William T. Papers, Virginia Historical Society, including correspondence 1926–28 with Harry Flood Byrd, Luther Gulick, and A. E. Buck.

Report of Citizens Committee on Consolidation and Simplification in State and Local Governments Submitted to the Governor of Virginia in Accordance with Act of General Assembly of 1926. Richmond, D. Bottom, 1927.

Report of the Commission to Suggest Amendments to the Constitution to the General Assembly of Virginia. Richmond, D. Bottom, 1927.

SECONDARY

Buck, A. E. "A Survey of Virginia State and County Government." *Social Forces* 6 (1928): 448–452.

Buck, Arthur E. *The Reorganization of State Governments in the United States.* New York, Columbia Univesity Press for the national Municipal League, 1938.

Fry, Joseph A. "Senior Advisor to the Democratic 'Organization': William Thomas

Reed and Virginia Politics." *Virginia Magazine of History and Biography* 85 (1977): 445–69.
Heinemann, Ronald L. *Harry Byrd of Virginia*. Charlottesville, University Press of Virginia, 1996.
Holsinger, Justus G. "The Process and Development of the Virginia Constitutional Revision of 1928: With Regard to the Reorganization of Administration." PhD diss., University of Virginia, 1935.
Holt, Wythe. "Constitutional Revision in Virginia, 1902 and 1928: Some Lessons on Roadblocks to Institutional Reform." *Virginia Law Review* 54 (1968): 903–60.
Morrissett, C. H. *Proposed Amendments to the Constitution of Virginia: A Statement Pointing Them Out and Explaining Them*. Richmond, Richmond Press, 1928.
Pate, James E. "Constitutional Revision in Virginia Affecting the General Assembly," *William and Mary Quarterly*, 2nd ser., 10 (1930): 105–22.
Spicer, George W. "Gubernatorial Leadership in Virginia," *Public Administration Review* 1 (1941): 441–57.

The Constitution of 1971

PRIMARY

Address of Mills E. Godwin, Jr., to the General Assembly, Wednesday, January 10, 1968, printed as Doc. 1 with *JS*, 1968 Sess.
Commission on Constitutional Revision. *The Constitution of Virginia: Report*. Charlottesville, Michie Co., 1969.
Proceedings and Debates of the Virginia House of Delegates Pertaining to Amendment of the Constitution, Extra Session 1969, Regular Session 1970. Richmond, Department of Purchases and Supply, 1973.
Proceedings and Debates of the Senate of Virginia Pertaining to Amendment of the Constitution: Extra Session 1969, Regular Session 1970. Richmond, Department of Purchases and Supply, 1971.
Records of the Commission on Constitutional Revision, Record Group 87, Library of Virginia.
Papers of A. E. Dick Howard for the Virginia Commission for Constitutional Revision, 1969–1971, Arthur J. Morris Law Library, University of Virginia.

SECONDARY

Canning, Bonnie. *State Constitutional Conventions, Revisions, and Amendments, 1959–1976, Bibliography*. Westport, CT, Greenwood Press, 1977.
Claiborne, Robert S. Jr. "Commonwealth and Constitution." *University of Richmond Law Review* 48 (2013): 415–77.
Cornwell, Elmer E., Jr., Jay Goodman, and Wayne R. Swanson. *State Constitutional Conventions: The Politics of the Revision Process in Seven States*. New York, National Municipal League, 1975.
Dinan, John. *The Virginia State Constitution*, rev., 2nd ed. (Oxford, 2014).

Dinan, John. "Amendments to Virginia's 1971 Constitution." *Virginia Magazine of History and Biography* 129 (2021): 322–45.

Dixon, Donald D. "Local Government and the 1971 Virginia Constitution." *Virginia News Letter* 49 (1973): 37–40.

Elazar, Daniel J. "Constitution Making: The Pre-eminently Political Act." In *Redesigning the State: The Politics of Constitutional Change*, edited by Keith G. Banting and Richard Simeon. Toronto, University of Toronto Press, 1985.

Friesen, Jennifer. *State Constitutional Law: Litigating Individual Rights, Claims, and Defenses.* 2nd ed. Charlottesville, Michie Co., 1995.

Grad, Frank P. "The State Constitution: Its Function and Form for Our Time." *Virginia Law Review* 54 1968): 928–73.

Howard, A. E. Dick. *Commentaries on the Constitution of Virginia.* 2 vols. Charlottesville, University Press of Virginia, 1974.

Howard, A. E. Dick. "Constitutional Revision: Virginia and the Nation." *University of Richmond Law Review* 9 (1974): 1–48.

Howard, A. E. Dick. "State Constitutions and the Environment." *Virginia Law Review* 58 (1972): 193–229.

Howard, A. E. Dick, and William Antholis. "The Virginia Constitution of 1971: An Interview with A. E. Dick Howard." *Virginia Magazine of History and Biography* 129 (2021): 346–89.

Libonati, Michael E. "Home Rule: An Essay on Pluralism." *Washington Law Review* 64 (1989): 51–71.

McCullough, Stephen R. "Article I Section 13 of the Virginia Constitution: Of Militias and an Individual Right to Bear Arms." *University of Richmond Law Review* 48 (2013): 215–33.

McCullough, Stephen R. "A Vanishing Virginia Constitution." *University of Richmond Law Review* 46 (2011): 347–57.

Mooe, Hullihen W. "In Aid of Public Education: An Analysis of the Education Article of the Virginia Constitution of 1971." *University of Richmond Law Review* 5 (1971): 263–310.

Pollock, Stewart G. "State Constitutions as Separate Sources of Fundamental Rights." *Rutgers Law Journal* 24 (1983): 707–22.

"Project Report: Towards an Activist Role for State Bills of Rights." *Harvard Civil Rights-Civil Liberties Law Review* 8 (1973): 323–50.

J. Y. P. Jr. "Toward a Constitutionally Protected Environment." *Virginia Law Review* 56 (1970): 548–86.

Spain, Jack, Jr. "The General Assembly and Local Government: Legislating a Constitution 1969–70." *University of Richmond Law Review* 8 (1974): 387–429.

Sturm, Albert L. "The Development of American State Constitutions." *Publius* 12 (1982): 57–98.

Sturm, Albert L. "The 1971 Revised Virginia Constitution and Recent Constitution-Making: A Standard for Comparison." *State Government* 44 (1971): 166–72.

Sturm, Albert L. *Thirty Years of State Constitution-Making, 1938–1968.* New York, National Municipal League, 1970.

Tarter, Brent. "The Virginia Constitution of 1971, The First Half Century." *Virginia Magazine of History and Biography* 129 (2001): 290–321.

INDEX

Act for Establishing Religious Freedom (1786), 71–72, 96–97, 122
Act to Provide for the More Efficient Government of the Rebel States (1867), 152–53, 161–62
Acts of Trade and Navigation, 16, 17, 25
Adams, John, 46–47, 58, 60
alcohol, 208, 220, 221, 285
Alexandria & Georgetown R. R. Co. v. Alexandria & Washington R. R. Co., et al (1870), 155
Almond v. Day (1955), 265
American Revolution, 69–70
Anderson-McCormick Act (1884), 189–90, 198
Anderson, William Alexander, 144, 204–5, 210
annexation, 273, 310–11
Antoni v. Wright (1872), 186
Archer and Johnson v. Mayes et al. (1973), 308
attorney general
 in Constitution of the colony, 15
 in Constitution of 1776, 46, 61, 68
 in Constitution of 1830, 96
 in Constitution of 1851, 123
 in Constitution of 1869, 177
 in Constitution of 1971, 286, 288–89, 300, 302
Ayers, Rufus Adolphus, 203, 205

Bacon's Rebellion, 10, 30–31
Baptists, 53, 71
Barber v. City of Danville (1928), 288–89
Barbour, John Strode, 264
Barbour, Philip Pendleton, 90
Barron v. Baltimore (1833), 75
Baugh v. Judicial Inquiry and Review Commission (1990), 303–4
Bayne, Thomas, 178
Beck v. Shelton (2004), 288–89
Berkeley, Sir William, 9, 15, 18–19, 21, 31

bicameralism, 19, 47
Bill of Rights, English, 51, 52
bills of attainder, 282
Black Belt, 199–201
Black Virginians: *see* freed people; racial segregation; slavery, suffrage
Blair, Frank S., 205
Blair, Robert William, 205
Bland, Richard, 28, 33; *Inquiry into the Rights of the British Colonies*, 5, 34–35
Board of Agriculture and Commerce, 267
Board of Agriculture and Immigration, 173, 228, 267, 281
Board of Public Works, 79, 121, 122, 172, 173, 231
Bodeker, Anna Whitehead, 166
Book of Common Prayer, 67
Booker, Sallie Cook, 253
Bostic v. Rainey (2014), 300
Bostic v. Shaefer (2014), 300
Botetourt, Norborne Berkeley, baron de, 14, 37
Botts, John Minor, 143–44
Bouldin, Wood, 210
Bowden, Lemuel J., 142
Brandeis, Lewis, 313
Braxton, Allen Caperton, 205–6, 207, 209–10, 264; State Corporation Commission 229–30, 232, 235–36, 294, 295
Braxton, Carter, 47, 60
Brenaman, Jacob, 187
Brennan, William J. "State Constitutions and the Protection of Individual Liberties," 2
Bristow, Joseph Allen, 204, 233
Brockenbrough, John White, 145–46
Brown v. Board of Education of Topeka (1954), 228, 265, 268, 275, 293
Bureau of Refugees, Freedmen, and Abandoned Lands, 152, 177
burgesses, 7–8

Burks v. Hinton (1870), 175
Burks, Edward Calohill, 175
Butler, Charles Wilson, 241
Byrd, Harry Flood, 244, 246–49, 262–63, 277, 310; Byrd organization, 244, 268–70, 272, 273, 274, 276–77, 284
Byrd, William, 14

Cameron, William E., 204
Campbell, Alexander, 92–93, 101
Campbell, Preston W., 205, 264
Canada, David, 165
Canby, Edward Richard Sprigg, 183
Carrington v. Rash (1965), 284
Cary, Archibald, 49
Case of the County Levy (ca. 1789), 65, 73
Catholics, 19, 221
Charles I, 9, 10–11
Charles II, 9–10, 19, 31
Chase, Salmon P., 152–53, 184
Chiswell, John, 36
Church of England, 8, 13, 26–28, 66-69, 71; clergymen, 32–33; parishes, 11, 26-28, 31, 71–72
church property, 180–81, 234
circuit courts, 123, 173–74, 223–24, 258, 289, 290
cities and towns, 29, 72, 225, 243, 273–74; independent cities, 226, 291
 in Constitution of 1776, 65
 in Constitution of 1830, 99–100
 in Constitution of 1851, 125–26
 in Constitution of 1864, 141
 in Constitution of 1869, 170, 177, 189
 in Constitution of 1902, 225–26, 238, 239
 in Constitutional Revision of 1928, 249–50, 258–59, 265, 266
 in Constitution of 1971, 291–92, 304, 310–11
 see also Dillon Rule
Citizens Committee on Consolidation and Simplification of State and Local Government (Reed Commission) (1926), 252–53
Civil Rights Act (1866), 166
Civil Rights Act (1964), 275–76
civil rights movement, 267–68, 275–76
Claiborne, William, 18

clergymen, 44, 121, 172
Coalter, John, 98
Coercive (Intolerable) Acts (1774), 37
Cohabitation Act (1866), 149, 181
College of William and Mary, 59
Colored Monitor Union Club, 159, 178
Colored State Convention (1865), 160
Combs, Everett Randolph, 269
Commission on Constitutional Revision (1968), 278–80, 285–86, 292, 294–95
Commission to Suggest Amendments to the Constitution to the General Assembly of Virginia (Prentis Commission) (1926), 252, 255–56, 257, 259, 262
common law, 69
commonwealth, 55
commonwealth's attorney, 125, 172
Commonwealth v. Caton (1782), 73
Commonwealth v. Dodson (1940), 222
Confederate States of America, 133, 138–39, 147, 148, 169, 170, 179, 182–83
Congress of the United States, 74–75
conservation, 297, 300
Conservative Party, 161, 165, 186, 187
constitutional conventions, 84, 312–13
 Convention of 1776, 43–44, 48–50
 Convention of 1829–30, 88–93
 Convention of 1850–51, 112–17
 Convention of 1861, 128–29, 196
 Convention of 1864, 135–37
 Convention of 1867–68, 162–67, 193, 195
 Convention of 1901–2, 191, 195–211
 Convention of 1945 (limited), 263–64
 Convention of 1956 (limited), 265–66
constitutional officers, 224, 225, 242, 266, 291
Constitution of Kentucky, 75–76, 312
Constitution of the United States, 2, 74–75, 169, 307–8
 Bill of Rights, 54, 75, 307–8
 First Amendment, 302, 303, 304
 Second Amendment, 283, 307–8, 308
 Ninth Amendment, 170
 Thirteenth Amendment, 191; Virginia ratification, 143
 Fourteenth Amendment, 166, 183–84, 191–92, 209, 215, 228, 265, 268, 275, 293, 308; Virginia ratification, 151–52, 183–84

Fifteenth Amendment, 192, 196, 203, 209, 215; Virginia ratification, 183–84
Seventeenth Amendment, 240
Nineteenth Amendment, 239, 240, 255
Twenty-Fourth Amendment, 267
Twenty-Fifth Amendment, 288
Twenty-Sixth Amendment, 301
Constitution of West Virginia, 130–31, 312
Constitutions of Virginia, 1–2, 312–13
of the colony, 5–12, 28–31, 32–39, 57, 69–70
of 1776, 31, 38–39, 40–41, 46–47, 49–50, 69–72, 78–87; proclaimed, 68–69
of 1830, 88–93, 100, 102–5; ratified, 100–2
of 1851, 112–17, 128–29, 133, 135; ratified, 126–27
of 1864, 132–33, 136–38, 141–42, 146–55, 212; legitimacy, 142–46, 154; proclaimed, 141–42
of 1869, 157–58, 162–68, 184–91, 193, 212; ratified, 181–83
of 1902, 202–12, 237–45; proclaimed, 206, 234–36
Revision of 1928, 247–52, 253–54, 263–67, 268–71, 270–71; ratified, 262–63
of 1971, 277–82, 297–98, 298–311; ratified, 298
constitutions of states, 1–3, 312
Continental Congress, 41–42, 43, 61
Cooley, Thomas M., *Treatise on the Constitutional Limitations*, 2, 172
corporations, 111–12, 121, 122, 202–3, 206, 226; *see also* State Corporation Commission
Council of State
colonial, 11, 12–13, 18–19; abolished, 51, 58, 63
commonwealth, 46–47, 58, 61, 62–63, 68, 84, 97, 103–4; abolished, 122
counties
board of supervisors, 176, 224
clerks, 15, 24, 25, 65, 125
constables, 65
county courts, 23–28, 98–99, 171–72, 176, 224

courts of oyer and terminer, 25, 64–66, 104
fee system, 31, 242–43, 251–52, 269
in Constitution of the colony, 23–28
in Constitution of 1776, 65, 125
in Constitution of 1830, 98–100
in Constitution of 1851, 125–26
in Constitution of 1864, 141
in Constitution of 1869, 173–74, 176–77, 188
in Constitution of 1902, 224–225, 250–52
in Constitutional Revision of 1928, 249–250, 250–52, 253, 258, 265, 266, 269, 372–74
in Constitution of 1971, 291–92
see also Dillon Rule
Court of Admiralty, 63, 64
Court of Appeals, 289–90
Court of Oyer and Terminer, 18
Court of Vice-Admiralty, 18
courthouse rings, 237, 242–43, 253, 269, 274
Cowling, William J., 136–37
Crenshaw and Crenshaw v. Slate River Company (1848), 98

Dale, Sir Thomas, 7
Dandridge, Bartholomew, 47, 48
Daniel, John Warwick, 198–99, 200, 203, 204, 205, 215, 242
De La Ware, Thomas West, baron, 7
Declaration of Rights (after 1864 Bill of Rights), 48–49, 50–54
in Constitution of 1776, 49–54, 73
in Constitution of 1830, 93
in Constitution of 1851, 117, 168
in Constitution of 1869, 168, 169–70, 188
in Constitution of 1902, 213–14
in Constitutional Revision of 1928, 254–55
in Constitution of 1971, 282–83, 299–300, 308
Declaration of the Rights of Man and Citizen (1789), 54
Declaratory Act (1766), 35–36
delegate, 41
Democratic Party: 19th century, 107, 110–11, 187, 200–1; 20th century, 197–202, 206, 309; 21st century, 309–10

demographic change, 78–79, 107–8, 155–56, 272–74
Dillon Rule, 243, 269, 291–92, 311
Dinwiddie, Robert, 32
District of Columbia v. Heller (2008), 308
double jeopardy, 213, 303, 308
Downs, L. McCarthy, 269
Dred Scott v. Sandford (1857), 191
due process of law, 229, 230, 282, 308
duels, 96, 171, 216, 285
Dunaway, Wayland F., 204
Dunmore, John Murray, fourth earl of, 38, 43

Eckenrode, Hamilton J., 143–44
economic change, 78–79, 86; *see also* State Corporation Commission
Edwards, LeRoy Griffin, 136, 142
Elijah R. Walker v. William H. Loving (1871), 144–46
Emancipation Proclamation, 135, 145
eminent domain, 282, 299–300
Enabling Act (1869), 155, 185
entail, 70–71
escheator general, 16
Ex Parte Lawhorne (1868), 154
ex post facto laws, 282

Fain, Sarah Lee, 253
Falwell v. Miller (2002), 302
fellow-servant rule, 231–32
First Military District (1867–70), 152–55, 161, 183, 184–85
Floyd, John, 104
Frederick Justices v. Bruce et al (1848), 99
freedom of assembly, 308
freedom of religion, 208; *see also* Act for Establishing Religious Freedom; Declaration of Rights
freedom of speech, 154, 69, 308
freedom of the press, 52, 169
freed people, 137–38, 149–51, 152, 158–60, 181, 243
Funding Act (1871), 185–86

Gates, Sir Thomas, 7
General Assembly, 20, 22, 61–62, 72, 186–87, 210–11, 302–3
  frequency of sessions, 21–22, 58, 139, 171, 189, 210, 238, 285–86
  apportionment of seats
    Constitution of the colony, 20
    Constitution of 1776, 59, 80–81, 83–84
    Constitution of 1830, 95, 112–13
    Constitution of 1851, 118–20
    Constitution of 1864, 139
    Constitution of 1869, 171–72, 189
    Constitution of 1902, 219–20
    Constitutional Revision of 1928, 274, 276, 284–85
    Constitution of 1971, 285–86, 301, 310
  bicameral, 19, 47
  constitutional revision, 249, 253–54, 277–80, 281
    in Constitution of the colony, 7–8, 10, 11, 13, 18–23
    in Constitution of 1776, 46–47, 58–62
    in Constitution of 1830, 95–97
    in Constitution of 1851, 120–22
    in Constitution of 1864, 139–40
    in Constitution of 1869, 171–72, 188–89
    in Constitution of 1902, 219–21
    in Constitutional Revision of 1928, 255–56, 267, 268–69
    in Constitution of 1971, 285–86, 289, 290, 294, 295–96, 302–3, 309, 312–13
  see also House of Burgesses, House of Delegates; Senate of Virginia

General Court: colonial, 13, 17, 19, 36; commonwealth, 61, 63–64, 74, 97, 123
George III, 37, 42–43, 56
gerrymandering, 309; Great Gerrymander of 1830, 95, 118–19, 128
Gillespie, Albert P., 203, 217–18
Glass, Carter, 210, 215, 218–19, 230, 242
Godwin, Mills E., Jr., 277–78, 298
Gooch, Robert K., 264–65, 270
Goode, John, 195–97, 204, 205, 210
governor
  amendments to bills, 211–2, 257, 287
  veto power, 14, 22–23, 58–59, 95–96, 172–73, 186, 221, 257, 287, 302–3; item veto, 221–22, 257
  in Constitution of the colony, 11, 12–16

in Constitution of 1776, 46–47, 58–59, 62–63, 68, 84
in Constitution of 1830, 97
in Constitution of 1851, 122–23
in Constitution of 1864, 140
in Constitution of 1869, 172–73, 177, 287
in Constitution of 1902, 221–22
in Constitutional Revision of 1928, 248, 256–57, 266, 268–69
in Constitution of 1971, 286–88, 290, 293, 302, 305, 309–10
Grant, Ulysses S., 183
Grattan, Peachy R., 154
Griffin's Executor v. Cunningham and Washington (1870), 155
Grigsby, Hugh Blair, 106

habeas corpus, 282
Hamilton, Alexander, 209
Harper v. Virginia State Board of Elections (1966), 216, 267, 275
Harrison, Albertis, 278
Hawxhurst, Job, 136
Hawxhurst, John, 136, 163
Henry, Patrick, 33, 34, 42, 47, 48, 52, 53, 67; governor, 68, 69
High Court of Chancery, 63, 97
Hill, Oliver W., 164, 278
Hinton, Drury A., 175
Holcombe, James P., 196
Holton, A. Linwood, 298, 310
Homestead Cases (1872), 180
homestead exemption, 180, 234, 261
House of Burgesses, 12, 18–19, 20, 21, 22, 29–30, 37–38
House of Delegates
  in Constitution of 1776, 59, 81, 95
  in Constitution of 1830, 95–96
  in Constitution of 1851, 118–20
  in Constitution of 1864, 139
  in Constitution of 1869, 171, 189
  in Constitution of 1902, 219–20
  in Constitutional Revision of 1928, 255–57
  in Constitution of 1971, 285, 287, 303
House of Representatives, 74, 96
Howard, A. E. Dick, 278, 279, 296, 297

Hunnicutt, James W., 163
Hunton, Eppa, 203, 209, 230

impeachment, 61, 64
independence, 48–49
interest rates, 179, 187–88
internal improvements, 79, 111–12, 121–22

Jacksonian Democracy, 84, 107
James I, 5–6, 8
Jamestown, 59
Jefferson, Thomas, 49–50, 67–68, 70–71, 106; Constitution of 1776, 45, 56, 58, 59, 80–81, 83–84, 99; *Summary View of the Rights of British America*, 35
Johnson, Andrew, 146, 147, 161
Johnson, Joseph, 123
Jones v. Montague (1904), 237
Joynes, William Thomas, 149
judges, 123, 140, 268–69; independent judiciary, 175; *see also* circuit courts, justices of the peace, Council of State; Supreme Court of Appeals
Judicial Inquiry and Review Commission, 290, 303–4
judicial review, 72–74, 98, 124, 174, 289
juries
  in Constitution of 1776, 52
  in Constitution of 1851, 117
  in Constitution of 1869, 169, 171, 188
  in Constitution of 1902, 210, 213
  in Constitutional Revision of 1928, 255
justices of the peace
  colonial, 23–25; commonwealth, 56–57, 65–66, 68, 84, 93, 98–99, 125

Keezell, George, 252
Kegley v. Johnson (1966), 284
Kelo v. City of New London (2005), 299
Kercheval, Samuel, 83
Kirkham v. Russell (1882), 243

Lawes Divine, Morall, and Martiall, 7
Lawhorne, James L., 154
Lee, Luther, 164
Lee, Richard, 15
Lee, Richard Henry, 40, 45, 46, 58, 60, 62, 67
Lee, Thomas Ludwell, 48

Leigh, Benjamin Watkins, 92, 94
Letcher, John, 108–9
lieutenant governor
    Constitution of the colony, 13–14
    Constitution of 1776, 62
    Constitution of 1830, 97
    Constitution of 1851, 120–21, 122
    in Constitution of 1869, 172
    in Constitution of 1902, 222–23
    in Constitutional Revision of 1928, 257
    in Constitution of 1971, 286, 287–88
literacy test, 190, 214, 284
Literary Fund, 177–78, 293, 304
local laws, 286
lotteries, 279, 281, 285, 298
Lottery Proceeds Fund, 306
Loving v. Virginia (1967), 300
Luther v. Borden (1849), 153

McCulloch v. Maryland (1819), 121
McDiarmid, Dorothy S., 280, 282
McIlwaine, Richard, 204
McKinley, William, 207
Madison, James, 53, 63, 67, 80, 89, 90, 91, 100
Mahone, William, 194
marriage, same-sex, 300
Marshall, John, 75, 89, 90, 98–99, 121
Marshall, Mary A., 280
Martin, Thomas Staples, 198–99, 242, 244
Mason, George, 44, 47, 49; Declaration of Rights, 50, 52–53; Constitution of 1776, 55–56, 60–61, 62
Mason, John Young, 115
massive resistance, 265, 276, 283
Mathews, Samuel, 18
Mercer, James, 47
Meredith, Charles V., 209–10, 235
Metropolitan Areas Study Commission, 274
Military Court of Appeals; *see* Supreme Court of Appeals
militia, 15, 52, 173, 308
Miller v. Ayers (1972), 304
Miller v. Ayers (1973), 304
Minor, John B., 146, 178
Mitchell, John, Jr., 197, 241
Moncure, Richard Cassius Lee, 149
Monroe, James, 89, 90

Morrissey, James, 164
Munford, George Wythe, 146

Nat Turner's Rebellion, 103–4
Nelson, Thomas Jr., 48
New State Ice Company v. Leibmann (1932), 313
New York Bureau of Municipal Research, 249–52, 252–53
Nicholas, Robert Carter, 49, 50
Norfolk, 59, 112
Norfolk and Portsmouth Belt Line Railroad Co. v. Commonwealth (1904), 240
Nott, Edward, 14

O'Flaherty, Daniel C., 202–3
Old Dominion Committee for Fair Utility Rates et al., v. State Corporation Commission (2017), 295–96

Page, John, 45, 48, 63
Page, Thomas Nelson, 104
Parson's Cause, 33
partisanship, 107, 110–11, 193, 309
Pedigo, Abraham L., 202, 204, 218
Pendleton, Edmund, 60, 65, 69, 70, 73; Constitution of 1776, 44, 47, 48–49, 51, 53, 55–56
Peter Kamper v. Mary Hawkins (1793), 72, 73–74
petition, 54, 70, 208–9
Pettit, William B., 205
Pierpont, Francis Harrison, 133–34, 135, 144, 148–47, 144, 149, 153–54
pistole fee, 32
Plessy v. Ferguson (1896), 276
poll tax, 275
    in Constitution of 1869, 188–89
    in Constitution of 1902, 214, 215–16, 233, 239, 241
    in Constitutional Revision of 1928, 263–64, 266, 267, 269–70
    in Constitution of 1971, 281, 283–84
Pollard, John Garland, 204, 205, 214, 216, 252
Pott, John, 23
Powell, Lewis F., 278
Prentis v. Atlantic Coast Line Co. (1908), 240
Prentis, Robert R., 252, 256

Presbyterians, 71
Price, James H., 268, 270
primogeniture, 70–71
probate of estates, 24, 224
public debt
  in Constitution of 1851, 121–22, 131
  in Constitution of 1864, 140, 149
  in Constitution of 1869, 179, 185–87
  in Constitution of 1902, 234, 239, 244, 247
  in Constitution of 1971, 277, 279, 293, 296, 298, 304
public schools, 92–93, 131
  in Constitution of 1869, 177–78, 186–87
  in Constitution of 1902, 208, 227–28, 238–39
  in Constitutional Revision of 1928, 259–60, 265–66, 266
  in Constitution of 1971, 277, 283, 293–94, 304, 306

racial segregation, 173, 178, 227–28, 244–45, 272, 275–76, 294
racism, 108, 195–97
railroads, 121, 185, 202–3, 229–30, 231–32, 236, 240
Randolph, Edmund, 49, 68; Convention of 1776, 49–50, 51, 52, 56, 57–59
Randolph, John, of Roanoke, 84, 100–101
Randolph, Peyton, 42
Randolph, Thomas Jefferson, 104
Readjuster Party, 175, 186–87, 189, 193
Reed, William T., 252
Reid, William Ferguson, 164, 280
religion
  in Constitution of the colony, 26–28
  in Constitution of 1776, 66–68
  in Constitution of 1830, 96–97
  in Constitution of 1851, 122
  in Constitution of 1902, 214, 220–21
  in Constitution of 1971, 302
representation, 40, 83–84, 85–87
  in Constitution of the colonial, 29, 33–34, 36–37
  in Constitution of 1830, 92, 94–95
  in Constitution of 1851, 112–14, 131
Representation Revolution, 276–77, 284, 285, 292, 309–10

Republican Party, 160–61, 203–4, 309, 309–10
Restored Government of Virginia, 130–31, 132–35, 149
Revenue Stabilization Fund (rainy day fund), 305
Revolutionary language of liberty, 70, 88, 107, 108
Rives, Alexander, 149
Roane, Spencer, 72, 84
Ruffner, William Henry, 178

Samuel, William H., 165
Schofield, John McAllister, 163–64, 182
Scott v. Commonwealth (1994), 283
Scott v. James, Secretary of the Commonwealth (1912), 238
secession, 128–29, 196, 213
secretary of the colony, 15
secretary of the commonwealth
  in Constitution of 1776, 46, 61
  in Constitution of 1869, 172
  in Constitution of 1902, 211, 222
  in Constitution of 1928, 248, 257
  in Constitution of 1971, 287
sectionalism, 78–79, 82–83, 85, 89–90, 91, 105, 109–12
sexual discrimination, 282
Selden v. Montague (1904), 237
self-incrimination, 308
Senate of the United States, 74
Senate of Virginia
  in Constitution of 1776, 59–60, 68, 81, 82
  in Constitution of 1830, 95, 96
  in Constitution of 1851, 118–20, 120–21
  in Constitution of 1864, 139, 141
  in Constitution of 1869, 171, 189
  Constitution of 1902, 219, 220
  in Constitution of 1971, 284–5, 287
separation of powers
  in Constitution of the colony, 11–12
  in Constitution of 1776, 47–48, 51, 56
  in Constitution of 1830, 93
  in Constitution of 1869, 155, 170
  in Constitution of 1902, 212
  in Constitutional Revision of 1928, 255
  in Constitution of 1971, 285
Sharpe v. Robertson (1849), 124–25

Sheppard, Eleanor P., 280
sheriffs, 65, 125
slave trade, 108, 128, 150
slavery, 74, 76, 108, 110–11, 131, 213; abolition, 131, 134–35, 137–38, 143, 148, 158–59, 191; taxation, 82–83, 121, 128–29
   in Constitution of the colony, 30
   in Constitution of 1776, 50–51, 69
   in Constitution of 1830, 85, 89, 91–92, 101, 104–5
   in Constitution of 1851, 113–14, 116, 119–20, 121, 128–29, 130
   in Constitution of 1864, 135, 137–38
   in Constitution of 1869, 169–70, 191
   in Constitution of 1902, 213
Smith, Captain John, 6
Smith, Meriwether, 47, 48
Special Courts of Appeal
   in Constitution of 1851, 124–25
   in Constitution of 1869, 174–75
   in Constitution of 1902, 223
   in Constitution of 1928, 258
   in Constitution of 1971, 289
Stamp Act (1765), 33–35
Staples v. Gilmer (1944), 263
Staples v. Gilmer (1945), 254, 264, 281
Starnes v. Cauoyette (1992), 302
State Board of Education, 177–78, 227 259, 293
State Corporation Commission
   in Constitution of 1902, 211, 229–32, 233, 236, 240
   in Constitutional Revision of 1928, 250, 260–61, 266, 268–69
   in Constitution of 1971, 288, 290, 294–96, 302
statute of limitations, 302
Staunton conventions, 81–82, 88
stay laws, 180, 234, 261
Strawberry Hill Land Co. v. Starbuck (1918), 61–62, 221, 256
Stuart, Henry Carter, 204, 252
suffrage, 109; Black Virginians, 159–60, 162–63, 170, 189, 210; poll tax, 188–89, 215–16, 241; property qualification, 29, 57–58, 86–87, 94, 216–17; woman, 87, 166–67, 208–9, 216–17, 239–40, 255
   in Constitution of the colony, 7–8, 20–21, 29
   in Constitution of 1776, 57–58, 86–87
   in Constitution of 1830, 94–95, 102–5
   in Constitution of 1851, 116–17, 118, 127–28
   in Constitution of 1864, 138–39, 147, 148
   in Constitution of 1869, 159–60, 162–63, 170–71, 182–83, 188–89, 189–90
   in Constitution of 1902, 196–97, 208–9, 214–19, 235–36, 239, 241
   in Constitutional Revision of 1928, 255
   in Constitution of 1971, 283–85, 300–1
   in Constitution of the United States, 192
Summers, George William, 123
superintendent of public instruction
   in Constitution of 1869, 177
   in Constitution of 1902, 211, 227
   in Constitutional Revision of 1928, 248, 259
   in Constitution of 1971, 293
Supervisors of Washington County v. Saltville Land Co. (1901), 226
Supreme Court of Appeals (after 1971 Supreme Court of Virginia): chief justice, 289, 290; docket, 98, 124–25, 174–75; judicial review, 72–74, 98, 124; Military Court of Appeals (so-called), 154
   in Constitution of 1776, 61, 63–64
   in Constitution of 1830, 98
   in Constitution of 1851, 123–24
   in Constitution of 1864, 140–41, 149
   in Constitution of 1869, 173–75
   in Constitution of 1902, 223–24, 228, 230
   in Constitutional Revision of 1928, 257–58
   in Constitution of 1971, 289–90, 295, 303, 308

taxes
   in Constitution of the colony, 10, 22, 33, 82–83, 86
   in Constitution of 1830, 94
   in Constitution of 1851, 121, 128–29

in Constitution of 1869, 178–79, 188
in Constitution of 1902, 232–33, 239
in Constitutional Revision of 1928, 248, 261, 262, 265
in Constitution of 1971, 277, 296, 304–7
Taylor v. Commonwealth (1903), 236–37
Taylor, John, of Caroline, 84
Terry, Alfred H., 151
Tertium Quids, 84–85
Texas v. White (1868), 152–53, 184
Thom, Alfred P., 209, 217, 240
Thompson, Lucas Powell, 149
Thorpe, George, 17
three-fifths clause, 96, 101, 120, 139
Tilton v. Herman (1909), 241, 263
treasurer
   in Constitution of the colony, 21
   in Constitution of 1776, 46, 61
   in Constitution of 1830, 96
   in Constitution of 1851, 122
   in Constitution of 1869, 173
   in Constitution of 1902, 211, 222
   in Constitutional Revision of 1928, 248, 257
   in Constitution of 1971, 287
Tucker, St. George, 50, 65–66, 99
Two-Penny Acts, 32–33
Tyler, John (1747–1813), 63
Tyler, John (1790–1862), 89

Underwood, John C., 142, 157, 163, 164, 166, 172, 181–82, 193, 194
Upshur, Abel P., 92

Vagrancy Act (1866), 150–51
victims of crime, 299
Virginia Association of Counties, 292
Virginia Committee of Safety, 42

Virginia Company, 5–8, 26; charters, 6–7, 10; Great Charter, 7
Virginia Municipal League, 292
Virginia Redistricting Commission, 301
Virginia State Woman Suffrage Association, 166
Virginia Union Association, 161
voting: by ballot, 118, 131, 190–91, 210–11, 284; registration, 162, 216, 237, 241–42, 266–67, 284, 301; voice voting, 20, 95, 118, 131, 138, 148
Voting Rights Act (1965), 275–76

Waddill v. Chamberlayne (1735), 30
Walker, Gilbert Carlton, 183–84, 184–85
Walton Act (1896), 190, 198
Washington, George, 1, 21
Washington, John Augustine, 47
Watson, Walter A., 207, 209–10, 215, 240–41
Webb, George, *Office and Authority of a Justice of Peace*, 24–25
Wells, Henry Horatio, 182–83
West Virginia, 130–31, 140, 148–49, 179
Whig Party, 110–11
Williams v. Mississippi (1898), 215
Williamsburg, 59
Willis, H. Parker, 230
Wilson, Norvell, 164
Winchester and Strasburg Railroad Co. v. Commonwealth (1906), 240
Wise, Henry Alexander, 116
women, 167, 238–39, 253, 278, 280, 284; woman suffrage, 87, 166–67, 208–9, 216–17, 239–40, 252; sexual discrimination, 255
Wyatt, Sir Francis, 9
Wysor, Joseph C., 210, 230
Wythe, George, 36, 49, 70, 73

www.ingramcontent.com/pod-product-compliance
Lightning Source LLC
Chambersburg PA
CBHW030516230426
43665CB00010B/644